PBH

Dreams and Experience
in Classical Antiquity

Dreams and Experience in Classical Antiquity

William V. Harris

HARVARD UNIVERSITY PRESS

Cambridge, Massachusetts, and London, England

2009

Library of Congress Cataloging-in-Publication Data

Harris, William V. (William Vernon)
    Dreams and experience in classical antiquity / William V. Harris.
      p. cm.
    Includes bibliographical references and index.
    ISBN 978-0-674-03297-2 (alk. paper)
    1. Dreams—Greece—History—To 1500.   2. Dreams—Rome.   I. Title.
BF1078.H2955 2009
154.6'30938—dc22   2008045081

for Silvana, Neil and Kelly

"Why, dreams ain't—nothing."

"Oh, yes they is!" she insisted, her eyes flaming . . .

W. E. B. Du Bois, *The Quest of the Silver Fleece* (1911), ch. 1.

Contents

List of Illustrations

Abbreviations

IGUR	*Inscriptiones Graecae Urbis Romae*
I. Knidos	*Die Inschriften von Knidos*, ed. W. Blümel (*IGSK* 41)
ILLRP	*Inscriptiones Latinae Liberae Rei Publicae*, ed. A. Degrassi
ILS	*Inscriptiones Latinae Selectae*, ed. H. Dessau
JRS	*Journal of Roman Studies*
P.Cair.Zen.	*The Zenon Papyri*, ed. C. C. Edgar
PG	*Patrologia Graeca*, ed. J.-P. Migne
PGM	*Papyri Graecae Magicae*, ed. K. Preisendanz
P.Goodspeed	*Greek Papyri from the Cairo Museum*, ed. E. J. Goodspeed
P.Herc.	*Herculaneum Papyri*, listed in M. Gigante (ed.), *Catalogo dei papiri ercolanesi* (Naples, 1979)
PL	*Patrologia Latina*, ed. J.-P. Migne
P.Leid.	*Papyri Graeci Musei Antiquarii Publici Lugduni-Batavi*, ed. C. Leemans
PLRE	*The Prosopography of the Later Roman Empire*, ed. A. H. M. Jones et al.
P.Oxy.	*The Oxyrhynchus Papyri*
RE	*Pauly's Real Encyclopädie der classischen Altertumswissenschaft*
SC	*Sources chrétiennes*
SEG	*Supplementum Epigraphicum Graecum*
*SIG*³	*Sylloge Inscriptionum Graecarum* (3rd ed.), ed. W. Dittenberger
SVF	*Stoicorum Veterum Fragmenta*, ed. H. von Arnim
UPZ	*Urkunden der Ptolemäerzeit*, ed. U. Wilcken

Preface

I am deeply grateful to the scholars who read all or most of a draft version of this book—though as usual I must avoid implicating them in the result. I should start with Suzanne Said, because her acute comments about every aspect of ancient dreaming go back to the beginning of this project. Our often differing points of view have constantly required me to rethink my opinions. Mary Beard, Angelos Chaniotis, Richard Gordon, John North, Philip van der Eijk, and the Harvard press's anonymous readers have provided invaluable help, all the more so, once again, because of our various differences of opinion. I also owe a particular debt to Gil Renberg for numerous conversations and for sending me his Ph.D. dissertation and his offprints (see the bibliography).

I also extend most sincere thanks to those rather numerous scholars who helped me to deal with particular problems or supplied useful information, especially to Glen Bowersock, James Davidson, James Hankins, Patrick Kragelund, Michael Lambert, Carol Lawton, Andrew Meadows, John Monfasani, Nicholas Purcell, Michela Sassi, Neslihan Senocak, Gregor Weber and Paul Zanker.

I have been extraordinarily fortunate to have all these learned and generous friends.

Finally I should like to thank the responsible persons at four institutions which helped this book along its tortuous path. The first three are St. John's College, Oxford, where I was a visiting fellow in 2002; the American Council of Learned Societies, which for the second time awarded me a research fellowship; and the Scuola Normale Superiore, where the idiosyncratic library has become almost a home away from home. And finally it is a pleasure to thank Harvard University Press, and in particular Sharmila Sen.

Dreams and Experience
in Classical Antiquity

Introduction: Then and Now

We can begin in fourth-century AD Egypt. Would you like to appear in someone else's dream? What you have to do is this. Say to your bed-side lamp (strictly speaking, it should probably be an oil-lamp) the following words: '*Cheiamopsei herpeboth*. Let MM, the daughter of NN, see me in her dreams, now, now, quickly, quickly'. Add your own message. Repeat frequently. Those at least are the instructions offered by a fourth-century Greek magical papyrus,[1] obviously in deadly earnest—it was not a game. Reading such texts seems to take us into a world entirely alien, superficially at least, from modern times.[2]

Yet very many people in the modern world think that there is 'something significant' about the content of their dreams, just as most Greeks did when Aristotle wrote on the subject.[3] As to *how* they are significant, if they are, that is nowadays very much a matter of opinion. By contrast, scholars have generally held that Greek and Roman beliefs about dreams were nearly unanimous, with only a few eccentric philosophers taking a different line. While most people thought that dreams were sent by the gods (that is not, be it noted, how Aristotle reported the general opinion) and could po-

---

1. *PGM* VII.408–410. It is assumed that the victim will be female.

2. We shall meet some similar texts, but it has to be admitted that dream-sending was not a major element in the magic of Greek or Roman times. The most elaborate such spells known to me appear together in a papyrus written in demotic and hieratic Egyptian: see Johnson 1977 (cf. Betz 1986, 325–326).

3. *On Prophecy through Sleep* 1.462b14–15. 'Since Freud', says one writer, 'we know in any case that a dream always means "something"', Gsteiger 1999, 375.

tentially provide valuable information or instructions, Aristotle and all the others who preferred naturalistic explanations of dreaming and/or rejected the predictive value of dreams,[4] were a small minority. At the heart of this book (Chapter III) is the claim that this scholarly model is excessively crude and inattentive to the nuances, not to say internal contradictions, of Greek and Roman attitudes.

The book does not set out to be a complete history of Greek and Roman dreaming, partly because that would require a huge tome,[5] partly because good scholars have already said a great deal of what needs saying (the subject has also provoked a considerable quantity of hot air).[6] Rather, certain interconnected problems have caught my attention, problems to do with the ancients' experience of dreaming and their comprehension of the phenomenon of dreaming (but also to do with our own comprehension of the same phenomenon). Like many ancient-history books, much of this one is about works of literature, a great variety of them, but it is the experience itself and how it was thought of that will be at the centre of my attention.

Scientific ways of understanding dreams enter into this historical account for a pair of reasons. One is that we cannot expect to describe properly how the ancients represented dreams unless we can say what dreams are like (were their descriptions almost entirely conventional?), and that is much harder than might be supposed—if you are in doubt, please read both sides of the recent and current debate among scientists as to whether dreams are 'bizarre' or not.[7] And there are sharply differing opinions about

4. It should be stated at once that these two positions are distinct from each other. In Chapters III and IV we shall meet those who thought that dreams could be predictive even though the gods did *not* send them. We shall also meet what seems to be an inconsistency in the thinking of Aristotle.

5. Antin 1963, 350—'quelle ampleur pourrait prendre une histoire du songe dans l'Antiquité!'.

6. There is perhaps little risk now that we shall be told that most of the Greeks and Romans thought that the experiences they had in dreams were as real as their waking experiences. Borret 1967, commenting on Origen, *Contra Celsum* i.48, imagined that 'until the Roman period' the ancients thought dreams and waking experience equally real. Michenaud and Dierkens 1972, 29, tended in the same direction. The idea partly derives from an older anthropology according to which 'primitives' cannot make distinctions (whereas, J. Z. Smith bracingly argued [1978, 437], they are/were obsessed with making distinctions).

7. For references see below.

the credibility of some famous and less famous dream narratives, partly because scholars have paid little analytic attention to what, in a dream narrative, constitutes credibility.

Secondly, there is the matter of ancient science, or as some might want to say proto-science. In Chapter IV, we shall set out what can be known about Greek and Roman attempts to reach a naturalistic understanding of the phenomenon of dreaming. The point is not of course to decide whether the Hippocratic school or Aristotle or Epicurus or Cicero or Galen (simply to mention a few of those whose ideas we shall encounter) deserve good marks, or whether they anticipated modern ideas on the same subject, but to trace the development of ancient ideas within their own cultural context. Ancient thinkers deserve to be treated seriously. And they were not always wrong. Take the question whether small children dream. Aristotle 'knew' that they do not. A recent and authoritative commentator pronounced that Aristotle was in error. As it happens, many, though not all, modern researchers agree with him.[8] On this and other questions we want to know how ancient thinkers 'knew', and why they formulated and more or less sensibly answered certain questions and failed to answer, or even formulate, certain others. One of their problems was that dreaming is, I think we can say, a difficult subject, psychologically and physiologically. The achievements of recent science, over the last fifty plus years in particular, may throw some light on the efforts of the Greeks in the same area—and the achievements of modern physiologists have indeed been impressive.

It is encouraging to see that historians have in recent times awoken much more to the possibility of learning from psychology, especially about the emotions.[9] There are risks, undoubtedly, in particular that the innocent historian will fall into the hands of a guide who is not widely accepted among the psychologists themselves. In this study we are fairly well insured

8. See Chapter IV.

9. Cf. L. Hunt 2002, 347–349. She could have mentioned that this trend is visible in many subfields, ancient, mediaeval, early-modern European, East Asian, and even American history. I do not agree, however with her belief (349–353) that the best way ahead for historians interested in psychology is through the history of 'selfhood' or 'personhood', partly because I find these to be artificial concepts, partly because I suspect that Foucault and his followers have largely exhausted the seam. This will not prevent me from speculating in Chapters I and II about how Greeks and Romans used dream-descriptions to establish their own identities.

against that risk, since the scientists who have written about dreams in recent times so conspicuously, as we shall see, disagree with each other about important matters.

This book has a leitmotiv, which is that there is more sense, common and otherwise, in what the ancients thought and wrote about dreams than scholars have sometimes recognized. It scarcely needs saying that the confusing phenomenon of dreaming caused a great deal of confusion in antiquity, that many people believed silly things about dreams and behaved superstitiously in reaction to them (Plato, and later Theophrastus and the Epicureans, complained about this), and that some of what was written about them was written by the exceptionally credulous. (I do not share Freud's admiration for Artemidorus of Daldis—though he will receive his due share of attention.) But what is remarkable about Greek and Roman writing on the subject of things seen in the night is, on the one hand, the artistry and sophistication of much of what was written by poets and others, and on the other hand the persistent and sometimes sharply perceptive efforts of those who, mainly from the fifth century BC to the first, wrote naturalistic accounts of dreaming.

✻   ✻   ✻

I shall start with a single convention that the Greeks and Romans, among others, employed as a framework for describing some of their dreams—the 'epiphany' convention as I shall call it. This type of dream consists of the appearance to the dreamer of an authoritative personage who may be divine or represent a god, and this figure conveys instructions or information. A dream such as that occurs very seldom in our experience and even in our literature—yet it was well-known to the Greeks and Romans and to some other ancient peoples, and, far from dying out in antiquity, it lived on into the Middle Ages and beyond. Did the Greeks and Romans actually dream epiphany dreams? What lies behind this pattern, and why did such dreams eventually disappear (Chapter I)? This inquiry will take us on an excursion far outside the boundaries of ancient history.

These problems lead to the question whether everything in Greek and Roman descriptions of dreams is a matter of convention and invention. Or can we sometimes know what the Greeks and Romans actually experienced in their dreams (Chapter II)? An expert on the extensive dream-literature of Byzantium has said that we have no single trustworthy dream-narrative anywhere in the history of that whole culture. Some classical scholars would probably say that the same is true for Greek and Roman times, yet scholars also make exceptions for their own favourites, whether it is the martyr Perpetua or the emperor Constantine. Since we cannot even be entirely sure about the truth, let alone the exactness, of the dreams we hear about from our own acquaintances, the possibility of finding out what the Greeks and Romans dreamt may seem practically nil. Yet we can construct some guidelines, and if we follow them some possibly surprising results emerge: not only are some famous dreams less historical than has sometimes been believed, we do also possess some descriptions of dreams that in all probability really occurred, or to put it more pedantically were remembered by the dreamer as having occurred as they are described. This inquiry will allow us to study further the conventions the ancients observed in describing dreams, their fibs, lies and fantasies. And it will show how very large and inviting the terrain of invention was, a terrain that was exploited with gusto by so many from Homer to Augustine (and of course later).

One reason why dreams were so subject to distortion and fakery in antiquity, and a reason why it was worth inventing them in general, was simply that many people believed that dreams sometimes revealed hidden truths, especially about the future. Indeed it is a widespread doctrine—often taken over without much thought from the 'authorities'—that almost everyone in the classical world believed this. Since belief in divination appears to have been one of the most conspicuously unmodern characteristics of that world, it is clearly important to know whether dreams were really judged to deserve so much faith (Chapter III). A more careful inspection of texts and social practices reveals a far more complex and interesting story than the one usually told. To begin with, we must establish what 'coming true' meant to the Greeks and Romans in this context. It is still more vital to analyse the notion of belief, especially religious belief, and to delve beneath the conventional notion that 'pagan' religion was largely or entirely a matter of practice rather than belief. We shall encounter all manner of intriguing characters, including sceptical tragic poets, highly educated doctors (one at least) who chose treatments according to what they dreamt, and historians on both sides of the fence.

Finally (Chapter IV), there is the matter of the intellectual achievement. No one will claim that naturalistic thinking about dreams was widespread in antiquity, even though Epicureanism enjoyed for some time a wide following for an intellectual movement in a largely illiterate society. And it is not as if the best researchers always offered a clear set of doctrines (even Aristotle's message is blurred, as we shall see).[10] The question I wish to pursue is not in any case *how many* people accepted naturalistic ideas on this subject, but how and why ideas developed. Nonetheless, human beings and their forms of communication will be at the centre of this inquiry.

✿   ✿   ✿

A neuroscientist writes that there is no longer any mystery about dreams: 'the work of sleep science is incomplete', but all is well, because 'for the first time in human history, we can see the regional activity of the brain as people wake, sleep, and dream. This is a true renaissance, a genuine revolution, and a major shift in the scientific theory of the brain and mind is to be anticipated.'[11] My point is not to deride such claims but to draw out the diversity of the interest that dreams evoke. If physiology is your concern, the above may hold true. If you are a philosopher, you may have an entirely different set of priorities. One contemporary philosopher asserts, for example, that there are three classic problems about dreaming:[12] whether it is possible to know for certain whether one is awake or dreaming (a problem first raised in Plato's *Theaetetus*), whether we experience dreams while we are asleep or make them up when we awaken, and whether it is possible to 'be immoral' in dreams.[13] To someone from another discipline, on the other hand, it may appear that these particular problems are trivial.[14]

In fact the modern science of dreams is in a much more fluid and attention-worthy condition than the quotation in the previous paragraph suggests.[15] There is a lot more to find out, a vast amount perhaps, even though the

10. Yet his achievement was remarkable, and I will not deny that an extra stimulus to write Chapter IV came from observing that the only person who mentioned Aristotle in a recent academic jamboree dedicated to dreaming got him quite wrong (Pagel 2000).

11. Hobson 2002, 158. The same author adopts a somewhat more cautious tone in scientific articles, e.g. Hobson et al. 2000a, 807.

12. Flanagan 2000, 163.

13. In their modern forms these three problems are the legacies of Descartes (who thought he had found the solution), of behaviourism and of Christianity respectively.

14. Some philosophers may think so too: at least I note that Austin (1962, 49 n. 1) spoke of 'the absurdity in Descartes' toying with the notion that the whole of our experience might be a dream'.

15. For the history of dream research since the mid–nineteenth century see esp. Hobson 1988, 23–51, Sophie Schwartz 2000 (with plentiful evidence of unconscious replication).

achievement has also been extraordinary. The humanists who still sometimes refer to Freud, and even Jung,[16] as the embodiments of modern research about dreaming, are particularly requested to pay attention here.

The turning point in the scientific study of dreams in the twentieth century, as is well known, was a paper less than two pages long published in the journal *Science* in 1953 under the title 'Regularly Occurring Periods of Eye Motility, and Concomitant Phenomena, during Sleep'.[17] Aserinsky and Kleitman at the University of Chicago had discovered the correlation between REM (rapid eye movements) and reports of dreaming, a correlation which implied that we dream far more than had previously been supposed.[18] Electroencephalogram (EEG) patterns during REM sleep are analogous to those of the waking brain. A night's sleep, for a normal adult, includes several prolonged episodes of REM, making up about one-quarter of total time slept,[19] and a person who is awakened during REM sleep claims, far more often than not, to have been dreaming, at least 80 percent of the time.[20] In other words, most of what we dream, we forget. There is also a certain amount of dreaming outside REM sleep, and NREM (non-REM) dreams present intriguing qualitative differences from REM dreams.[21] Earlier observers had known of course that dreams are easily forgotten (Freud, however, tended to minimize the fact, in accord with his belief in the royal importance of dream memories),[22] but they vastly underestimated the phenomenon.

What have subsequent developments amounted to? They have been exhilarating or disappointing, according to one's interests. But first let us note

16. Few recent writers about Greek or Roman dreams have attempted to apply Jungian ideas (but see Amat 1985, Gollnick 1999, 91–104); Näf 2004, 187–189, nonetheless held that his book required two (neutral) pages on the Jungians.

17. Aserinsky and Kleitman 1953.

18. Refinements were soon added, e.g. by Dement 1955, Dement and Kleitman 1957.

19. 22 percent: McNamara 2004, 1. As to how episodes of REM are distributed during a normal night's sleep see Walker and Stickgold 2004, 122.

20. Cf. Belicki 1987, 187.

21. Herman, Ellman and Roffwarg 1978; Hobson 1988, 143. How much dreaming there is in NREM sleep is disputed: see among others Solms 2000a, 844–845.

22. He argued in *The Interpretation of Dreams* (1954 [1900], 517) that 'the extent of this forgetting is as a rule over-estimated'. His reason was that 'not infrequently . . . in the middle of the work of interpretation an omitted portion of the dream comes to light and is described as having been forgotten till that moment' (518). And it is undeniable that apparently forgetting (part of) a dream is not always final.

a major side-effect of the discovery of the correlation between dreaming and REM, an effect owed also to other causes, namely the complete marginalization, in the scientific community, of the Freudian view of dreams. The inability of the Freudians to meet ordinary standards of scientific proof,[23] combined with the contextualization of Freud himself (not to mention Freud's appalling treatment of his patient 'Dora'),[24] helped in the 1970s to cause a drastic decline in the popularity of the Freudian view,[25] even in its modified later form.

In his book of 1900, Freud had set out his view that dreams were all wish-fulfilments, though in a very specialized sense: an internal censor usually turns our real wishes, sexual or aggressive,—the 'latent' content of our dreams—into relatively innocuous 'manifest' content.[26] In an essay of 1923, he continued to maintain that all dreams were wish-fulfilments, except those that occur 'in a traumatic neurosis'.[27] By that time he was also able to fit dreams into his tripartite structural theory—dreaming reflected strife between what are conventionally called in English the id and the superego.[28]

The Freudian view once exercised a very strong appeal, since it seemed to promise the true unveiling of a mystery. But by the 1970s and 1980s the more fair-minded of Freudians were beating a retreat, indicating for example, and it was a crucial admission, that they were interested in the manifest content of dreams for its own sake and not simply as a means of gaining access to their supposed latent content.[29] Psychiatrists began to point out that analysts were giving ludicrously contradictory interpretations of the same dreams.[30] One specialist writes that in 1973 one could still

23. Cf. Hobson 1988, 55.

24. The literature on Dora is now extensive: the revisionist view seems to have started with a literary critic—Marcus 1975, 286–290.

25. Symptomatic was the paper of McCarley and Hobson 1977 on the neurobiological origins of Freud's dream theory.

26. See Freud 1954 [1900], esp. 550–609.

27. Freud 1923a, 118. On the mainly unchanging character of Freud's views about dreams after 1900, see Hobson 1988, 59–60.

28. Freud 1923b.

29. See Fosshage 1987, for instance.

30. Zane 1971. The whole volume in which that paper appeared led in the same direction.

attempt to 'salvage . . . Freud's methodology'.[31] But from the late 1970s onwards the literature shows quite clearly that psychoanalytic research and practice were seeking very un-Freudian ways of explaining dream content.[32] The strongest claim that one is likely to hear now is that a Freudian view is not inevitably incompatible with the known physiology of dreaming.[33] But positive exponents are few.[34] The neuropsychologist Solms has argued that 'new clinicoanatomical and functional imaging findings . . . suggest that Freud's hypothesis to the effect that dreaming is instigated by the arousal of instinctual mechanisms during sleep is more tenable than we previously thought'; and that it is now possible to test Freud's hypothesis that dreams function to protect sleep.[35] However, this is a long way from being a revival of the major controversial elements in the old theory.[36]

Readers of this book will have no difficulty in seeing that I am to a great extent in sympathy with this Freud-diminishing trend. But there has been too much glee in some quarters over the Freudian decline, enough to make one suspect that the Freudians were sometimes right to claim that their opponents were merely in denial ('resistance'). For the fact is that Freud was, among his other talents, quite brilliant at describing some of the most characteristic features of dreaming, features that in several cases remain almost as mysterious now as they were in 1900—*Mischbildung*, for instance,

31. Foulkes 1996, 617.

32. Note in particular Fosshage and Loew 1986. J. Hopkins 1991 and indeed the entire *Cambridge Companion to Freud* amounted to a rearguard action.

33. B. E. Jones 2000.

34. But not extinct. On the centenary of the publication of the *Traumdeutung* an Italian psychiatrist (Bolognini 2000, 18) wrote, echoing Freud himself, that the book had had an effect on western culture as great as that of the discovery of America or the work of Copernicus or Darwin. An embattled Italian view, one might think. In the 'jamboree' mentioned above, the Freudian representatives considered themselves to be taking a 'decidedly minority position' (Shevrin and Eiser 2000, 1005); cf. Žižek 2006. Since 1999 a journal has appeared that seems hospitable to neo-Freudianism, *Neuropsychoanalysis*, but it is hard to find and appears in only thirteen libraries worldwide, according to WorldCat; it scarcely symbolizes a revival. The claim of Budd 2004, 257 (a British psychoanalyst) that 'modern dream research . . . has confirmed many of Freud's views' is undocumented and very misleading.

35. Solms 2000b, 1039.

36. Yet for fairly clear reasons such revivals are to be expected from time to time.

a person or place appearing in a dream with more than one identity, and condensation, the tendency of dreams to pack together multiple allusions.

The results of physiological research about dreaming have caused exhilaration, as we have already seen. A combination of techniques, some older, some more recent such as positron emission tomography (PET),[37] have allowed the physiologists to formulate much more detailed hypotheses about how the brain works during dreaming.[38] I am incompetent to judge such results, or to weigh the significance of continuing disagreements within that field; I simply note that physiology has not settled either of two other questions that are directly relevant to the present inquiry: it has not resolved the problem of the functions of dreaming, and it has not given us a fully satisfying account of all the salient subjective features of the phenomenon of dreaming itself.

What purpose does dreaming serve? It is not impossible that brain researchers will one day produce an incontrovertible theory about the function or functions of dreaming, but at present sharply divergent theories have their defenders.[39] One idea, ingenious but implausible, has it that our dreams are a vestige of Pleistocene man's (adaptive) unconscious training sessions for meeting the main danger in his life, attacks by wild animals.[40] This theory has the great merit of focusing attention on earlier stages of human evolution: a theory of function needs to distinguish between an original phase and current utility.[41] It would certainly be intriguing if it could be

37. Maquet et al. 1990 and many later publications.

38. Here I will note some work produced in and since 2000, and mention some critics: Hobson et al. 2000a and 2000b summarize the work of the most prominent group of American researchers in this field (for an easily understood visual summary see 2000a, fig. 7); for a different view see Solms 2000a and 2000b in the same volume. For critiques see among others Cartwright 2000 ('blind men describing an elephant', 914), Franzini 2000, B. E. Jones 2000, Nielsen 2000. McNamara 2004, 1–5 offers a brief account concentrating on REM.

39. 'It has been conjectured that dreams are the safety-valve of an overloaded mind; that dreams are used to clear the neural network of superfluous information acquired during the time we are awake; that dreams keep the organism in a state of constant alertness; that dreams stabilize memory traces after learning; that they have the role of preserving mental identity' (Casati 1998). For a review of other theories see Domhoff 2003, 156–167 (effectively demolishing 'problem-solving' theories about the function of dreams), McNamara 2004, chs. 6 and 9.

40. Revonsuo 2000 and elsewhere. See further Zadra et al. 2006; Valli et al. 2008.

41. Gould and Lewontin 1979, 581.

shown that dreams somehow echo the adaptive needs of early man, but it is simply nonsense to say that dreams do in fact do that, still more to say that they rehearse useful solutions to Pleistocene man's real problems about eating and being eaten. They simply do not provide *practice* at anything (except at thinking about insoluble problems). Of course we have plenty of anxiety dreams, but it is not even established that our anxiety dreams mostly concern our most serious waking anxieties (they frequently concern quite trivial ones),[42] and it is quite obvious that they do not normally help to *resolve* our anxieties.[43]

If there is to be a theory about the function of dreams based on the experience of prehistoric or anthropological populations, it should be based on what we actually know about the societies in question. For millions of years, humans lived as hunter-gatherers. Did dreaming serve any adaptive purpose in such a world?[44] It is certainly noteworthy that when a sophisticated anthropologist lived closely with hunter-gatherers (V. Pandya among the Ongees in the Andaman Islands), he found that they made regular use of their dreams and dream-descriptions to deal practically with their real-life anxieties and desires (they had a spirit medium to help them, and a marked tendency to make everyone's dreams agree with each other).[45]

The theory that currently has most support, however, declares that dreaming serves to consolidate memory. Dreaming might do this, for example, by clearing away superfluous information we have gathered while we are awake, removing 'certain undesirable modes of interaction in networks of cells in the cerebral cortex',[46] or it might somehow stabilize in our memories things that we are going to remember. It is not of course *obvious* that dreaming does either of these things. Dreams do not, for example, rehearse information that we possessed before we went to sleep, and if you have recently learned something, say the paradigm of the complicated

42. Is it not remarkable that no one has attempted to establish experimentally whether people's natural anxiety dreams reflect their deepest anxieties, even though a good deal of effort has gone into finding out whether dreams reflect the dreamers' 'concerns' (e.g. Saredi et al. 1997)?

43. For detailed refutation see Gunderson 2000, Thompson 2000 (with some weak arguments too) and other contributors to the same volume.

44. The question was asked, though not answered in a way I can fully understand, by Wax 2004.

45. Pandya 2004. This was a vital contribution.

46. Crick and Mitchison 1983.

Greek verb *histemi,* or how to play the violin, you are most unlikely to dream about the matter in detail,[47] or to remember your new-found skill any better as a result of a dream.

The problem is still very much under discussion. One view claims that 'aside from the REM rebound effect [that is to say, an increased need for REM sleep itself], no significant psychologic or biologic [*sic*] effects are noted with REM deprivation—at least for short-term REM deprivation in humans'.[48] (If you deprive rats of REM sleep for long enough, they die.) Yet the same author wrote that 'the cumulative effects of converging lines of experimental evidence suggest . . . that both REM and NREM [the author evidently means REM and NREM *sleep*] participate in memory processing. This, however, does not necessarily speak to the evolutionary functions of sleep'.[49] A highly lucid review-article observes that given the types and stages of memory consolidation and the several stages of sleep,

> one is faced with a truly staggering number of possible ways that sleep might affect memory consolidation. . . . It is only by asking whether a specific stage of sleep affects a particular aspect of memory processing for a given type of memory that one can ask scientifically answerable question<s> concerning sleep-dependent memory processing.[50]

The authors of an older article entitled 'The Case against Memory Consolidation in REM Sleep'[51] argued among other things that the techniques used to deprive experimental subjects of REM sleep, including drugs, have themselves been responsible for disrupting memory (and that dreaming serves to keep the brain alert during sleep). They admitted, however, that there was some evidence in favour of the theory they were attacking. The review-article quoted above concluded, inter alia, that

> human studies have provided examples where increases in REM sleep are seen following training, where REM, SWS [slow-wave sleep], or stage 2 NREM deprivation diminishes subsequent performance, and where overnight improvement correlates with REM, SWS or stage 2 NREM sleep.[52]

---

47. Which has led Flanagan (2000, 937) and others to deny that dreaming helps memory.
48. McNamara 2004, 94. Cf. Cartwright 2000, 915.
49. McNamara 2004, 99.
50. Walker and Stickgold 2004, 123. See further Hu et al. 2006.
51. Vertes and Eastman 2000.
52. Walker and Stickgold 2004, 130. Schredl 2005 gives a clear summary of the evi-

But REM sleep is not identical with dreaming, and none of this yet tells us whether dreaming in itself, with all its specific characteristics of fantasy, anxiety and story-making, is what serves these functions. There have been very many more or less plausible theories about why we dream, and as has been said, 'all of them are highly speculative and difficult to refute in a definitive way, and they therefore linger despite a lack of evidence for any of them'.[53] The same author concludes that 'it seems highly unlikely that dreams have any adaptive function'.[54] Yet both these statements are somewhat exaggerated: there is *some* evidence, and it seems much too early to say that an adaptive function is 'highly unlikely'.

No doubt it has always been the tendency of modern biologists to assume that every biological activity has a meaning or function. (Some have attributed this point of view to Aristotle,[55] wrongly, I think, for all he assumed was that there was a *reason* for every biological phenomenon, including dreaming,[56] which is crucially different.) Others have pointed to the side-effects of evolution, and the architectural metaphor 'spandrel' has enjoyed a certain amount of popularity.[57] But we know why buildings have spandrels, and we cannot yet say with confidence why we dream. I point this out to help us understand why the Greek science of dreams did not progress further than it did.

✿   ✿   ✿

A critic will certainly want to complain by this point that by introducing contemporary scientific accounts of dreaming into a discussion of the Greeks and Romans I am presupposing that dreaming is a kind of human constant. On one level, such a charge is simply false, since throughout this study I take it as obvious that every society understands dreams in its own way, or rather in its own selection of ways (the ancients disagreed heartily

---

dence for supposing that REM sleep strengthens 'procedural', as distinct from 'declarative', memory.

53. Domhoff 2003, 157.

54. 167. For a similar view see Blagrove 2000.

55. Mayr 1982, 89.

56. See Chapter IV.

57. 'The triangular space between the outer curve of an arch and the rectangle formed by the mouldings enclosing it, frequently filled in with ornamental work', *OED*. Gould and Lewontin 1979 applied the concept to evolution and Flanagan (2000 and elsewhere) has insistently applied it to dreaming.

among themselves). On the level of dreaming itself, however, the charge deserves a somewhat fuller response. This response comes in three parts: in the first place, I am entirely willing to believe that there have been changes—in fact a large part of the point of Chapter I is to explore the likelihood (as I see it) that Greeks and Romans from time to time dreamed a kind of dream that we do not dream and have not for several hundred years. Secondly, dreaming is—though scholars in some fields do not like to face the fact—a physiological phenomenon, which means that radical changes that are supposed to have taken place in a relatively short evolutionary time-span had better have some good evidence in their favour. Thirdly, every one of the thirteen features of dreaming in the list that follows is indeed attested in antiquity;[58] the reasons why some of them are not attested very often will emerge in Chapter II. Greek and Roman dreams had no common and credible feature—apart from the epiphany dream—that modern dreams lack.

✿   ✿   ✿

It is hard enough to agree what dreams are like now, from the point of view of the dreamer. Once again, some are confident: 'the content of dream reports . . . is in large measure a coherent and reasonable simulation of the real world'.[59] For the moment I leave aside our difficulties in remembering dreams, in remembering them clearly, and in continuing to remember them (see Chapter II), except to observe that the word 'report' may suggest more accuracy than even the most clear-headed and honest dreamers usually achieve.

A dream is normally a life-like sequence of images (occasionally a static image) seen while one is sleeping or half-awake. Yet dream images have some other specific qualities, some that are invariable, others that are occasional, and in each case there is likely to be some variation between the different phases of sleep.[60]

58. Item 5 may possibly be a minor exception: people sometimes dreamt of reading or writing, according to Artemidorus (i.53, iii.25).

59. Domhoff 2003, 19.

60. I had to devise this list for myself, on the basis of five years of reading, my own experience and that of some of my friends and students. It is not exhaustive: in particular I am not sure how to describe or analyse the phenomenon that Freud called 'condensation' (1954 [1900], ch. VI).

(1) It is universal or nearly so that the dreamer has no control over what he/she attends to while dreaming. In waking life I feel that I am free to stop typing and look around my study, go out for a walk, or do any of a million other things; in my dreams I have no such sense of freedom. I cannot alter my field of vision, or decide to do something else.[61]

(2) One's self-control is often weak: we often say and do things we would not permit ourselves to say or do if we were awake.[62] Can there be any adult who has not behaved outrageously in sleep?

(3) Dreams are more or less inventive, sometimes startlingly so; they are never or hardly ever reruns of remembered experiences,[63] though strangely enough—so at least it is widely believed[64]—they can occasionally be reruns of earlier dreams.

(4) Nonetheless they quite often contain elements from the dreamer's very recent experience—sometimes selected quite at random it seems. The 'day's residue' *(Tagesreste)*, a topic much discussed by Freud,[65] has been the subject of recent research, with somewhat divergent results. But two credible studies concluded that 'about half' and about 48 percent of young adults identified some day residue, defined as residue of the immediately preceding day.[66]

(5) A negative feature may be included: even scholars and scientists ap-

61. This matter of will is not mentioned much in the contemporary scientific literature, but the older literature refers to it from time to time, e.g. Macario 1857, 21 (which I learned of from Sophie Schwartz 2000).

62. The night before I wrote this I dreamt that I told a colleague what was really wrong with his work.

63. Exceptions are sometimes claimed: Fosse et al. 2003, 5.

64. Cf. Solms 1997, ch. 22, Hobson 2002, 122.

65. 1900, esp. ch. V, sec. A.

66. Botman and Crovitz 1989–90, Harlow and Roll 1992; cf. Fosse et al. 2003. There is also very strong evidence of a 'dream-lag' effect, that is to say reminiscences of waking life six days and more before the dream: Marquardt et al. 1996. See further McNamara 2004, 134–135. The attempt of Roussy et al. 2000 to show that there is in fact little 'continuity between waking and dreaming life' was methodologically flawed: having defined continuity as continuity with the previous day's experience, the researchers made the mistake of relying on their subjects' (N = 13!) 'event descriptions' to know everything that passed through their minds on the preceding day. Reading *Ulysses* might have suggested to them what a day's mental experiences may be like.

pear to dream no more than rarely of reading or writing, or perhaps even of any 'highly focussed cognitive activity'.[67]

(6) Dreams normally involve human interactions with other living creatures.[68]

(7) They are far more likely to be forgotten than waking experiences.

(8) The visual image may be vivid but it is often out of focus or inadequate (though one can commonly identify a person without looking carefully, just as in waking life). Some exceptionally careful research concluded tentatively that while 'most dreams do not depart very radically [in quality] from normal waking imagery', there is a tendency towards colour desaturation (which is presumably the main reason why some people are not sure whether they dream in colour) and a tendency towards poor background clarity (compare feature 1).[69]

(9) The other senses seldom seem to do much—even hearing enters in less than in waking life.[70]

(10) Futility and incompleteness are common.

(11) Dreams often have emotional impact, leaving us in a particular frame of mind, afraid, wondering, depressed or disgusted.

(12) An ancient typology of dreams that still works and is sometimes reproduced in a contemporary form features anxiety dreams and wish-fulfilment dreams as the two most easily recognized types apart from 'recent memory' dreams,[71] which can coincide with either of the others. It is not to be expected that there will be any agreement about how many of our dreams fall into these two categories. More interesting in any case than the quantitative question is that the fact that anxiety dreams very often reflect *not* the

67. To use the language of Schredl and Hofmann 2003.

68. McNamara 2004, 127.

69. Rechtschaffen and Buchignani 1992, 154.

70. According to the studies reviewed by Snyder 1970, esp. 139, virtually all dreams involve visual sensation, 69 percent hearing, 11 percent touch (median figures).

71. Such dreams bulk large in most scientific taxonomies, ancient and modern: see for instance Busink and Kuiken 1996, who argue with considerable care for the following groupings: 'existential dreams' (which many would include among anxiety dreams), 'anxiety dreams', 'transcendent dreams', which are I think wish-fulfilments under another name, and 'mundane dreams'. Antiquity knew of these phenomena too, of course, as we shall see in detail in Chapter IV.

dreamer's serious anxieties but petty or nonexistent ones (the gravest problems of youth do not include appearing at school with no clothes on, and the gravest problems of old age do not include losing one's luggage). The contrary is often asserted,[72] but there seems to have been no good research, even though the answer might well have some clinical importance in psychotherapy. However, a recent scientific writer has noticed that we dream about 'incomplete arrangements' and not about certain 'emotionally salient' anxieties.[73] Does something similar apply to our wish-fulfilment dreams?

(13) Finally, a feature more contentious than any of the above. Everyone knows that dreams have a tendency to be bizarre or illogical, and in certain particular ways: places and people can have more than one identity, Rome may simultaneously be New York, the sun may also be the moon, Sigmund may at the same time be Siegfried (Freud called this phenomenon *Mischbildung*).[74]

Some researchers, however, have presented for decades the counterintuitive claim that dreams are not bizarre after all. In the beginning there was a discovery—that dreams dreamt in laboratory awakenings are not as bizarre as dreams that are spontaneously remembered;[75] which may leave a historian unconcerned, since in so far as we are concerned with actual dreams they are not laboratory dreams.

72. Greenberg et al. 1992, 545, claim to have shown that 'manifest dreams deal with issues that are problematic for the dreamer', but they scarcely do so, still less do they establish that the 'issues' concerned are the *most* problematic ones. For a relatively strong statement see Revonsuo 2000, 881 ('there is overwhelming evidence showing that dream content indeed reflects the current emotional problems of the dreamer'). For a relatively limited statement see Domhoff 2000, 930 ('much of dream content is . . . continuous with past or present waking emotional concerns', referring to his 1996 book, ch. 8, for the proof; there, however, he rightly observes that 'much more research needs to be done before this conclusion [not an identical one, but let that pass] can be stated with confidence', 189). Cartwright 1996, 182, merely says that 'the judges found significantly more negative-feeling dreams among the depressed subjects than among those who were not depressed'.

73. Hobson 2002, 154.

74. Freud 1954 [1900], ch. VI sec. C. I leave aside 'condensation' and 'displacement' as not being immediately observable; but Freud's sections on these topics (A and B in the same chapter) are still of very great interest.

75. Snyder 1970. But since his research had not even attempted to define or investigate the bizarre, his conclusion was to say the least impressionistic.

But the quarrel has spread to dreams in general. It is in part a fairly simple matter of verbal confusion, in part a rather less simple matter of inappropriate methodology. There is no agreed definition of dream bizarreness, a definition that has to cover eeriness and implausible behaviour as well as the suspension of the laws of physics and biology. It has become a commonplace that 'relatively few dreams are very bizarre',[76] but such statements are invariably based on inadequate definitions of the bizarre (a term that is itself scarcely adequate to the strangeness of dreams). This is scarcely surprising in view of the fact that even those specialists who do recognize dream bizarreness have not succeeded in describing it comprehensively (they are particularly weak on psychological improbability— cf. feature 2).[77] A systematic account[78] lists as the components of bizarreness (a) discontinuities,[79] (b) improbable combinations (essentially the suspension of the laws of physics and biology), and (c) improbable identities (Freudian *Mischbildung* apparently). Which is fine as far as it goes, but leaves out, among other things, psychological improbability (inappropriate speech and action), absurdity, and sheer oddness of subject matter (when I tell myself that the word for 'swordfish' in Chinese, a language I do not know, is such-and-such).

It would take too long to analyse the many poor conceptualizations of this problem that have found their way into print. I will simply take two fairly recent examples.[80] One study found that only 15–20 percent of the 'elements' in dream reports 'were classified' (scientists love passive

76. Rechtschaffen 1978, 97. One can understand what leads someone to write that 'nocturnal dreaming is a well-organized and generally realistic simulation of waking experience' (Foulkes 1985, 28), yet that word 'generally' conceals a serious distortion.

77. Hobson 1988, 257–269, Mamelak and Hobson 1989, Rittenhouse et al. 1994 (with useful bibliography, 101).

78. Reinsel et al. 1992, esp. 184.

79. 'For example, in a mentation report [this is psychospeak for a description of a conscious mental experience] the subject says that he was talking with his brother in an apartment and then, with no transition reported, says he was speaking with a woman in the hall'. The vagueness of this criterion is evident.

80. Domhoff 2003, 152–153, does not trouble to offer a definition of any kind, criticizes others for failing to achieve an agreed definition, and relies largely on a forty-year-old piece of research by one of his own collaborators that is regrettably unfindable as referenced; it is said to have shown that 'only 10% of 815 home and lab dream reports had at least one bizarre element' (153), which is not consistent with the other evidence available.

verbs!) as bizarre.[81] But no one ever pretended that a high proportion of 'elements' in dreams were bizarre (everything in Penelope's famous dream in *Odyssey* XIX was quite normal—except that her husband was an eagle). A highly salient characteristic of dreams is that most of them have something in them that makes them quite unlike waking experience, lived or remembered. It is still possible to write that dreams 'are mental simulations of the world and the dreamer's lifeworld',[82] but such misleading statements are destined, I think, to retreat to the fringes.[83] Some empirical research done twenty years ago showed convincingly that in a sample of 117 REM dreams, only 23.9 percent had no bizarre features.[84]

The wish to deny that dreams are to a significant extent bizarre may partly derive from a subconscious desire to quieten the ghost of Freud. On a rational plane, it derives from the misuse of a social science technique known as 'content-analysis'. A historian who hears for the first time that in the 1990s people were still advocating the use of content-analysis is likely to be startled. Some American historians *circa* 1959 thought that content-analysis—which amounted to little more than counting the number of times a given expression occurred in a given text—was a mildly useful technique worth borrowing from sociology, but it rapidly turned out that at best it could only be used to suggest lines of inquiry, and it sank without the slightest trace (in another sense, of course, what historians do all the time is analyse content). Something similar seems to have happened in anthropology.[85] Those who have applied content-analysis to dreams have discovered a great deal—of wholly inconsequential and uninteresting information. They know, or at least claim to know, how often Americans dream about their dogs and cats.[86]

81. Revonsuo 2000, 1066, referring to Revonsuo and Salmivalli 1995.

82. McNamara 2004, 107.

83. States 1993 (he claims, 14, that he does not deny that dreams are ever bizarre, but that is not consistent with his title). States 2000 marks a certain retreat.

84. Haas et al. 1988. Whether this work was underattended to in Anglophonia because it was in German I do not know; the results are also presented in Strauch and Meier 1996 [1992], 96–103.

85. See Tedlock 1991, 162–163, offering good reasons. This practice lives on in social psychology, apparently: C. R. Smith 2000.

86. Domhoff 2003, 108–109. Some of the questions asked by this school are potentially more interesting, such as how often the dreamer behaves aggressively in his/her dreams

But they have not shown, or even come close to showing, that the common experience of mankind—not to mention the views of many other scientists—according to which dreams occurring in natural conditions are often (and I attempt no definition of 'often') bizarre, illogical or fantastic, is an illusion.

❖   ❖   ❖

Two lessons can be learned. The scientific achievement of the last half century with respect to dreams has been notable (there had already been some marked progress in the nineteenth century). As is usual in all fields of inquiry, the quality of the work has been variable—and we have not taken into account the lunatic fringe, which in the case of dreaming always threatens to be a little more than a fringe.[87] And the drive to discover things about dreaming is quite naturally not as strong as the drive to make more practical discoveries. That may also have been true in antiquity, as we shall see in Chapter IV. But we now possess an impressive amount of quantified knowledge.

The second lesson, however, is that there is a great deal of disagreement, even about describing the phenomenon under discussion, let alone explaining it. That should help us to maintain a sense of proportion when we come to consider what the Greeks and Romans thought about dreaming, and how they theologized and theorized on the subject.

❖   ❖   ❖

What follows is not a full cultural history of dreaming in classical antiquity, but a more limited attempt to answer specific questions. Nonetheless the project is methodologically quite exigent, partly because it requires one to take account of the scientific debates described above, but also for several other reasons.

First of all there is the fragmentary nature of the evidence, so familiar that we are sometimes in danger of forgetting it. In Chapter III, in particular, but also in every other chapter, I shall be speaking about notions entertained by the more articulate Greeks and Romans and trying to trace

---

(see Domhoff 73). But such questions are probably too loaded, morally speaking, to elicit reliable answers (Domhoff 41–46 notwithstanding).

87. My nightmare is that an American billionaire(ss) will take it into his/her head to devote $200 million to an institute dedicated to proving that dreams are—whatever he/she believes they are.

how these notions developed from period to period, but often we ancient historians are like people trying to collect their possessions after a hurricane. There is no need to harp further on this theme.

Any attempt to write a chapter of the cultural history of the Greek and Roman world also faces the difficulty that, from the time of Alexander of Macedon onwards, many of its inhabitants were Greeks or Romans only in some attenuated sense. One can of course choose to study the people whose primary identity was Greek or Roman, and that is what this book does; but matters are not so simple, particularly because Christian, and therefore Jewish, beliefs are also part of our subject-matter.

The next hurdle is literary form. Now, not all the evidence that we are going to use is literary (and the epigraphical evidence too has its conventions). But literary form is not a barrier to this inquiry, it is in effect part of the subject matter. The difficult part is that so many genres and so many individual imaginations are involved. Some questions are obvious—how, for instance, should a historian approach romance (in the literary sense)? Other questions concern particular authors and, though they can be of great interest, cannot be fully discussed in these pages—what, for instance, did Vergil mean to convey when he made such extensive use of the convention, Homeric and non-Alexandrian, of the epiphany dream? The aim is to describe the flow of ideas and conventions about dream-description, which—it is to be hoped—will help others to understand what Greek and Roman writers built on and reacted to.

The religious assumptions of Greek and Roman antiquity are another complication. Even in lands where religion is still powerful, the twenty-first-century person does not see the divine order, or the gods' role in the world, as the Greeks and Romans did. Their attitudes, though very far from uniform even before the spread of Christianity, cannot be summed up in a few phrases. Suffice it for the moment to say that, free of fantastic dogmas, the adherents of traditional Greek and Roman religion were free to speculate about the activities (if any) of the gods in the affairs of humans but generally assumed that the gods were benevolent unless provoked to anger; and only a few offences provoked them.

The last hurdle that deserves discussion concerns the empathy of the historian with the flesh-and-blood people he/she is writing about, a question often raised, though never resolved, by the late Keith Hopkins.[88] Can a cold-blooded rationalist write about ancient religion? It depends what

---

88. See especially K. Hopkins 1993. See further Harris forthcoming.

you mean by 'rationalist'. I recognize the Stoics as rationalists (and the purists at least were extremely cold-blooded by our standards), and believe that a modern academic, if he/she is endowed with a strong imagination, knows the sources perfectly and makes an enormous effort, can understand them. With respect to dreaming, however, the difficulty is more severe. I cannot possibly become Aristotle, Artemidorus or Synesius. What I can do is to set out for myself the psychological characteristics and literary habits of the ancients I know about, and with certain problems and their possible solutions in mind launch into an analysis of such evidence as survives. With the aim of making history out of it.

I

From Epiphany to Episode: A Revolution in the Description of Dreams

Epiphany or Messenger Dreams

A form of dream-description that was very common in classical antiquity is now, apparently, very rare indeed in the western world. Many dreams were described as what we can call *epiphanies:* an authority figure visited the sleeper and made a significant pronouncement, and that was the dream. In modern times, all or most dreams are described as what we can call *episodes,* sequences of events.[1] This chapter attempts to refine the above description of this remarkable change in the representation of dreams, and to answer the obvious questions—first, what changed—people's dreams, the conventions used to describe them, or both? Why did such a strange convention last so long? When did it die out, if it really did? And can we say why?

Scholars have written generously about this peculiar form of Greek and Roman dream-description. The work of the Hellenist E. R. Dodds more than half a century ago still stands out; but even Dodds, who had much to say about the epiphany dream,[2] did not date or account for its demise.[3]

---

1. I see no alternative to making these two words technical terms. They will be defined shortly. For the term 'epiphany dream' see Schwabl 1983, 18 (which he contrasts unsatisfactorily with *bildhaft* dreams, which he calls 'symbol-dreams'—but very many of these were not seen as symbolic). I use the term 'episode' without any implication that the dreams in question are coherent or intelligible.

2. Dodds 1951, ch. 4. On some other aspects of Dodds's thinking about ancient dreams see Harris 2003, 19.

3. He suggested a cause, however, which will be discussed at the end of the chapter.

Neither has anyone else. I shall argue that there is a degree of continuity between the way the Greeks and Romans, on the one hand, and mediaeval Europeans, on the other, represented dreams, more continuity than we might have expected given the official attitude of Christianity towards meaningful dreams, which was often suspicious. Later I shall contend that the disappearance of the epiphany dream was part of the widespread secularization of European thought in the sixteenth and seventeenth centuries. And the story which begins in the ancient Near East seems to end with, of all books, *Robinson Crusoe*. Yet outside the 'modern west' the epiphany dream still lived on in the twentieth century.

Let us first explore how 'epiphanies' differ from 'episodes', and establish that a change has in fact taken place. No one will dispute that Greek and Roman texts, when they describe dreams, often represent them as admonitory epiphanies, that is to say as the sleeper's experience of a visitation by an individual, often a divine being or a divine messenger but sometimes simply an authoritative person or a ghost, who brings instructions or important information.[4]

A few examples will illustrate the pattern. In *Iliad* II, in the first dream-description in Greek literature, Zeus sends a personage called 'dire Dream' in order to mislead Agamemnon:[5] Dream 'stood over the head' of the Achaean king 'in the semblance of Nestor the son of Neleus, whom Agamemnon most honoured among the elders'.

> 'You sleep [he said], son of warlike Atreus tamer of horses. A man should not sleep all night if he bears the burden of office, a man to whom armies are entrusted and who has so many cares. Now quickly take note of what I say: Know that I am the messenger of Zeus, who though he is far off cares for you and pities you greatly. He commands you to arm your long-haired Achaeans, to attack in full force, for now you could capture the wide-streeted city of the Trojans. The immortals who live on Olympus no longer debate the matter, for Hera with her prayers has prevailed on them all, and upon the Trojans troubles from Zeus are fixed. Keep you this in your mind, and don't forget it when sweet sleep leaves you'. So saying, he departed, leaving the king imagining things that were not to come to pass. He thought

4. The figure may be conceived of as an image *(eidolon)*: cf. Dodds 1951, 104. Hanson 1980, 1410–1411, gives a useful description of the epiphany dream, to which he gives the awkward name 'audio-visual dream-vision proper'.

5. On the personification of dreams in Homer (and later) see Kessels 1978, 7–10, 174–185, 199–200.

he would capture Priam's city that day, the fool . . . He woke from sleep, but the divine voice was poured around him.[6]

Another instance of the epiphany form is the stunningly powerful dream in which Aeschylus' Avenging Furies see and hear the dead queen Clytemnestra.[7] In Herodotus, to take a more typical example, a tall fine-looking man,[8] presumed by those who saw him to be speaking for the gods, appeared in two successive dreams to King Xerxes, and then once to his counsellor Artabanus, to tell them to reverse their policy and invade Greece.[9] Another case: when Socrates was in prison awaiting his death, so Plato tells us, he informed his follower Crito that a 'fine and beautiful woman, dressed in white' had appeared to him in a dream and told him exactly which day he would be executed ('she approached, called me, and said . . .').[10] This, by the way, is the first time we hear of an epiphany dream being afforded to someone of less than royal status.[11]

6. Lines 1–41. When Agamemnon describes the dream to the council of the Achaeans, he describes the visitor as Dream in the shape of Nestor (56–58), and adds the details that Dream flew away and that he woke up (71). For Nestor's reaction see Chapter III. The other epiphany dreams in Homer are listed below. Homeric dreams are usually epiphany dreams (Schwabl 1983, 19). Brillante 1990a shows how artfully Homer played with this narrative pattern.

7. *Eum.* 94–178. The other known occasion when a dream figure appeared on the tragic stage like this was when the dead Polydorus appeared to his mother in Euripides' *Hecuba*, with the difference that Polydorus speaks directly to the audience (cf. Cederstrom 1971, 163, Jouanna 1982, 43).

8. The beauty of the epiphany figure, common in Greek and Roman texts (cf. Dulaey 1973, 197–198), has Near Eastern parallels (Oppenheim 1956, 189), and, I think, roots. Cf. Oppenheim 198–199.

9. vii.12–18. Xerxes tells Artabanus that if a god has sent the dream, it will come back (vii.15), and of course it does; Artabanus, on the other hand, thinks that dreams are mostly 'remains of the day' (vii.16), but comes to accept that this one was 'sent by the god' (vii.18). I have started with some misleading dreams, since so many scholars keep on repeating that the Greeks and Romans all believed in the truthfulness of predictive dreams. Other epiphany dreams that were pieces of divine trickery: *Il.* x.496–497; Herodotus ii.139 (cf. Harrison 2000, 136 n. 52).

10. *Crito* 44ab. She did so simply by quoting *Il.* ix.363, a plain message in the context. For a good commentary on this dream-description see van Lieshout 1980, 106–107. The closest parallel is with *Apol.* 33c, where Socrates tells the jurors that dreams were one of the means that 'the god' used to tell him to spend his time cross-examining those who think they are wise but are not really so (but these are not explicitly said to have been epiphany dreams). We shall return in Chapter III to Plato's opinions about dream-knowledge.

11. In the case of Xenophon's King Cyrus it is less remarkable that a superhuman figure appeared in a dream to warn him that death was near (*Cyr.* viii.7.2).

Athena appeared in dreams, four times in all, to priests or ex-priests of hers at Lindos on the island of Rhodes.[12] Ptolemy Soter, king of Egypt, dreamt of a statue of the god Pluto that, as it turned out, was situated in the city of Sinope; the statue ordered him to take it as quickly as possible to Alexandria, where the Egyptians recognized it as an image of the god Serapis.[13] In a recently published epigram by Posidippus of Pella,[14] Ptolemy's daughter Queen Arsinoe (II) is imagined appearing in a dream to a young woman.[15] Several times a certain Zoilos of Aspendos, in the mid–third century, received dream-instructions from Serapis.[16] Diodorus the Sicilian gives a relatively full account, attributing it to the Egyptians, of how Isis appears to those who seek her medical aid through the procedure of 'incubation' (about which we shall shortly say more).[17]

The Hellenistic literary dream was often of a quite different type,[18] but Callimachus evidently claimed to have dreamt of the Muses.[19] The fragments of Ennius' Annals show that he in turn described an epiphany dream featuring Homer.[20] Vergil reverts to, or rather surpasses, the Homeric

12. So said the temple's inscribed chronicle: Blinkenberg 1941, 182–187, FGrHist 532 F 1, section D. The first record (when she saved the Lindians from the forces of Darius in 490) is fully preserved, the others only in part; but the first three epiphanies were certainly supposed to have been in dreams. For parallels and useful commentary see Higbie 2003, 273–284.

13. Plutarch, De Iside et Osiride 28 (Mor. 361f–362a), Tacitus, Hist. iv.83–84 (not a statue but a larger-than-life young man), etc. A Greek text from Egypt describing a sort of epiphany dream that appeared to King Nectanebo II (359–342)—a character who incidentally had a long future in the Alexander Romance—is thought to have been based on an Egyptian original and suggests how local traditions may have reinforced the Greek model (P.Leid. I.396 = UPZ 81; see most recently Gauger 2002, Ryholt 2002).

14. Fr. 36 in the edition of Austin and Bastianini.

15. Contrast fr. 33.

16. P.Cair.Zen. I.59034, reprinted in Totti 1985, 160–162.

17. Diodorus Siculus i.25. A Hellenistic text in the pseudonymous little-known letters of Hippocrates describes a dream in which Asclepius and Truth ('tall and beautiful') make successive pronouncements (Ep.15; for the date see W. D. Smith 1990, 29).

18. See among others Perutelli 1994.

19. Aetia 2 (for the likelihood that the vision was described as a dream cf. Cameron 1995, 138), but that was something of a special case. As to whether the vision Hesiod had of the Muses (Theog. 22–34) was meant to be a dream-description see M. L. West ad loc. (there is no clear indication to that effect).

20. Book 1, lines 2–11 Skutsch—he made quite a lengthy pronouncement, so it seems from Lucretius i.126 (cf. Fronto, De eloquentia 2.12).

method: all the rather numerous dream-descriptions in the *Aeneid,* bar one or one and a half, are epiphany dreams.[21] Ovid invents an elaborate story about Morpheus, a son of Sleep, to explain at length how Alcyone came to dream of an epiphany of her dead husband King Ceyx.[22]

Eunus, the leader of the rebellious Sicilian slaves, said that he was visited and informed by the gods, both in his dreams and while awake too.[23] Cicero included in his *De Republica* a long account of a dream of Scipio Aemilianus, in which the latter's grandfather Scipio Africanus is supposed to have appeared in order to pass on his political wisdom; the so-called *Somnium Scipionis* is the most elaborate of all the epiphany dreams to have survived from antiquity.[24] On a more modest social level, the elder Pliny wrote that an unspecified god had recently told the mother of a praetorian guardsman of a cure for rabies (the root of the dog-rose, *cynorrhodon,* suitably enough), just when he needed it.[25] Plutarch tells numerous dream-epiphany stories, how for instance in Asia Minor 'the mother of the gods', named here as Dindymene, appeared to Themistocles and gave him a warning that saved his life, and led him to build her a temple.[26]

In the Acts of the Apostles,[27] Paul, while in the Troad, dreamt of a Macedonian, whom he took to be a divine representative, who told him to cross over to Macedonia to help the people there.[28] Apollonius of Tyana ex-

21. Cf. Steiner 1952, 49–50, Berlin 1994, 25. There are ten epiphany dreams. The exception is Dido's dream in *Aen.* iv.465–468 (but see also the simile at xii.908–912), on which see among others Weidhorn 1970, 64–65. In the case of Palinurus, Sleep is said to bring him 'somnia tristia' and to appear in the form of the Trojan Phorbas, so there are major elements of an epiphany dream, but Palinurus is still awake when he sees Phorbas (*Aen.* v.838–861).

22. *Met.* xi.583–709. Juno sends Iris to tell Sleep to send a dream, and he sends Morpheus, who specializes in appearing as a human in the dreams of royalty. In *Ex Ponto* iii.3 Ovid varies the convention by delivering a speech to Amor, who appears in a dream, before the god is able to speak.

23. Poseidonius, *FGrH* 87 F 108 = Diodorus Siculus xxxiv/xxxv.2.3.

24. Macrobius explains why Cicero converted Plato's myth of Er into a dream—the resuscitation of Er was more susceptible to mockery than a dream-story, *Comm. in Somn. Scip.* i.1.9.

25. *Natural History* xxv.16–18. A rather convincing dream, perhaps, since it was supposed to have contained the day's residue, for the dreamer had been attracted by such a rose the previous day.

26. *Them.* 30. For other instances of epiphany dreams see *Rom.* 2, *Alc.* 39, *Alex.* 2, *Pyrrhus* 11, *CG* 1, *Luc.* 10 and 12.

27. Acts 16:8–10.

28. According to Josephus, Alexander of Macedon had crossed into Asia after dreaming

plained his visit to Crete by recounting, similarly, that he had seen a personified female Crete in a dream:[29]

> He came to Cape Malea in early spring, with the intention of sailing for
> Rome. This was his project, but he had a dream that a tall, elderly lady embraced him and asked him to stay with her before he went to Italy. She
> claimed to be the nurse of Zeus, and she wore a crown adorned with every
> product of land and sea [!]. Apollonius thought the vision over and realized
> that he must first sail to Crete.

According to Suetonius, Iuppiter Capitolinus himself appeared in a dream to Augustus—who was not overawed but replied to the god's complaint.[30] Among the ninety-five dreams written up by Artemidorus in Book V of his *Oneirocritica* (examples of dreams that 'came true'), there are only four epiphany dreams,[31] but that is not surprising since Artemidorus considers that the meaning of such dreams is so obvious that they are not worth discussing by a dream-interpreter such as himself. Two scenes of just this kind appear as miniatures in a Vatican manuscript of Vergil produced about 400 AD: in one of them two Penates and in the other Hector appear to the sleeping Aeneas (Plates 1 and 2).[32]

Augustine tells a tale about a young man ('I heard for certain while I was in Milan . . .') who dreamt that his dead father appeared in a dream and showed him the whereabouts of some highly useful legal documents.[33] But most late-antique epiphany dreams are religious and Christian. In the year 415, in Palestine—to take a random example—a priest named Lucianus

---

of a priest who encouraged him (*AJ* xi.333–335); just before Alexander and the High Priest met, in strained circumstances, god appeared to the latter and told him all would be well (*AJ* xi.327–328).

29. Philostratus, *Vita Ap.* 4.34.

30. *Div.Aug.* 91; see also ch. 94. All the dreams in which gods or others appeared in the dreams of Roman emperors are catalogued by Weber 2000.

31. Dodds 1973, 178 n. 1, says nine, but only the ones in chs. 9, 72, 89, and 92 really qualify. The story in ch. 13 might count in a pinch, and perhaps the ones in chs. 50 and 61. One is briefly recounted in iv.80, where a man prays to Serapis to give judgement on an ambiguous dream and the latter obliges with another dream (see further Nock 1934, 71–72).

32. Vat. Lat. 3225, f. 28r and f. 19v. See further Wright 1993. The dreams are described in *Aen.* iii. 147–178 and ii. 268–297 respectively.

33. *De cura pro mortuis gerenda* 11 (*CSEL* 41.642).

Plate 1. The Penates appearing to dreaming Aeneas, an epiphany dream described in *Aeneid* iii.147–178. From Vat.Lat. 3225 of about 400 AD, f. 28r. Photo © Biblioteca Vaticana.

dreamt three times of a tall elderly man dressed in white who identified himself as the angel Gamaliel and told Lucianus where to find the bodily remains of the saint Stephen.[34]

34. The text of Lucianus' letter is in *PL* 41, but it is best read in Vanderlinden 1946, 194–197.

Plate 2. Hector appearing to dreaming Aeneas, an epiphany dream described in *Aeneid* ii.268–297. From Vat.Lat. 3225 of about 400 AD, f. 19v. Photo © Biblioteca Vaticana.

The epiphany dream also lent itself to parody: at the beginning of the life of Aesop, the goddess Isis, along with all the Muses, appears to the lowly slave.[35] In the *Golden Ass,* the newly converted Lucius is visited by Isis every single night.[36]

35. *Vita Aesopi G* 6–7 (ed. B. E. Perry, pp. 36–37); but Isis could not go to the length of addressing Aesop directly—she speaks to the Muses. See further the *Vita Aesopi* edited by G. A. Karla (Wiesbaden, 2001), ch. 7 (Tuche [Chance] appears to Aesop). There are also epiphany dreams in Babrius' fables (10, Aphrodite; 30, Hermes; 49, Tuche).

36. Apuleius, *Met.* xi.19. A number of scholars have pointed out that Lucius makes him-

We know in fact that this was very far indeed from being an exclusively literary convention, mainly because of the epigraphical and also sculptural evidence. Gods, especially Asclepius and Serapis but others too, were commonly held to have appeared to dreamers, and to the waking as well, and to have required commemoration of the event. But the figure who is most often said to have appeared in epiphany dreams is without doubt the healing god Asclepius. The texts from Epidaurus are well-known to historians of ancient religion and medicine,[37] but it is worth quoting two examples:[38]

> Ambrosia of Athens, blind in one eye. She came as a suppliant to the god. As she walked about in the temple she laughed at some of the cures as incredible and impossible, <and at the notion> that the lame and the blind should be cured by merely seeing a dream. In her sleep she had a vision. It seemed to her that the god stood by her and said he would cure her, but that in payment he would ask her to dedicate in the temple a silver pig as a memorial of her ignorance [*amathia*]. After saying this, he cut the diseased eyeball and poured in some drug. When day came she walked out in good health.[39]

> Euphanes, a boy from Epidaurus. Suffering from stone he slept in the temple. He dreamt that the god stood by him and asked 'What will you give me if I cure you?' 'Ten dice', he answered. The god laughed and told him that he would cure him. When day came he walked out sound.[40]

Van Straten[41] and Renberg have painstakingly collected the epigraphical evidence from the whole Graeco-Roman world (some of the inscriptions refer explicitly to dreams as distinct from visions); they cover the entire period from the fifth century BC to the fourth century AD.[42] Inscriptions

---

self ridiculous with such claims (see most recently Hunink 2006, 26–27). Yet Isis must sometimes have been quite generous with her appearances, because the *only* persons who were allowed to enter her shrine near Tithorea, 'the holiest one the Greeks have made for her', were those she had summoned by dreams (Pausanias x.32.13, where the next sentence, which quotes a similar practice at a shrine of the gods of the underworld, seems to guarantee that epiphany dreams are involved [*oneiraton opseis*]).

37. *IG* IV².1.121–127, reedited by Herzog 1931. For selections see Edelstein and Edelstein 1945, LiDonnici 1995, Girone 1998.

38. Another example will be quoted in Chapter II.

39. *IG* IV².1.121 (Edelstein and Edelstein 1945, I, 230, T.423), no. IV, LiDonnici 1995, 88–89).

40. Ibid. no. VIII.

41. Van Straten 1976.

42. Renberg 2003, 143. Few of the Greek inscriptions are pre-Hellenistic; none of the

occasionally give details of what had happened: at Cnidos, at some time in the fourth century BC, Hermes appeared to a mother in a dream and told her that her (presumably deceased) daughter 'was serving the goddess' (Demeter);[43] Apollo Ptoios, at some date in the next century, appeared to a seer and promised him, with a smile, the gift of truthful *(apseude)* prophecy.[44] It is notable that these instructions, apart from the ones received in health shrines, always regarded religious obligations.

The best-known reliefs representing the dream-visitations of divine beings date from the fourth century, and that may have been their heyday. For example, a relief from the shrine of Asclepius in the Piraeus shows an incubation scene in which a woman is being treated by the god, assisted by Hygieia (Health) (Plate 3; compare Plate 9, page 158).[45] But the tradition continued. Van Straten began his path-making study with a third-century BC relief from Cos that depicts the dedicator's dream of Four Charites (Graces) (Plate 4).[46] And this convention too lent itself to parody. That is, I think, the only way to explain a Hellenistic relief now best known from a Hadrianic version in Boston: it shows a naked Siren copulating with a sleeping and evidently dreaming shepherd-like figure, perhaps Silenus (Plate 5).[47]

Latin ones are republican. Few in either language are later than 250 AD. Renberg maintains (144) that the chronological distribution of the dated Latin texts corresponds to the prevalence of the 'epigraphic habit'; in my view, there is a disproportionate increase in the number of Greek texts in the second century AD and later on a similar increase in the Latin ones (see below, p. 215). For the Roman period see also the brief account in Schörner 2003, 20–22.

43. *I. Knidos* 131. On the text see Rigsby 2003.

44. The inscription: Guillon 1946 (Boeotia); cf. Van Straten 1976, 5.

45. Van Straten 1976, 3, and fig. 6. Näf 2004, 51, seems to me unduly cautious about this interpretation. Van Straten provides numerous parallels.

46. But nothing entirely proves that he was asleep when he saw the Graces, or that they spoke to him. See van Straten 1976, 1–2.

47. Erotic scenes need no explaining, but their forms may do so. See among others Vermeule 1964, 334, Hofstetter 1997, no. 89b, C. Stewart 2002, 286. It is a pity that its earliest provenance is the collection of the undiscriminating collector of erotica Edward Perry Warren, but its substantial authenticity is guaranteed by the Begram plate (see below). It has sometimes produced strange reactions: Devereux 1976, 339, was inclined to think that the male figure was being raped. In the Kabul museum the same scene is shown in a plaster cast from Begram (= Alexandria) of what was originally a Hellenistic metal relief (Richter 1958, 372).

Plate 3. Asklepios appearing to a dreaming female patient. The figure on the right is Hygieia (Health). Relief from the Asklepieion of Piraeus, fourth century BC. Piraeus Museum, inv. 405. Photo © Piraeus Museum.

Plate 4. Four (!) Graces appearing to a dreamer, Daikrates, who in consequence of what was apparently an epiphany dream made this dedication to them. Relief from Cos, first half of third century BC. The inscription: van Straten 1976, 1–2. Museum of Cos. Photo: Hartwig, Koppermann, Deutsches Archäologisches Institut, Athens.

Definition and Origin of the Epiphany Dream

In high classical Greek there was no distinct term for the epiphany dream.[48] Under the Roman Empire Artemidorus calls epiphany dreams *chrema-tismoi*,[49] and some later authors follow the same usage, but this word is not attested in the sense of 'divine injunction' prior to isolated appearances in the third and second centuries BC.[50] Some Latin-speakers used the term

48. Apparently: but Poseidonius' third category of dreams, which we know of only from Cicero, *De div.* i.64, occurs when 'ipsi di cum dormientibus conloquantur' (fr. 108 E-K). This is an approximate description of the commonest form of epiphany dream.

49. Artemidorus i.2, p. 6 Pack (all subsequent page references to Artemidorus will be to this edition). R. J. White translated *chremistismos* as 'oracular response', but that is not quite right.

50. *P.Cair.Zen.* I.59034, line 6, of 257 BC; 2 Macc. 2:4. So it was a little misleading of Dodds to write of the 'the Greek *chrematismos*' (1951, 109). According to Engelmann

Plate 5. A Siren-like figure copulating with a dreaming shepherd, perhaps Silenus. Is this a parody of an epiphany dream? Marble relief, provenance somewhere in Italy, probably Bay of Naples area. Hadrianic or Antonine version of a Hellenistic original. The object is quite small (breadth 39 cm., height 40 cm.). Boston, Museum of Fine Arts, RES 08.34c. Photo © 2009, Museum of Fine Arts, Boston.

1975, 18 the verb *chrematizein* was the usual expression in Ptolemaic Egypt for such a dream-revelation. See also *IG* XI.4.1299 (Delos, about 200 BC). For later uses of the verb in this sense see the references amassed by Robert 1989 [1974], 292. When gods appeared in dreams, the Greeks of Hellenistic and Roman times could refer to the event as an *epiphaneia* (Pfister 1924, 278, Kyriazopoulos 1997, 559).

admonitio, others *oraculum,* but there was no universal agreement about the Latin terminology either.[51] An alternative name for them in English might be 'pronouncement dreams'.

The defining qualities of such descriptions are in any case these:

(1) Attention is all or mostly focused on a single visitor to the sleeper, or on a very small set, such as the two Penates who appear to Aeneas in Vergil (there is little or no 'setting').

(2) The visitor is authoritative—he/she/they may be deceptive, and the dreamer may resist, but the dreamer always knows that the visitor is likely to be truth-telling or to deserve obedience. In Homer, for instance, the visitor is a god or a god's agent, or a ghost (Patroclus),[52] or Odysseus. Artemidorus, intent on giving an exhaustive list, says that persons who appear in dreams should be believed and obeyed if they are gods, priests, kings *(basileis)*, rulers *(archontes)*, parents, teachers *(didaskaloi)*, seers[53]—except of course for those who do not tell the truth[54]—also the dead, children, the elderly, and animals.[55] Macrobius gives a more concise list.[56] A friend might be a god in disguise.[57] The visitant's appearance, when specified, is usually splendid.[58]

---

51. Cicero, *De div.* i.55, but there is no sign that he is employing a technical term. Chalcidius, *Comm. in Timaeum,* ch. 256, says that a dream is an *admonitio* 'cum angelicae bonitatis consiliis regimur atque admonemur, spectaculum, ut cum vigilantibus offert se videndam caelestis potestas clare iubens aliquid aut prohibens forma et voce mirabilis.' But according to Macrobius, *Comm. in Somn.Scip.* i.3.2, such a dream is an *oraculum;* it is an *oraculum* 'when the dreamer's parent, or some other august or impressive person, or a priest or even a god, reveals openly what will or will not happen, or should or should not be done' (i.3.8).

52. For the latter see *Il.* xxiii.62–101. A ghost such as Polydorus in Euripides' *Hecuba,* appearing in a dream (1–58), can at least bring authoritative information about his own death.

53. Artemidorus ii.69, p. 195. Admittedly it is not clear whether he speaking about epiphany dreams: in theory they are not part of his subject (i.2), but the reference to obedience in this chapter suggests that he is thinking of them nonetheless.

54. At this point Artemidorus pronounces a little tirade against those scoundrels who attempt to foretell the future by palmistry, etc., etc., instead of dreams.

55. The snake that becomes an eagle in Themistocles' dream in Plutarch, *Them.* 26 is almost but not quite an epiphany.

56. See note 51.

57. Dodds 1951, 109; but his idea that dreams about acquaintances may 'often' have been interpreted in this way is far-fetched indeed.

58. Cf. Hanson 1980, 1410, Kyriazopoulos 1997, 560–561.

(3) The visitor conveys an admonition or pronouncement, the meaning of which is clear to the dreamer or eventually becomes clear.[59]

In the Graeco-Roman context, certainly, the 'epiphany' mode of representing dreams seems not at all surprising. For the gods were both intensely anthropomorphic—by this I mean that they felt human emotions as well as looking like superior humans—and, according to the general opinion, willing to take an interest in human affairs (think of Athena, in the form of Mentor, micromanaging Telemachus at the beginning of the *Odyssey*). A well-established belief gave them an important role in producing dreams: Achilles says in the *Iliad* that a dream is 'from Zeus',[60] and many other texts throughout antiquity reflect the idea that some dreams at least come from the gods or a god.[61] (Eventually, however, it became a mere figure of speech to say that something was 'god-sent'.)[62] At all events, most Greeks and Romans had a more vivid anthropomorphic idea of their gods than is normal for modern Christians, let alone Jews or Muslims. This did not necessarily mean that the dreams would sometimes be in epiphany form, but it certainly supported that kind of description.

And how did a powerful ruler exercise power in preliterate archaic Greece? He sent messengers, though not usually in disguise.[63] And it is evident from the Homeric poems that archaic Greeks had no difficulty at all in supposing that the gods were willing to disguise themselves, and were willing to make use of messengers, in itself a very human activity: so you could believe that you had been instructed by a god even if the actual visitor looked less-than-divine.[64]

In some Ancient Near Eastern cultures the gods were said to have appeared in dreams in their own likenesses.[65] One can only speculate as to

59. Sometimes too late, however, to do the dreamer any good, as in Herodotus v.56 (Hipparchus' dream the night before he was assassinated).

60. i.63.

61. This scarcely needs documenting, but see e.g. Plato, *Symp.* 203a, Xenophon, *Anab.* iv.3.8–13, Herophilus in Aetius, *Placita* v.2.3 (cf. Dodds 1951, 124, von Staden 1989, 386), Cicero, *De div.* i.58.

62. Artemidorus remarks (i.6) that, in his time, saying that something was *theopempton*, 'god-sent', could merely signify that it was unexpected.

63. And this was still so in the late fifth century, I believe (Harris 1989, 78).

64. A divine *epiphaneia*, even when it was experienced by an individual who was awake, did not necessarily require the visitant to be personally visible (Versnel 1987, 49–51).

65. See Oppenheim 1956, Noegel 2002. For a divine epiphany dream from Egypt, reign of Thutmosis IV, see Szpakowska 2003, 189; another, from the reign of Rameses II, 195–196.

whether this was a feature of Minoan or Mycenaean culture.[66] In Homer, as it happens, an Olympian god does this only once, when Hermes warns King Priam to leave Achilles' camp and return to Troy.[67] A tabulation of the epiphany dreams in the *Iliad* and the *Odyssey* follows on page 40.

A fragment of Sappho may possibly (it depends how you spell and punctuate it) refer to a dream encounter with Aphrodite.[68] Alcman saw Apollo in a dream, apparently.[69] At all events the next fully preserved Greek account of a god's appearing in person to a dreamer, after the *Iliad,* is in Pindar's *Olympian* XIII (of 464 BC), where Athena is said to have appeared to Bellerophon while he slept on her altar.[70] But whatever the chronology of the overtly divine dream, it is probable that its origins were outside Greece, whether in Asia Minor, Ugarit or Egypt.

It might be suggested that statues of the gods, being familiar physical presences, are likely to have been the origin of the classical epiphany dream. The reluctance of the early Greek gods to appear to dreamers in person seems to argue against this notion. But whether this theory is correct or not—and the question is far from being resolved[71]—it does seem

---

66. It is at least intriguing that 'the most peculiar and characteristic feature of the Minoan experience of the divine is . . . the epiphany of the deity from above in the dance' (Burkert 1985 [1977], 40), while the dance element in the iconography in question is often mere guesswork.

67. *Il.* xxiv.673–690. N. Richardson, in his note on 677–686, says (like some others) that Homer is 'surely' not describing a dream here, but this must be wrong: see Lévy 1982, 27, and in most detail Brillante 1990a, 41–45. The poet does not say in 689 that Priam awoke, but he had no need to spell that out; 682 makes it altogether clear that a dream is being described. Hermes was probably already thought of as the 'bringer of dreams' (*h.Hom.* 4.14), and so felt no inhibitions about appearing in person. Earlier in the book he had done so in 'reality'. Hundt 1935, 98–99, and Walde 2001, 42 n. 65, have this more or less wrong.

68. 87 Bergk = 134 Voigt.

69. 47 Page = 117 Calame. The story about Heracles appearing in a dream to Pherecydes of Syros (Diogenes Laertius i.117 = 7 A 1 D-K) was probably invented much later than Pherecydes' time.

70. *Olympian* xiii.65–82. The word *auta* (78) emphasizes that it was really her. The *Vita Ambrosiana* says that Pindar dreamt of Demeter and afterwards wrote her a poem (fr. 37).

71. Part of the trouble is to know how widespread large images of the gods were in Mycenaean or 'Dark Age' Greece. Burkert 1985 [1977], 88 points out that 'in many places the most important gods of the Mycenaean period, Zeus and Poseidon, did without cult image and temple, down into Classical times'; on the other hand, most of the Near Eastern cultures that are relevant here did make use of such cult statues. Of course nothing *proves* that the Greek epiphany dream was much older than Homer. The story in Schol.

likely that the existence of temples inhabited by anthropomorphic statues of superhuman size from Homeric times onwards[72] contributed at least to the survival of the epiphany dream.

The same applies to 'incubation'. For most of antiquity many people had faith in the procedure by which a sick or troubled person visited a shrine of Asclepius, Serapis, or some other god with appropriate powers, and, after some preparatory ritual, slept there in the hope of being cured, or at least (and naturally this happened more often) of receiving instructions in a dream.[73] Such practices seem to presuppose that the epiphany dream was already an established form of dream-description. Incubation was practised in some places in the Near East in the second millennium,[74] and Dodds argued that in the Greek world it went far back into the Bronze Age,[75] but there is no real evidence earlier than the passage of Pindar just mentioned. Incubation is, I think, unlikely to have been the source of the epiphany dream, for it was in a loose sense democratic, during historical times: in principle, almost anyone with the necessary funds could approach. The epiphany dream on the other hand had started out quite differently, as a princely prerogative;[76] gradually it became less exclusive, but throughout antiquity the recipients were normally persons of distinction, either social or religious or literary. Furthermore incubation was always highly ritualized. The Pindar passage, however, could hardly have been understood unless incubation was already being practised:[77] by this time, it

---

Pindar, *Pyth.* iii.77 about Pindar's encounter with a statue of Demeter is of interest, but only for much later times.

72. Burkert 1985 [1977], 88–90, Gladigow 1990, 98 (there were probably no over-life-sized cult statues until the eighth century, he asserts).

73. For a general account of incubation see most recently Wacht 1998; see also Gorrini 2002–2003, Renberg 2003, 256–263. For some similar practices in Greece and elsewhere see Dodds 1951, 110.

74. Among the Hittites, for instance: see further Oppenheim 1956, 187–188, Gnuse 1996, 61; in Mesopotamia: Butler 1998, 218–239. In dynastic Egypt the evidence is sparse: according to Szpakowska 2003, 142–147, it is largely 'late' (i.e. after 664 BC).

75. Dodds 1951, 110–111. It was unknown to Homer (though some scholars have seen evidence for it in *Il.* xvi.235); cf. Wacht 1998, 182–183.

76. Nestor does not deny that other people can have such dreams, but 'if any other Achaean were to tell us a dream, we would call it a lie and keep away from it' (ii.80–81).

77. The medical use of incubation was satirized in the early fourth century by Aristophanes, *Wealth* 659–748. In Herodotus incubation had been a practice of the distinctly 'barbarian' Nasamones (iv.172.3; it also features as an emergency procedure in a tale that Egyptian priests told him about king 'Sethos', ii.141).

Table 1. Epiphany Dreams in Homer

	Sender	Visitant/apparent visitant	Recipient
Il. ii.1–40	Zeus	'Dream', a messenger resembling Nestor	Agamemnon
Il. x.496–7	Athena	Diomedes	Rhesus
Il. xxiii.62–101		*Psuche* (spirit) of Patroclus	Achilles
Il. xxiv.673–690	Hermes	Hermes	Priam
Od. iv.795–841	Athena	*Eidolon* (image) in the form of Iphthime, Penelope's sister	Penelope
Od. vi.20–51	Athena	Athena disguised as one of the recipient's friends	Nausicaa
Od. xix.535–50		Odysseus disguised as an eagle	Penelope

probably tended to sustain the epiphany form of dream-report, for stories about incubation, fortified by the inscriptions put up at the shrines themselves, encouraged people to describe their dreams in epiphany form.

Varieties of the Epiphany Dream

The epiphany dream-description included a number of complications and variations, and indeed the line separating it from the episode-dream is somewhat blurry. Surviving accounts of dreams sometimes leave it more or less unclear whether an epiphany was supposed to have taken place. When Eumenes of Cardia claimed (it was an invention no doubt) that he had dreamt of a battle in which one side was helped by Demeter and the other by Athena, neither of whom spoke to the dreamer,[78] the dream should not be classified as an epiphany. But the two tall fine-looking women who appeared in a dream to the Persian queen-mother in Aeschylus' *Persians* are characteristic epiphany figures, even though a quite complicated story follows.[79] When in Sophocles' *Electra* Clytemnestra is said to have dreamt of her murdered husband, who brought her a message, though without words, that we might or might not count.[80] Lactantius, to take another murky example, says that the emperor Constantine was given certain instructions in the dream he supposedly dreamt on the night before the Battle of Saxa Rubra in 312 ('commonitus est in quiete Constantinus'):[81] Lactantius may have supposed that Constantine had dreamt an epiphany dream—but it is also possible that Constantine had spoken of a dream more episodic in form which he *interpreted* as a divine order.

There were also variations on the usual pattern. There can be a group visitation: Callimachus wrote of a visit from the Muses, Vergil of the two Penates, Pausanias of the two Nemeseis (local goddesses) who told Alexander to refound the city of Smyrna (Plate 6),[82] Lucian a little differently of the two symbolic ladies who came to claim his allegiance, Sculpture and Culture. Three Nymphs visited Daphnis to give him instructions in the romance *Daphnis and Chloe*.[83]

---

78. Plutarch, *Eum.* 6.
79. Aeschylus, *Pers.* 176–199.
80. Lines 417–423.
81. *De mort.pers.* 44.5. See Chapter II.
82. Pausanias vii.5.1–3.
83. ii.23.

Plate 6. Alexander of Macedon dreaming of the two *Nemeseis* (local goddesses). While he slept under a plane-tree, they instructed him to refound the city of Smyrna, and under the Roman Empire, from Antoninus Pius' time onwards, this was sometimes commemorated on the city's coins. Bronze coin of the reign of Philip the Arab (B. V. Head, *Catalogue of the Greek Coins of Ionia,* London, 1892, Smyrna no. 452). Photo © The Trustees of the British Museum.

A much more interesting variation is the visitant who comes to several interconnected dreamers, in sequence or at the same time. We have already met the dream experienced successively by both Xerxes and Artabanus. On one occasion many of the inhabitants of Ilium had the same dream of Athena, Plutarch says.[84] Both Roman consuls once dreamt on the same night that they would win a battle if one of them agreed to die.[85] Many such stories were told,[86] and the tradition persisted: before the Battle of the Frigidus (394), a soldier as well as the emperor Theodosius saw the crucial encouraging dream[87]—possibly because Constantine's extremely convenient dream prior to the Battle of Saxa Rubra had encountered some disbelief. The monk Benedict appeared to two of his followers in the same dream on the same night.[88] And epiphany dreams are quite commonly repeated.[89]

84. *Luc.* 10 end. 'And the people of Ilium used to point out a *stele* with many inscribed decrees on this subject'.

85. P. Decius Mus and T. Manlius Torquatus: Livy viii.6, Zonaras vii.26.6, etc.

86. Wikenhauser 1948, Frenschkowski 1998, 34–39.

87. Theodoret, *Hist.Eccl.* v.24.

88. Gregory the Great, *Dial.* ii.22.1–5.

89. See the references given by Hanson 1980, 1411. Add the famous case of Socrates, Plato, *Phaedo* 60e. This phenomenon was already described in ancient Mesopotamia (Noegel 2001, 48), and continued in late antiquity (Dagron 1985, 41). For more cases see

The visitation might be deceptive, as in *Iliad* II and Herodotus VII, and there was disagreement about how to tell the difference: Artemidorus said that a god seen in a dream was authentic if he/she appeared with the proper attributes,[90] whereas Aelius Aristides thought that Asclepius had visited him even when he had not seen him in his conventional form.[91] The latter is probably nearer to the actual practice of incubation shrines throughout antiquity—the appearance of the god was recognized even if he was, so to speak, in disguise.[92]

The dreamer was sometimes said to have dreamt that he/she had spoken to the visitant.[93] Penelope questioned her sister Iphthime when the latter appeared to her in a dream sent by Athena.[94] Not only that: what are undoubtedly epiphany dreams sometimes have an active role for the dreamer.[95] Aelius Aristides, for example, once dreamt that after Asclepius gave him instructions, he did what he was commanded to do (walked around with no shoes on), and then shouted out 'Great is Asclepius! The order has been obeyed'.[96] Germanicus was said to have dreamt that after he had killed a sacrificial victim his grandmother Livia appeared and gave him a highly propitious gift.[97] We shall meet many other instances.

An occasional characteristic of the epiphany dream was that the visitant guaranteed the dream was authentic by leaving a physical token, known as an 'apport', such as a letter.[98] The earliest one we know of is Bellerophon's dream in Pindar: Athena left a golden bridle. Was that because fifth-century Greeks would have been tempted to doubt that a real goddess would deign

---

Renberg 2003, 246–249. Six times in the case of Athena appearing at Lindos in 305: Blinkenberg 1941, 187, *FGrH* 532 F 1, sec. D (p. 513 end).

90. iv.72; cf. ii.44, but the text there is somewhat defective. According to Brillante 1991, 96, this was the usual opinion.

91. *Or.* xlviii.9, 18, etc.

92. Cf. Frankfurter 2005, 239–240.

93. But this does not normally happen (cf. Hanson 1980, 1411).

94. *Od.* iv.795–841.

95. Cf. Björck 1946, 311, but not all his examples were well chosen.

96. *Or.* xlviii.7.

97. Tacitus, *Ann.* ii.14.1. People were sometimes said to have dreamt of engaging in sex with someone who might be thought of as an authority figure (men with their mothers especially: Sophocles, *OT* 981–982, Herodotus vi.107, Plato, *Rep.* ix.571c, Artemidorus i.79), but such dreams lack the essential 'pronouncement' component.

98. But it is not accurate to say with Van Lieshout 1980, 13, that the epiphany figure 'often' leaves an apport.

to appear in a dream?[99] Letters were more typical: Serapis might leave one under the dreamer's pillow.[100] The apport might be used as evidence that the worshipper had not dreamt but had really been visited by a god such as Asclepius: such was the story told in connection with a ruined temple of this god—a poetess named Anyte thought she had dreamed of Asclepius, but for Pausanias, who tells the story, an apport in the shape of a writing tablet proved that the god had *really* visited her.[101] Jerome could not go so far as to say that angels had visited him while he was awake: rather, he dreamt of being interrogated at the Last Judgement, of being admonished for his love of Cicero, and of being beaten, and to prove it he assured Eustochium that afterwards his shoulders were black and blue with bruises.[102]

People could always of course dream of individual gods who remained silent, and since such dreams were enigmatic it is plausible to suppose that they were really dreamt sometimes.[103]

Then there is the matter of waking visions: for long periods of ancient and medieval history, miraculous visions and apparitions—usually helpful or supportive ones—were as credible to many people as meaningful dreams.[104] Sometimes, it is true, such stories were situated in the mythic past: Athena visited Telemachus by night (but he was not asleep), and Odysseus too.[105] But Herodotus tells us as a solemn fact that the runner Philippides or Pheidippides met divine Pan on the way from Athens to

99. See further Dodds 1951, 106.

100. *IG* X.2.1.255.

101. x.38.13.

102. 'liventes habuisse me scapulas', *Ep.* 22.30 end (where 'post somnum' makes it clear that Jerome was claiming that he had dreamt all this).

103. Artemidorus attends to dreams of the gods esp. in ii.34–39 and iv.71–77. When the gods made numerous dream-appearances at Miletus at a certain juncture in the first or second century AD (*I.Didyma* 496, with van Straten 1976, 17; other bibliography: Weber 2000, 61 n. 35), there is no indication that they made pronouncements; in fact the puzzlement of the priestess from whom we know this suggests otherwise.

104. For a stimulating account of the classical world's apparitions see Lane Fox 1986, 104–123.

105. *Od.* xv.1–45, where the poet skillfully emphasizes the urgency of the matter by setting the scene for a dream but keeping Telemachus awake; the visit to Odysseus: xx.30–55 (he too was lying awake). In the ideal world of the Phaeacians the gods show themselves to mortals without disguise, vii.199–206.

Plate 7. Dedication of a gilded bronze ear to Asklepios the Saviour, by Fabia Secunda 'according to a dream', a thank-offering for improved hearing. Pergamum, second century AD (?). The inscription: Habicht 1969, 118–119 (no.91), with bibliography on ear-dedications. The object is small (9 cms. high); similar ex-votos are still dedicated in Greek churches. Pergamum museum, inv. M 1959, 17. Photo: Deutsches Archäologisches Institut, Istanbul.

Sparta (no doubt this was already a popular story), and such tales were not rare.[106]

Now a waking vision or apparition may be easiest to believe if it consists of the appearance of a singular individual: shepherd girls see the Virgin Mary, not the Last Judgement. This kind of narrative, and epiphany dream-narratives, presumably supported one another—notwithstanding the fact that both ancient dreamers and personages who appear in epiphany dreams sometimes make a point of claiming that the epiphany is real and not merely a dream.[107] A high proportion of the dedicants who are epi-graphically recorded as having made dedications on divine instructions—the so-called *ex visu* inscriptions now catalogued by Renberg (Plate 7, from Pergamum, provides an example)—did not trouble to explain how exactly

106. Herodotus vi.105. For some other classical pagan examples see Dodds 1951, 117, Pritchett 1979, 11–46 (many stories of gods appearing during battles), Sinos 1993, 79–80, Renberg 2003, 28–29. Literary men from Hesiod onwards described their own waking meetings with divinities: see Nisbet and Hubbard 1978, 315, for a list.

107. Thus the eagle (= Odysseus) in Penelope's dream in *Od.* xix.547, Aeneas in Vergil, *Aen.* iii.173–174 (concerning his dream of the Penates), Asclepius in Aelius Aristides, *Or.* xlviii.18.

they had received a divine command.[108] The Via Latina catacombs in Rome show the famous scene from Genesis in which Abraham's god appeared to him in the heat of the day in the form of three men.[109] Another extraordinary case occurs in the Imouthes papyrus (second century AD), in which the author tells how Imouthes/Asclepius appeared to his mother as she kept watch over him, and he, as he slept, simultaneously experienced exactly the same vision.[110] But let us keep the matter of waking visions in proportion: for most ancient people, no doubt, 'belief in divine epiphanies [to those who were awake] depend[ed] on their happening in some far-off place, to a friend of a friend or a very long time ago'.[111]

This was no longer so in western Europe in the Middle Ages: waking visions grew commoner. Many of them were not simple epiphanies, but more or less complex descriptions of the world to come. Some, however, closely paralleled dream epiphanies.[112]

Distinguishing the Epiphany Dream from the Modern Dream

We, on the other hand, usually describe our dreams as sequences of events or experiences; there may be a principal actor (often the dreamer him/herself), and there may be a lesson to be learned, but what we describe is an episode, though often a very brief one.[113] This is a difference in structure, not just in subject-matter, and it is a cultural convention too, one that to a certain modest degree simplifies our experience, for our dreams, as re-

108. Renberg 2003, 27–28.

109. Genesis 18.1–5; illustrated in Näf 2004, fig. 3 (p. 30).

110. *P.Oxy.* XI.1381, republished a number of times, e.g. in Edelstein and Edelstein 1945, I, 169–175, and Totti 1985, 36–45. This was a sign of particular divine favour, just like Isis' simultaneous appearance to the ass and to her priest (in dreams). The text states that it had been translated from Egyptian (lines 32–35). For a summary of the story see Bresciani 2005, 109–111.

111. Harrison 2000, 91, with bibliography; his focus is on high-classical Athens, however. On later times see esp. Kyriazopoulos 1997.

112. See esp. Dinzelbacher 1981, who classifies the material I have in mind under 'Erscheinungen' (33–36) not 'Visionen'.

113. To check this assertion I consulted www.dreambank.net (30 July 2006), which contains dreams in English and German, as well as printed sources. Rumours of epiphany dreams in the 'modern west', for instance in H. T. Hunt 1989, 231, have always turned out to be false. I know of one literary exception (in Sciascia's story *La morte di Stalin*) and one subliterary case from a late nineteenth-century Russian Jewish context.

membered, may for example be abstract or static.[114] To assume, as some investigators have,[115] that a dream is normally a 'story' is a slight but significant misuse of the language. Modern dream-typologies, when constructed by psychologists, seldom if ever make any space for anything that even resembles an epiphany dream.[116] The one modern kind of dream report that sometimes resembles an epiphany dream consists of dreams of encountering friends or near relatives after their deaths.[117]

There are exceptions outside the 'western' tradition, and they will later on be important to the argument. There is especially strong evidence from Haiti, Mayan Mexico, Morocco and Zululand—also from rural Greece as recently as the 1930s.[118] On the basis of Haitian field-work carried out about 1950, a careful investigator stated that 'dreams which are labelled as such, or as things that happen in sleep, seem on the basis of the data collected to refer almost exclusively to two classes of entities: the dead and the gods, both of which come in order to convey a message to the dreamer'.[119] A researcher among Tzotzil-speaking Mayans in the 1950s found that the shamanistic healers there dreamt of appearing before the ancestral gods to receive instruction.[120] In Morocco in the 1960s and 1970s, an anthropologist whose work carries conviction encountered among his mainly illiterate

114. While writing this chapter, I once dreamt of two reindeer standing side by side, doing nothing; that was the whole dream.

115. Cipolli and Poli 1992, for example.

116. See e.g. Busink and Kuiken 1996.

117. For dreams of the dead in antiquity see Dodds 1951, 111; among the Christians: Dulaey 144. The murdered dead might return to tell their stories, e.g. Apuleius, *Met.* viii.8. Dreams of the dead in the contemporary world: Barrett 1991–1992. Some work by Adams (2005), though it is methodologically flawed, seems to suggest very interestingly that children may sometimes dream epiphany dreams.

118. For evidence concerning dreams about the Panagia on Naxos see C. Stewart 2003, 491–492. For a dream about her on Tinos at the time of the Greek War of Independence see www.greeka.com/cyclades/tinos/tinos-churches.htm; see also www.in2greece.com/english/places/summer'islands/leros.htm (both accessed 5 March 2008) (information from Angelos Chaniotis). Since writing these lines I have encountered further evidence concerning traditional Hawaii (Craighill Handy 1936, 123). For material from traditional Madagascar see Bloch 1998, 97.

119. Bourguignon 1954, 264. She goes on to explain that the living dream figures in question are commonly familiar humans routinely interpreted as gods who have taken possession of them.

120. Fabrega and Silver 1973, 31. Not much is clear, however, about what was actually supposed to have been dreamt. I owe this reference to Richard Gordon.

subjects a strong tradition of what he called 'visitational dreams', involving the appearance of saints, demons, and 'other spiritual beings'.[121] Even in this case, however, epiphanies are embedded in what I call here 'episodes'—which in turn suggest the possibility that what the ancients were often doing when they described epiphany dreams was extracting a single element from a more complex experience. For traditional Zulus, finally, the shades of the dead appear quite frequently in dreams, apparently 'always bring[ing] good news'.[122] (There are also cases from modern literate Islamic societies).[123]

This difference between 'epiphany' dreams and 'episode' dreams, or something like it, has naturally been remarked on by other students of dreaming. Some of them have labelled epiphany dreams as 'external' and episode dreams as 'internal'.[124] They have also formed the notion, which is quite close to the central premise of this chapter, that dreams as external visitors *were replaced by* dreams as internal phenomena,[125] without realizing how long the epiphany dream really survived. What concerns us here, however, is not a distinction between dreams of this origin or that, but between forms of description; and while all epiphany dreams are necessarily 'external', an episode dream was sometimes regarded, in both antiquity and the Middle Ages, as having been sent by a divine or daemonic being,[126] which made it, too, 'external'. Conversely, even those who knew that dreams were internal, sometimes make reference to epiphany dreams[127]—for in classical antiquity you could hardly pretend that such dreams did not occur at all.

---

121. Crapanzano 1975, esp. 150; cf. Crapanzano 2001, 246. This was largely confirmed by the work of Kilborne, summarized in 1987, 185–189. For a somewhat similar phenomenon in Sudanese Dinkaland in the 1940s, divinities who spoke in dreams, see Lienhardt 1961, 57; but the divinities were 'formless'.

122. Berglund 1976, 98. I owe this reference to Michael Lambert (University of KwaZulu-Natal).

123. Turkish and Indian in particular: see the ahistorical account by Schimmel 1997, 60, 67, 69–70.

124. Hey 1907–1908, Hundt 1935, Pelling 1999. For criticism of this classification see Björck 1946, 311 n. 1, van Lieshout 1980, 59 n. 70.

125. The two forms coexisted and interacted over a long period.

126. Penelope already takes it for granted in *Odyssey* XIX. We shall meet a number of examples, such as the dreams of Perpetua, in the next chapter.

127. Cicero, *De div.* ii.135–136; for the speaker's denial that dreams come from the gods see ii.124. But he naturally questions the authenticity of as many epiphany dreams as possible (136).

One of the most perceptive of modern writers about ancient dream-lore has suggested another somewhat unsatisfactory classification. What are called here epiphany dreams he labels 'objective' dreams, subcategory 'passive'.[128] Up to a point, this is certainly in accord with the thinking of many Greeks and Romans. But the term 'objective' unnecessarily obscures the fact that this kind of dream could be recognized as false, and it is not reliability that is in question here but the manner in which the dream is described.

A better attempt to grasp the classification I have in mind is the 'message' versus 'symbolic' distinction employed by the great historian of ancient Near-Eastern dreams, A. L. Oppenheim,[129] and still popular in that field.[130] The first label is better than the second; Oppenheim's 'message' dreams are my 'epiphany' dreams, but my 'episode' dreams may or may not be symbolic—in fact they were *not* usually taken in that way in classical antiquity.

Other Kinds of Greek and Roman Dream Reports

From the time of Homer onwards, there were other, nonepiphany, kinds of dream reports.[131] As indeed there had been in earlier Near Eastern societies, for we possess at least a modicum of evidence for the episode dream-

128. Van Lieshout 1980, 13–14: 'active' objective dreams occur when the soul goes off to visit; in truth van Lieshout was concerned with the mechanism of dreaming not the nature of the dream-report. See also Weidhorn 1970, 46–47, who distinguishes between 'objective' dreams caused by an outside agency and 'subjective' dreams that arise 'from the dreamer's own inner faculties'.

129. See Oppenheim 1956, 186–197.

130. See Butler 1998, 15–18, Noegel 2001, 45–46; for a critical view see esp. Szpakowska 2003, 4.

131. So it is better not to follow Brillante 1996 in calling this kind of dream 'the Homeric model'. Hanson 1980 appears to claim that the epiphany form of the dream-report was virtually universal from the beginning of classical antiquity to the end: he says (1396) that the form was 'fairly consistent'; on 1400 it is 'the' form; and it 'does not significantly change from the Homeric poets to the end of late antiquity' (1396). This was simply an aberration. Kessels, in the service of his view that 'the Greek attitude towards the phenomenon of dreaming underwent a radical change in the period between Homer and Plato' (1978, 198), rather exaggerates (198–207) the retreat of the epiphany dream in postarchaic times. Van Lieshout 1980, 14, reached the conclusion that in Greek literature down to and including Plato, omitting what he calls 'the material recorded in philosophical and scientific writings', sixteen 'objective' (that is epiphany) dreams are described, and ninety-five 'subjective' ones, with fourteen borderline cases.

description in both ancient Mesopotamia[132] and dynastic Egypt.[133] The Greeks and Romans, in other words, made cultural choices in this matter. An erotic dream, such as the one Penelope dreamt about Odysseus,[134] we might be willing to count as a special kind of epiphany as well as a wish-fulfilment. But Homer was entirely familiar with dreams that were quite as episodic as anything that is dreamt nowadays, as he shows in *Iliad* XXII when he compares Achilles' still futile pursuit of a futilely fleeing Hector to a dream-sequence.[135] What may be the most famous dream in the Homeric poems, Penelope's dream about the eagle and the geese in *Odyssey* XIX, is something of a hybrid: it describes an episode—Penelope's twenty geese were eating and she was enjoying the sight, when an eagle swept down and killed them all, to her dismay. Then there follows a kind of epiphany: the eagle returned, and in a human voice explained that he was Odysseus come to inflict vengeance on the suitors.[136]

Some Greek and Roman authors are of course fonder of epiphany dreams than others. In the *Iliad* and the *Odyssey*, they are more numerous than the episode dreams (that is a fact about the poetry of Homer, as it should hardly be necessary to say, not about the proportion of epiphany dreams actually dreamt in the eighth or seventh century BC). There is some tendency in the scholarly literature to suppose that the Greeks fairly early on turned away from the epiphany dream-description, but this notion needs to be guarded against, for as we have already seen it lived on, and not only in epic poetry.[137]

There were, it is true, archaic Greek ideas about dreams that had apparently expired by the fifth century BC: the *demos oneiron* of the Odyssey

132. See most recently Noegel 2002, 167–169.

133. See Szpakowska 2003, esp. 47. Dodds (1951, 109) was apparently in error when he wrote that 'most of the dreams recorded in Assyrian, Hittite, and ancient Egyptian literature' are epiphany dreams.

134. *Od.* xx.88–90.

135. xxii.199–201. There will be more on this simile in Chapter II.

136. xix.535–550. It is strange that Dodds should call this 'a simple wish-fulfilment dream' (1951, 106), since it is plainly an anxiety dream as well, even if Rankin 1962 and others are wrong to think that Penelope had in fact grown fond of her ill-behaved suitors (there is something in Rankin's case; for the contrary view see Rozokoki 2001).

137. This is not of course to suggest that conceptions of dreaming remained static: Herodotus and his slightly later contemporaries give evidence of some interesting evolution in the terminology of dreaming, for which see Kessels 1978, 200–203, and there were further changes under the Roman Empire.

(the 'country', or perhaps 'people', of dreams),[138] a concept which Homer seems to take for granted,[139] never appears again except as a learned allusion (Lucian had a wonderful time correcting Homer's account and filling it out);[140] the same with the *phulon oneiron* (tribe of dreams) mentioned by Hesiod.[141]

Yet there were difficulties. The most famous sceptic among the Preplatonic philosophers was Xenophanes of Colophon, and we know that he was a sceptic about prophetic dreams.[142] It has been argued that his scepticism began in some sense with divination,[143] and stories about gods appearing to mortal men certainly provoked him.[144] By the time of Empedocles and Democritus, some reflective Greeks had begun to realize that many or most dreams had natural causes (see Chapters III and IV), but Democritus took epiphany dreams into consideration, and it would be an exaggeration to suppose that a rising tide of naturalistic speculation made the old stories untenable.[145]

It hardly causes much surprise that epiphany dreams are largely absent from the major analytic texts about dreams that survive from high classical antiquity, the Hippocratic *On Regimen* IV[146] and Aristotle's essays in the *Parva Naturalia*.[147] But although the Epicureans did not believe that gods sent dreams, epiphany dreams are entirely familiar to Lucretius and helped

138. *Od.* xxiv.12.

139. And they are all the more interesting because whereas some other early Greek ideas about dreaming are also found in the Ancient Near East, those cultures never imagined the dreamer as a traveller (see Husser 1996, 1494).

140. *Vera Historia* ii.32–35. The personified Oneiros (Dream) of the *Iliad* did not have much of a future, though Pausanias (ii.10.2) reports that he had a statue in the shrine of Asclepius at Sicyon.

141. *Theogony* 212. On the *demos* and the *phulon* compare Hundt 1935, 74–77.

142. This is clear from Cicero, *De div.* i.5.

143. Lesher 1978.

144. He of course denied that the gods were of human form (21 B 14 D-K).

145. Burkert 1985 [1977], 313 seems to go a little too far when he says that for Herodotus it 'is certain, that gods cannot be of human shape', where the most important texts are i.60.3 and i.131.

146. Yet there may be an allusion in iv.89, where the author refers to dreams of receiving things from gods (cf. van der Eijk 2004, 198 n. 32). This text is generally dated about 400 (see R. Joly's edition, pp. xiv–xvi)—but it might be somewhat later.

147. He sometimes seems to take it for granted that a dream represents an event or a sequence of events, and he rejected any notion of divine origins. Gallop, however, argued (1996, 9) that 'a trace of the old "dream-figure" concept may be detected in his approach'.

him (and other Epicureans) to formulate their theory about the origins of religion.[148] About one-third of the prophetic dreams described by the 'believer' 'Quintus' in Cicero's *On Divination* Book I are epiphany dreams—which is not hard to explain.[149] Philo of Alexandria's book *On Dreams* is indeed somewhat concerned with epiphany dreams, but the dreams in question are from outside the Graeco-Roman tradition. Artemidorus intentionally excluded epiphany dreams from consideration (though not because he refused to believe that they occurred).[150] Aelius Aristides is a more complicated case, to which we shall return later.

Such stories may have seemed to the analytically minded to be somewhat lacking in intellectual respectability, notwithstanding their prominence in Homer, Vergil and elsewhere. The late-antique experts, on the other hand, Chalcidius, Synesius of Cyrene, and Macrobius, are perfectly aware of the epiphany dream, though they offer no clue as to whether they thought such dreams were common in life as well as literature.[151]

The Force of Convention

What then determines how in a particular age people describe their dreams in a particular form? Both patterns of representation, epiphanies and episodes, coexisted throughout antiquity, though not always in the same proportions in all ages.[152] Why in fact was classical antiquity rather fond of the epiphany form of dream-description? We have already considered certain factors—the inheritance from the Near East, and the anthropomorphic nature of the Greek and Roman gods. We may consider aspects

148. v.1169–1193, but line 1173 leaves it a bit unclear what kind of dream is meant. His theory about the part played by *simulacra* (emanations, images) in causing dreams of the dead (iv.29–43) suggests that he thought of dreams as often consisting of apparent visitations. Another first-century Epicurean allusion to divine figures that appeared in dreams: 'Velleius' in Cicero, *De natura deorum* i.46.

149. Of the twenty-five prophetic dreams that 'Quintus' lists in i.39–59, for instance, eight at least are epiphany dreams (i.48, 49, 52, 53, 55, 56 [two], 59). The Quintus character, a supporter of dream-divination, was likely to emphasize dreams in which gods appeared.

150. Cf. Blum 1936, 68–69. But we might consider that some of the dreams listed in Book V (v.9, for instance) belong in this category.

151. For Chalcidius and Macrobius see the passages referred to in n. 51; for Synesius, see *On Dreams* 4, 12 beginning and 15 beginning (apparently).

152. Cf. Kessels 1978, 175.

of the actual dreaming experience and the actual religious experience of
the Greeks and Romans, and then the instrumental factors—reasons why
it was convenient to represent dreams in this fashion.

Faced with the question whether the Greeks and Romans actually did
dream epiphany dreams, we can respond in one of three ways: *either* the
question does not matter, because almost all dreams are in principle inaccessible and the texts present us with quite enough historical problems to
be going on with, *or* we cannot know, because the evidence is in the end in-
sufficient, *or* it is likely that from time to time they did indeed dream
epiphany dreams.[153] I exclude the first answer for reasons explained in the
introduction—ancient experience interests me. In what follows I shall argue tentatively for the third answer as against the second.

This was the view taken by Dodds in his classic work. He adopted from
the anthropologist J. S. Lincoln the idea of a 'culture-pattern' dream. What
Dodds meant by this expression was a 'type . . . of dream-structure which
depend[s] on a socially transmitted pattern of belief, and cease[s] to occur
when that pattern of belief ceases to be entertained.' This 'pattern of belief' existed, so he thought, 'in many primitive societies'.[154] In other words,
there was a genuine and major difference in experience. In a later work,
however, without explaining why, he retreated somewhat from this position.[155]

There are certainly strong reasons for doubt. The force of convention
may account for the whole tradition. However the Greeks and Romans
dreamt, they had clear reasons to *represent* their dreams as epiphany
dreams from time to time. To start with, they were as likely as anyone else
to engage in what Freud called 'secondary elaboration', thereby on some
occasions making dreams that were only approximately epiphany dreams
into impressive divine appearances; priests and pious bystanders will also
have done their bit.[156] People who believed that some dreams at least had,
to put it no more strongly, 'something significant' about them—to use Aristotle's phrase again—may have been especially likely to describe to others

153. Clearly no one is going to say that they *cannot* have had such dreams.

154. Dodds 1951, 103–104. Attached to the word 'socially' was a healthily anti-Jungian
footnote that need not concern us here. Dodds presented his case, 104–109.

155. He was 'less sure now than I was . . . that the "divine" dreams so often recorded
in antiquity reflect a difference in the actual dream-*experience* of ancient and modern'
people (1968, 39).

156. 1951, 114–115.

a dream in which a god, a messenger from a god or some other authority figure seemed to deliver a pronouncement. If a god or a credible messenger appeared, that might seem to guarantee the 'truth' of the dream, which could in various ways be extremely important.

There were practicalities. When supernatural intervention was needed, it was more forceful if a supernatural being or other authoritative personage made a pronouncement that had little or no need of interpretation. The epiphany dreams dreamt by Homeric rulers presumably reflect the fact that an archaic monarch could use his dreams to justify his decisions.[157] Yet as we shall see in Chapter III, few Greek or Roman rulers ever did this. Josephus justified both his rebellion against Rome and his surrender to the Romans by means of epiphany dreams.[158] We know that military commanders sometimes sought to encourage their troops on the day of battle by announcing that gods, or their surrogates, had appeared in their dreams assuring them of victory: Alexander, Scipio Africanus and Constantine are prominent examples;[159] but we may think that only an exceptionally prestigious commander could get away with it.

Other dream stories circulated that gave added standing to rulers or to charismatic figures. Plutarch's lives include many epiphany dreams that contribute to the stature of their subjects, and some of them, a few, are likely to go back to the subjects' own life-times.[160] The whole history of Roman imperial times is studded with such dreams, some of which, once again, derived from contemporary propaganda or myth-making, such as the story about Germanicus we met earlier and the stories put about by Septimius Severus and his helpers to justify, along with other omens, his usurpation of power.[161] The physician Soranus said that a dream was what told Hippocrates to move to Thessaly,[162] just as a dream had in effect told

157. He would have said something like what Cyrus is made to say in Herodotus i.209.4: 'the gods take care of me and tell me in advance everything that is going to happen to me: last night I dreamed . . .'

158. *Vita* 208–219, *BJ* iii.352–3 (where, however, he is less than clear about what he had supposedly dreamt).

159. See Harris 2005a. Only the more megalomaniacal commanders attempted this; others, like Xenophon, used episode dreams.

160. E.g. the ones in *Sull.* 28 and 37.

161. Weber 2000, 202–210.

162. *Vita Hipp.* 4.

Paul to go to Macedonia. It is admittedly true that a 'status-conferring' dream did not *have* to be an epiphany. Agariste, following a common pattern, dreamt that she gave birth to a lion—that is to say, Pericles[163]—and the story undoubtedly circulated while Pericles was in power;[164] but it was not an epiphany dream.

Socrates may have made use of the dreams that told him to philosophize publicly or 'to do *mousike*',[165] and Plato, notwithstanding his generally low estimate of the knowledge that might be gained from dreams, glorifies his hero when he describes the epiphany dream that Socrates dreamt while he was awaiting death.[166] Immodest poets, as we saw, inserted themselves into the canon by dreaming of the Muses or a famous predecessor.[167] The writer who like the elder Pliny or Cassius Dio claimed to be following an order given in a dream[168] was mainly, I suppose, attempting to aggrandize himself.

From a literary point of view too, the epiphany dream was enormously useful, in the first place by providing a narrative with justification and hence intelligibility.[169] Why did Agamemnon order an attack at the wrong moment? Because a dream told him to. Presumably the historical Hannibal felt no need of excuses for invading Italy, but historians provided him with one anyway—a dream in which he received orders from Jupiter.[170] Vergil's Aeneas, on the other hand, most definitely needed an explanation for the fact that in the end he somewhat unheroically fled from burning

---

163. Herodotus vi.131.2.

164. See G. Nenci's commentary. On giving birth to a lion see Dyson 1929.

165. In *Apol.* 33c he is made to say that he was instructed to carry out his questioning of the pseudowise 'by god through oracles and dreams *(enhupnia)* and in every manner by which divine power has ever commanded a person to do anything'; it is not certain that Plato was thinking of epiphany dreams. Similarly, the famous dreams in *Phaedo* 60e–61a had appeared differently on different occasions *(allot' en allei opsei phainomenon)*, and I am not sure that they were meant to be epiphany dreams. (Socrates had understood the dreams to refer to philosophy, he says, but now thinks that they may have referred to musical composition.)

166. Above, p. 25.

167. Cf. Propertius iii.3.

168. Pliny *Ep.* iii.5.4 (the order was given by an *effigies* of the late Drusus); Dio lxxii.23 (the *daimonion*, superhuman power, ordered him).

169. See too Artemidorus ii.70 end.

170. Cicero, *De div.* i.49, etc. We shall return to this dream in Chapter III.

Troy: his excuse was that Hector had come to him in a dream and told him to leave.[171] Almost all ancient epiphany dreams that are described in literary texts are explicable as attempts to bestow prestige or to explain action, or as some combination of the two.

One investigator has perceptively written that this kind of dream is also 'a way of presenting in palpable dramatic form the inner promptings of a divided or malicious mind'.[172] Thus a hesitant hero such as Aeneas has particular need of them, and sure enough almost all the dream-descriptions in the *Aeneid* are epiphany dreams.[173] After his failure in Crete, Aeneas needed guidance: he duly dreamt that the two Penates gave him instructions;[174] later, father Anchises directed him to visit the underworld.[175] In *Aeneid* VII the poet skilfully uses the Fury Allecto not just to give Turnus a reason to act but to stir him to rage.[176]

Novelists played amusingly on this convention. Should the heroine sleep with the hero now or later? Achilles Tatius, who purports to take predictive dreams seriously, shows us Artemis instructing the heroine to hold on to her virginity.[177] It is the virgin goddess once again who by means of later epiphany dream makes a crucial contribution to the inevitable happy ending.[178] Chariton was perhaps less interested: he recounts only one epiphany dream, which was perhaps intended to create oriental atmosphere.[179] We shall consider Heliodorus a little later.

---

171. *Aen.* ii.268–297. Cf. Steiner 1952, 33. For the sake of variety Aeneas addressed the epiphany before it had time to speak. The lengthy description of Aeneas' armed resistance (336 to 452 or even 633) suggests that Aeneas' withdrawal made Vergil a little uneasy. Indeed Aeneas needs other epiphanies, not dreamt, to get him on his way (560–620).

172. Weidhorn 1970, 126, who was referring, however, to the dreams he defines as 'objective' dreams (see above, n. 128).

173. Cf. Berlin 1994, 25.

174. *Aen.* iii.147–191. For commentary see Steiner 1952, 37–44.

175. v.720–740. When Silius Italicus (xv.18–128) presents the visitation of Scipio Africanus by Virtus and Voluptas [Pleasure], he avoids dream terminology—it would not have fitted such abstract powers (Lucian decided differently, as we have seen). Raphael converted this visitation into a dream (*The Dream of the Night,* London, National Gallery).

176. vii.413–466.

177. i.3, iv.1 (with nice complications, including a dream of Aphrodite; see the commentary of Bartsch 1989, 89–93).

178. vii.12, 14 (with Bartsch 1989, 92–93).

179. vi.2; cf. vi.8.

An expert on Greek dreams, while admitting apparently that archaic Greeks may have dreamt epiphany dreams,[180] has maintained that they were, in the main, part of the old 'epic machinery'.[181] (In view of the copious use of the epiphany dream by most of the great European poets, and many others, down to the seventeenth century, the phrase seems a little derogatory.) The sheer force of tradition was no doubt part of its survival power, partly manifested in the attraction and prestige of great literary men, for Homer and Plato, Aeschylus and Callimachus, Ennius and Vergil, had all recounted epiphany dreams. Ennius' dream about Homer might be known only to *viri doctissimi* such as Cicero and Fronto, but the dreams recounted by Homer and Vergil were known to everyone who had been to school for a few years, and perhaps to some others too. In antiquity and in the Renaissance the use of an old motif attached one to the poetic tradition and offered a challenge: could it still be used effectively? In the case of the epiphany dream, Milton at least still thought so.

Actual Epiphany Dreams?

Dodds was too acute to base his argument that the Greeks sometimes dreamt epiphany dreams on the claim that any particular Greek epiphany dream must really have been dreamt.[182] Only a small proportion of ancient dream narratives of any kind has a good claim to credibility, as we shall see in the next chapter. Nor did Dodds deny that Homer's epiphany dream-descriptions were already very stylized, rather he denied that they were mainly a matter of poetic convention. And some thoroughly prosaic ancient authors are on hand to show that epiphany dreams were a fact: thus the pseudo-Platonic text *Epinomis*, for instance, takes it for granted that

---

180. Van Lieshout 1980, 19.

181. Van Lieshout 1980, 14. Hundt 1935, 42–43, seems to have been the first to formulate in any detail the notion that the epiphany dream was mainly the product of literary needs. The idea was developed further by Björck 1946, who contrasts the epiphany dream with the dream-descriptions in the Icelandic sagas (which also reflect a culture that believed in predictive dreams).

182. Whereas Schwabl 1983, 19–20, maintained that Socrates' epiphany dream in the *Crito must* really have been dreamt, since it cannot, he says, have been a literary invention. But the anecdotal tradition about Socrates was going strong while he was still alive, and, more importantly, Plato had a quite specific set of views about dreams (see Chapter III) that gave him a strong motive to elaborate such a story.

people really do encounter superhuman beings in their dreams,[183] and Cicero too, notwithstanding his scepticism about the interpretation of dreams, takes the fact for granted in *On Divination*.[184]

Two further considerations help to make it likely that epiphany dreams really were dreamt from time to time. In the first place there is the widely attested Greek and Roman custom—mentioned earlier—of making dedications to the gods in accordance with a dream or after one had seen a dream. The earliest evidence that this was a fairly widespread phenomenon appears in Plato: women especially, says the philosopher prejudicially, and people who are ill or in danger or difficulty, and people who have had some good luck too, are constantly dedicating altars and sanctuaries in private, and one reason they do this is because of their dreams. (Plato disapproves, and at this point in the *Laws* he is in the process of forbidding private cults.)[185] A large body of Hellenistic and Roman-imperial inscriptions seems to confirm the fact, without of course wholly clarifying its psychological basis: many ordinary Greeks and Romans made dedications because of their dreams.[186] Asclepius and Serapis in particular, because of their healing functions, were the commonest dedicatees.

Not all of these 'instruction' dreams—only a small proportion of them perhaps—will have been epiphany dreams, for, as we have already seen, classical Greeks and Romans commonly thought that some episode dreams too were sent by the gods.[187] So a dedication made in response to a dream does not necessarily refer to an epiphany dream. Poseidonius for his part explained that there were three different ways in which the gods brought about dreams, and one—but only one—of the three produces the occasions when 'they speak with those who are asleep'.[188] Relatively few of the *visu/iussu* inscriptions just alluded to say that the dreamer had actually

183. 985c. The author has just established a complex typology of such beings.

184. *De div.* ii.138.

185. *Laws* x.909e-910a. He does not specify any particular kind of dream.

186. See above, p. 31.

187. Dulaey 1973, 197, has this wrong, notwithstanding her erudition.

188. Fr. 108 E–K = Cicero, *De div.* i.64: 'tribus modis censet [Posidonius] deorum adpulsu homines somniare: uno, quod provideat animus ipse per sese, quippe qui deorum cognatione teneatur; altero, quod plenus aer sit immortalium animorum, in quibus tamquam insignitae notae veritatis appareant, tertio quod ipsi di cum dormientibus conloquantur'.

seen a divinity or a divine messenger.[189] And we shall find later that Aelius Aristides often interpreted episode dreams as messages from Asclepius,[190] and in this respect at least he seems to have been normal.

Dodds also argued in favour of the historicity of the epiphany dream that other cultures too, both archaic and anthropological, sometimes show the same tendency to report not only 'culture-pattern' dreams, but dreams of the epiphany type, the implication being that they help to demonstrate that the Greeks too quite often actually dreamt epiphany dreams.[191] He was not able to present this case in a strong form. The Ancient Near Eastern texts may be as conventional as the Greek and Roman ones.

The anthropological evidence is in the end more helpful. It is true that the evidence that Dodds was aware of established at best that 'culture pattern' dreams have existed in some parts of the world.[192] And since his time, older anthropological methods have to say the least become suspect[193]— in fact it something of a tiresome anthropological topos that earlier researchers did not learn the languages well enough, did not integrate themselves into the lives of their study populations, and so on. But the Haitian, Mayan, Moroccan and Zulu evidence cited earlier would be hard to fault in this respect. It shows beyond reasonable doubt that deep cultural and especially religious differences can sometimes be associated with differences in the form of actual dreams. Outside the secularized western world, quite different kinds of dreams can be found, or could until recently.

Dodds could also have argued, I think, that the Greeks and Romans had specific ideas about the dead that always encouraged them not only to pass on stories about the appearance of dead individuals in dreams but actually to dream about them. It is striking how often in some of the great classics of the Greek imagination such dreams evoke more or less latent feelings of guilt, from the appearance of Patroclus to Achilles in *Iliad* XXIII onwards. The

---

189. Cf. Renberg 2003, 239.

190. Cf. Dodds 1968, 42 n. 2.

191. See Dodds 1951, 103–104, 109.

192. For a type of dream 'corresponding to the Greek *chrematismos*', which 'appears among the dreams of contemporary primitives, who usually attach special importance to it' (109), he relies on Seligman 1924, 35–46, and Lincoln 1970 [1935], 24, 94, who do not in fact provide evidence that satisfies modern criteria.

193. Tedlock 1991 expresses anthropologists' distrust of older anthropological reports about dreams. Dentan 1986, 317–322, sets out many of the difficulties.

dreams in the *Eumenides* and in Sophocles' *Electra* are other examples. Admetus, in Euripides' *Alcestis*,[194] looks forward to his dead wife's return to his bed in the form of a dream. Propertius, in a different cultural context, dreams at length of the dead Cynthia's reproaches.[195] Lucan imagined how Pompey dreamt of his late wife Iulia, who came to upbraid him during his civil war against her father.[196] Much later, we find Augustine paying attention to the phenomenon of dreams of the dead in which they complained that they had not been buried.[197] All this means that ancient writers easily supposed that a person who felt culpable, to some degree, with respect to someone dead was quite likely to be visited by that person in sleep. Not that the appearance of the dead in dreams *always* evoked guilt: they could be a positive omen, and the author of *On Regimen* IV robustly recommends that the treatment for negative dreams about the dead is running, walking and a light diet.[198]

Two other religious practices clearly favoured the dreaming of real epiphany dreams. One was incubation, about which it is unnecessary to say much more for the moment. Common sense seems to suggest that visitors to incubation shrines are sometimes likely to have dreamt about receiving messages from the presiding deity, since they earnestly wished to do so, and since they may have been in an especially emotional condition, encouraged by the surroundings, including the statue of the god, and by the ritual preparation.[199] But this argument elides a crucial step—do we dream of the things we want to dream of, or (something different) of the current influences that are pressing in upon us? We know surprisingly little about either question. Neither is identical with the question of the 'day's residue', which we considered in the introduction. Such credible research as there has been seems to suggest that presleep concerns do not in fact appear consistently in our dreams—but the subjects of the research were, to say the least, remote from the world of the ancients.[200]

194. 354–356.

195. iv.7. He takes her epiphany to mean that there is life of some kind after death.

196. Lucan, *Phars.* iii.8–35. There is no need here to parse Pompey's dismissive comment (38–40). Alcyone, whose dream was mentioned earlier, ought perhaps to have saved her husband from shipwreck since she was the daughter of Aeolus god of the winds (Ovid, *Met.* xi.431, 728). For other Roman cases see Kragelund 1991, 264 n. 29.

197. *De cura pro mortuis gerenda* 10 (*CSEL* 41.639).

198. [Hippocrates], *On Regimen* iv.92. Throughout antiquity 'it is taken for granted that people tend to dream of those they miss or love' (Kragelund 1991, 261).

199. This is the argument of among others Lane Fox 1986, 152–153.

200. Roussy et al. 1996 ('there was no overall group pattern suggesting continuity of dream content with presleep ideation', 121). The sample was minute (N = 8!!). It seems to

From incubation to magic. Graeco-Roman magic, at least as it is known from Egypt, sometimes included summoning spirits, and summoning them to appear in dreams.[201] Now at least according to conventional views, not many Greeks or Romans believed that major or even minor deities could be manipulated in this fashion. But those who deeply desired to receive a dream-visit from say Hermes—the god most interested—may possibly have succeeded on occasion in obtaining one.

Statues of the gods may have haunted the imaginations of pious persons more generally (which makes one wonder whether the inhabitants of seriously Catholic lands often dream of the Madonna, and whether devotees of the Buddha recall his statues—the Vairocana Buddha at Nara is 52 feet tall—in their sleep). A statue such as that of Athena Polias in the Parthenon, some 39 feet tall[202] and largely made of ivory and admittedly exceptional, made a lasting impression, without doubt, on those who saw it.[203] The same might apply on a smaller scale in countless other cases, all the more so because many statues of divinities were at the centre of rituals. Gods who appeared in epiphany dreams often resembled their cult-statues.[204] Sometimes in fact it is the statue that seems to speak rather than a living being: we have met one case (Ptolemy Soter) and shall meet another (Aelius Aristides).[205] It would therefore be possible to reverse the opinion of Democritus and the Epicureans that humans believed in gods because they had seen them in dreams, and argue that they dreamt of gods because they had seen them in their waking lives—in temples. But this will not do as a full explanation of the continued survival of the epiphany dream, even if we concede that the latter was a fact as well as a convention.

---

be widely accepted that dreams dreamt in a sleep laboratory are affected by the setting (cf. Bulkeley 2001, 369).

201. Cf. Miller 1994, 120–121, Renberg 2003, 249–250. How to summon Hermes himself: *PGM* V.370-445, XII.144–152 ('show me a form [*morphe*] of yourself', lines 149–150). For sending a god or spirit to appear in what would clearly be an epiphany dream see IV.1842–1869 (the spirit is told to appear to the victim 'looking like the god or *daimon* she worships', lines 1858-1859; cf. 2500–2501), XII.121–144, esp. 136. All these texts are from the fourth century.

202. 26 cubits: Plin. *NH* xxxvi.18.

203. As to how often and in what circumstances people saw cult statues see among others Burkert 1985 [1977], 91–92, Lane Fox 1985, 154, P. Stewart 2003, esp. chs. 4 and 5.

204. Brillante 1988, 17–18, Renberg 2003, 240.

205. For further instances see Renberg 240–241; but in truth the total is not very large. It is worth remembering that many Romans went to sleep in the presence of lamps, metal or terracotta, that represented gods: see P. Stewart 2003, 195–207 for the material.

It is after all part of the essence of an epiphany dream that there should be a pronouncement, and although the statues of the Greek and Roman gods did occasionally give miraculous signs of life,[206] they did not talk much. Many dream visitants are not gods at all, or at least do not look like them. And once again we need to recall that we are dealing with a *form* of dream-description, not a mere matter of common content.

There was also, I suggest, a cognitive aspect. There can be little doubt that, quite apart from memory problems, many people find it difficult to describe their dreams—it is enough to read the often jejune reports of those who have slept in sleep laboratories while taking part in experiments.[207] The epiphany dream was a simplifying or structuring formula, which may help the dreamer to get confused recollections into orderly shape. I have already suggested why it is likely that ancient dreams were as 'illogical' (that is a shorthand term) as modern ones (more on this in Chapter II);[208] and if so, they presented their narrators with real problems.

We should not overestimate the strength of our evidence that Greeks and Romans sometimes actually dreamt epiphany dreams. Our most prosaic sources generally 'knew' of such dreams not on the basis of scholarly or scientific investigation but from literary texts, for most ancient reasoners took their first evidence about the world from the established canon of anecdotes, that collection of good stories that was such an important part of ancient thinking about abstract questions.[209] Cicero in fact points out the poor quality of the sources.[210] But the most plausible conclusion is probably that the Greeks and later the inhabitants of the Roman Empire *did* occasionally dream epiphany dreams. They probably remembered and recorded such dreams in disproportionate numbers, and they probably elaborated some other dreams into the epiphany form. The reasons why they dreamt in this way, when they did, is that they desired instruction from a superhuman source, and given both the nature of the gods and the prevailing religious practices, they almost inevitably received 'epiphanies', in our sense, from time to time; and it became a convention.

206. MacMullen 1981, 175 n. 42, Barasch 1992, 36–39.

207. The raw material is, understandably, not printed very often.

208. Above, p. 14.

209. Just for this reason the ancient classifiers of dreams are of little use for present purposes; cf. Dodds 1951, 107–108, who does not see the significance of the material he describes.

210. *De div.* ii.136; cf. Dodds 1973, 183.

The Epiphany Dream in Danger

What told against the epiphany dream? As we have already seen, secular reflection about dreaming probably made it more difficult to make use of the epiphany dream,[211] as early perhaps as the times of Xenophanes, Heraclitus and Empedocles.[212] Democritus, who attempted another naturalistic explanation of the origins of dreams, may not, however, have weakened the tradition, since it was part of his teaching that 'images of huge size . . . foretell future events to people by appearing to them and speaking'; it was this phenomenon that made early man believe that there were gods.[213]

No one would want to exaggerate the influence of philosophers. I would suppose that few people in classical Athens claimed to have been visited in their dreams by gods or divine messengers and that it would have seemed arrogant and presumptuous and not very convincing. If it happened at an incubation shrine, many people who heard the story will have been inclined to believe (see Chapter III for more on this problem). Epic figures of the past had had such dreams, and a heroic figure, such as Socrates was for his followers, might have epiphany stories attached to him. But Plato and Aristotle, while they do not reflect popular opinion, give some hint of it, in all likelihood, when they in their different ways make the truth-telling dream a special prerogative of the few. But the ancient world was not about to be taken over by rationalism or secularism. After Aristotle, or at latest after Epicurus, there was little progress in the naturalistic understanding of dreams. It would be quite wrong to imagine that the ancient world grew progressively more sceptical about authentically god-inspired or predictive dreams—on the contrary, as we shall see, there is good reason to think that trust actually increased in fourth-century Athens, and again in many parts of the Roman Empire after 100 AD (different chronologies in different

211. Dodds 1951, 117, spoke of this as 'a more rational attitude towards dream-experience', but we have become more cautious about diagnosing rationality. Who would now want to say that Homer (the only archaic Greek whose thinking about dreams we can be said to know) was 'irrational' about them? He reacted intelligently to what was generally thought in his time. 'We should expect', says Dodds, '. . . that by the end of the fifth century the traditional type of "divine dream", no longer nourished by a faith in the traditional gods, would have declined in frequency and importance' (118); but this wave of mass scepticism about the gods is a mirage. We should see analytic thought as an addition rather than as a replacement.

212. On all the philosophers mentioned in this section see Chapters III and IV.

213. Sext.Emp. *Adv. math.* ix.19 (*testimonium* 175b in Taylor 1999); cf. 68 B 199 D-K.

places). Meanwhile the epiphany dream still had its *raisons d'être,* and indeed sometimes entered into the discourse of the most admired philosophers, Poseidonius for instance.[214] Cicero must have been correct to assume that those people of education who believed in predictive dreams could, on some level, accept epiphany stories.

Galen and Aelius Aristides

Two authors in particular can help us to understand the status of the epiphany dream among educated persons in the high Roman Empire. Where a man of science might end up on this issue is nicely illustrated by the language used by Galen. Galen reverenced Asclepius, and believed that one might learn an effective cure from a dream. He was no doubt loosely associating himself with the divine when he claimed that a dream *(enhupnion)* had found fault with him and told him to write certain material,[215] though he was also making an authorial excuse for prolix and difficult prose. It must be on purpose that he avoids the full epiphany form here—it would have seemed solemn, pretentious, poetic; it was just the dream, not in so many words a god, that instructed him. Similarly, he took seriously the dreams dreamt by his father to the effect that he should become a doctor[216] but he does not say explicitly that his father's dreams were of a god or a spokesman for a god. That too would have been to veer off into the world of the poetic, or the superstitious. Asclepius, he says, has from time to time given instructions aimed at circumscribing the passions,[217] and he was presumably thinking of instructions given in dreams, but again he does not explicitly say so—for Asclepian epiphany dreams did not suit the image of himself he was intent on maintaining. Explaining how he excused himself from accompanying Marcus Aurelius on a military campaign, he refers somewhat vaguely to an 'order' he had received from Asclepius.[218]

214. See above, p. 58.

215. *De usu partium* x.12 = III.812–813K. I have tried to use the best editions of each of Galen's work (for a catalogue see Fichtner 1985) but have normally referred to Kühn's edition only, since it is the easiest for most readers to consult.

216. *De ordine librorum suorum* 4 = XIX.59K (Singer 1997, 27–28), *On Prognosis* ii.12 (XIV.608K), *De methodo medendi* ix.4 (X.609K). (It is repeatedly stated that Galen speaks of a single dream, but that is an error.)

217. *De sanitate tuenda* i.8.19–21 = VI.41K.

218. *De libris propriis* 2 = XIX.18–19K (Singer 1997, 8). When he describes receiving advice to cut an artery (*De curandi ratione per venae sectionem* 23 = XI.315K), he speaks of vivid dreams without mentioning their nature.

Galen's contemporary the great sophist Aelius Aristides was temperamentally quite different, and at first sight seems to have known no such restraint. He describes, by my count, some 163 dreams of his own,[219] approximately one-tenth of which might, on a generous reckoning, be counted as epiphany dreams.[220] (Many others, more than fifty, contained orders from Asclepius but are not said to involved his appearing in person; still others are anonymous orders which Aristides may well have thought of as emanating from the god.)[221] The identity of the visitant might be multiple—an interestingly realistic touch: 'he was at the same time Asclepius and Apollo, both the Clarian one and the one who is called Callitecnus'.[222] Yet it may seem surprising, in view of Aristides' passionate devotion to the god, that he registers only three other epiphany dreams of Asclepius (one of which the god shared with Serapis and perhaps Isis).[223] Here is one of them:[224]

> when the god appeared, I grasped his head with each hand in turn and entreated him to save Zosimus [his foster father] for me. The god refused . . . for the third time I grasped him and tried to persuade him to assent. He neither refused nor assented but told me certain phrases. . . . [Zosimus recovered].

As will be seen at once, this was not a classic epiphany dream, but it was fairly close. Other characters who appeared, besides Serapis, were Asclepius' son Telesphorus, Athena, the gods of the underworld, and in an exceptional case a philosopher named Rhosandros.[225] My view is that in spite

---

219. Some very briefly indeed. Behr 1968, 171, gives a total of 130.

220. Occasionally someone else's epiphany dream is mentioned, e.g. in xlviii.9 (Asclepius in disguise).

221. It is fairly plain in fact that he took all or most of the anonymous orders he said he received in dreams to have come from Asclepius: see xlvii.55, where he asks Asclepius for a clarification. Since this is the first time I have had occasion to mention xlvii, i.e. the first of Aristides' *Sacred Tales,* I may add that Dorandi 2005 has convinced me that while almost all of it was written by Aristides, it was put together in its present chaotic form by some *post mortem* editor.

222. xlviii.18.

223. xlvii.56 (a brief appearance in the guise of the temple-warden Asclepiacus), xlvii.71, xlix.46; xlviii.31–33 cannot be counted, since Asclepius seems not to have said anything even though he was thought to be present (sec. 32 beginning).

224. xlvii.71.

225. xlix.47 (statue of Serapis), xlix.23 (Telesphorus), xlviii.41–42 (Athena), xlix.47 (the chthonic gods), l.19 (Rhosandros). We could also count the five short dreams about various gods mentioned in l.39–40.

of his hypochondria and his vanity, Aristides was not wholly lacking in shrewdness and knew that he was in some danger of not being believed if he exaggerated his personal contact with Asclepius.[226] When he dreamt of Athena, he became aware that the two friends and the servant he informed were afraid that he was delirious *(paraleron)*:[227]

> not much later, Athena appeared with her aegis and beauty and size and overall form as in the statue by Phidias in Athens. There was also the sweetest possible scent[228] from the aegis, and it was like a kind of wax, and it too was marvellous in beauty and size . . . She reminded me of the *Odyssey*,[229] and said that these were not idle tales, as could also be judged from the present circumstances. It was necessary to persevere.

Late-antique Stimuli

In late antiquity the epiphany dream received some new stimuli, and although it sometimes also found itself on the defensive, it may be said to have survived and flourished.

A relatively detailed discussion is to be found in the work of the Neoplatonist Iamblichus *On the Mysteries of the Egyptians*:[230] while he may consider epiphany dreams inferior to waking visions of the gods, he most certainly accepts that the gods really do appear in dreams—Asclepius appears, and other gods have done so—'but what need is there', he asks, 'to go through such occurrences one by one, when things that happen every day provide greater clarity than any story?'[231] Labelled by Dodds 'a manifesto of irrationalism',[232] *On the Mysteries* is almost Christian in its willingness to detect the manifold interest of superhuman beings of various kinds in the lives of humans. Iamblichus in fact has a theory about 'god-sent' dreams, by which he seems to mean epiphany dreams (for in such dreams 'one can hear a voice that guides us on the subject of our duties'); they take

---

226. At all events the information set out here ought to calm the *Schwärmerei* of certain religious historians ('nightly screening of the gods', Lane Fox 1986, 164).

227. xlviii.41.

228. A sign of authenticity.

229. In which of course she had constantly helped Odysseus.

230. iii.2–4. See esp. Athanassiadi 1993, 124–127.

231. iii.3 end (p. 103 Des Places).

232. Dodds 1951, 287.

place in the transitional state between sleeping and waking.[233] Iamblichus continued to be read, if only by philosophers and the emperor Julian.

None of this had anything to do with Plato. But the classical tradition carried epiphany dreams within it, so that as long as and wherever Homer, the *Dream of Scipio* and the *Aeneid* continued to be respected their readers were familiar with narratives of this kind. Libanius and his like knew all the classic examples. Augustine was familiar, from boyhood on, with the story of the quasi-epiphany of Phorbas to Palinurus in the *Aeneid*.[234] We shall shortly meet another dream of Augustine's with classical overtones. Synesius naturally remembered that dreaming poets had met the Muses.[235] Both he and even more Macrobius display their learning on the subject of Penelope's Goose Dream.[236]

What difference did Christianity make? For a long time, not very much, since Christians were few (probably not many more than two hundred thousand in the entire Roman Empire around 200 AD)[237] and their cultural influence was marginal. It is only after about 300 that they need to be taken into account. But the origins of their ideas about dreams certainly concern us, not only because they eventually came to dominate but also because of a continuing doctrinal conflict.

Yahweh preferred to be heard but not seen,[238] and consequently perhaps, though there are prophetic dreams in the Old Testament, most famously Jacob's Ladder (in which the god of Israel does appear), relatively few of them take the form of a classic epiphany.[239] The epiphany dream announced by Judah Maccabee on the morning of the Battle of Adasa (161 BC),

233. iii.2. These chapters deserve further analysis, but this is not the context. For specific epiphany dreams supposedly dreamt by Alexander and by Lysander see iii.3 end. For more epiphany dreams in the Neoplatonist tradition see Marinus, *Vita Procli* 30.

234. *De cura pro mortuis gerenda* 10 (*CSEL* 41.641).

235. *On Dreams* 4.

236. *On Dreams* 13 (he also remembered the visit of Oneiros to Agamemnon in *Iliad* II); Macrob. *Comm. in Somn. Scip.* i.3.17–20.

237. Hopkins 1998, esp. 195.

238. Husser 1996, 1506–1507. Even the Hellenized tragedian Ezechiel felt this (*Exagoge* 101–103).

239. Genesis 28:12–13. Abimelech's dream (Genesis 20.3–7) qualifies, as do the dreams of Solomon in I Kings 3:4–15 and 9:1–9. How to classify the dreams of Jacob and Laban in Genesis 31 is less clear. Husser 1996, 1483–1544, and Gnuse 1996, 68–96, provide detailed accounts of Old Testament dreaming (see Husser 1996, 1506–1516, on 'message dreams').

featuring both the high priest Onias III and the prophet Jeremiah,[240] had no known Jewish precedents.[241] God, it is true, had promised prophetic powers, according to a famous passage of Joel: 'your old men shall dream dreams, and your young men shall see visions'.[242] The apocalyptic *Ethiopic Book of Enoch*, an originally Aramaic text (as it seems) that goes back to at least the first century, contains an imperative dream that was probably thought of as an epiphany.[243] But Philo's dream taxonomy seems to have no room for epiphany dreams,[244] and the fact that Josephus recounted some[245] has been attributed to Greek influence,[246]—which was of course also powerful among the first generations of Christians.

Dreams have a minor and curious role in the Gospels, being concentrated, with a solitary exception, in Matthew's account of Jesus' birth, which includes at least three and perhaps as many as five brief epiphany dreams.[247] The other birth-narrative, in Luke, knows nothing of such stories. Since Matthew is so insistent, it seems likely that this inconsistency was a result of a difference of opinion about the value of dreams. In Acts, waking visions are important, dreams less so; Paul dreamt of the Macedo-

240. II Macc. 15: 11–17.

241. The whole passage reeks of Greek rhetoric; this should not surprise us (see Seth Schwartz 2001, 35). For some further discussion see Weber 1999, 24–27.

242. 2:28 (quoted in Acts 2:17 and Tertullian, *De anima* 47, among other places; see Amat 1985, 40); cf. Numbers 12:6. The contradiction between the latter passage and Zechariah 10:2 is discussed in the Babylonian Talmud (*Berakoth* 55b—see Miller 1994, 63–64). Job 33:15–16 contains a statement by Job's instructor Elihu that Jehovah speaks to men in dreams. The OT has much else to say on the subject. Later, Ecclesiasticus 34:1–8 speaks strongly against believing in dreams—'unless they are sent by intervention from the Most High' (6).

243. 13.8–10. M. A. Knibb translates 'and I saw a vision of wrath, (namely) that I should speak to the sons of heaven and reprove them . . . I spoke before them all the visions which I had seen in my sleep.'

244. *On Dreams* i.1–2, ii.1–2.

245. Above, pp. 27 n. 28, 54.

246. Gnuse 1996, 198.

247. Matthew 1:20–24, 2:13, 2:19–20 (in each case a messenger from god appears to Joseph). The less clear cases are 2:12 and 2:22. The exception is the dream dreamt by Pilate's wife, Matthew 27:19, which adds to the impression that Matthew (or a source) was at odds with the other synoptic writers on this topic. The claim of Gnuse 1990, 118, that Matthew used the dream motif because 'it highlights a distant, transcendent deity' carries no conviction at all; it is more plausible to suppose (ibid.; cf. Gnuse 1996, 99) that Matthew wishes to suggest for a Jewish audience that Jesus was the new Moses.

nian (in truth, it seems a very Greek story in this context) and three times, apparently, of Jesus, who brought encouragement and instructions.[248] There is no dreaming at all in Paul's letters, either on his part or anyone else's.[249]

The first Christian text to make extensive use of dream-language is the *Shepherd* of Hermas (probably a production of the mid–second century), so much so that it has even been referred to as a 'dream-book'.[250] Though it is unclear how many of the author's five visions should be considered as dreams, he several times refers explicitly enough to dreams,[251] and always to epiphany dreams (with the variant that he sometimes talks to his visitants); and the experience was clearly thought of as a rare privilege.[252] Now, no Christian apologist attempted to delegitimize such texts, and most of them must have recognized that dreams could lead to conversions (see below). Some scholars think that Christianity attempted to demonstrate its respectability by distancing itself from dreams (which has interesting implications for the way in which dreams were valued in the wider culture).[253] It was one of their notions that demons sometimes create belief in pagan deities by means of dreams *(oneiroi)*.[254] But it will be argued in Chapter III that Christian attitudes towards dreams resembled in many respects those that prevailed in the wider culture.

As far as the epiphany dream is concerned the *net* effect of the spread of Christianity was undoubtedly to give it a new set of functions and a very

---

248. Visions: Acts 5:19, 8:26, 9:3–9 (where it is clear that the recipient is supposed to be awake; see further 22:6–11, 26:12–19; what Paul was supposed to have *seen* on the road to Damascus was simply light), 10:1–8 and 30–34, 11:4–12, 12:6–11 (the divine messenger woke Peter before addressing him), 22:17–21. We call these events visions, but notice that in 12:9 the author distinguishes between a real angel's being there and a (mere) *horama*. Dreams: 6:9: (Paul and the Macedonian, a *horama*), 18:9, 23:11, 27:23–26. In Acts 2:17 Peter quotes the passage of Joel which favours prophetic dreaming.

249. I put off till Chapter III the question of the early Christians' estimation of the value of predictive dreams and concentrate here on their use of epiphanies.

250. Miller 1994, 132.

251. *Horaseis* [*Visions*] 1.1 (he sees a female accuser who speaks on behalf of god), 2.4 (a 'fine-looking young man' gives him instruction), 3.10 (two apparent instances); and cf. Miller 133.

252. For a different reading of Hermas' dreams see Amat 1985, 55–61.

253. Miller 1994, 64–65.

254. Justin, *Apology* i.14 (cf. Athenagoras, *Legatio* 27 end); Tatian, *Oration to the Greeks* 18 (in ch. 21, the MSS seem to imply that god ensures that all dreams are intelligible, but there is probably a textual fault here; see M. Marcovich's edition, 1995).

long future. Modalities changed: neither god the father nor, more surprisingly perhaps, Jesus appeared very often.[255] But that removed a hindrance, for it would have been still harder for the Christians to maintain discipline among themselves if it had been accepted that each of them could receive personal appearances from the saviour;[256] and there were plenty of messengers available. At least four features of Christianity supported the epiphany dream: its followers believed more strongly than most non-Christians did that the divine beings were interested in them as individuals; they made very abundant use of the miraculous; the most committed Christians were often in difficulties of one kind or another—doctrinal disputes, impossible commandments, occasional persecution—so they needed warnings and encouragement;[257] and last, they tended very strongly towards hierarchy, which meant that the leaders could mark themselves off by this privileged form of communication and be recognized by the other faithful.

Theologians were aware that some epiphany dreams might come from evil sources, but they tended all the same to be accepting. Tertullian's opinion was that some dreams came from god and turned out to be true (he has a long list of secular examples, none of them epiphany dreams), though other dreams came from demons or the devil.[258] Epiphany dreams occur, and they even occur to quite ordinary people.[259] He even writes that 'almost the majority of mankind' learns of god through visions,[260] no doubt

255. Here I diverge from Stroumsa 1999, 197, who appositely cites the *Vision of Dorotheos*, an enigmatic text of about 300 AD (*P. Bodmer* 29) which narrates a dream about the Christian god (see Kessels and van der Horst 1987, 316–317, for the date), but does not consider the full range of the evidence. Justin in the second century and Novatian in the third argue that god himself does not appear in visions or dreams (cf. Ps.-Clement, *Hom.* 17.16); see further Nock 1934, 73. In the dreams of Perpetua and Cyprian he appeared in disguised form; on all this see Amat 1985, 113. In a dream attributed to Constantine, a natural reading of the source (Sozomen, *Hist.Eccl.* ii.3.3, early fifth century) indicates that god himself appeared, though nothing is said of his appearance.

256. As to why discipline and conformity were so important to the early Christians see Hopkins 1998, 217–222.

257. Hence they are fairly frequent in martyr acts. See in addition to the acts of Perpetua the *Passio Mariani et Iacobi* (chs. 5, 6, 7, 8) and the *Passio Montani et Lucii* (chs. 7, 8, 21), both third- or fourth-century texts. Not all of these are obvious epiphany dreams.

258. *De anima* 46–47. On Tertullian's dream theories see esp. Amat 1985, 93–99.

259. Christian sinners in *De idololatria* 15.7 (a vision by night, probably a dream), *De virginibus velandis* 17.3.

260. 47.2.

thinking in part of epiphany dreams (and incidentally borrowing an idea from the much detested Epicureans). Origen similarly asserted that many had been converted to Christianity by waking visions or dreams,[261] and although he does not specify that these were normally epiphany dreams, that is rather likely to have been what he had in mind. Cyprian can accept the validity of *nocturnae visiones*.[262]

Dream-descriptions served multiple Christian purposes, for example in explaining conversions,[263] where the epiphany form, since almost by definition it gave a clear-cut message from an undoubted authority, was especially valuable.[264] When Augustine's mother Monica was assured in a dream by a 'splendid young man' that her son would become a Christian too,[265] that was an epiphany dream, even though in this adaptation a third person appeared (Augustine himself). Conversely Natalius, a 'heretic' mentioned by Eusebius,[266] disobeyed epiphany dreams of Jesus (they are called *horamata*), and was subsequently scourged by angels, like Jerome later.

The epiphany dream-description also allowed Christian writers to convey lengthy moral instruction, as in the case of Hermas. Jerome wrote about one Praetextata, who was threatened by an angel for having had the temerity to give her niece a stylish coiffure—the punishment was paralysis of the hands, shortly followed by death.[267] Cyprian used this method to

261. *Contra Celsum* i.46: 'a certain spirit having presented images *(phantasiosantos)* to them while they were awake or asleep'.

262. *Ep.* 16.4. Pontius' *vita* (ch. 12: *CSEL* 3.3.ciii–civ) quotes a dream-description of Cyprian's which is a variant on the epiphany form.

263. See Dulaey 1973, 160, Amat 1985, 114–115. This tradition lasted an extraordinarily long time: for sixteenth-century France see Bokdam 1990, 139.

264. Gregory of Nyssa was converted to a life of contemplation after an epiphany dream featuring the Forty Martyrs: *In XL martyres* pp. 167–168 ed. O. Lendle (*Opera*, ed. W. Jaeger, X.1) = *PG* 46.785ab. The same text p. 166 = 784c shows their shrine at Ibora being used for incubation. They later appeared to the empress Pulcheria (399–453) to tell her where their relics were: Sozomen, *Hist.Eccl.* ix.2.

265. *Conf.* iii.11, cf. viii.12.

266. *Hist.Eccl.* v.28.11–12.

267. Even though she had been ordered to do so by her husband. Jerome's story (*Ep.* 107.5) is characteristically even more violent than the one told by Tertullian, *De virg.vel.* 17.3, in which a young woman dreams that an angel appeared in a dream to reproach her for being imperfectly veiled in church, and struck her. One recalls the violence in his famous *Ciceronianus es* dream (*Ep.* 22.30). It is best to pass hastily by the comment of

moralize against the fear of death.[268] Chastity was also assisted: Abba Elias, a figure in the *Lausiac History* of about 400, dreamt of being castrated by three angels.[269]

Variants and improvements on the descriptive pattern were always possible. Augustine, for instance, knew how to make a combined epiphany-episode dream a rhetorically effective method of instruction, as in his account of the dream of Tutulismeni of Hippo:[270] Tutulismeni demanded money from a debtor, then dreamt that he appeared before a 'tall and admirable' judge[271] who interrogated him, instructed him, and ordered him to be beaten (he bore the marks of this the next day). Anyone who behaves like Tutulismeni after my sermon, says Augustine, will be committing a much greater sin. The judge before whom Tutulismeni had appeared was god—but Augustine avoids saying so. When Augustine described how a 'fine-looking young man' appeared to Gennadius,[272] it was an epiphany dream, or rather a pair of epiphany dreams, but they were not simple ones because in the first the young man showed Gennadius, who was sceptical about life after death, a city representing 'heaven', and the second dream attempted to use the phenomenon of dreaming itself as proof that there really is an afterlife.[273] The author of the *Miracles of Saint Thecla*, a person of some education writing in Cilicia in the mid–fifth century, tells how one Orention claimed to have dreamt an epiphany dream in which the saint rather improbably bestowed on him the pretty girl he had seen at the saint's festival; a little later, a demon duly flayed him alive.[274]

Pious tales were in fact constantly cast in the form of epiphany dreams. In his life of Martin of Tours (about 396), Sulpicius Severus describes how, the night after the man of god, while still a soldier, had 'divided his cloak'

Miller (1994, 212) that Praetextata's alleged dream 'allowed' her 'to reflect . . . on the meaning of [her] actions'.

268. *De mortalitate* 19 (but though he uses some of the conventions of the epiphany dream in this case, he also seems to imply that the subject was awake); cf. Dulaey 1973, 171.

269. Palladius, *Lausiac History* 29.3–4.

270. *Serm.* 308

271. Clearly therefore a divine figure: Dulaey 1973, 173.

272. *Ep.* 159.3.

273. Dulaey 1973, 158, thinks that it is by design that Augustine does not say that god sent these dreams, though he does say 'Quo docente nisi providentia et misericordia dei?' These dreams appear again in Chapter II.

274. Miracle 33. See the edition by Dagron (1978), 376–81, with his comments (104). For date, authorship and context see 13–30.

with a beggar, he was rewarded with a dream-appearance of Jesus,[275] which, he hastens to add, did not make Martin proud.[276] The narrative thus forthrightly claimed that Martin was one of the elect, and afterwards by implication Sulpicius included himself.[277] Later on, epiphany dreams might give authoritative plans for the foundation of monasteries.[278] Sometimes epiphany dreams partake of the miraculous: they may help the pious to find the bodies of saints—for a practice already known in the Greek world in the mid–fourth century spread westwards in the next generation (Ambrose of Milan was led to the bodies of the saints Gervase and Protasius).[279] More generally they may reveal the whereabouts of relics.[280]

The dead seem to return more than ever in the dreams of the living.[281] Augustine explains that they are no more aware that they are doing so than living people are aware of the fact that they are being dreamt of.[282] How then to explain that what the dead say in dreams is sometimes (usually) right? 'Angelical operations', he says.[283] But he himself dreamt of dead acquaintances who spoke to him.[284]

There continued, however, to be a more negative Christian view about dreaming, and this ambivalence continued throughout the Middle Ages.[285]

---

275. *Vita S. Martini* 3.2–5.

276. 'Quo viso, vir beatissimus non in gloriam elatus est humanam, sed bonitatem Dei in suo opere cognoscens . . . ad baptismum convolavit'. Later (5.3) another dream gave Martin instructions, but its form is not indicated.

277. In *Ep.* 2 Sulpicius describes how he himself dreamt of Martin just before receiving the news of his death. The form of the 'pronouncement' was that Martin held forward a copy of Sulpicius' biography and blessed him. The literary antecedents of these dreams are traced at length in the edition of J. Fontaine (Paris, 1967–1969). On these texts (the only dreams in the *Vita*) see also Le Goff 1985, 205–207.

278. Gregory the Great, *Dial.* ii.22.1–5.

279. Dulaey 1973, 148, Amat 1985, 283–290. Ambrose: Augustine, *Conf.* 9.7.16, *Epist. ad Catholicos* 19.50 (*CSEL* 52.297) (not quite the first case in the West: see Dulaey). But it is not clearly identified as an epiphany dream.

280. Above, n. 257, for example. Cf. Dagron 1985, 41.

281. Often in Augustine, see Dulaey 1973, 144–146. Waking visions of the dead are commonly attested in Roman Africa in this period: Dulaey 145. See also the life of Saint Thecla, ch. 17 (Dagron 1978, 236–239).

282. It is clear, however, from the story in *De cura pro mortuis gerenda* 17 (*CSEL* 41.655–656) that not all agreed: a holy man said that he would appear in a person's dream and he did so.

283. *De cura pro mortuis gerenda* 10 and 13 (*CSEL* 41.639–641, 647).

284. *Ep.* 158.8.

285. Cf. Kruger 1992, esp. 75–78.

Jerome also took a relatively restrictive view: he criticized those who thought that all dreams are divine revelations, for such dreams are only available to the saints and the servants of god;[286] in a polemical context, he even dismisses all dreams as *vanae imagines*.[287] Not that Jerome was entirely consistent about this, since the 'sinner' Praetextata, like Tutulismeni, was also a chosen recipient.[288] But this is now the orthodox doctrine: god chooses a few people to send meaningful dreams to.[289] It was probably from pagans that Constantine had learned how to make military and political use of dreams[290] and he had no claim to saintliness, but Lactantius had little choice but to accept the emperor's account of what had happened the night before the Battle of Saxa Rubra. Eusebius may have been more dubious, since he plays down dreams in his *Ecclesiastical History* and ignores this particular one.[291]

Eusebius at one point recalls an epiphany dream from Matthew, but he regards *oneiropompoi* (bringers of dreams) in a bad light if they had called themselves Christians.[292] Christian emperors, beginning with Constantine, legislated against divination, and Constantius II made it explicit that dream-interpretation was included among the forbidden practices.[293] Not that there is any evidence of prosecutions on this latter count, except when the accused had apparent political motives.

The testimony mentioned in the preceding paragraphs demonstrates that there were plenty of people, including Christians, who believed in revelatory dreams. Jerome's words, in particular, suggest that there was a steady supply of epiphany-dream reports. A proliferation of them is also suggested in 401 by the attempt of the bishops of Africa to discourage the spread of martyr shrines that had been set up 'per somnia et per inanes

286. *In Hierem.* iv.59–60 (*CC-SL* 74.225–226): 'revelationem . . . quae proprie sanctis et servis dei aperitur'. Cf. *Ep.* 22.16.

287. *Contra Rufinum* i.31 (*SC* 303.86). For the context see Miller 1994, 212.

288. See the exceedingly unpleasant story told in *Ep.* 107.5.2. Add the dream dreamt by Pilate's wife, *In Matheum* 27.19 (*CC-SL* 77.266).

289. Gregory of Nyssa, *De hominis opificio* 13. For a detailed reading of this text cf. Miller 1994, 47–51.

290. In Gaul in 311, Apollo, in a vision or dream, had promised him victory (*Pan.Lat.* 6 (7).21.3–4); Harris 2005a, 492.

291. Lactantius' account: *De mortibus persecutorum* 44.5. Eusebius' description of the battle: *Hist.Eccl.* ix.9.2–8.

292. *Hist.Eccl.* i.8.16, iv.7.9. For fourth-century Christian censure of dream-based prophecy see Dagron 1985, 39.

293. *C.Th.* ix.16.6 = *C.J.* ix.18.7. See Sandwell 2005, 114–115.

quasi revelationes quorumlibet hominum',[294] 'as a result of dreams and the practically valueless revelations of certain persons', though these dreams may of course not have been strictly epiphanic.

At the same time, pious and self-confident Christians were quite content to record more or less miraculous dreams, their own and other people's. Ambrose of Milan speaks at length about encountering his deceased brother Satyrus.[295] We mentioned earlier a tale Augustine tells about a young man in Milan who received some thoroughly secular help from a dream appearance by his deceased father. And he tells of a rather famous dream in which he himself appeared to his ex-student Eulogius and explained a passage of Cicero which Eulogius had to teach the next day.[296] 'How such things occur, I do not know', he frankly says, but he has no doubt that they do occur. God can send true dreams, even to non-Christians,[297] but they are not a way of knowing god, and demons can create phantoms that they somehow put into the minds of sleeping humans.[298]

Epiphany dreams continued to perform practical functions for non-Christians and Christians alike. Julian seems to have expected his supporters to believe—and be encouraged—when he told them that a figure resembling the Spirit of Rome (the *genius publicus*) had appeared to him in a dream the night before he was proclaimed Augustus and went into open rebellion.[299] Before the Battle of the Frigidus in 394, Theodosius announced that the apostles John and Philip had appeared to him in a dream, promising victory.[300] Incubation shrines continued to function, in some important cases taken over—not without conflict—by Christian saints: Saint Thecla, for instance, took over from Apollo Sarpedonius at Cilician Seleucia (the formal difference was that no *divine* figure now appeared), and other saints gained control of the shrines of Isis at Menuthis (outside Alexandria) and of Bes at Abydos.[301]

Skilled writers were still well aware of the literary tradition and knew how to manipulate it. We have just seen how Augustine did this. A nice

---

294. *Concilia Africae a.345–a.525*, canon 83, ed. C. Munier (*CC-SL* 149.205).

295. *De excessu fratris sui Satyri* 72–74 (*PL* 16.1313).

296. *De cura pro mortuis gerenda* 11 (*CSEL* 41.642).

297. Augustine, *Epist. ad Catholicos* 19.49 (*CSEL* 52.296).

298. *De civ. dei* xviii.18.

299. Ammianus Marcellinus xx.5.10.

300. Above, p. 43.

301. See the vivid account of Athanassiadi 1993, 125–127. Cf. also Dulaey 1973, 186–188.

example unaffected by Christianity—even if the author was in fact a bishop—appears in the last and most sophisticated of all the Greek romance-writers, Heliodorus. Wanting to give the brigand chief Thyamis an interesting dream which he can *mis*interpret (that helps the novelist to create complications), he perceives that it needs to be authoritative, definitely divine.[302] So Thyamis enters the sanctuary of Isis at Memphis—thus it is in part an episode dream—and the goddess tells him what is going to happen—so it is in part an epiphany dream.

Finally the scholar Macrobius, not surprisingly, was aware that a narrative such as the *Dream of Scipio,* the long philosophical dream with which Cicero ended his *Republic* and on which Macrobius wrote a commentary, could partake of more than one dream-type. For him it was both an epiphany dream, an *oraculum* (because 'Paulus and Africanus, who were both his ancestors [*uterque parens*], both sacred and authoritative figures who had exercised priestly functions, announced his future to him', i.e. to the younger Africanus) and also *not* one, since some of its features were anomalous.[303]

Epiphany Dreams in the Middle Ages

Those who are expert on the dream as it appeared in mediaeval literature concur that the epiphany dream made up a significant part of the very extensive body of dream-description.[304] Many will remember that the famous stained glass of Chartres cathedral (twelfth- and thirteenth-century) is studded with epiphany dreams.[305] In the present context, it will be enough to indicate twelve other examples summarily, ranging over some eight cen-

302. i.18. See Bartsch 1989, 94–98.

303. *Comm. in Somn. Scip.* i.3.12.

304. Manselli 1985, esp. 223–224. He uses categories somewhat different from mine, but most of the dreams he classifies as 'premonitory' are epiphany dreams, though sometimes quite elaborate ones as in the case of the dream written up by Emperor Charles IV (*Karoli IV Imp.Rom. Vita ab eo ipso conscripta,* ed. K. Pfister and W. Bulst, ch. 7) (the dream he dreamt at Terenzo near Parma on 15 August 1333; for commentary see Dinzelbacher 1989). For his perception of roughly what I have called the 'episode dream' see further 237–238, 242. He remarks (242) that the mediaeval sources are disproportionately interested in what are in effect epiphany dreams. For other discussion see Dinzelbacher 1981, 40–45.

305. For a good account see Deremble-Mannes 1989.

turies. The point is to demonstrate both continuity and some of the functions of dreams of this type. The background includes both wide acceptance of waking visions, and also (the paradox is only superficial) a strong and continuous tradition of Christian selectiveness about meaningful dreams. It must always have been obvious that dreams were a special danger to monks, and John Climacus warns strongly against martyrs who appear in epiphany dreams—they are demons in disguise.[306]

(1) Gregory of Tours recounts many dreams. An angel appeared to Saint Gall when he was bishop of Clermont, and promised that for the eight years more that the saint was destined to live his diocese would be exempt from the plague then afflicting the rest of the country.[307] This was written in the last quarter of the sixth century, probably in the 580s.

(2) According to Gregory the Great, Saint Benedict while still alive chose to deliver a message to two of his subordinates by appearing to each of them in a dream; they took no notice of the dream until Benedict revealed what he had done.[308] Date of the text: 593–594.

(3) Bede tells how Saint Germanus, injured in the foot, dreamt one night that a person dressed in pure white visited him, held out his hand and told him to stand: he was cured.[309] Date of this text: 731.

(4) A Greek manuscript from Constantinople in the Bibliothèque Nationale contains the *Homilies* of Gregory of Nazianzus,[310] and among the illustrations is the Dream of the Magi, represented more explicitly as an epiphany dream than it was in the text of the Gospel.[311] In

306. *Scala Paradisi* 3 = *PG* 88.670–672 = I, pp. 95–97 Trevisan (when real angels bring dreams, they are dreams of punishments, judgements and 'separations', i.e. from god), also 20 (II, p. 31) and 23 (II, p. 65). The date is late in the sixth century or early in the seventh.

307. *Historia Francorum* iv.5. For another epiphany dream see vii.22. For some other cases in Gregory's writings see Le Goff 1985, 207–208 (misusing the term 'incubation').

308. *Dial.* ii.22.1–5. This book contains more than fifty dream and vision descriptions (Bartelink 2006, 80).

309. *Hist.Eccl.* i.19.2. See also ii.6.1 (with marks of scourging as an apport), iv.11.2. A. Crépin lists other examples in his edition (2005) (I, p. 43), but does not trouble to distinguish between dreams and waking visions.

310. Paris BN gr. 510.

311. f. 137r, illustrating Gregory's reference to Matthew 2:12. As Brubaker 1999, 66, points out, the artist's angel is not mentioned in the original; she discusses sources and parallels.

accordance with Artemidoran terminology, the scene is described as the *chrematismos ton magon*.[312] Date: ninth century.[313]

(5) Geza, the father of King Stephen I of Hungary, having turned to Christianity, dreamt that a 'young man delightful to look at' appeared and made authoritative pronouncements about his future son.[314] The dramatic date: 975.

(6) A Burgundian monk, Raoul [Rodulfus] Glaber, wrote in his *Historiae* about a certain Vilgard of Ravenna who was excessively devoted to the *ars grammatica*—just like an Italian. One night demons appeared to him as Vergil, Horace and Juvenal, and thanked him for his devotion; they 'proclaimed him a blessed herald of their immortal fame and promised him a share in their glory'. But all ended well, because he was condemned as a heretic.[315] Date of the text: 1020s.[316]

(7) The foundation legend of Waltham Abbey in Essex had it that a blacksmith dreamt, three times in all, that Christ ordered him to guide the parish priest and his parishioners to a distant hilltop, where they would find a marvellous cross. This story is known from a chronicle written in the second half of the twelfth century,[317] but it probably goes back to the eleventh.[318]

(8) While the First Crusade was fighting at Antioch in 1098 Saint Andrew appeared, more than once apparently, to a Provençal named Pierre Barthélemy to tell him where the 'Holy Lance' (the spear employed at the Crucifixion) was to be found, and what to do about it; the discovery of this relic did wonders for the invaders' morale.[319]

---

312. Brubaker 1999, fig. 18.

313. For many other Byzantine examples of epiphany dreams see Dagron 1985.

314. See E. Szentpétery (ed.), *Scriptores Rerum Hungaricarum* II (Budapest, 1938), 379–380; Manselli 1985, 224.

315. *Historiae* 2.12 (p. 92 in the edition of J. France, Oxford, 1989).

316. France p. xlv.

317. Schmitt 1999, 281. The source is *De inventione sanctae crucis Walthamensis*, ed. as *The Waltham Chronicle* by L. Watkiss and M. Chibnall (Oxford, 1994).

318. For an important eleventh-century narrative of dreams and visions see Otloh von St. Emmeram, *Liber Visionum* (ed. P. G. Schmidt, Weimar 1989), whose dreams are sometimes in epiphany form (with an explicit allusion to Jerome's Cicero dream, Visio 3, p. 46 Schmidt). For an eleventh-century healing epiphany see F. Metcalfe (ed.), *Passio et Miracula beati Olavi* (Oxford, 1881), 100.

319. Manselli 1985, 223, Riley-Smith 1997, 150–151.

(9) Another manuscript in Paris, this time French, illustrates a story from the life of Abbot Hugh of Cluny, according to which Saints Peter, Paul and Stephen visited the paralysed monk Gunzo in a dream with instructions to tell the abbot to build a new church ('Cluny III', officially founded in 1088) (otherwise, they said, the abbot would become paralysed too).[320] Date of the text: twelfth century.[321]

(10) Federico III of Aragon, King of Sicily, repeatedly dreamt of his mother, who said to him 'My son, I give you my blessing, so that you may devote yourself to serving the truth'.[322] He consulted his personal physician, Arnaldus de Villa Nova (to give him his Latin name; he was in fact a Catalan), one of the leading medical men of the age, who wrote an interpretation. After which a whole saga began, for which there is no space here. Date: 1309 or shortly afterwards.[323]

(11) The majority of the dreams in the *Divine Comedy* are not epiphanies, but the poet's dream of the Siren in *Purgatorio* XIX,[324] the 'femmina balba', the 'stammering female', is a fine if not typical

---

320. BN lat. 17716. See in detail Carty 1988, who also provides numerous parallels. She could have included the dream of Rahere, the founder of St. Bartholomew's Priory in London, which was recounted in the church's *liber fundationis* between 1174 and 1189 (see Dinzelbacher 1989, 82–85), where the most interesting feature is the author's hesitation about the value of dream-visions. The Cluny story is known in various versions. Carty argues (115–116) that the monks knew from the books in their library what to think about dreams; also (116) that the dream-story provided authoritative justification for the heavy expense of rebuilding. The healing of the monk served as a kind of apport proving the dream's authenticity.

321. See Carty 120 n. 3, 121 n. 19. Another twelfth-century case (c. 1115) occurs in the autobiography of Abbot Guibert of Nogent: his mother dreamt of the Virgin, who in effect gave instructions (1.16) (*De vita sua*, ed. E.-R. Labande, Paris, 1981). He recounts fourteen other dreams, of which three or so others are epiphanies (I leave out the knight who, having usurped the fishing rights of Nogent's monastery, dreamt that the Virgin boxed his ears), as well as a similar number of waking visions (cf. Schmitt 1985, 294).

322. Iacobus de Voragine, *Legenda Aurea*, is a text of the 1250s or 1260s constellated with epiphany dreams: see, at random, the entries for 25 December, 30 March, 21 October. For an epiphany dream attributed to the miracle-working craftsman Facio da Cremona see Vauchez 1972, 42.

323. Arnaldo's *De somniorum interpretatione* was eventually printed in Toulouse in 1485. On the whole case see Manselli 1985, 230–233.

324. Lines 1–33. *Purgatorio* makes extensive use of other kinds of dreams.

example. She is instructive, even though she does not give instructions. Date of the text: 1310s.[325]

(12) At the beginning of his *Trionfi*, Petrarch sinks into sleep and begins
a prolonged epiphany dream of a 'vittorioso e sommo duce', Amore.[326]
Date: 1352–1357.

Throughout western mediaeval literature, as this list suggests, one en-
counters imaginative manipulations of the epiphany dream form. In the
Song of Roland, for example, Charlemagne dreams four prophetic dreams,
two before and two after the disaster at Roncevaux. The first pair are both
episode dreams,[327] and Charlemagne fails to understand them—he had no
special reason to trust them. The second pair are episode dreams too, but
they are brought by the angel Gabriel, 'who stands at his head the whole
night', in the classic pose of the dream-visitor, and this time they are more
comprehensible, and, because Gabriel is there, more trustworthy.[328]

There are countless other mediaeval dreams that might be discussed
here.[329] But Weidhorn's discussion of Chaucer's dreams brings out an especially important point. In his early works the poet makes liberal use of
the traditional dream framework, but in other poems he 'transcends the
trite mechanism of falling asleep at the beginning of the work and awakening at the end'. He 'alters the conventional to achieve verisimilitude, the
real unreality of dreams'.[330] There had been too many epiphany dreams.

One more example will be enough, from Thomas Malory: when in *The
Most Piteous Tale of the Morte Arthur saunz Guerdon* the king's nephew
Sir Gawain, with 'a number of fair ladies', appears to King Arthur, and
Arthur recognizes that he is a messenger from god, this is an epiphany
dream, in Macrobian terms an *oraculum*—all the more clearly so because

325. On dreams in the *Vita Nuova* that may be counted as epiphany dreams see Baldelli
1985.

326. *Triumphus Cupidinis* I, 13. See the commentary of V. Pacca (1996), esp. p. 52, for
many mediaeval parallels not listed here.

327. Lines 717–736.

328. Lines 2525–2569 (note esp. 2529–2530, 2568). For Gabriel as Charlemagne's protector during sleep see 2847–2848. I do not underestimate the difficulties posed by these
passages.

329. For wide-ranging discussions see especially Paravicini Bagliani and Stabile 1989
and Kruger 1992. Neslihan Senocak points out to me that epiphany dreams were often
listed among the post-mortem miracles in canonization reviews.

330. Weidhorn 1970, 51. The *Book of the Duchess* is his chosen example.

it takes place at an important moment in the story and comes true in spite of the king's efforts.[331] Yet it is also somewhat anomalous in various ways, not only because of Gawain's attendants; the king, for instance, initiates the conversation (correct court etiquette, no doubt).[332]

The Late-medieval and Early-modern Demise

The epiphany dream-narrative gradually lost its credentials over a long period, from the fourteenth century to the eighteenth. To explain such a cultural change, which affected both Protestant and Catholic Europe, is sure to be difficult, even if we limit ourselves, as we are practically bound to, to the world of the literate. How can we tell individual aberrations from a general trend? The obvious master-narrative in the concluding sections of this chapter would pronounce that what killed the epiphany dream was a more secular attitude towards dreaming, generated and practised by intellectuals and others, both during the Renaissance and even more afterwards.[333] And that is part of the truth. But there are many complications. Consider to begin with two facts that fail to fit comfortably into such an explanation.

(1) One of the most 'rational' texts about dreaming ever written before the Scientific Revolution was the work of Albertus Magnus (ob. 1280): his *De somno et vigilia*[334] is closely modelled on Aristotle's three short pieces in the *Parva Naturalia* (for which see Chapter IV), arguably the high point of ancient thinking about dreaming (that was Albert's opin-

---

331. *The Works of Sir Thomas Malory*, ed. E. Vinaver (Oxford, 1954), 865–866. On dreaming in Malory's work see Goyne 1997. She errs, however, in saying that this dream does not come true (84): Gawain warns Arthur that if he fights Mordred next day, he will die. He does not mean to fight, but he does, with the inevitable result, reminiscent of the trickster oracular replies of antiquity.

332. In the early hours of the morning, 'he fell on slumbering again, not sleeping nor thoroughly waking', i.e. he was in the half-waking condition in which many people sometimes dream (readers who have not experienced this could consult Foulkes 1985, 64–77).

333. Books that help to show the range of Renaissance writing about dreams include Charpentier 1990 and Brown 1999. Browne 1979, 126 n. 14, says that 'the relative lack of interest of Renaissance writers in the ... [Macrobian] *oraculum* [see above, n. 51] can probably be explained by the relationship of dreams of this type to features of Greek culture, such as incubation', ignoring the Roman and mediaeval history of the phenomenon.

334. In *Opera Omnia* ed. A. Borgnet, IX (Paris, 1890), 121–207. For an account of this text see Gregory 1985, 121–133.

ion).[335] He used other sources too, and explicitly criticized the master. What he did not do was to mention the Bible or the church fathers.

(2) Throughout the sixteenth and seventeenth centuries, there continued to be an enormous production and consumption of dreambooks.[336] Robert Wood's translation of Artemidorus' *Oneirocritica*, first published in 1606, went into its twentieth edition in 1722 (and it was not the last).[337]

But let us concentrate on the epiphany dream. I offer some markers of its strength and weakness, before returning to the matter of explanation.

Nicolas Oresme (c.1320–1382), bishop of Lisieux, is often treated as the greatest scientific intellect of the fourteenth century, and among his scholarly works is the *Livre de divinacions* (1361–1365), in which he set out with vigour to debunk astrology,[338] more or less incidentally rejecting most predictive dreams at the same time.[339] But the same scholar on at least one occasion made spectacular use of a dream epiphany. In the volume in which he debates at length, in a wholly rational manner, about what he calls the measurability of the movements of the heavenly bodies,[340] he abruptly

335. *De somno et vigilia* iii.1.1 (p. 178 Borgnet). Epiphany dreams apparently belong in the sixth and seventh of his thirteen categories (iii.1.10, pp. 191–192 Borgnet).

336. For France and Italy in the sixteenth century see Cooper 1990a (who also includes sceptical authors such as Aristotle and Cicero). For Germany in the sixteenth to eighteenth centuries see Lenk 1983, 159.

337. *The Interpretation of Dreams by the Most Celebrated Philosopher Artimedorus* [*sic*], *and other Authors* (London, 1722). It was translated from French not Greek. See Thomas 1971, 128–130, for ample evidence that Britons prior to the Restoration often took dream-predictions seriously, with the strict Puritans objecting (but the correct date of Wood's Artemidorus is as given here). In 1657 the pious Philip Goodwin observed that God seemed to send fewer meaningful dreams than in ancient times (Goodwin 1657).

338. For the text and a translation see Coopland 1952. The editor raises the interesting question (6–7) whether astrology was especially popular at the time. The decision to write in French not Latin shows of course that Nicolas had a semieducated audience in mind.

339. That dream-interpretation was not his major target is evident from ch. 1 end; but see chs. 3, 7, 12, and esp. 11: 'although a person may sometimes, by nature, be able to see what is absent or to come, either in dreams or in sickness, or when they have been put out of their senses by magic art . . . yet such visions are often false or occult, without certainty, and dangerous to accept, and there is still less certainty in the other arts I have mentioned'. There is some ambivalence here.

340. *Tractatus de commensurabilitate vel incommensurabilitate motuum celi,* ed. E. Grant (*Nicolas Oresme and the Kinematics of Circular Motion*, Madison, Milwaukee and London, 1971).

turns to a kind of *deus ex machina* for a solution. He dreamt of a god,[341] and what a god! For it is Apollo, who has not been seen for some time in this story, accompanied on this occasion by the Muses and the Sciences. But even Apollo, though he smiles upon the dreamer,[342] does not give a clear answer to Oresme's astronomical problem but allows Arithmetic and Geometry to dispute it. Geometry seems on the whole to prevail.[343] We are left to think that Nicolas has made skilful and somewhat ironical use of an antique convention—as Dante and Petrarch had done decades before, but with a clearer implication of a claim to authority. His model, I suggest, is likely to have been the *Dream of Scipio*,[344] but what matters is that an epiphany dream is still judged to be highly acceptable.

It is already relatively rare to find true epiphany dreams in the imaginative dream literature of the late-fifteenth or sixteenth century.[345] Francesco Colonna, at the end of his fantasy *Hypnerotomachia Poliphili*,[346] which is cast in the form of a vast dream, seems to acknowledge the existence of the epiphany form of dream. The trouble-making demon Alecto in Tasso's *Gerusalemme Liberata* is also a descendant rather than a copy of ancient dream-visitants (specifically of Allecto in *Aeneid* VII); but later in the poem god sends a dream to make a pronouncement to Goffredo, the crusaders' commander.[347]

341. P. 284 Grant: 'ecce mihi, quasi sompniatori, visus est Apollo'. That he meant to describe a dream not a waking vision is confirmed by the ending (p. 322).

342. P. 288.

343. Cf. Kruger 1992, 146.

344. The *Somnium* discusses astronomy among other matters, as Oresme knew (*Livre*, ch. 5). For Oresme and Cicero cf. Coopland 1952, 27. There is a nice additional irony in the fact that Oresme was certainly aware (Coopland 139) of the passage in Cicero, *De div.* ii.115–116, where the author accuses Apollo of ambiguity and obscurity—and incidentally says that he never spoke Latin.

345. This emerges clearly enough from Charpentier 1990. James Hankins has pointed out to me the unfinished dialogue of Aeneas Silvius Piccolomini (Pius II, ob. 1464) in which he imagines being led in a dream to the Elysian Fields, where the emperor Constantine complains to Jesus at length that Constantinople has fallen to the Turks, and receives an answer (see Hankins 1995, 133–134). This fantasy owes something to the epiphany dream model.

346. Published in Venice in 1499, but written more than twenty years earlier.

347. In VIII, stanzas 57–62, Alecto appears in a dream to the Italian knight Argillan, and in the guise of the deceased Rinaldo demands that Argillan exact revenge from Goffredo. The later dream: XIV, stanzas 1–19. It comes not through the Gate of Horn, but through a crystal gate in the East: 'da questa escono i sogni, i quai Dio vòle/ mandar per grazia a pura e casta mente' (XIV.3). Cf. Weidhorn 1970, 63.

That enterprising physician and astrologer Girolamo Cardano (1501–1576) shows, paradoxically, that the epiphany dream was in some difficulty.[348] He believed that dreams had great predictive force—it was no accident that the classical writer on dreams who most interested him was Synesius, who unlike most others thought that *all* dreams had meaning. In his monograph of 1562, Cardano relates a number of epiphany dreams from classical texts, but his powers of observation are too much for him when he comes to describe dreams dreamt by himself or by people he knew (which he does often): here he almost always avoids the epiphany form.[349] He seems to wish to minimize the number of genuine epiphany-form dreams.[350]

Another, much shorter, account of dreaming has something of a modern ring to it: in the third book of his *Essais* (1586–1587), Montaigne, a faithful Catholic, casually devoted a well-known autobiographical page to the subject:[351]

> I seldom dream; and then it is of fantastic or grotesque things, the product of thoughts that are usually pleasant, being ridiculous rather than melancholy. And I believe it to be true that dreams are loyal interpreters of our inclinations; but there is an art in sorting and understanding them. [He quotes Accius, from Cicero]. Plato, moreover, says that it is a prudent to draw from them prophetic instructions for the future. I see nothing in this, were it not for the marvellous experiences that Socrates [*sic*], Xenophon and Aristotle relate on this subject, men of unimpeachable authority. . . . I exercise little choice at table.

In English literature in the seventeenth century epiphany dreams are rare, and grow rarer.[352] There are perhaps three in Shakespeare, amid a

---

348. For the role of dreams in Cardano's own life cf. Grafton 1999, 165. Browne 1979 gives a rather decontextualized account of his book on dreams.

349. His filial piety was only just equal to accepting the extravagant fantasies of his father Fazio (see Grafton 1999, 167). I am taking Cardano's *idolum* dreams to be almost all of them epiphany dreams in the sense used here.

350. *Synesiorum somniorum omnis generis insomnia explicantes libri IV* (*Opera Omnia* V, 593–728). According to Boriaud 1999, 223, he thought there were few or none. But I read 2.18 (p. 690) a little differently: 'non negaverim in quibusdam huiusmodi idola à Diis velut & in defectu artis medicae sanationes, immitti: quale illud: Surge, & tolle puerum, & vade in Aegyptum: sunt enim qui animam pueri quaerant. Sed miracula sunt, & extra artis considerationem, sicut & sanationes illae, *& reliqua huiusce generis*' (italics mine).

351. III, Essay XIII, 'De l'experience [*sic*]' (ed. A. Micha, Paris, 1979, 310). This passage accurately reflects the opinions he expressed elsewhere; see Mathieu-Castellani 1990.

352. On the latter point cf. Weidhorn 1970, 119.

wealth of 'episode' dreams, and it may be a sign of their questionable status that they all appear in what are commonly considered to be Shakespeare's 'romance' plays.[353] Almost the last English epiphany dream in a literary text of any importance may be Eve's dream in Books IV and V of *Paradise Lost*:[354] Satan, 'close at the ear of Eve', manages to instil into her a dream in which a false Adam appears and misleads her.[355] The real Adam explains:

> Oft, in her [i.e. Reason's] absence, mimic Fancy wakes
> to imitate her; but, misjoining shapes,
> wild work produces oft, and most in dreams,
> ill matching words and deeds long past or late.[356]

In subliterary texts of the same period epiphany dreams appear to be equally uncommon.[357]

Explaining the Change

What caused the epiphany dream to disappear?[358] This is a question about representation but also, as we saw earlier, about actual dreams.[359]

(1) As we noted at the outset, E. R. Dodds did not attempt to explain in any detail the disappearance of the epiphany dream, a development which

353. *Cymbeline* 5.4.29–150, *Pericles Prince of Tyre* 5.1.240–250, *The Winter's Tale* 3.3.15–46. *Henry VIII* 4.2.80–94 is somewhat different.

354. For epiphany dreams brought about by the devil in the works of some minor English poets of this period see Weidhorn 1970, 125–129.

355. IV.799–1014, V.1–128. On the poet's opinions about dreams, and his use of dream-descriptions: Weidhorn 1970, 130–155.

356. V.110–113.

357. Take for example the material discussed by Burke 1973. Crawford 2000, 134, in an intriguing paper about women's dreams in England, mentions an apparent case in a religious pamphlet of 1695. For a few other cases earlier in the seventeenth century see Crawford 2000, 137–138.

358. I offer the following hypothesis to those who know more about the history of the fourteenth to seventeenth centuries than I do.

359. Incubatory practices to some extent survived the Christianization of the Roman Empire, but they were never more than marginal in the empire's western half (cf. Renberg 2006) and are virtually unheard of there after the sixth century (occasional assertions to the contrary are based on mistaken use of the terminology). Carty 1988, 120 n. 5, looked carefully but did not find much. Rightly observing that 'incubation was not foreign to Christianity', she cites only one other site in use later than the time of Gregory of Tours (eleventh-century miracle cures attributed to Sainte Foy that did not involve dreaming).

he left undated. But he took over from the anthropologists whose work he knew the notion that its continuance was to be associated with 'the old solidarity of the family'—he saw the visitants as essentially father-figures— and its demise with 'our more individualised society'.[360] He seems to equate the patriarchal family with the close-knit family. But few historians if any would confidently assert that either patriarchality or family solidarity declined in the era in question.

The figure of the dreamer, the recipient, deserves careful attention. Consider who, outside incubatory contexts, is said to have experienced an epiphany dream. It is the man of power or the man of god, the great poet, the queen or princess, or at least the brigand chief or the literary heroine. The exceptions are intriguing, but they are few. The epiphany dream can only have wide currency in a world in which it is taken for granted both that divine power takes a strong interest in charismatic individual humans, and that such a human is to be believed when he or she makes an unsupported claim about his/her inner experience.[361] The second of these conditions prevailed less and less, I suggest, from the sixteenth century onwards.

(2) Western Christendom in the Middle Ages was profoundly ambivalent about dreaming, and if you want to, you can catch the most lucid of its spokesmen, from Gratian to Thomas Aquinas, 'contradicting' themselves—and indeed you can do the same for some of the best minds of classical antiquity, as we shall see in Chapter IV. But this state of affairs might have gone on indefinitely.

The mediaeval historian J.-C. Schmitt writes that it was Descartes who first 'described a physiology of dreams that reduced the process . . . to the individual and the brain and nervous system, *wresting it away from the old interpretative framework which laid stock in supernatural forces as well as in the collective and ritual dimension*'.[362] But Descartes in fact represented only one stage in a long process, and the words italicized here send us back much earlier, almost 400 years earlier. Between the twelfth century and the thirteenth some of the philosophical thinkers of western Christendom

360. Dodds 1951, 109. He depended here on Lincoln 1970 [1935], who described, with the carelessness about sources that was permitted among anthropologists at that time, a certain number of epiphany dreams from around the world (e.g. Tonga [46], Borneo [59–63]), and by contrast other cultures in which he thought they were unknown.

361. Septimius Severus, Constantine and Julian could hope, at least, that their dreams would be believed.

362. Schmitt 1999, 281.

adopted a new approach to dreams, less religious and more in accord with contemporary philosophy.[363] It is too simple to say that 'during the Renaissance the dominant strain of oneiric thought ceased to be religious',[364] for essentially secular dream-books had already begun to gain a certain footing in the twelfth century. Nonetheless a more secularized approach certainly did have some effect on how people recounted their dreams as well as on how they thought about them.

We have already referred to Albertus Magnus and Nicolas Oresme; Albert in particular is especially incisive. The interest of such church authorities in naturalistic explanations of dreaming was all the more important because, as the reader will have noticed, all but the last three of the twelve mediaeval epiphany dreams listed above were written up and propagated for *religious* reasons (Federico III's case was driven by politics). No theologian could deny that the saints had received truth-telling epiphany dreams, but they were no longer a phenomenon of modern times.

Truly thorough dream-sceptics were probably still rare in the fifteenth century, however, and none of the great Italian humanists of that era is known to have been one. The increasing presence of Aristotle's *Parva Naturalia* in Italian libraries[365] is suggestive but no more. Was it a sign of the times that when Ulric von Ellenbogen,[366] a Bavarian physician who copied the famous mediaeval dream-book, the *Somniale Danielis*, for Rupert of Bavaria, also wrote a tract (1459) in which he argued that it was not really written by Daniel, and that the addressee should take no notice of dreams since most of them are deceptive?[367]

The real wave of naturalistic thinking seems to follow the Reformation, though it does not come from the Protestant reformers (Philipp Melanchthon, for example, wrote a preface for an edition of Artemidorus and was

363. See esp. Gregory 1985, 113, with references to twelfth-century texts.

364. Rupprecht 1993, 124.

365. Bolgar 1954, 466–468, under 'before 1459', '1468', 'before 1475', '1475', 'before 1482', '1490'. But George of Trebizond, who translated a number of Aristotle's *libri naturales* into Latin (Monfasani 1976, 176–177) did not translate the *Parva Naturalia*, so John Monfasani has kindly told me. It would be worth knowing more about the diffusion of the Hippocratic *On Regimen*, in the same period; it seems to have been printed for the first time in Rome about 1481 (Cooper 1990a, 261).

366. Udalricus Ellenbog: Chevalier 1903–1907, II, 4591.

367. See L. T. Martin in his edition of the *Somnium* (1981), 48–49. The MS is Vatican Pal.Lat. 1880.

far from being a sceptic).[368] In fact the challenge to the traditional Catholic view of dreams could come from diverse directions; Pietro Pomponazzi, a wide-ranging rationalist, wrote in 1521 that it was the movements of the heavenly bodies that caused predictive dreams and what are called here epiphany dreams (the author he cites for examples is Plutarch).[369] The elder Scaliger must have intended to promote a secular approach when he published a commentary on the Hippocratic book *On Regimen* IV (*On Dreams*), in Lyon in 1539. Auger Ferrier (1513–1588), who wrote what was at the time the longest treatise on dreams since Albertus Magnus, was quite the opposite of a sceptic, but his opinion that 'no dreams are meaningless' was as subversive as scepticism itself.[370] All these men were Catholics.

Four years after Ferrier a German Protestant, the physician and mathematician Kasper Peucer (1525–1602),[371] published the first edition of a longer and more complex work, his *Commentarius de praecipuis divinationum generibus* (*Commentary on the Main Types of Divination*).[372] What is striking about Peucer's career is that he spent twelve years in prison for having the wrong theological opinions; what is striking about the section of his *Commentarius* that deals with dreams is that while it starts out conventionally, dividing dreams into those with physical causes, those that come from god, and those that come from the devil, the central section seems to reveal what interests him most of all about dreaming, namely its physiology. We should not, however, lose sight of the fact that Peucer and his readers were above all in keen pursuit of reliable ways of discovering the secrets of the future.

By the late sixteenth century, in England at least, a sceptical view of dreaming seems to have been fairly commonplace among literary minds, even though it is obviously unsafe to cite such acrid personalities as

368. *Opera quae supersunt omnia* XX (ed. C. G. Bretschneider and H. E. Bindseil, Brunswick, 1854), cols. 675–684 (it is true that he wrote many other prefaces). For his views about dreams see Lenk 1983, 190–193, Brosseder 2004, 97–99.

369. *De naturalium effectuum causis, sive de incantationibus* (Basel, 1556, but written thirty-five years earlier according to the title-page; Pomponazzi died in 1524).

370. *Liber de somniis* (Lyon, 1549) (but it is not much more than five thousand words in length). He published it together with translations of 'Hippocrates', Galen, and Synesius. 'Somnia nulla sunt vana' (26). On Ferrier on dreams see Cooper 1990b, 56–60.

371. A son-in-law of Melanchthon.

372. Wittenberg, 1553.

Thomas Nash and Thomas Hobbes as proof that this was so,[373] and we have already seen that many of their educated contemporaries were still able to believe. But for the most part 'the age in which the validity of a dream was readily established had long since passed'.[374]

Thus we come to Descartes, without examining the sources of his thinking about human nature or the methods of science—his biology has been branded as 'sterile physicalism' in a well-known history of the subject[375]— and without assessing the extent of his influence. It is a fairly well-known paradox that while Descartes gave a secular account of the human organism, and of dreaming in particular, he gave great weight to some of his own dreams and in particular to the three he dreamt on the night of November 10, 1619 (the first of which shows some traces of the epiphany form).[376] Furthermore he took these latter to have come to him from above (d'en haut): they were supernatural.[377] It is reasonably clear in fact that the philosopher grew up with some traditional assumptions (he was twenty-three at the time of the famous dreams) which he eventually discarded. But what concerns us here is his developed scientific method, and in particular his manner, in his mature work, of dealing with dreams:[378] it is strictly physiological. Descartes' continuing awe of religious authority was not strong enough to make him return to traditional ways of thinking about this subject.

(3) Renaissance men of letters did not for the most part write in isolation from the great philosophers of the age.[379] But there was, I think, a purely literary factor at work in the disappearance of the epiphany dream. In its simplest form it was already unsatisfactory to Dante, Chaucer, and Malory:

373. Bacon seems to have taken a naturalistic view of dreams: *De augmentis scientiarum* (I used the Amsterdam, 1662, edition), III.368, IV.376–7. On Nash see Weidhorn 1970, 34, and on Hobbes 35–36.

374. Weidhorn 1970, 123, referring to seventeenth-century England.

375. Mayr 1982, 98.

376. Cf. Holland 1999, 127. Among the commentaries on Descartes' dreams I have found Hallyn 1990 especially helpful. The English translators of *The Philosophical Writings of Descartes* (1985) repeat a fable when they say that the famous dreams included a 'new mathematical and scientific system' (I, p. xi); see Hallyn 46–47.

377. Hallyn 1990, 48–49.

378. The partial displacement of the word *songe* by the word *rêve* from the seventeenth century onwards is always mentioned in this context, but the weight of such a linguistic change is hard to measure.

379. On Dante's knowledge, for example, see Gregory 1985, 123.

all of them knew of the convention but avoided it or reshaped it. As the classical canon widened and became better known, certain conventions became harder to use in any serious context. At the same time, many of the mediaeval stories about epiphany dreams became steadily harder for most people to accept. Even religious poets, perhaps more inclined to conservatism than others in this respect, showed some inclination to get away from the old conventions of dream-description.[380] But Robinson Crusoe still dreamt an epiphany dream of a kind: 'a Man descend[ed] from a great black Cloud, in a bright Flame of Fire . . . his Countenance was most inexpressibly dreadful . . . he moved forward towards me, with a long Spear or Weapon in his Hand, to kill me . . . he spoke to me . . . "Seeing all these Things have not brought thee to Repentance, now thou shalt die"'.[381]

The Romantics were deeply interested in dream narratives, but seldom if ever wrote of epiphany dreams. The convention was dead, after several millennia of life, as far as the 'west' was concerned.[382] But it lived on in traditional unmodernized Greece and outside the Graeco-Roman tradition.

380. Cf. Bokdam 143–144 on Marguerite de Navarre (1492–1549) and François Habert (c.1508–c.1561).

381. Quoted from M. Shinagel's second edition (New York, 1994 [1719]), 64–65. As Armstrong and Tennenhouse 1989–1990, 473, remark, Defoe started out with a 'pure convention' and added a 'modernizing twist'. By 1788 epiphany dreams seemed archaic: a pseudonymous 'Elihu', writing in that year about the U.S. Constitution, remarked that 'no deity comes down to dictate it, not even a God appears in a dream to propose any part of it' (American Mercury, 18 February, p. 3).

382. One might ask, however, whether the apparitions of the saints, not sleeping apparitions but flesh-and-blood visitations, that have flourished to a bizarre degree in modern Europe—all students of comparative religion know the names of San Sebastian de Garabandal (where visions of the Madonna and Saint Michael started in 1961) and Medjugorje (where the Madonna has frequently been observed since 1981)—meet an atavistic need for epiphanies.

II

Greek and Roman Dreams That Were Really Dreamt

Is This Tale Tall?

We asked whether people really dreamt epiphany dreams, but in answering that question we sidestepped another one—whether we can *ever* know what was really dreamt in antiquity.

Here are three classical texts that claim to describe real dreams dreamt by real people:

(1) Alexander of Macedon was campaigning in India, when Ptolemy, one of his officers, and some of the troops he commanded, were affected by the enemy's poisoned weapons. They were dying. Alexander, however, dreamt of a snake which 'carried a plant in its mouth, and showed him its nature and power, and the place where it grew'. Alexander woke up, found the plant, made some medicine; Ptolemy and the rest duly recovered. So writes Diodorus Siculus,[1] on the basis no doubt of Ptolemy's memoirs.

(2) On the eve of Julius Caesar's assassination, so Suetonius informs us,[2] the dictator's wife Calpurnia dreamt that the gable of their house collapsed,[3] and that Caesar was run through while he lay in her arms (many variant versions appear in other authors). A story of this kind was already circulating in the times of Nicholas of Damascus a generation later.[4]

---

1. xvii.103. Also Strabo xv.723. For another dream that identified a desperately needed medicinal plant, see above, p. 27.

2. *Div.Iul.* 81.3.

3. An old dream motif: Euripides, *IT* 44–51.

4. *FGrH* 90 F 130.83.

(3) Our hypochondriac friend Aelius Aristides included among the approximately 163 dream-descriptions in his *Sacred Tales,* the following (for 11 January 166 AD):[5]

> I dreamed that some barbarians had got me in their power, and one of them approached me and seemed about to place a tattoo mark on me. Then he inserted a finger right in my throat and poured in something, according to some local custom, and called it *oxusitia,* 'heartburn'. Later on I was recounting [still in the dream] that I had dreamed this, and my hearers were startled and said that the cause of my being thirsty but unable to drink was this, that my food [*ta sitia*] turned to bitterness [*oxos*]. Vomiting was recommended, and the barbarian ordered that to-day I abstain from bathing and produce one servant as a witness of this'.

Now, it seems to me likely that the last of these descriptions is, most of it anyway, close to a dream actually dreamt, and obvious that the stories about Alexander and about Calpurnia are inventions. But are there solid reasons for making these judgements, and do there exist usable methods for assessing the credibility of these and the thousands of other Greek and Roman dreams which the sources recount to us? As we have just seen, there seems to have been at least one important dream-type in the classical world that is now practically unknown, so our investigation promises to be quite complex.

An Essential Question

Writing about dreams in twelfth-century Europe, a fine scholar observed a few years ago that whether a historian studies such matters as evolving attitudes towards dreams, past theories of the dream, or the literature or iconography of dreams, 'the same perhaps unanswerable yet unavoidable question keeps on returning: what were the dreams of mediaeval people like, and what were they about?'[6] For the ancient and the mediaeval world alike, that task seems quite beyond us. But there may at least be a reward

---

5. *Or.* xlvii.9.

6. Schmitt 1985, 291. His response was to attempt a microhistorical analysis of the dreams described in the *De vita sua* of the monk Guibert de Nogent (above, p. 79). The further aim should be, he suggests, to understand how, in a given historical setting, dream and society affect each other.

for deciding whether some particular dream narratives are likely to be wholly or partially true.

Some other scholars probably do not think so. The epistemological status of dreams is plainly and notoriously peculiar (no one can check the veracity or accuracy of anyone else's account of a dream—but that can also be true about some other claims we may make about our thoughts). So much so that the attempt to judge the truth of a dream report is widely thought to be futile. It is elementary, after all, not only that dreams are, with minor exceptions, wholly interior experiences,[7] but that they are hard to remember accurately and that they are subject to easy misrepresentation. A contemporary scholar discounts the question of what was really dreamt by Roman emperors,[8] and in the main he was right to do so, since no one wrote down an emperor's dream without some ulterior motive.[9] Yet the reasons he puts forward, which apply equally to nonimperial dreams, are scarcely cogent:[10] the first is that there is no determining test of authenticity—of course not, but there are probabilities, and probabilities are the historian's currency, above all in ancient history. The second argument is that since we meet historical dreams in the form of texts not actual experience, we can never check directly that the text is true—but that is simply one of the historian's normal problems in a particularly intense form.[11]

Literary scholars, in particular, may hesitate to follow us here, but those who read ancient accounts of dreams need to know what really occurred. For those who think that dreams reveal something about the dreamer's personality, this is straightforward and obvious. For those who are more sceptical, the question is nonetheless a fertile one: few subjects indeed reveal more about the tastes of classical authors than the way they (mis)rep-

---

7. Wet dreams are exceptions, and dreams in which the dreamer speaks or makes other sounds may be (I am not aware of any research as to whether such sounds actually correlate with dreams).

8. Weber 2000, 10–11. Contrast his attitude in 1998, 29.

9. Marcus Aurelius may have done so, but his interest in the subject was limited (see Chapter III).

10. They derive from Dutton 1994, 24–26, also preoccupied with the dreams of rulers, in his case of Carolingian times.

11. None of this prevents Dutton 1994, 28, from saying that 'it may generally be true that the oracular dream was more frequent in the ancient world than it is in our own'. Nor does it prevent Weber 2000, 536, from generalizing implausibly about the nature of ancient dreams (see below, n. 61). For a more sensible approach to dream-reports see Kilroe 2000, 127–128.

resent particular dreams. Just as you need to know ancient warfare to understand the literature of the subject, so you need to know ancient dreams, their reality and their conventions and what was invented, in order to understand the men of letters who wrote about them.

The question of authenticity is in any case unavoidable: some famous Greek and Roman dreamers such as Aelius Aristides, Artemidorus of Daldis, the martyr Perpetua, the emperor Constantine and Augustine of Hippo—but others too—have been subjected to very diverse scholarly judgements. Some have also argued that the dreams reported from incubation shrines may really have been dreamt, under the influence of 'suggestion',[12] and as we saw in the last chapter it is plausible to suppose that occasionally—but only occasionally—the pilgrims dreamt something that could be turned into the sort of record that the recording priests found useful.

Even careful scholars have the kindly but scarcely logical habit of asserting the authenticity of the dreams which they *wish* were genuinely dreamt—the biggest offenders here being the pious historians of early Christianity who cannot imagine that Constantine's dream before his decisive battle in 312, let alone the reported dreams of Perpetua, were inventions.[13]

The reported dreams of some ancient dreamers—the five people mentioned above, among others—have been taken very seriously by some scholars as truth-telling reports. In what follows I shall attempt to establish criteria for judging the authenticity of historical dream reports, and then I shall apply them to particular texts. Authenticity may be partial, since dream-reports are subject to 'secondary elaboration' as well as invention, and (a point less often noted) they are subject to simplification too. Hence a dream-report does not have to be either true or false—it may very commonly be somewhere between the two. Penelope disagreed, for according to her, and according to Vergil, dreams came *either* through the Gate of Horn *or* through the Gate of Ivory—a harmful dichotomy (implicitly recognized as such, centuries later, by Lucian), which we, however, can easily avoid.

12. Taffin 1960, but without real evidence.

13. For those who find authenticity in the dreams described in the *Shepherd* of Hermas see Miller 1994, 134 n. 23; Miller 66 judges the virgin's dream described by Tertullian, *De virg.vel.* 17.3 (see above, p. 71 n. 267), to be an actual dream.

Meanwhile we shall not lose sight of the fact that historically important dreams do not have to be true. Most of the dreams that have had any known impact on the affairs of the human race—Constantine's dream is the prime example—are in fact demonstrably invented.

The Matter of Authenticity

So what did the Greeks and Romans actually dream about? An initial answer is easy: everything that they could imagine. No doubt their dreams are reflected to some extent in the themes which Artemidorus most pays attention to in his handbook, such as teeth, dancing, wearing garlands, sex, fire, the gods, and flying.[14] On the other hand it will certainly *not* do to say that Artemidorus' having given over a whole chapter of his book to dreams of sexual acts with one's mother 'guarantees' that this was a common dream[15]—on the contrary, it may have been rare but considered fascinating.

We may suspect that they had more health-related and medical dreams than we do, though it would be little more than a guess. It would be readily understandable if they were more prone than we are to medical anxiety dreams. Greek and Roman doctors were frequently unable to help their patients, but both they and the devotees of healing cults (two overlapping groups) encouraged people by their various practices to believe that cures might be forthcoming. In the richer parts of the modern world, most people do not have to worry about their health until they approach old age, and up to that time they tacitly suppose that there is a remedy for every ill. No one could reach adulthood in antiquity without knowing that serious sicknesses were common and frequently sudden and could seldom be cured by routine procedures—yet there was often hope. Asclepius was very much needed, and dreams were his preferred means of communcation.

But do we in fact have any means of knowing what anyone in antiquity ever dreamt? There are two separate questions here, one about the authenticity of particular dream-reports, the main subject of this chapter; the other concerns *types* of dreams. A few words first about the latter.[16]

14. See i.31, 76, 77, 78–80, ii.9–10, 37–39, 68, respectively.

15. Guidorizzi 1988, xxvi. The same fallacy generalized: his 1985, 169.

16. As to how well classical writers, particularly the most intelligent of them, succeeded in typologizing dreams, that is a question worth answering in detail, a task I reserve for Chapter IV.

In the previous chapter I argued that epiphany dreams probably did occur sometimes in antiquity, but that is merely a probability. We are on firmer ground with wish-fulfilment dreams, erotic and otherwise,[17] and with anxiety-dreams:[18] classical texts offer us many examples, and we scarcely need to prove that such things really occurred. And no one will have any difficulty recognizing what Plato was writing about when, in describing 'the tyrannical man', he says that there are terrible desires in all of us, 'as becomes clear from our dreams'.[19] Devereux went further, arguing that the great tragic poets of Athens were in effect pre-Freudians, intuitively understanding how to express their characters' latent wishes in so-called 'manifest' dreams;[20] Atossa's dream in Aeschylus' *Persians*, for instance, reveals that she suffered from a 'counter-Oedipal Jocasta complex'.[21] This is altogether far-fetched. It is also of course a distortion of Freud's method of interpretation, which assigned a central function to the analysand's self-observing 'associations'.[22]

It is nonetheless true up to a point that skilled poets, playwrights and novelists knew how to invent convincing dreams, convincing in both form and content.[23] But the conventions of classical literature, untouched by the gothic, the romantic or the modern, made it almost inevitable that fictional dream-descriptions would usually be too tidy and too pointed. You have to wait for Federico Fellini to find an artist who knew how to create dream-like scenes with no apparent point (but plenty of meaning). The ancient artist could demonstrate his surpassing excellence by combining the fantastic and the apposite. The Greek novelist Achilles Tatius insists, at the beginning of *Leucippe and Cleitophon,* that dreams come true, and then makes up a rather plausible dream narrative:[24]

17. Erotic examples are numerous of course: Homer, *Od.* xx.88–90, Aeschylus, *Ag.* 420–422 (frustrated not fulfilled), Euripides, *Alc.* 354–356, Meleager 117 Gow-Page (*Anth.Pal.* 12.125), Horace, *Od.* iv.1.37–38, not to mention Lucretius or Artemidorus.

18. The texts are innumerable: the *locus classicus* is Lucretius iv.1020–1023.

19. *Rep.* ix.572b. Cf. 571b, 574e–575a. He supposes that the man in whom reason is dominant will not have such dreams (571d–572b).

20. It is fairly evident that Homer achieved something like this with Penelope's Goose Dream; see Rankin 1962, and p. 50 above.

21. Devereux 1976, 17.

22. Freud 1954 [1900], 96–121.

23. Imagined dreams 'may represent the same patterns and symbols with which the [Greek] artist is familiar', according to Wijsenbeek-Wijler 1978, 7.

24. i.3.

I had a dream in which I seemed to have grown into one with Calligone [the narrator's half-sister] from the waist downwards, while above we had two separate bodies. Then there stood over me a tall woman of fearful appearance; she had a savage face, bloodshot eyes, hairy cheeks, and snakes for hair; in her right hand she held a sickle and in her left a torch. She advanced angrily upon me, brandishing the sickle, and then struck with it at my waist, where the two bodies joined, and so cut the maiden away from me. In mortal fear, I jumped up, terrified.

When in his book about the art of poetry Horace pronounces that the macabre, or rather certain kinds of the macabre, should be excluded,[25] he seems to reveal that there were poets who disagreed with him (and we hardly have to look any further than Ovid's *Metamorphoses*). But it was always the prevailing taste to exclude incoherence and some kinds of bizarreness, and when Horace expresses a rule of this kind, he sums up what is to be avoided as 'like the dreams of a sick man'. The truly dream-like, in other words, was thought uncouth.

The Problem of Memory

I referred in the introduction to the difficulty we encounter in remembering our dreams and continuing to remember them. There is much more that can be said about the difficulties of remembering and reporting. Even a well-remembered dream may be hard to turn into a narrative. Psychologists' systematic research confirms what everyone knows: when we wake up, our dreams 'fad[e] quickly if no effort is made to remember [them] by rehearsing [their] content'.[26] It is worth being more explicit: (1) People remember more if they pay careful attention to their dreams *immediately* after waking, which they are evidently more likely to do if they believe that dreams are important; (2) the slightest distraction within this time-frame usually drives the memory away; (3) once the memory has fled, there is no getting it back, except occasionally by more or less chance reminders.[27]

25. *Ars Poetica* 1–9; cf. 338.

26. Crick and Mitchison 1983, 112. For an unorthodox account of dreaming, denying this, see Cohen 1979, 178–182.

27. For a good though not recent survey of work on what influences dream recall see Goodenough 1978. See also Butler and Watson 1985, Schredl et al. 1995, Schredl 2002, Schredl and Piel 2003.

Some would add—rather few perhaps in these post-Freudian times—that
(4) repression mechanisms may help to prevent dream-recall.[28] The further point has been made in recent research that we should distinguish between the ability to recall a dream and the ability to recall its details,[29] but
that seems mostly to be another way of making the banal observation that
we commonly remember a dream *in part*.

Something which psychologists theoretically know, but often—paradoxically—avoid applying to dreams, is that 'self-report data are . . . unreliable
on everything from voting to church attendance to eating habits',[30] and, the
quoted author might have added, particularly if sex is involved. And we often behave in embarrassing ways in our dreams, which further lowers the
likelihood that dream-descriptions will be full and accurate.

Scholars have sometimes asserted that the ancients were better at remembering their dreams than we are,[31] on the grounds, broadly speaking,
that they took them more seriously than we do. On a simple quantitative
level, there is no answer, for while recent research has refined how often
we remember dreams (a decreasing number with age, supposedly),[32] no
ancient writer seems to have a clear opinion about this.[33]

It is quite widely and credibly held that Freudian and similar kinds of
psychotherapy, by strengthening the patient's motives for remembering
dreams, has often had the effect of improving dream recall.[34] That may en-

28. Cf. Goodenough 1978, 125–129, Segall 1980, Stewart 2002, 281–282, etc.

29. Wolcott and Strapp 2002.

30. Domhoff 2003, 41. He proceeds to argue that this does *not* apply to dreams, on the
specious grounds that 'people do not feel responsible for their dreams' (as if Freud had
never existed), and that 'the dream experience is so direct, immediate, and compelling that
a report on it is not likely to be distorted by filtering it through cultural beliefs'. This is a
fantasy. Such evidence as there is (Cartwright and Lerner 1963) suggests that people readily lie about their dreams when it suits them to do so.

31. Behr 1968, 116, and Gigli 1977, 220 n. 33, following the suggestion of Björck 1946,
307. By the time of Aristotle it is evident that some people had reflected about the problem of remembering a dream: *On Dreams* 1.458b19–24.

32. Cf. Segall 1980, 741. Two to three a week: Belicki 1987, 187. Schredl 2002 shows
that women remember more dreams than men do, and that recall declines with age (persons aged from thirty to forty-four are said to remember on average 1.91 per week).

33. I no longer think, as I did previously (2005b, 249), that Cicero's opinion that we
dream almost every night (*De div.* ii.121) (if that is what he meant) has any relevance here.

34. Cf. Rechtschaffen 1978, 103.

courage us to think that those ancient writers who attributed great importance to their dream lives in general (and not just to isolated prophetic dreams), people such as Aelius Aristides and Synesius, were for that reason unusually good at remembering their dreams—a hypothesis we shall later test.

Contemporary research has sought to establish whether there is some correlation between 'dream recall frequency' and what has been very vaguely called a 'positive attitude toward dreams'. One author concluded that there are 'small but measurable relationships between DRF and personality'.[35] But a further study from the same stable[36] concluded that 'the attitude scale correlated weakly with dream recall frequency'.[37]

It is no doubt true that most classical Greeks thought that dreams could have 'something significant about them', in Aristotle's words, and many later Greeks and Romans thought so too. But we immediately need to qualify these statements. Van Lieshout has examined the criteria used in classical Greek texts to determine whether a dream was in fact significant or should be dismissed:[38] the most relevant is whether the dream was dreamed at a critical moment in the dreamer's affairs[39]—but how then are we to know what counted as critical moments? Battles and severe illnesses concentrate the mind but much smaller crises may do so too.

What the Greeks and Romans believed about the predictive power of dreams is the subject of the next chapter. To put it in one paragraph, the conclusion of that investigation is that the entire question of belief is in danger of being falsely stated, both because 'belief' itself is a complicated concept and because a dream might turn out to be true, according to Graeco-Roman thinking, even if it had not literally foretold the future. The majority of Greeks and Romans thought that *some* dreams had 'something

35. Schredl 1996, 616 (see also Robbins and Tanck 1988, Tonay 1993). Those who show a 'positive attitude', according to this writer, are those 'who like dreaming, give dreams a meaning, think over them, tell them to other people or record dreams'. This is a widespread view (Beaulieu-Prévost and Zadra 2005, 920).

36. Schredl et al. 2003. This paper gives a useful bibliography (153) on personality traits that may influence dream recall.

37. Schredl et al. 2003, 152. The authors followed the psychologists' usual custom of taking psychology students as their subjects (147).

38. Van Lieshout 1980, 195–200.

39. Van Lieshout 1980, 200.

significant about them', and could be impressed by what seemed to be a significant dream; but few of them acted as if they thought that dreams were reliable sources of information. Some well-educated people accepted or were prepared to countenance that some dreams could in some sense be truth-telling, but the practically minded did not rely on *oneirokritai* or *coniectores*. So the ancients' motives for remembering their dreams may not have been much stronger than ours. As we have already noted, there is no shortage of people in the here and now who have a 'positive attitude toward dreams'. Thus we have no reason to believe in a sharp ancient/modern divide with respect to the capacity to remember what one saw in the night, and indeed the ancients *may* even have remembered less than we do.

Meanwhile classical habits of mind encouraged the invention of dreams for real-life as well as literary purposes. We have already seen how a dream might be invented to encourage soldiers, or to add to a ruler's or a usurper's prestige. Sertorius was admired for having invented dreams that improved the morale of his troops.[40] Menander Rhetor, writing about speech-making in the late third century AD, states explicitly that the orator should invent propitious dreams to glorify the object of his eulogy.[41]

What is oddest about ancient dream-descriptions is how un-dream-like they usually are.[42] When we consider our own dream-experience, we are likely to say that many of our dreams are somehow bizarre or illogical, as we saw in the introduction. As we also saw, the matter is disputed, but I see no reason, as far as remembered dreams are concerned, to reject the historic view of this matter. The ancients perhaps underestimated the sheer difficulty of describing a kaleidoscopic dream, even if one remembers it well: at any rate, no writer before Synesius of Cyrene seems to be much concerned with the problem.[43]

---

40. Gellius xv.22.

41. ii.371, lines 11–14 (flattering the emperor is the business in hand); see further Weber 2000, 14.

42. Weber 2000, 536 glimpses this but makes nothing of it. Gordon 1997, 84, noticed the relative absence of bizarre elements from ancient dream-descriptions, and interestingly suggested that such elements were seen 'as part of the "frame" and not the content of the experience', which seems to ignore the fact that real-life dream-narrators commonly put the bizarre elements at the centre of their descriptions. Only one scholar, I think, has attempted to measure ancient dream reports against modern ones in any detail: Gigli 1977, on Aelius Aristides.

43. See Synesius, *De insomniis* 18 and and 19. He is concerned in part about presenting dreams in proper rhetorical language.

Dream-like Dreams

Classical literature is certainly not without dream-like dreams.[44] When in *Iliad* XXII the poet compares Achilles' still futile pursuit of a futilely fleeing Hector to a dream-sequence,

> when a man can't catch another fleeing on ahead
> and he can never escape nor his rival overtake him—

we immediately recognize what he is talking about (it may be significant, however, that his commentator Aristarchus did not).[45] Many readers of Aeschylus have no doubt felt that he was deeply interested in the phenomenon and also understands it rather well[46]—Menelaus dreaming of the departed Helen comes to mind, and the fearful dreamt spider in the *Supplices,* as well as the dream of the Furies mentioned in the previous chapter.[47]

When Medea dreams of Jason in *Argonautica* III (he really came to Colchis for *her,* not for the Golden Fleece, and she chooses to run away with him), most readers are likely to find the story psychologically convincing to the highest degree, all the more so perhaps because she has only just laid eyes on him for the first time.[48] In the *Aeneid,* we are once again likely to experience recognition when we read of Dido's nightmare, in which she imagines herself 'always travelling an endless road' in futile and lonely search for 'her Tyrians'.[49] One of the marks of Aristophanes' skill in invent-

44. Oppenheim 1956 was generally sceptical about the possibility of detecting dreams really dreamt in the Ancient Near East, but argued (204) that a dream of Nabonidus, King of Babylon, had a 'tang of authenticity' about it (for the text see 250, no. 13). It would not pass the tests outlined in this chapter.

45. *Il.* xxii.199–201 (trans. Fagels). Wilamowitz 1916, 100–101, discarded these lines, but for trivial reasons. See Dodds 1951, 123 n. 20, Kessels 1978, 49–52.

46. Cf. Rousseau 1963, who, however, exaggerated.

47. *Ag.* 420–426, *Supp.* 886–888.

48. Apollonius of Rhodes iii.616–632: 'deceitful, harmful dreams assailed her . . . she dreamt that the stranger had accepted the challenge, not in order to win the ram's fleece . . . but in order to carry her off to his own home to share his bed. Then it seemed that it was she who was standing up to the bulls and she found it easy to manage them . . . And in a trice she chose the stranger, paying no heed to her parents' (I only quote a small part of the dream). For the literary antecedents see R. L. Hunter's commentary. Compare Propertius ii.26.

49. *Aen.* iv.465–468: 'agit ipse furentem/in somnis ferus Aeneas, semperque relinqui/sola sibi, semper longam incomitata videtur/ire viam et Tyrios deserta quaerere terra'. Björck 1946, 306, quoted the Homer passage and this one to make the same point. The

ing the opening scene of the *Wasps* is that the dream-narratives which the two slaves exchange are surreal as well as topical.[50]

Most of the dream-like dream-narratives in Greek and Roman authors, we can say—apart, it will be suggested later, from those contained in the writings of Aelius Aristides—come from works which we consider to be fictional. The potential exceptions are some of those reported in inscriptions from temple sanctuaries. Particularly striking are some of the dreams described in the papyrus and ostracon 'archive' of Ptolemaios son of Glaucias, a religious functionary of some kind who flourished at the Serapaeum of Memphis in the 160s and 150s BC: whatever Ptolemy's motives were, his dream-descriptions are not distorted by any intention of propagandizing for Serapis, and in two cases at least they exhibit dream-like elements;[51] I shall shortly quote an example.

But the vast majority of ancient dream-descriptions are lacking in dream-like illogicality. That was in part an inevitable consequence of the fact that most of those who found something significant in dream-descriptions were on the look-out for something relatively straightforward and comprehensible (even if only symbolically), not for the rigmarole which one experiences in the longer kind of real dream.

And there are other reasons too for suspecting large numbers of Greek and Roman dream narratives. Since dreams were commonly thought to be of divine origin and/or to possess 'significance', a dream could provide authority in a wide variety of circumstances, whether it was Agamemnon in the *Iliad* giving orders to his army, or Perpetua (if it really is her voice we hear in her martyr-narrative) encouraging her coreligionists, and herself, in the face of persecution. A meaningful dream, furthermore, could establish an agreeable complicity between narrator and audience—they know what is going on, even if the character who has dreamt is mystified.[52] Gradually,

---

dream which Ennius gave to Ilia has some such features, as Cicero apparently noticed (*De div.* i.42).

50. Xanthias: 'I dreamt that a huge eagle flew down into the market place, seized a bronze shield in its claws and carried it up into the sky—and then Cleonymus threw it away' (15–19). Sosias: 'I dreamt that I saw sheep seated in the Pnyx to hold an assembly meeting, wearing cloaks and carrying walking-sticks. Then I dreamed that these sheep were being harangued by an all-consuming whale', etc. (lines 31–35).

51. *UPZ* I.77–81. The editor U. Wilcken discussed the question whether incubation was involved (pp. 349–350).

52. Pelling 1997, 199.

it seems, classical writers also came to realize that dreams could be used to illustrate a dreamer's frame of mind: Medea's dream about Jason, mentioned just now, is an early example;[53] Vergil clearly understood this, as did Tacitus.[54] So narrators, or rather some narrators, were inclined to accept or elaborate or invent them. But whereas a modern novel or film sometimes ends in mid-air, the Greeks and Romans abhorred incomplete stories, which set them at odds with many actual dreams and favoured the improvement and hence distortion of dream-descriptions.

On the other hand we should not hold it against classical writers that they quite often describe dreams as epiphanies rather than sequences of events. As we saw in the last chapter, it is plausible to suppose that Greeks and Romans occasionally dreamt more or less in that manner; and even if they did not, they could scarcely escape from a cultural convention of such power—Homer, Vergil, and so many others having helped to establish its credentials.

One might also be tempted to say that the Greeks and Romans do not narrate a sufficient number of nightmares, but that is probably a false impression which one receives from the fact that they use technical terms such as *ēpialos, ep(h)ialtes* and *incubo* no more than rarely. In an unclear passage of Aristophanes, the *ēpialoi* are apparently said to join with fevers to 'throttle fathers by night and strangle grandfathers', but the word is never used in this sense in later periods.[55] *Ephialtes* was the title of a play by Aristophanes' contemporary Phrynichus, but the word was almost never used except occasionally by medical writers, and even some of them, Galen for example, avoid it.[56] The only writer known to have used the word *incubo* in this sense before 200 AD is the (medical) writer Scribonius Largus. But Greeks and Romans seem in fact to describe a reasonable number of dreams which we might describe as nightmares: it was a matter of classification.[57] Some of the dreams already mentioned in this chapter,

53. Pelling 1997, 199, emphasizes Plutarch's fondness for this sort of dream, instancing *Marc.* 28, *Thes.* 6, *Brut.* 13.

54. See for instance the dream of Caesellius Bassus, *Ann.* xvi.1–3, where, however, the mental state of most interest is not that of the dreamer but of Nero.

55. *Wasps* 1038–1039. In the mime poet Sophron fr. 67 K-A (PCG I, p. 222) *ēpialēs* seems to be a personified throttling nightmare (cf. fr. 68).

56. Note how the word is also avoided by, e.g., Plutarch, *De superstitione* 3 (he uses the adjective *dusoneiros* several times to convey the same concept), Lucian, *Vera Historia* ii.33. Ephialtes and Pan are considered to be identical: Artemidorus ii.37 (cf. ii.34). The fullest account down to his time seems to be that of Paul of Aegina, *Seven Books* iii.15.

57. Stewart 2002 misses this point.

Calpurnia's on the night before the Ides of March for instance, or the dream of Dido in the *Aeneid,* can easily be described as nightmares. Ovid tells us that he dreamt terrifying dreams, as well as wish-fulfilments, as an exile.[58] Macrobius classified under the heading *insomnia* ('ordinary dreams', we might say) many dreams we would consider to be nightmares,[59] whereas he includes the *ephialtes* under the heading of *phantasmata* or *visa,* by which he means bizarre figures seen just as one is going to sleep.[60] The most likely explanation of the Greek and Roman classificatory system is that *ēpialoi, ephialtai* and *incubones* were the evil counterpart of epiphany dreams, and therefore quite uncommon in real life.

It is not, I think, to be supposed that the nature of the dreaming experience, as distinct from the subject-matter of dreams, was much different in antiquity.[61] One writer has claimed that since the sources, Artemidorus for instance, sometimes report that two people or even hundreds of people dreamed the same dream at the same time, the world must have been very different[62]—and if they did, it certainly was. It is possible that even within historical times the characteristics of the subjective experience of dreaming have evolved to a certain extent;[63] but all the thirteen main features of dreaming noted in the Introduction were known in classical antiquity.[64] And all the ancient evidence is explicable without any such hypothesis. There is some risk of circularity here, of assuming that classical dreams had

58. *Ex Ponto* i.2.41–56.

59. *Comm. in Somn. Scip.* i.3.4–6.

60. i.3.7.

61. As e.g. Guidorizzi argues, 1988, ix. Weber (2000, 536), having disowned all interest in what the ancients actually dreamt (above, n. 8), asserts that it was a characteristic of ancient dreams to be 'realitätsnah', by which he evidently means like *waking* life, and he denies that they often included contraventions of the rules of time and space, or incoherence. This is in the highest degree improbable.

62. Guidorizzi 1988, ix, who shares the credulity of Artemidorus (i.2 p. 10 Pack) in this respect. For Guidorizzi the story of the marvel-loving historian Phylarchus (*FGrH* 81 F45) according to which the magistrates of Sybaris, after sacrilegiously killing ambassadors from Locri, all experienced the same nightmare on the same night 'ha un aspetto verosimile'. We shall return to shared and collective dreams in Chapter III. Aelius Aristides xlviii.28–35 shows the power of this cultural pattern, as he turns two *similar* dreams (one dreamt by himself, the other not) into the *same* dream.

63. Hartmann 1998, 209–214, attempted to imagine how, feebly it must be said.

64. With the possible exception of our negative feature 5, that we do not dream of reading or writing. See p. 14 n. 58.

the same characteristics as modern ones (even though there was at least one big difference, as we saw in Chapter I); but there are in fact reasons for supposing that these characteristics were present.

We may in fact suppose, on the basis of documentary texts as well as literary ones, that the dream-like qualities of dreams were broadly the same in antiquity as they are now. Here is a Greek text of the second century BC, from the Ptolemaios of Memphis mentioned earlier:

> On the 14th I dreamed that I was in Alexandria on top of a great tower. My face was beautiful and because of its beauty I did not want to show it to anyone. And an old woman sat beside me and there was a crowd to the north of where I was and to the east. They shouted out that a man had been burned to a cinder with much [a gap in the text]; and she said 'Stay for a little and I will lead you to the *daimon* Knephis, so that you can bow down before him'. And I seemed to say to an old man: 'Father, don't you see the vision that I have seen?' I told him about it. He gave me two straws. When I looked I saw Knephis.'[65]

That seems as illogical a dream as one could wish, and rather plausible as a real dream.

What is at issue here is the quality of dream-experiences, not the subject-matter of dreams. Presumably the Greeks and Romans dreamt in part about different subjects from the ones we dream about: I assume that there were more gods, more gladiators (for the Romans), and more homo-erotic couplings. What we cannot suppose on the other hand is that ancient dreams were deficient in eeriness, illogicality or inconclusiveness.

More systematically, we can say that a dream-description is suspect (though not necessarily to be rejected) if

(1) It claims to describe someone else's dream, not the writer's own experience

(2) It in any way serves the narrator's conscious or unconscious purposes

(3) It makes a fully coherent story[66]—notwithstanding the fact that one of the most extraordinary feature of dreams is that even quite unimag-

---

65. *UPZ* I.78, lines 28–38 (159 BC). The dream described in lines 1–28 is similar in style.

66. Particularly of course if the dream forms part of a familiar type of story: Calpurnia, for instance, resembles a tragic heroine (Kragelund 2001, 55).

inative people regularly report dreams that are connected life-like episodes[67]

(4) It lacks dream-like qualities, such as 'bizarreness' in the special sense described above or weakened self-control

(5) It in any way predicts an event which subsequently occurred

(6) It was dreamt 'on demand' (let us say, on the first night in the sanctuary of Asclepius)—if in other words it was what Artemidorus called a 'petitioning' (aitematikos) dream.[68]

An ancient dream-description *gains* credibility if the opposite conditions are fulfilled.

A dream narrative may also be more plausible if it describes a common type of real-life dream such as an anxiety dream or a wish-fulfilment dream, or if it includes 'residue' of the dreamer's recent waking experience. But this kind of plausibility is of very limited use for the simple reason that, as we have already seen, a skilful writer knows very well how to invent dreams of this kind.

A dream-description also gains considerable credibility, if (as happens rather seldom in classical dream-descriptions)

(1) It was written down or told to someone immediately after waking

(2) It puts the narrator in a shameful or embarrassing light

(3) The narrator admits to some failure of memory.

Mendacious Historians and Biographers

In theory we could hope that historical writers might help us. But it is evident at once that the historical and biographical writers of Greece and Rome are unlikely to provide us with many reliable dream-descriptions. Partly this was because of their very imperfect respect for what we conceive to be truth, a story well told by Wiseman in his paper 'Lying Historians: Seven Types of Mendacity',[69] but partly also for the elementary reason that dreams dreamt by historical characters seldom had much interest unless they 'came true' (at least in some loose sense: Calpurnia's dream both

---

67. This has often been pointed out, and it has sometimes led to the neglect of incoherence.

68. Artemidorus iv.2, p. 246 Pack.

69. Wiseman 1993.

did and did not 'come true'), or, alternatively, were spectacularly misleading. When Herodotus, Xenophon or Plutarch in his biographical mode recounted dreams, they normally fell into one of these categories—and are very unconvincing as real dreams (we shall meet some instances in Chapter III), while at the same time revealing a great deal about their authors and a certain amount about their imagined readers.

When Germanicus, according to Tacitus,[70] had a propitious dream before the Battle of Idistaviso, it rather obviously fails our tests, even though it had an element of wish-fulfilment about it: he dreamt that he sacrificed and that some of the blood got on his toga, but grandmother Livia gave him a finer one. One wonders who edited or invented the story, and whether Tacitus really thought that it was true (he will have been aware of the historical precedents for generals' announcing propitious dreams before important battles). Like the story of Calpurnia's dreams before the Ides of March, this one is likely to have been invented quickly, quite possibly by Germanicus himself to encourage his troops (which will mean that some but not necessarily all of them took such matters seriously).

Some Strong Candidates

Many Greek and Roman dream-descriptions that purport to be factual are plainly nothing of the kind—they are historically interesting, but they hardly enter into the present discussion. I have chosen instead to put to the test some of the dream-descriptions that have some degree of plausibility, and I will then proceed to examine the five famous dreamers mentioned earlier, Perpetua, Artemidorus, Constantine, Augustine and Aelius Aristides. Like a long dream, these texts will lead us through some unexpected twists and turns.

We can start in late-fourth-century BC Epidaurus, where the priests of Asclepius had dozens of Asclepius' cures recorded in a set of inscriptions that have in good part survived (there were probably several hundred recorded in all). A high proportion of these cures involved dreams in which the patients encountered the god himself. Here is a fairly typical example of the longer kind of 'record':[71]

---

70. *Ann.* ii.14.

71. *IG* IV². 1.121 (and Herzog 1931, 8–10, Edelstein and Edelstein 1945, I, 422 (T.423), no. III, LiDonnici 1995, 86–87).

A man whose fingers, with the exception of one, were paralysed, came as a suppliant to the god. While looking at the tablets in the temple, he expressed incredulity regarding the cures and scoffed at the inscriptions.[72] But in his sleep he saw a vision: it seemed to him that, as he was playing at dice below the temple and was about to cast the dice, the god appeared, sprang upon his hand and stretched out his fingers. The god stepped aside, and [the suppliant] bent his hand and stretched out his fingers one by one. Then the god asked him whether he still refused to believe the inscriptions on the tablets in the temple, but he denied it. 'Since, then, you were formerly incredulous of the cures, though they were not incredible, in the future', he said, 'let your name be Apistos [Incredulous]'. When day came, he walked out in good health.

An extensive literature has grown up around such texts.[73] In the first place, they do not come directly from the dreamers themselves but from those who had a strong vested interest in promoting Asclepius' miracles.[74] On the other hand, the priests probably chose to inscribe the experiences of those, a minority undoubtedly of those who sought Asclepius' aid, who reported dreaming something about him (and in this suggestive environment, they will not have been very rare).[75] Adaptation followed.[75] In this case, no clearly dream-like elements survived, except that the suppliant dreamt about the building in which he was actually asleep,[76] and we should suspect that the 'report' has little to do with what was actually dreamt,[77] even though the underlying medical event is relatively easy to accept.[78]

Let us move to a less shadowy informant. In the first book of his dialogue *On Divination*, Cicero represents his younger brother Quintus as recounting

72. This is a feature paralleled in some of the other Epidaurus texts.

73. See Girone 1998 as well as the works just cited.

74. Cf. Herzog 1931, 46.

75. Compare the perceptive pages of Vlastos 1949, 277–280.

76. Like the many experimental subjects reported by Dement et al. 1965 who dreamt, on their first night there, of the laboratory in which they were sleeping.

77. Rousselle 1984–1985, 347, was evidently inspired by a strong desire to find psychoanalytic evidence in these texts to conclude that they 'are fairly accurate records of actual dreams'.

78. There is a choice between supposing that the suppliant suffered from a normal case of Dupuytren's contracture, which (he and) the priests persuaded themselves had improved, or that the disease was a 'conversion disorder' of psychological origin (which can produce paralysis), alleviated by the religious experience (cf. Herzog 1931, 99), or that it was a temporary paralysis with a physical origin.

that he, Marcus, once claimed to have dreamt a prophetic dream about the great C. Marius, and the sceptical Marcus implicitly accepts the story (though not Quintus' understanding of it).[79] Marcus was fleeing into exile, and dreamt one night that he was wandering sadly in a lonely place when Marius—who had made a strong impression on him when he was a youth some thirty years before[80]—asked him why he was sad; after Cicero explained, Marius took him by the right hand, gave him words of encouragement, instructed one of his attendants to take him to his own *monumentum* (by which meant the temple he had built for Honos and Virtus), and told him that there would be salvation for him there. Thus: a first-hand narrator who apparently recounted the dream or at least *a* dream at the time; but it was a coherent and useful dream, which furthermore contained a correct prophecy (for in 57 the Senate's crucial vote in Cicero's favour took place in this very temple). Cicero may have dreamt a Marian dream, but if so it was drastically refashioned.

The younger Pliny recounts a dream dreamt by his recently deceased friend C. Fannius:[81] 'He foresaw the event long before. He dreamt that he was studying in bed and had a desk in front of him as usual. In came Nero and sat down on a couch. The late emperor took out the first volume of the work which Fannius had published about his crimes, unrolled it to the end, did the same with the second and third volumes, and then left. Fannius was afraid, and realized that he would not write any further than Nero had read; so it turned out'. Now this was someone else's dream, it made a tidy story within a highly literary context, and it was taken to be a prediction. All this is on the debit side. On the other hand, the dream did not itself purport to be prophetic, it apparently contained residue of the day (Fannius 'had a desk in front of him *as usual*'), and it compressed time (Nero apparently read three volumes at unreal speed). We may tentatively conclude that Fannius experienced an anxiety dream, which he and/or Pliny elaborated (or possibly simplified).[82]

Here is a rather later dream-report from the Temple of Aesculapius at Rome: 'To Iulianus, who was spitting up blood and had been despaired of by everyone, the god revealed that he should go and take from the threefold altar the seeds of a pine cone and eat them with honey for three days.

79. *De div.* i.59, ii.137, 140.

80. *Post Red. ad Quir.* 19–20.

81. *Ep.* v.5.

82. For another somewhat credible dream, dreamt by one of Pliny's freedmen, see *Ep.* vii.27.12.

And he was saved.'[83] Numerous parallels survive. This dream may seem particularly implausible: the proprietors of the shrine were in effect putting up an advertisement, and no dream-like elements are included. But the important point here is a different one, namely that we are not in fact told the content of the dream at all, simply what it was thought to command. As we shall see when we examine the evidence of Aelius Aristides, the god could be held to have 'revealed' something even if the patient did not literally dream of him at all. Quite probably Iulianus really did dream one night on the Tiber island—but what he dreamt is unknowable.

Perpetua

Let us turn to our five famous dreamers. The dreams of Perpetua—four of them, included in what is normally taken to be a prison diary within the *Passio Sanctae Perpetuae*—are sure to remain an object of contention. Recent writers have for the most part taken their authenticity and even accuracy for granted.[84] They form part of what the *Passio* says in so many words was an account written in Perpetua's own hand.[85] And it is undoubtedly true, as indeed this *Passio* demonstrates, that dreams were important in African Christianity in the era of Tertullian,[86] when the *Passio* was probably written; but far from proving that the Perpetua's dream-descriptions are authentic, this fact can just as easily be held to suggest that they were wholly or largely invented.[87] Some scholars have indeed argued that the

83. *IG* XIV.966 = *SIG*³ 1173 = *IGUR* 148, lines 11–13; Van Straten 1976, 7–8. Moretti (in *IGUR*) dates the text to the early third century.

84. Robert 1982, esp. 254–255 n. 101, Amat 1989 (this study is worth reading, but it fails to come to grips with the problem) and 1996, Shaw 1993, 26–27, Miller 1994, 150 and 154, Bremmer 2000, 100. Farrell 2001, 76, claims that these dreams are 'more dream-like . . . than any others we know from the ancient world'. But see Kraemer and Lander 2000.

85. 2.3 ('ordinem totum martyrii sui iam hinc ipsa narravit, sicut conscriptum manu sua et suo sensu reliquit', 14.1 ('hae visiones insigniores ipsorum martyrum beatissimorum Saturi et Perpetuae, quas ipsi conscripserunt'). The Greek version says substantially the same.

86. Amat 1996, 41.

87. The other standard arguments *in favour of* the authenticity of these dreams include (1) variation in clausula patterns between the sections attributed to Perpetua and Saturus, and between each of them and the language of the redactor (Shewring 1931, Fridh 1968)—but such an argument can at most suggest multiple authorship; and (2) the supposed fact that the text was old enough to be known to Tertullian about 210 (*De anima*

whole autobiographical narrative as an invention,[88] and it will be argued here that the dream-descriptions are at least for the most part apocryphal.

Perpetua's four dreams[89] are quite long; I will translate the first in full and summarize the others.

(1) Perpetua's Christian brother points out to her that she can learn whether she is to be put to death by praying for a vision (*visio, optasia*). She takes it for granted that her prayer will be answered, and it is:

> I see a bronze ladder of marvellous size, reaching right up to heaven, narrow so that you could only climb it one at a time, and its uprights had every kind of sharp weapon sticking out of them, swords, lances, hooks, scimitars, and spears, so that any who went up it carelessly or without looking upwards would be lacerated and pieces of their flesh would stick to the weapons. At the foot there lay a dragon of marvellous size who waited in ambush for those who wanted to ascend, and tried to scare them into not ascending. The first to go up was Saturus, he who later gave himself up freely on our account, because he had instructed us but had not been present when we were arrested. He reached the top of the ladder, turned round, and said to me: 'Perpetua, I am waiting for you; but take care, do not let the dragon bite you'. 'He will not harm me', I said, ' in the name of Jesus Christ'. And from underneath the ladder, the dragon stuck his head out slowly, as though he were afraid of me. And as if I were stepping on the first step, I trod on his head and went up.[90] Then I saw an enormous garden, and in the middle a white-haired man dressed like a shepherd, tall, milking his sheep; and standing around him were many thousands of people dressed in white. He raised his head, looked at me and said to me 'Welcome, child'. He called me to his side and from the curds of his milk he gave me something like a mouthful. I accepted it with joined hands and ate it. All who stood around said 'Amen'. At the sound of their voices, I awoke.

55.4)—but he either muddled Perpetua's last dream with her first or (more probably) had in mind an earlier and simpler version of the *Passio*.

88. Notably E. Schwartz 1905, 23: he asserts that such documents were made up (I quote his exact words, the book being quite rare) 'ut earum locum teneant vel orationum quas in paganorum historiis condemnati sive in senatu sive ad amicos habere solent, vel narrationum quae ut plus admirationis et misericordiae commoveant'.

89. *Passio* 4, 7, 8, 10.

90. The ladder is reminiscent of the one Jacob had dreamt of. A Christian in Rome could have seen the latter scene visually represented (see the painting from the Via Latina catacombs illustrated in Näf 2004, fig. 5 [p. 32]), and perhaps a North African Christian could too. Bremmer's alternative explanation (2002, 99–100) is much less likely.

(2) Perpetua next dreamt of another brother, Dinocrates, who had died at the age of seven: he emerged hot and thirsty from a dark place, but she could not reach him; nor could he reach up to the rim of a pool of water that stood nearby. (3) She dreamt of Dinocrates again, now cured and now able to reach the water, which he drank from but without reducing the amount that remained. (4) The day before her horrific death in the arena, she dreamt that she was taken there but not exposed to wild animals; she had to box against a hideous Egyptian,[91] which was easier because she became a man. A trainer of superhuman size said that if she won he would give her a branch. This duly happened, and she walked with glory to the gate of life.

Some dubious arguments have been used against Perpetua's authorship. Augustine insinuated that the narrative was inauthentic, speaking of 'Perpetua, or whoever it was who wrote it'[92]—but he had a doctrinal motive for doing so,[93] so his testimony has little value. A recent study pointed out, correctly, that the language attributed to Perpetua is that of a retrospective narrator, *not* that of a day-by-day chronicler or diarist,[94] but the author does not in fact claim to have kept a prison diary,[95] and it is conceivable that she wrote the whole text (nearly fifteen hundred words) at one sitting. It is just possible—though not very likely.

To return to the criteria we set out earlier, it is plain that we are faced, as in all martyr acts, with a text that serves the author's purposes and offers a satisfactory story. Furthermore, the first dream-narrative recounts a 'sought' dream,[96] and there are at least two bogus predictions (that is, elements in the dream narratives designed to 'come true' in the aftermath).[97] Dodds

91. Representing the devil: see Amat 1996 ad loc.

92. *De natura et origine animae* i.10 (12) (*CSEL* 60.312).

93. Since he supposed that the unbaptized, such as Dinocrates, could not be cleared of 'original sin' (ibid. iii.9 (12) = *CSEL* 60.369). He harps on Dinocrates. Athenaeus slighted another female writer, Erinna, with a phrase like Augustine's, vii.283d.

94. Heffernan 1995, 322–323. It makes no difference here whether the Greek or the Latin version was the original, a much debated problem (see Amat 1996, 51–66).

95. Dolbeau 1996. Eventually there is said to have been some improvement in the conditions of Perpetua's imprisonment (sec. 16), which is not implausible, given her apparently high social rank, but this detail may have been added precisely in order to lend plausibility. Bremmer 2002 and Castelli 2004, 85, continue to refer to the text as a diary.

96. 'Crastina die tibi renuntiabo. et postulavi, et ostensum est mihi hoc', 4.2. The second and third dreams were not strictly 'sought', as Dodds claimed (1968, 50).

97. This is a marked feature of the first and fourth dreams. Cf. Dodds 1968, 49–50.

considered that Perpetua's dreams were 'entirely dreamlike',[98] and they certainly include some dream-like details (in Dream IV Perpetua becomes a man, and there seems to be an instance of time-compression in Dream I),[99] but they are in general straightforward tales of Christian commitment, its dangers and rewards. Every single detail in all four descriptions fits tidily into the story.

The most individual element is the narrative about Perpetua's dead brother, the child Dinocrates (in Dreams II and III). Why, asks Dodds, would any pious redactor have invented it?[100] That is not too difficult to answer: it provided a response to a pressing question of the age of proselytism—was there nothing a Christian could do to bring salvation to dead pagans, such as Dinocrates, who had had no opportunity to embrace the new cult and had not been baptized?

We might be making a mistake if we applied conventional modern ideas of authorship to this text. Perpetua may possibly have written a memoir of some kind, and it may have described one or more dreams. But the existing memoir should be taken as at least in large part the work of a pious survivor. And if Perpetua wrote these dream-narratives, she at the very least improved the story.

Artemidorus

Now for Artemidorus, who may look as if he should be our great witness, since he claims to have listened to immense numbers of dreams in Greece, Asia, Italy 'and in the largest and most populous of the islands'.[101] Furthermore he sounds serious: 'the *oneiros* must be examined with precision, how it is, for the outcome is altered by the slightest addition or omission'.[102] And not all is bad: he knows about a lot of transformation dreams, for instance.[103] Occasional touches are bizarre and undignified enough to make us at least want to believe: 'I know a household slave who dreamt that he

98. Dodds 1968, 50.

99. 4.9.

100. Dodds 1968, 51. That Dinocrates appeared in a real dream may be supported by the fact that he is represented as having just appeared in her waking thoughts (7.1); hence he is part of the day's residue.

101. i pr. p. 2 Pack.

102. i.9. See also i.12, iv.4, iv.28.

103. i.50.

struck some frogs with his fist. This man became overseer of his master's household and of the other slaves in it. For the pond represented the house, the frogs the servants in it, and the punch his command over them';[104] it could have been dreamt.

In most of his book, Artemidorus is not even claiming to describe particular dreams[105]—in fact he makes it explicit that his interest is in types of dreams, or rather in single elements in dreams:[106]

> It was not possible to record dreams that have come true and their fulfilments [*apobaseis*] in a treatise on dream interpretation that is didactic and scientific. In my view such an account would have been subject to disbelief, even though Geminus of Tyre (three books), Demetrius of Phalerum (five books) and Artemon of Miletus (twenty-two books) have recorded a large number of dreams and especially prescriptions and medical cures given by Serapis.

And while Artemidorus describes many bizarre dream-events, he provides us with little that is illogical or eerie in the way of narrative, as distinct from explanation; this has sometimes been recognized, at least in part.[107]

Unfortunately Artemidorus was not only a man of monumental gullibility (whose book would have aroused the scorn of many other ancients),[108] but a man with a determined mission, which he states as follows:[109]

> I shall join battle with those who are trying to do away with divination in general and its various forms [who were they, one wonders, in the age of the Antonines], bringing to bear my experience and the proof furnished by the fulfilment of particular dreams. . . . Secondly, for those who look to prophecy for advice . . . I will provide a treatment that will save them.

In other words, he was convinced of a case which could only be made plausible by means of misinformation. Moral snobbery was another impedi-

104. ii.15.

105. Cf. Lloyd 1987, 32 n. 97.

106. ii.44 end. On the difficulty of dealing with multiple features occurring in a single dream: iii.66. It is in fact quite wrong to say that 'Artemidorus discusses thousands of dreams and their outcomes' (Oberhelman 1997, 58).

107. Del Corno 1988 [1975], 152. Artemidorus' insistent use of colour terms (documented by Kasprzyk 2002) also makes one suspicious, given the tendency towards colour desaturation often noted in real dreams (see the Introduction).

108. Guidorizzi 1985, 167, asserts that Artemidorus is sometimes brilliantly intelligent, without giving examples.

109. i pr. p. 1 Pack.

ment: 'people who practise a virtuous and moral way of life', he says, 'do not have dreams that are merely meaningless'.[110] Furthermore, *hoi polloi* have different dreams from those of the experts: 'whatever the masses want or dread, they also see in their sleep, whereas those who are qualified experts in this field see their wishes expressed in symbols [*semainousin*]'.[111] He even describes a dream that 'could not have been dreamt'.[112] A pity that he never describes in full a dream of his own.

When he recounts a particular case, Artemidorus usually writes 'I know someone', or 'I know *of* someone who dreamt that . . . ,'[113] where the vagueness of Greek *oida* may leave us in some perplexity—did Artemidorus have the story directly from the dreamer or not? In Book IV some of these possible acquaintances even have names. But very few of these descriptions of images can be anything like full accounts of dreams.

Constantine

Few ancient dreams have caused more confusion than the one supposedly dreamt by the usurper Constantine during the night before the Battle of Saxa Rubra on 28 October 312, the battle that in effect completed his conquest of the western empire and ensured that an emperor who was a Christian, in some sense, would rule it all.[114] The most important source is Lactantius' *De mortibus persecutorum*,[115] now generally thought to have been written in 314 or 315 (in other words, very soon after the event by the standards of ancient writers about the past):[116]

> he moved his whole force nearer to Rome and camped in the general area
> of the Milvian Bridge. The anniversary of the day when Maxentius had

110. iv pr. p. 239 Pack.

111. iv pr. pp. 239–240 Pack.

112. iv.63: 'For you know well that there are some dreams which it is completely impossible to have. For example, they say things like this: a man who lost a slave dreamt that someone said to him, 'Your servant dwells among those who are exempt from service'. His servant was found in Thebes, since the Thebans, alone of the Boeotians, did not fight in the war against Troy'.

113. i.15, 24, etc.; about thirty times in all.

114. For a fuller account of this dream see Harris 2005b. And see Bremmer 2006a.

115. 44.5.

116. For the textual problem in this passage and for the following comments see Harris 2005b, 489–490.

seized power was approaching, namely October 27th, and his fifth anniversary celebrations were coming to an end [there are errors here]. Constantine was advised in a dream to put the celestial sign of god [*caeleste signum dei*] on the shields of his soldiers and so to join battle. He did as he was ordered, and by means of an X with its top turned around he marked Christ on their shields.

Such a story, when recounted by Lactantius, is not likely to have lacked direct or at least indirect imperial approval: it was a delicate matter to write about the living emperor's divinatory pronouncements.

A few scholars, but only a few, have believed Lactantius' account.[117] Nothing should lead us to doubt that Constantine claimed on the morning of the battle that he had dreamed a significant dream. But it is overwhelmingly likely that he either made it up or brusquely adapted an actual dream. Real-life dreams do not show up when they are convenient. They also tend to be illogical and inconclusive and to have other characteristics wholly lacking in Constantine's Saxa Rubra dream-description. The dream was too convenient, and it adapted a traditional ruse of Roman generals designed to raise the soldiers' morale at a crucial juncture. Before his Italian campaign Constantine had claimed, so it seems, to have seen a vision or dream at a famous shrine of Apollo in Gaul; Apollo promised him victory.[118] In other words, Constantine knew how to make use of such mechanisms. And in the period after the Saxa Rubra battle, the eastern emperor Licinius imitated Constantine's procedure, announcing a propitious dream before his showdown with Maximinus at the Battle of Campus Ergenus.[119]

Augustine

The case of Augustine deserves mention mainly because the authenticity of some of his dream narratives has been defended by an exceptionally careful scholar, Martine Dulaey.[120] First, the rather well-known dream of his

117. Alföldi 1948, 18, Lane Fox 1986, 617.

118. Panegyrci Latini vi (vii).21.3–4, a speech delivered not long afterwards. The anonymous panegyrist does not say that Constantine *dreamt* what he saw, but see Harris 2005b, 492.

119. Lactantius, *De mort.pers.* 46.3–11.

120. But the uncertainty of her method of dealing with this subject is shown by the fact that while she sees Jerome's 'Ciceronian' dream as 'very literary' (1973, 153 n. 75) she also denies there is any reason to doubt its authenticity (62 n. 109; cf. Amat 1985, 219–222). For the latter view see also Miller 1994, 211 (but she has no reasons worth debating). John Milton, who famously favoured the freedom to read almost anything, suggested in the *Are-*

friend Gennadius (which was mentioned in Chapter I): 'everything', says Dulaey, 'leads us to believe that Augustine here faithfully transcribes the dream of Gennadius', and 'it is unlikely that Gennadius had embellished it'.[121] On the contrary: the dream is a consummate example of the Latin rhetorician's art;[122] furthermore it serves Augustine's purposes,[123] is entirely and suspiciously coherent, and in spite of its great length contains not a single clearly dream-like feature.[124] We are probably faced in fact with one of the *most* embellished of all classical accounts of a 'real-life' dream.[125] Mother Monnica's dream implying Augustine's future conversion[126] has even less claim to be authentic: it fails all our first five tests.[127] Dulaey's arguments in its favour are in large part subjective and valueless.[128] Yet she was right to point out that, according to Augustine's story, the dream, whatever it consisted of, had a specific effect—it made Monnica willing to share Augustine's table (though nine more years elapsed before he fell in with her doctrinal wishes); the likelihood is that she had a dream which she and

---

opagitica that Jerome's dream was either the work of the devil or a 'fantasm bred by the feaver which had then seis'd him' (*The Complete Prose Works of John Milton,* II [New Haven and London, 1959], 510).

121. Dulaey 1973, 154. The text is Augustine, *Epist.* 159.

122. This hardly needs to be demonstrated at length, but note how Augustine makes uses of the 'repeated epiphany dream' motif (for he describes two epiphanies of the same personage: Dulaey 1973, 155 and 198–199 herself gives the parallels), how the 'fine-looking young man' leads the sceptical doctor into *aporia* before giving his explanation of the fact that the dreamer can see even while his senses are not working, and how the writer enlivens his narrative with lengthy 'quotations' in direct speech. There was even a tradition of making up dreams to convince people of the immortality of the soul (Cicero, *De Rep.* vi.24–26, Philostratus, *Vita Ap.* viii.31). Other traditional elements: Dulaey 1973, 156.

123. The whole point was of course to prove the existence of an afterlife.

124. Dulaey 1973, 155, sees as marks of a real dream the statement that Gennadius eventually realizes in his dream that he is dreaming (the notorious 'lucid dream'), but the dream within the dream had long been a banality of classical dream-descriptions. 'De même, en rêve, nous n'avons pas besoin de parler pour nous faire comprendre: ici, le jeune homme répond à des questions [*sic*] non formulées de Gennadius (155)'. But whether the question ('What is all that singing?') had been made clear, in words or otherwise, is hidden by Augustine's rapid narrative.

125. Dulaey 1973, 155, claims it as a sign of authenticity that Augustine says, in recounting the first dream, that he has forgotten what else the dreamer saw 'sinistra . . . parte' in the heavenly city. She could have added that Augustine is unlikely to have upset his friend by distorting what he had reported.

126. *Conf.* iii.11.

127. See further Dulaey 1973, 159–161.

128. It was 'sober' and 'simple' (161).

her son were able to adapt more or less drastically to their religious and literary needs.

Aelius Aristides

It may be that the unloved Aelius Aristides is after all a relatively credible narrator.[129] Sometimes this has simply been asserted without argument. Festugière wrote that 'it is impossible to doubt for an instant the sincerity of Aristides',[130] but it is not only his sincerity that is in question, as Festugière in effect pointed out a page later. He found it incredible that Aristides dreamt about Asclepius 'night after night'—but in fact Aristides hardly ever claims anything of the kind.[131] It is not particularly implausible to suppose that he had a recurrent dream that Asclepius gave him instructions about bathing,[132] since he believed that bathing and not bathing made a great difference to his health. Another critic, who claimed that Aristides' dreams were 'subjected to a rather heavy-handed "secondary elaboration"' and another occasion referred to his 'dreams' in inverted commas did not descend into details.[133]

As has often been observed, Aristides' narrative falls partly into an established tradition that those who visited the sanctuaries of the healing deities should record their (appropriate) dreams.[134] Furthermore the dream-descriptions in the *Sacred Tales* are not, or at least are not for the most part, transcriptions of the reports he wrote down soon after the dreams took place—they are part of a narrative.[135]

But Aristides wrote down his dreams over a period of many years, for 'immediately from the beginning the god ordered me to commit my dreams to writing *(apographein)*':[136]

---

129. Cf. Del Corno 1978, 1616–1617, who, however, says that Aristides is free of any 'suspicion of intentional secondary elaboration' (1616); that is going too far.

130. 1954, 97.

131. In *Or.* xlvii.6 he says that 'on the twelfth of the month, the god instructs me not to bathe, and the same on the next day, and the same on the day after that'; in xlviii.75 that Asclepius, some twenty years earlier, had appeared to him on two successive nights.

132. For the constant references to bathing in his dream-descriptions see Behr 1968, 38.

133. Devereux 1976, xxv, xxxiv.

134. Nicosia 1988, 175–176.

135. Pearcy 1988, 390.

136. xlviii.2.

I made a copy of my dreams, dictating them whenever I was unable to write myself. However I did not add the circumstances in which each dream came to me, or what resulted after them. . . . Furthermore, as if I was annoyed by the fact that I did not start to write down everything[137] from the beginning I also neglected the rest. . . . But I found other ways of thanking the god, since I think that there are at least 300,000 lines of writing in my copy book.[138] But it is not, I may say, easy to go through them or to fit them together chronologically. Besides some things have been scattered through various losses and confusion at home during these times. The only thing to do is to give a summary account, as I remember different things from different sources.[139]

In other words, Aristides kept contemporary records, but he distinguishes them carefully from the account he offered to the public:[140] 'But if someone wishes to know precisely what has happened to us by the god's doing, it is time for them to seek out the parchment books [*diphtheras*] and the dreams themselves.' In fact he is in some ways strikingly scrupulous. When Asclepius recommended a potion made of four ingredients, he specifies the two he can remember—and 'we shall add the other two if (the records of) the dreams should show up'.[141] On the one occasion in the *Sacred Tales* when he repeats a dream he has described before, he gives substantially the same account, even though some twenty-five years have passed.[142]

Aristides' longing for help would certainly have debased the value of his dreams in the eyes of Artemidorus.[143] But what seems to tell against his actual credibility more than anything else, apart from his enormous vanity, is his passionate desire to justify the ways of Asclepius by showing that the god really had provided help for his devotee. He is much concerned that

137. I.e. (apparently) the circumstances and outcomes of his dreams as well as the dreams themselves.

138. I take it that this total refers to all his interactions with Asclepius, not only his dreams.

139. xlviii.2–4.

140. xlviii.8.

141. xlix.26. See also xlvii.38, xlix.30, l.25.

142. This observation I owe to Behr 1968, 117, who compares xxviii.116 and l.52.

143. Artemidorus i.6: 'It should be understood that the things that appear in dreams to people who are anxiously concerned about something and have asked the gods for a predictive dream do not correspond to their anxieties, since those dreams that are similar to the dreamer's waking thoughts are without significance'.

his narrative should not offend Asclepius,[144] and it is quite clear that nothing even remotely unfavourable to the god could possibly have entered one of his dream narratives.

What this means, however, is simply that there is an area of inhibition. And it is clear, certainly, that Aristides has left out anything that would, by his standards, reflect badly either on his own importance or on his loyalty to Asclepius. In every other respect he seems convincing. The typology of his dreams, to begin with, is instantly credible. They fall into three main blocs: anxiety-dreams, wish-fulfilments (what Dodds impatiently calls 'pathetic megalomaniac' dreams),[145] and divine-advice dreams. His language corresponds to that of authentic dream reports, and his frequent confessions of difficulty ('somehow', 'in some way', and similar expressions) add greatly to his credibility.[146] And Aristides is capable of admitting in so many words that his memory of a dream had been defective—'such more or less was the dream, to recollect it dimly'[147]—which is another positive indication.

But what tells most strongly in favour of a great deal of this material—not all of it—is its dream-like nature, with persons and places changing identity, unexplained behaviour and inexplicable concatenations of events.[148] Take this for example:[149]

> And once I thought that the poet Sophocles came to my house. When he came, he stood before the room where I happened to be passing my time. While he stood there in silence, his lips of their own accord seemed to make the sweetest possible humming noise. His whole appearance was that of a handsome old man. I was glad to see him, and rising, I welcomed him and asked 'Where is your brother?' And he said, 'Do I have a brother?' 'It's Aeschylus', I said, and at the same time I went out with him. And when we appeared to be at the front door, a sophist, one of the most distinguished ones of our time, fell and lay on the ground off to the left, a little further away from the door.

144. *Or.* l.50.

145. Dodds 1968, 41–42.

146. Examples are numerous: xlvii.7, 9, 11, 13, 25, 26, 43, 45, 71, etc. Cf. Gigli 1977, esp. 220–221.

147. xlix.21. See also xlviii.18 and 27, xlix.5, l.15 and 80. Cf. Gigli, 1977, 223.

148. See Nicosia 1988, 180–181, quoting xlvii.22, and referring to xlvii.10–14, 36–40, 42–45, 46–50, li.56–67.

149. l.60–61.

There are plenty of other instances: in fact the great majority of Aristides' longer dream-descriptions are of this type. Not wishing to labour the obvious, I will quote only two more examples, which in my judgement at least are all the more convincing because they are not dramatic:[150]

> I dreamed that I was in Smyrna and went in the evening to the temple of Asclepius in the district of the Gymnasium. I went with Zeno.[151] And *the temple was larger* and covered as much of the portico as was paved. At the same time, I was also thinking about this temple *as if it were a vestibule*. While I prayed and called upon the god, *Zeno said 'Nothing is more gentle'*, and speaking of the god, he named him as a refuge and such things. In this sort of vestibule I examined a statue of myself. At one time I saw it as if it were me, and *again it seemed to be a large and beautiful statue of Asclepius*. Then I told Zeno the things I had been dreaming of. And the part about the statue seemed to bring me great honour. Again I saw the statue *as if it were in the long portico of the Gymnasium*.[152]

Or again:

> He appeared to me <in a dream> . . . He was *at the same time Asclepius and Apollo, both the Clarian and the one who is called the Callitecnus at Pergamum* (the one who has the first of the three temples). Standing before my bed in this form, when he had extended his fingers and calculated the time, he said 'You have ten years from me and three from Sarapis', and at the same time the thirteen *appeared by the position of his fingers to be seventeen. He said that this was not a dream but a waking state*, and that I would also know it. And at the same time he commanded me to go down to the river that flows before the city and bathe. He said that a young boy would lead the way, and he pointed out the boy.[153]

We may conclude that Aristides, though exceedingly vain and egocentric, is a relatively credible witness. The conclusion is necessarily an uneasy one, for the *Sacred Tales* are the most educated and literary of the five texts and sets of texts we have been examining. What distinguishes their author is not his seriousness or even his intelligence, for Augustine was not defi-

---

150. One other was quoted at the beginning of the chapter.
151. Identity unknown.
152. xlvii.17. I have italicized the dream-like elements in these two passages.
153. xlviii.18.

cient in those respects, but a crucial willingness to admit that the world and its phenomena was sometimes beyond his understanding.

Writing Good Stories

We may wish that Coleridge had really dreamt the text of *Kubla Khan,* all the more so because some of the poem has a certain ghostly quality— 'where Alph the sacred river ran/through caverns measureless to man/down to the sunless sea'—but alas he did not.[154] However, the claim that he did dream it all tells us something about how Coleridge thought about dreams, and even something about the minds of his expected readers.

This chapter has not unearthed many historical ancient dreams, but it may help us to draw some conclusions on a larger scale about the mental and discursive practices of articulate Greeks and Romans. (1) The widespread invention of dreams underlines once again the difference between ancient conceptions of statements about past events and our own. Consciously inventing or improving facts is for us lying and/or diplomacy. Such activities may be perfectly justified, but only by some supposedly higher interest. Antiquity was less severe, especially but not only with regard to the murky world of dreams. (2) Greek and Roman taste strongly disliked stories with loose ends or incoherences, and so was predisposed to distort dream-descriptions. (3) The people who were said to have received significant dreams tended—though there were exceptions—to be the great: it was a mark of their greatness that they dreamt wonderful dreams, as Alexander of Macedon dreamt of a vital antidote and Constantine of how to win the battle that gave him Rome. (4) Since many Greeks and Romans had at least an uneasy suspicion that dreams, at least on some occasions and to some people, might reveal a hidden truth or even bring an important instruction from above, they had a powerful incentive to invent or embellish.

It is to assessing this suspicion or belief that we now turn.

154. See among others Flanagan 2000, 188.

III

Greek and Roman Opinions about the Truthfulness of Dreams

What They Believed and What We Believe

Most humans need gods in order to endure a world full of war, sickness, death and uncertainty, and they have to be gods with whom they can communicate. If and when the gods are well-disposed, they will reveal things that people want to know, especially about the future. Now, neither Greeks nor Romans took it for granted by any means that the gods were always well-disposed,[1] though philosophers and the philosophically inclined often argued, or at least asserted, that they were benevolent: Aristotle in fact makes use of this assumption when he argues that they do *not* send dreams.[2] But it was a large part of religious practice to maintain divine good-will, and some of the time it worked. The gods communicated, and one way they did so was by sending dreams.

Careless writers have often said that almost everyone in Greek and/or Roman antiquity believed that dreams came from the gods and predicted the future.[3] One says that in the ancient world dream-interpreters had 'a

---

1. Martin 2004 has argued that for most of antiquity 'intellectuals' were sharply divided from ordinary people on this issue, the former taking the more optimistic view, but his line is far too distinct: most Greeks and Romans of all types, the Epicureans aside, knew that the gods had to be placated, but most Greeks and Romans seem to have had confidence in what Richard Gordon has called 'the fundamental benignity of the moral order' (1972, 52). But see also Veyne 1986, and Padel 1995, 26 (on the contradictory nature of Greek gods, helping and hating).

2. See Van der Eijk 2005, 189–190.

3. 'Only the Epicureans and the adherents of the New Academy objected' to the belief

central function in human history'.[4] Their doctrine is in effect that the Greeks and Romans were far removed from the modern world in which every sane person supposedly knows that dreams have no predictive value. In this respect, however, the distance between ancient and modern is shorter than is often suggested.

Modern beliefs are themselves problematic: in one corner are the scientists, notwithstanding the sharp divergences of opinion we noticed earlier, in the opposite corner are the far more numerous people who write and consult books of innocent superstition with titles such as *1001 Dreams*,[5] or better still *The Element Encyclopedia of 20,000 Dreams*,[6] that are scarcely distinguishable from the manual of Artemidorus. Many studies have shown that belief in predictive dreams is widespread in modern western societies.[7] As a professor of English recently wrote, 'the feeling that dreams do convey messages . . . has always survived'.[8] But there is a third corner in this confusing contest, where you find the psychoanalytically inclined, those— Freudians, post-Freudians and others—who believe that dreams reveal something profound about the dreamer's psyche;[9] and there is a fourth one too, except that it is occupied by noncontestants, that is to say the normal people who, while they may not be above recounting dreams at the break-

---

that dreams were sent by the gods, 'but even they did not necessarily reject the prophetic and revealing character of dreams' (Edelstein and Edelstein 1945, II, 157) (but neither the Epicureans nor the 'New Academy', which is represented for us, on this subject, mainly by Cicero's *De divinatione,* hedged at all on the subject of prophetic dreams). Cf. Oberhelman 1993, 122, Manuwald 1994, 22. 'The dream was a real phenomenon in which people firmly believed . . . politicians and army leaders based vital decisions on dream-experiences', Del Corno (1982, 55; he gives no instances). According to Frenschkowski and Morgenthaler 2002, 31, popular belief never questioned 'belief in dreams', and important people, including 'almost all Roman emperors', based important decisions on dreams. Even a careful scholar such as van der Eijk (2005, 189) writes that it was 'generally accepted' in Aristotle's time 'that dreams are sent by a god'.

4. Näf 2004, 13. He goes on to point out, however, that their interpretations were often doubted.

5. J. Altman (London, 2002).

6. T. Cheung (New York, 2006); this was produced by a large commercial publisher.

7. Tedlock 1991, 163, listed nine items of bibliography. See further Holy 1992, 86.

8. Spearing 1999, 20.

9. It is customary to say that ancient dream-interpretation considered only what events were indicated, especially future events; but from at least Plato's time some considered that dreams and character were strongly linked: an evil person was liable to dream evil dreams. See below, p. 6.

fast-table, assume that what they saw in their sleep has no large significance whatsoever.

Some very good scholars tend to hypothesize an essential dichotomy in the ancient world between a small intellectual minority that was unwilling to admit that dreams came from the gods, and a large majority that assumed the contrary, with respect to some dreams at least.[10] And that majority is often held to have included almost all of the educated: thus an expert on the role of dreams in ancient medicine argues that ancient physicians, 'from Hippocrates to Galen', accepted 'the significance of the reality of diagnostic and even mantic dreams'.[11] One historian of Graeco-Roman religion writes carefully that 'the existence of predictive dreams was generally accepted in the ancient world',[12] which may possibly be nothing worse than an exaggeration. There have been a few dissenters, however: an outstanding expert on Greek dreaming concluded, atypically, that, in classical Greece, 'only in exceptional cases was serious attention paid to dreams by normal people in normal daily life'.[13] And most historians recognize that whereas in monarchical regimes dreams may sometimes have had practical effects on public affairs, in other kinds of regime they very rarely exercised any influence (we shall consider both halves of this proposition).

The truth about Greek and Roman dreams is in fact much more interesting than the blanket assertion that almost the whole population believed that dreams predicted the future, for their reactions to the world of dreams were marked by contradictions, doubts, inconsistencies, hopes, fears and other human phenomena that we shall encounter as we go along; as indeed were the reactions of mediaeval Christians.[14] Most classical people thought that *some* dreams, though only a small proportion of them, were in some fashion revelatory; but there were also plenty of people who thought that dreams were very seldom, or never, grounds for action of any kind.

'Exceptional cases'—that is a pregnant phrase: one hypothesis might be that most Greeks and Romans only paid attention to the predictive poten-

---

10. See van der Eijk 2004, 191, on the Greeks, for instance.

11. Oberhelman 1987, 48. In fact he admits that the Methodists did not (47 n. 3, referring to Galen, *De fac.nat.* i.12 = II.29K); his view of the Hippocratics is as we shall see one-sided, to say the least. The difference between the 'diagnostic' and the 'mantic' use of dreams is of course enormous.

12. Price 1986, 11.

13. Van Lieshout 1980, 6.

14. See Dagron 1985, Manselli 1985, Schmitt 1985.

tial of dreams in life-threatening circumstances, or when they were faced with very unusually important dilemmas.

The weight of tradition, for many people, must have strengthened the urge to believe. To be thoroughly sceptical required one to reject a very great number of more or less authoritative stories, as Cicero was well aware during the composition of his sceptical *On Divination*. And most figures with cultural authority either told meaningful dream-stories themselves (Homer, Euripides, Plato, leading Stoics, Vergil) or left some room for predictive or informative dreams (Democritus, Aristotle, some physicians)— or in extreme cases provided explanations of dreaming that also required a measure of faith (Epicurean *eidola* or images).[15]

The aim of this chapter is to judge how far and how deeply Greeks and Romans put faith in dreams. This will involve us periodically in some wider questions, how, for instance, belief in dreams fits into the history of classical 'divination' in general, given all the other available means of obtaining revelations. In so far as true dreams were supposed to come from the gods, what sort of theology accompanied the supposition? (It may not be guaranteed that the gods are benevolent enough to wish to supply us with useful revelations.)[16] And can we know anything substantial about *what determined* levels of belief at particular epochs, or the intensity of associated practices such as incubation?

In investigating this matter, we clearly need to make some distinctions of time and place, probably also of class and gender.[17] Still more importantly, we need to ask what counted as a prophetic dream in the classical world, what it meant to 'believe', and how one might find out what was believed by 'almost everyone'.

15. For these naturalistic explanations see Chapter IV.

16. Some—Artemidorus is a conspicuous example—supposed that dreams conveyed truths even though they were not messages from the gods.

17. This was well appreciated by Brelich 1966, 293: 'it is not possible to talk of a general Hellenic attitude towards dreams without differentiating'. That is still more obviously true of the Roman Empire. Buxton 1999, 4–5, challenges us not to talk about the cultural history of classical Greece without thinking of 'the woman working with her husband in the fields of the island of Chios', 'the Arcadian goatherd', and the slave in the Laurium silvermines, which is fair enough, but dreams are I think an aspect of the mental world of such people that is beyond our grasp—and we should recognize that. Even generalizing about the way women understood dreams is I think scarcely possible (even in the social elite), since it was a regular *topos* from Penelope onwards that women were especially likely to misunderstand their dreams.

Truth

The gods, even at their most benevolent, were fond of indirect or disguised communication. A Homeric story told how Iphthime appeared in a dream to reassure her sister Penelope, truthfully, that her son was still alive—but it was an image *(eidolon)* of Iphthime, sent by Athena and claiming the authority of Athena; furthermore, it refused to say whether Odysseus was also alive.[18]

Much more broadly, there was the problem of symbolism and interpretation (already present in Penelope's Goose Dream): a predictive dream would often need to be interpreted before it could be said to yield up truth.[19] The *oneirokritai* and *coniectores* could make almost anything sound true,[20] to some people. But no one can have been unaware that the right interpretation was often doubtful.

There was truth and truth. To suppose that a dream had been truthful was by no means necessarily to suppose that it had predicted an event that subsequently took place. A dream's validity was considered to have been established in a variety of ways, some of which had nothing to do with correct prediction. As far as archaic and classical Greece are concerned, Van Lieshout attempted to classify the kinds of information a dream might provide,[21] which could be about the past, the present or the future, as was the case with several other ancient methods of divination.[22]

But a still more basic classification would set apart the numerous dreams that did not make statements but issued instructions. For not only dream-statements but dream-orders too raised questions about truth and authenticity. Nestor says of Agamemnon's dream in which he, Nestor, had appeared

18. Homer, *Od.* iv.795–841.

19. Gnuse 1996, 110–111, catalogues (with some errors) a sample of thirty-seven symbolic dreams drawn from authors ranging from Homer to Cassius Dio.

20. See, for instance, Bouché-Leclercq, 1879–1880, I, 317–321, on fantastic ways of interpreting numbers in dreams.

21. Van Lieshout 1980, 8–12. Cf. also, for divination more widely, Bouché-Leclercq 1879–1880, I, 7–13.

22. For expressions of this kind see Euripides, *IT* 1264–5, and many other texts. Information about the past: Plato, *Rep.* ix.572a, *Tim.* 72a; the present: both of these passages and cf. Homer, Od. xiv.495 (apparently) (an invention by Odysseus). It is almost a commonplace that in many cultures prophets earn their reputations by knowing hidden truths about the past and the present as well as about the future (see for instance E. Fraenkel 1950 on Aeschylus, *Ag.* 1185).

(an instruction-dream) that 'we would have called it false *(pseudos)*' if it had been dreamt by anyone else.[23] When the image of Patroclus gave Achilles instructions about his burial,[24] that was probably thought of as a truth-telling dream (though Homer uses no such expression).[25] When Juno, in a dream, uttered a threat in her own interest, it could be considered definite that it was really she who had spoken, and the dream was categorized as 'true'.[26] If the dreamer disobeyed what might be a divine instruction and afterwards suffered, the dream was normally, I assume, considered by Romans to have been 'proved', *comprobatum* (a technical term).[27] Sulla is said to have told Lucullus that divine orders in dreams were 'the most secure' things (we shall consider later whether Sulla's social milieu is likely to have agreed).[28] In Chapter I we encountered the claims of literary men to have received divine instructions in their dreams. The fifth-century BC sculptor Onatas was said to have made a statue of Black Demeter for the Phigaleans partly on the basis of her appearance in a dream.[29] Would not all these dreamers have claimed that their dreams were 'true'?

Dream instructions might come from a mere human: Drusus appeared in Pliny the Elder's dreams and told him to write the history of the German wars;[30] it was a valid dream though not a prediction. But a dream might also be considered divine if it had served as a means of telepathic communication between friends.[31]

It is also a very important point here that a dream was considered, by some people at least, to have been prophetic if it was simply followed by a favour-

23. *Il.* ii.81. Fictionality need not come into the discussion here.

24. *Il.* xxiii.62–107.

25. Formal parallels: *Od.* vi.20–49 (Athena, in disguise, told Nausicaa to do the laundry); [Aeschylus], *PV* 645–657 (dreams told Io to go to a certain place to have sex with Zeus); Herodotus ii.139, vii.12–18 (where the word for an authentic instruction-dream is 'divine'), 15.3, 16.β.2, 16.γ.1 and 2); cf. Herodotus iii.149, viii.54. There could be still more complicated questions of authenticity: Pelias, wanting to get Jason out of the way, told him that Phrixus had instructed him in a dream that the Golden Fleece must be recovered: all this was in a poem by Pindar (*Pyth.* iv. 157–163), who does not categorize the dream as true or false.

26. Cicero, *De div.* i.48, 60.

27. *De div.* i.55.

28. Plutarch, *Sull.* 6, *Luc.* 23.

29. Pausanias viii.42.7. For another legend of the same kind see Athenaeus xii.543f.

30. Pliny, *Ep.* iii.5.4, with interesting details (cf. Önnerfors 1976). For receiving instructions as the typical form of the dream that had some claim to validity see Cicero, *De div.* ii.122 beginning.

31. For an instance see Cicero, *De div.* i.57, with Pease's commentary.

able turn of events, or by an unfavourable one. It was not merely a question of symbolic truth—the eagle who is a husband, or the snake who is the murderous son Orestes (we shall meet him shortly)—but of a vaguer signal of coming good or evil. 'What trouble is in store for me after seeing a dream like that?' asks one of the slaves at the beginning of Aristophanes' *Wasps*.[32] The author of the pseudo-Hippocratic *On Regimen* says that seeing the sun, the moon, the heavens and the stars 'pure and bright' portends good health.[33] According to Artemidorus, an *oneiros* (which in his language is supposed to be a dream which has a truthful message, *apobainei*) 'signifies good or evil things in the future',[34] and he constantly takes dreams to have done this when they are in his language 'allegorical', in our language 'symbolic'. 'The experts say that' one must judge to be propitious everything in a dream that is in accord with nature, law, custom, occupation, names, and time.[35] Thus part of the population at least set the barrier quite low. And they in fact set it still lower than this, for as Artemidorus explains[36] dreams that seemed positive in themselves could predict negative events and vice versa.

Epicurus, who denied altogether that dreams had any predictive value, nonetheless said that they were 'true'[37]—in the sense that we really see them (then we start drawing false conclusions). No doubt he enjoyed subverting an old superstition.

Belief

Someone may wonder whether we should be concerning ourselves with 'beliefs' at all. Older scholars, for whom Christianity was supposedly the only religious model, concentrated on beliefs,[38] but when anthropological research began to have an effect on the study of ancient religion, in the early twentieth century, it tended to promote ritual and marginalize what

32. Lines 24–25; cf. line 47.

33. [Hippocrates], *On Regimen* iv.89.

34. i.2, p. 5 lines 17–18.

35. i.3, p. 11 lines 7–9. The similarities between these two texts—the one concerned with health, the other with life in general—were already analysed well by Fredrich 1899, 207–213.

36. i.5, p. 15 lines 3–18.

37. Diogenes Laertius x.32 (Canon fr. 36 Usener). Cf. Sextus Empiricus, *Adv.math.* vii.203–205.

38. Wilamowitz's last book was *Der Glaube der Hellenen* (1931–1932). The second volume of M. P. Nilsson's authoritative *Geschichte der griechischen Religion* still in 1950 laid great stress on belief, incidentally classifying trust in dreams among the 'lower' beliefs.

people thought.[39] Dodds, in *The Greeks and the Irrational* (1951), wrote
sarcastically about 'drawing up a list of recorded "beliefs"', and for a time, at
least, his attitude became orthodoxy.[40] A modern book about non-Christian
religion in antiquity is still unlikely to concern itself explicitly with belief to
any great extent.[41] We *might* see our task as the investigation of a practice,
not a belief—the practice of speaking of one's own dreams and other people's
as sources of genuine information. But that is not the view taken here.

It has become a frightful cliché to juxtapose traditional ancient religion
as a religion of practice, and Christianity as a religion of belief. This anti-
thesis has great disadvantages, including a tendency to homogenize the
quite kaleidoscopic world of Greek and Roman 'paganism'. More recent
fashions have also belittled belief: one writer tells us that, for such writers
as Artemidorus, 'dreams can be occasions not for "belief" but rather for reflection on constructions of self-identity',[42] which in so far as it means anything suggests a wholly false dichotomy.

In these circumstances one might hanker for Durkheim, who once
wrote as follows: religion 'is merely a form of custom. . . . What perhaps
best distinguishes this from all others is that it asserts itself not only over
conduct but over consciousness. It not only dictates actions but ideas and
sentiments. In short, religion starts with faith, that is to say with any belief
accepted or experienced without argument'.[43] Yet this formulation has its

39. Harrison 2000, 18 n. 73, traces this back to William Robertson Smith.

40. Dodds 1951, viii. Neither he nor his followers seemed to be concerned with the
racism inherent in the supposition that anthropological populations are incapable of thinking about religion. For more recent proponents of this orthodoxy, and some dissenters, see
Harrison 2000, 18–19. Wittgenstein 1967, reacting against Frazer, insisted that the 'primitives' did not have religious opinions.

41. This is beginning to change: see Harrison 2000, and also Feeney 1998 (ch. I), Janko
2002–2003, King 2003. In Burkert's survey of classical Greek religion (1985 [1977]), belief
is entirely subordinated to practice; but see 313–317. 'Practice not belief is the key', says
Price 1999, 3. In consequence neither offers any clear account of how the Greeks esti-
mated the value of their various methods of divination. Beard, North and Price 1998, I, 43,
maintain that belief was relatively unimportant in Roman religion because it did not bestow identity, but this is not very satisfactory since religious practice did not do so either
except in rare instances; they agree in any case that there is such a thing as 'the history of
Roman religious ideas' (I, 151). Scheid 2005, a study of Roman sacrificing with the challenging title *Quand faire, c'est croire*, presents in effect a sophisticated version of the standard late-twentieth-century view (see esp. 276–282).

42. Miller 1994, 127.

43. From a review published in 1886, quoted in Pickering 1975, 21 (but my translation
diverges from his at one point).

weaknesses: in particular, it involves a perilous reification of belief—which can be highly unstable.[44]

A new book could be written on the subject of religious belief in antiquity, as also on the subject of religious 'experience'. Thomas Harrison has well observed that 'to avoid the term "belief" on the grounds of its association with Christianity is . . . to privilege Christianity . . . unduly'.[45] By the late fifth century BC, at the latest, the Athenians did attach some importance to actual belief: no reader of Aristophanes' *Clouds*[46] or of Plato's *Apology* is likely to doubt it (though there remains the old question whether Plato accurately represents Athens at the time of Socrates' trial).[47] Classical and Hellenistic Greeks devoted enormous efforts to discovering the right ways to think about higher beings. Educated Romans inherited this tradition: in Cicero's *On the Nature of the Gods* the conservative Cotta harps on the rigidity of his own *opiniones*.[48] Dreams were part of this problematic.

There was belief and belief. This is not only a matter of how strong beliefs were, varying from the kind of firm conviction that led to action to a faint suspicion that something might be true—which might also lead to action—though that is very important.[49] Nor is it only a matter of propositional belief (belief that . . .) versus generalized faith or confidence (belief in . . .), though that has some relevance too.[50]

A brilliant passage in Ryle may help us to notice some more of the complexities:[51]

> Beliefs, like habits, can be inveterate, slipped into and given up; like partisanships, devotions and hopes they can be blind and obsessing; like aversions and phobias they can be unacknowledged; like fashions and tastes

44. Cf. Arnold 2005, 19. But his account of mediaeval European belief concerns a world of doctrinal policing very remote from classical antiquity.

45. Harrison 2000, 20; his five pages on this problem are, I think, the best account of the matter so far. King 2003 is an important contribution on the Roman side. Cf. also Flower 2008, 10–11.

46. For belief see for instance lines 329, 819, 1279.

47. Price 1999, 85, among others, considers that Plato's version of what Socrates said is likely to be nearer to Socrates' real speech than Xenophon's version.

48. iii.5.

49. Such uncertainty might lead a Greek to ask an oracle, such as the one at Didyma, whether a dream was true: Robert 1968, 586–589.

50. Many have ruminated on this difference, e.g. Needham 1972, 86–89. Sperber 1997 advocates a dichotomy between intuitive and reflective beliefs that does not seem to offer much to a cultural historian.

51. Ryle 1949, 128–129.

they can be contagious . . . belief might be said to be . . . 'propositional'; but
this, though not far wrong, is too narrow . . . [belief] is a propensity not only
to make certain theoretical moves but also to make certain executive and
imaginative moves, as well as to have certain feelings.

We have no need to embrace the classic behaviourist credo, yet it cannot
do ancient historians anything but good—tied as we mostly are to a body of
literary texts—to think about propensities to action, in both public and private life.[52] If someone professes to see 'something significant' in (some)
dreams, but never acts on them, we ought to be suspicious. Circumstances
mattered of course, for anxiety inevitably made people more inclined to
take notice of prophecies,[53] and might lead to hesitant trust in dreams: going into painful exile, Cicero took notice of his dream of Marius;[54] Pliny the
Younger was not sure that his client Suetonius was right to be alarmed by a
dream about a forthcoming trial, but nonetheless undertook to get its date
changed[55]—better not to take risks over such an important though not life-
threatening matter. It was not a subject over which people had to have
more or less consistent views. Scholars often look for a stable 'attitude'
towards dreams, even where there may have been so such stability.

The problem of stability arises in another form too: folk-beliefs about
dreams may have remained more or less the same from generation to generation, yet they may also have changed, and certainly the views prevailing
among the educated could vary from time to time. A marked feature of the
important history of Roman religion by Beard, North and Price was the authors' willingness to detect fairly short-term changes of religious attitude.[56]
Scholarly accounts of ancient dreaming are often flat and synchronic. But
in the end, the ancient world's slowness of communication, by modern
standards, is bound to make us cautious about major changes of belief,
especially in the general population.

One's reactions to a dream might not be analytic or intellectual in the
very least, but simply a matter of a particular mood; if that mood went as
far as depression or fear on the one hand, or elation and hope on the other,

52. Weber 1998, 23, well suggests that we should look for the consequences people
drew from dreams for their ordinary life.

53. Cf. Seneca, *NQ* vi.29.3.

54. Cicero, *De div.* i.59, ii.137, 140.

55. *Ep.* i.18.

56. Beard, North and Price 1998, e.g. I, 110, 113, 150.

then one was taking the dream seriously. And there is quite a lot of evidence in the Greek world, from Pindar to Nonnus, that dreams felt to be threatening or propitious caused the dreamer to take various actions, including making libations and even sacrifices.[57] A famous play, the *Choephori,* centres around the libations Clytemnestra ordered after a loathsome dream. What in all this, we may ask, was theatrical or 'literary' behaviour, or a sign of unusual superstitiousness, and what was the reaction of the ordinary god-fearing Athenian or Roman? Texts that concern themselves with everyday reality show that reactions might include prayer,[58] sacrifice,[59] the building of shrines and altars,[60] or (according to Plutarch) immersions and ablutions of various kinds.[61] All this must have been meant to bring relief from genuine anxieties.[62]

There is still more, however, in particular 'poetic belief',[63] or much better 'literary belief'. We know that we cannot say about the historical Vergil or the historical Ovid that they believed that the gods behaved just as they behave in the *Aeneid* or the *Metamorphoses,* and we know that we cannot assume that they thought as their actors do about the interpretation of dreams. The same applies to Plutarch's biographies, among other texts.[64] There is a real risk of underestimating the force of literary tradition and the opportunities it created, factors which helped to form every single literary text we shall be using.

Closely related to, but not quite part of, the literary tradition, is the story about the remote past (which may also be a story about a remote country). We shall encounter many examples of stories about long ago that classical

57. Much of the evidence was collected by A. D. Knox in W. Headlam's ed. of Herodas, pp. 381–382, and by Parker 1983, 220 n. 171. Neither attempted to differentiate in any way between the fictional and the nonfictional. They did not include the Roman instances in Cicero, *De div.* ii.130, Valerius Maximus i.7.3, Petronius, *Sat.* 104, Martial xi.50.8; cf. Propertius iii.10.13, etc.

58. [Hippocrates], *On Regimen* iv.89 end and 90 end (instructions to pray to various deities, but this is in brief after two long chapters of physical remedies), Theophrastus, *Char.* 16.11, Plutarch, *De superstitione* 3 (*Mor.* 166a).

59. Xenophon, *Anab.* iv.3.9, Plato, *Laws* x.909e, Artemidorus v.66.

60. Plato, *Laws* x.910a.

61. Plutarch, l.c.; cf. Aristophanes, *Frogs* 1331–1340.

62. Cf. Dodds 1973, 183.

63. The pages of Veyne on this subject (1983, 33–34) are more convincing than the rest of that book. Perkell 1989 discusses poetic truth in Vergil's *Georgics.*

64. Plutarch himself seems to have been quite sceptical: see below.

authors would more or less clearly have refused to credit if they had taken place in their own times. Take for example Diodorus the Sicilian on the Egyptian king he calls Sabacon (who lived in the eighth century BC): Sabacon dreamt that 'the god in Thebes' told him in a dream that he would not be able to rule Egypt happily for long unless he cut all the priests of Egypt in half and marched between the halves; Sabacon recoiled from the deed and abdicated.[65] Would Diodorus have believed this if a similar story had been told about a Roman consul of his own time?

The Interpreters

An elementary error to avoid is the presumption that because Artemidorus, and apparently quite a few people before him,[66] wrote keys to dream-interpretation, a lot of people supposed that dreams frequently foretold the future.[67] Perhaps they did believe that; but whereas in the modern world the extensive sales of a book or a type of book may provide a valuable indication of widespread beliefs, ancient book distribution was all on a very small scale.[68] And both Artemidorus and the whole genre of *Oneirocritica* fail a major test of their popularity: the long list of Greek literary papyri found in Egypt contains no dream-books at all (whereas even palmomancy, the art of reading hands, *is* represented).[69] Artemidorus refers

65. Diodorus Siculus i.65. Another version of this story had appeared in Herodotus ii.139.

66. Many Greeks and Romans wrote specialized books about the interpretation of dreams—Del Corno 1969 lists some twenty-three authors other than Nigidius Figulus (who wrote the only attested Latin work on dream-interpretation, Del Corno 1969, xi) and Artemidorus (cf. also Bouché-Leclercq 1879–1880, I, 277 n.). It would be possible, however, to doubt the existence of some or all of those nine of Del Corno's authors who are attested exclusively by Artemidorus (and one of the others, Theophrastus, was probably a dream-sceptic). We are in any case more concerned here with what was read than it what was written.

67. This error in its crude form: Boriaud 1999, 216.

68. Plastira-Valkanou 2001 entirely fails to show that the novelist Xenophon of Ephesus' readers were conversant with texts such as that of Artemidorus. Pomeroy 1991 maintains that Artemidorus' approach was the popular one.

69. Pack 1967. Cf. Guidorizzi 1985, 159. Weber's counterargument (1998, 35 n. 49) is unintelligible. The Roman-period texts written in hieratic or demotic (Volten 1942, 5; Zauzich 1980; Bresciani 2005, 139–151) somewhat modify this picture. Artemidorus denounced palmomancy (ii.69 p. 195), but apparently he had written or was to write a book about it (Suda s.v.), which seems unlikely to have been critical.

to 'the deeply despised diviners [*manteis*] of the market-place' with whom he had 'consorted for many years',[70] and he expected that his book would encounter plenty of scepticism. It might possibly be argued that the literate classes, at least in Roman Egypt, were much less interested in dream-interpretation than the uneducated (and it is presumable that at all social levels dream-interpretation will mainly have taken place face to face), but nothing in this chapter suggests that literacy inoculated one against dream-credulity any more than it did against palm-reading.

Interpreters like these *manteis* may give us some important clues, however. Since it was always obvious to Greeks and Romans that not many dreams predict the future *in a literal sense,* interpretation was constantly necessary, and *oneiropoloi,* skilled dream-interpreters, are already mentioned in Homer.[71] They continued to exist in a more or less humble way in some classical Greek cities, including Athens, where they were a standard feature of life in 422 BC;[72] and in the fourth century a *mantis* could be prosperous.[73] Having gained the dignified name of *oneirokritai* ('dream-judges'),[74] dream-interpreters lived on in Hellenistic and Roman times, at least in religious centres. The most famous Hellenistic evidence is the shop sign of a Cretan who practised dream-interpretation at Memphis (Plate 8).[75] And there was more paid dream-interpretation in the Greek

70. i prooem.

71. *Il.* i.62–63.

72. Aristophanes, *Wasps* 52–53: 'Now why don't I pay you a fee of two obols, since you're so good at interpreting dreams?' Such persons were immediately available to Hipparchus, if we can rely on Herodotus v.56. Lysimachus, the grandson of Aristides the Just, was extremely poor and practised dream-interpretation at Athens out of a writing tablet (*pinakion*), according to Plutarch, *Arist.* 27 (on the authority of Demetrius of Phalerum). The fact that Aristotle wrote a treatise *On Prophecy through Sleep* [*De div. per somnum*], saying that it is 'not easy to despise it' (1.462b13–14), suggests that they had many clients.

73. See Isocrates xix.5–6, for instance.

74. Theophrastus, *Char.* 16.11, and Clearchus fr. 76b are the earliest attestations, but the importance of the verb *krinein* in relation to dreams is already attested in Homer, *Od.* xix.555 *(hupokrinasthai),* and in other authors; and Aristotle, *De div. per somnum* 2, uses the noun *krites* in this connection. By the time of Galen (XV.442K), *oneiropolos* was no longer current usage.

75. See Rubensohn 1900, Rostovtzeff 1941, pl. CI, Thompson 1988, pl. VII, Näf 2004, 77, etc. The most interesting aspects of this text: its location, and the fact that it is written at all (which suggests some prosperity). For *oneirokritai* in second-century or early-first-century Delos see *I. Délos* 2072 (= *SIG*³ 1133), 2073 (the same person evidently), 2105 (= *SIG*³ 1127; he came from Nicomedia and had a client with a Latin name), 2106, 2110, 2120,

world than we may at first realize, since the practitioners sometimes appeared in various other guises: Aristander of Telmessus, for instance, who was for a time Alexander of Macedon's favourite dream-interpreter, was a multipurpose seer, not simply a dream-interpreter.[76] The generic figure of the *mantis* is far commoner in the sources than the specialist dream-interpreter.

Mid- and late-republican Rome had its paid *coniectores* or interpreters of dreams (what they practised was called *coniectura*),[77] some of those of the late Republic being *Isiaci coniectores*,[78] who presumably interpreted the dreams which devout Isis-worshippers received through incubation.[79] Quintus Cicero, even though he is represented in his brother's *On Divination* as putting the case *in favour of* divination, professes to despise both types,[80] and this is likely to have been the general attitude of the literate classes. Juvenal expresses contempt.[81] Yet the interpreters, a certain number of them at least, stayed in business, in Italy as in Greece.

The interpreters sometimes showed great ingenuity. Part of their art, for example, was to tell you when the dream meant *the opposite* of what it seemed to mean.[82] Since this technique of theirs was quite well-known—

2151. One notes that all these inscriptions came from major religious centres. For a woman *oneirokritis* in Roman Athens see *IG* III.162. None of these people is likely to have been poor. Other literary texts that more or less confirm the existence of *oneirokritai:* Zenodotus in Aristonicus on *Il.* i.62, Chrysippus fr. 1202 Arnim (from Photius), Ps.-Theocritus xxi.33 (even fisherman look down on them), Dorotheus of Sidon [first century AD] 362 Stegemann, Ptolemy iv.4.3, iv.4.11, Alciphron iii.23 (with a note of scepticism). This is a fairly small harvest of evidence for several centuries of Greek history.

76. Cf. too Theophrastus, *Char.* 16.11. On seers see esp. Parker 2005, 116–119 (emphasizing the shadiness that attached to selling religious knowledge but also the respectability of some practitioners, mentioning also that Athens lacked a local oracle to give help over everyday worries).

77. Plautus, *Curculio* 246–250, *Miles* 693 (female—possibly a joke, according to Traill 2004, 123), Cicero, *De div.* i.45, ii.123.

78. The reference to *Isiaci coniectores* and *interpretes somniorum* in Cicero, *De div.* i.132, falls outside the quotation from Ennius given there (see Pease's comm., p. 336).

79. Renberg 2006 implies that this cannot be so because Isis did not yet have a temple in Rome, but Isis and Serapis certainly had some shrines in Italy by this time (cf. *ILLRP* 159, 518, line 6, etc.). What rituals were practised in them is of course uncertain.

80. *De div.* i.132 again (cf. ii.145).

81. vi.546–547.

82. This kind of interpretation is widely attested in the anthropological literature: see Dentan 1986, 330. Amat 1985, 30, was mistaken to say that it typically 'Latin'.

Plate 8. Shingle of a Cretan dream-interpreter, with a metrical inscription: 'I interpret dreams, having a command from the god. With good fortune. The interpreter is Cretan'. From Memphis, early Hellenistic. This object too is small: breadth 26 cm., height 35 cm. Egyptian Museum, Cairo, stele 27567. Photo: Deutsches Archäologisches Institut, Cairo.

we can date it back at least to the fifth century and one of the earliest authors of a book of dream-interpretation, possibly the earliest, namely the sophist Antiphon[83]—ordinary dreamers must sometimes have wondered which way an apparent indication of the future was going to jump:

> a runner preparing to set off for the Olympics dreamt that he was riding in a four-horse chariot; in the morning he told a dream-interpreter [*coniector*], who said 'You will win, for that's the meaning of the speed and power of the horses'. But then he went to Antiphon, who said 'You will certainly lose, for it's obvious that four ran ahead of you'.[84]

In the hands of a sceptic, interpretations of this kind could serve as ammunition,[85] but it was probably always part of the Greek and Roman tradition of dream-understanding that dreams were sometimes tricking and ambiguous, like oracles: Hamilcar the Carthaginian, while besieging Syracuse, was said to have dreamt that he would dine in the city next day, and he did—as a prisoner;[86] just as Pompey, before the Battle of Pharsalus, supposedly dreamt that he was decorating the temple of Venus Victrix with trophies, which he duly did—as the loser.[87] Artemidorus quite often describes surprise outcomes of this kind.[88]

(Some readers will have recalled that Freud, a reader of Artemidorus, followed much the same procedure when he justified, with very elaborate

---

83. Stories about deceptive dreams go back to Homer, as we have already seen. Van Lieshout 1980, 224–229, seriously overestimated Antiphon's contribution to the understanding of dreams, in my opinion.

84. Cicero, *De div.* ii.144 = Antiphon 87 B 80 D-K = fr. 80 (a) Pendrick. Antiphon provided another similar example, and Cicero comments that the books of Chrysippus and Antipater are full of such interpretations. I have no special wish to contest the usual opinion that equates the 'Antiphon the Athenian' who wrote *peri kriseos oneiron* (87 A 1) with the sophist of that name (see e.g. Pendrick 2002, 24–26); but I note that that the Suda distinguishes them (for discussion see Del Corno 1969, 129–130).

85. It was probably with this intention, I think, that Diogenes of Oenoanda, a dream-sceptic (see below), cited the second of this pair of interpretations from Antiphon (fr. 24; see M. F. Smith 1993, 186–187). Previous interpreters (cf. Pendrick 427) have seen the citation of Antiphon as the tactic of an unnamed opponent with whom Diogenes is supposed to have been debating.

86. Cicero, *De div.* i.50.

87. Plutarch, *Pomp.* 68. There is plenty of other evidence that this form of interpretation was well-known: see for example Pliny, *Ep.* i.18, Apuleius, *Met.* iv.27.

88. i.5, etc.

arguments, his opinion that anxiety dreams are really expressions of re-pressed wishes.[89] The arguments in question provoked Sebastiano Timpa-naro to call them the 'most capricious and scientifically dishonest of all'.)[90]

The expectations of the clients of dream-interpreters were not necessar-ily high, even among those who were inclined to suppose that dreams might contain genuine revelations. Dreams were indeed like oracles, or worse, but Greeks and Romans were accustomed to recognize that divine communications with mankind were also, rather often, 'ambiguous, in-scrutable, opaque'.[91] Animal entrails were undoubtedly considered more important signs than dreams in high classical Greece.[92] As to the kinds of people who turned to dream interpreters (women more than men?), and the circumstances in which they did so (mainly in times of crisis?), we must distinguish milieux.

Metaphors

The Greek and Latin languages also suggest, at least in some periods, that expectations were low. Dreaming was often a by-word for falling victim to the insubstantial and the deceptive.[93] This is especially significant because it was the decision of the population at large, not of an intellectual elite, that both Greek and Latin words for dreaming regularly serve as meta-phors for thinking or talking nonsense. This disdainful attitude was visible when Pindar wrote that 'man is a dream of a shadow'.[94] Others too com-pared humans to insubstantial dreams.[95] When the tragedians compare

---

89. See Freud 1954 [1900], chs. 3 to 5 and 7, 1957 [1910], and 1963 [1916–1917], 178–180.

90. Timpanaro 1976 [1974], 115.

91. Gould 1985, 22. He says that they were 'systematically' so, which is an exaggeration, as is the claim that this applies to all types of divination. Fontenrose 1978, 236, argued that Delphi had no reputation for ambiguity until very late.

92. See Pritchett 1979, 76, 78–81, Burkert 1985, 113; the latter maintains that seers had less influence in Hellenistic warfare.

93. Yet these terms are not synonymous: so when Homer compares the shade of Anti-clea, whom her son Odysseus is unable to embrace, to a dream (*Od.* xi.207), that tells us nothing about the question at issue in this chapter.

94. *Pyth.* viii.95–96. The sense is 'a dream dreamt by a shade' (Bieler 1933).

95. [Aeschylus], *PV* 448, 548 (see below, p. 143), Aristophanes, *Birds* 687 (with N. Dun-bar's n.).

useless old men to dreams—as Euripides does four times[96]—that tells us something about how little they valued dreams as well as old men. It was only perhaps in the late fifth century that this disdain was fully absorbed into the language: for Plato dreams epitomized obscurity,[97] and an *enhupnion* or something achieved *onar* (in a dream) corresponded to a delusion,[98] although this did not prevent him from also using the word *enhupnion*, once, in reference to a splendid ideal.[99] This Greek usage continues throughout high classical times,[100] the prettiest illustration being the practice of Aelius Aristides, a man of high culture who thought of his own dreams as enormously valuable.[101] None of this would make sense except against a background of widespread scepticism—which leaves plenty of room, however, for good stories and a certain amount for actual belief.

Latin *somniare*, from Plautus onwards, quite often meant 'to have illusions'.[102] 'What I want to know is whether you're insane or dreaming on your feet', says a Plautine character.[103] This usage may have been influenced by Greek models, but a number of later Latin texts allude to dream-

96. Aeschylus, *Ag.* 79–82, Euripides, *Heracles* 112, *Phoen.* 1543–1545, 1722, *Aeolus* fr. 25 Kannicht. Cf. Cederstrom 1971, 83, Brillante 1991, ch. 5.

97. *Symp.* 175e. But van Lieshout 1980, 104–105, goes wrong, I think, in supposing that such casual expressions are the best guide to *Plato's* opinions—rather they are a guide to the opinions of the *general community* that created such expressions.

98. Plato, *Plt.* 290b, *Ly.* 218c, *Tht.* 208b (cf. Menander, *Aspis* 358–359); also *Rep.* iii.414d5 *(oneirata)*.

99. *Rep.* iv.443b. We shall shortly return to Plato's opinions.

100. For the connection between dreams and cheating and delusions compare the use of the verb *oneiropolo* in Aristophanes, *Knights* 809 and Demosthenes, *Phil.* i.49, and innumerable later texts easily located through a TLG search for ὀνειροπολεῖν. Some later texts where the language suggests a 'negative' attitude towards dreams: Philo, *Legum Alleg.* iii.226, Plutarch, *Mar.* 46, Dio Chrysostom vii.42, xi.129.

101. He sometimes speaks of dreams in a derogatory tone when it is simply a matter of metaphor (ii.400, xxiii.63, xxvi.43, xxviii.69); on this matter see above all Leuci 1993, 121–122.

102. Mazzoli 1995, 57–59, explains well how Plautus makes use of this theme.

103. *Cist.* 291 (like the two following passages, this refers to a woman). Cf. *Amph.* 696–697 ('She's raving. . . . Or is she dreaming while she's wide-awake?'), *Men.* 394–395 ('Are you in your right mind [*sanan es*]? Certainly this woman is dreaming on her feet like a horse'), *Capt.* 848 ('This man is dreaming on his feet'), *Merc.* 950 ('Come on now, what dream are you telling me [there is a minor textual uncertainty here])? This fellow is not in his right mind'). In *Curc.* 546 *somniare* means 'to talk nonsense about'. Cf. Terence, *Adelph.* 724–725 ('You fool, you're dreaming that I'm talking about a musician-girl . . .'). *Somnium*, dream, is common in Terence in the sense 'delusion' or 'day-dream'.

ing in a similar fashion,[104] and precisely because the habit is for the most part casual it seems to disclose a somewhat sceptical, though not a systematically sceptical, point of view.

The Greeks before the Sophists

From the beginning, known Greek opinion about the truthfulness of dreams was variegated. Homer apparently expected a hero to believe in the divinatory power of (some) dreams: Achilles suggests that a prophet or priest or *oneiropolos* could tell the Achaeans why Apollo was angry, 'for an *onar* is from Zeus'[105]—yes indeed, and before long Zeus sends one that is not just hard to interpret but intentionally misleading.[106] While supposing that a king might go to battle because of a dream, the poet calls Agamemnon a fool for having believed in this one.[107] The Homeric gods seem to enjoy deceiving humans, sometimes with bloody consequences: Athena kept Rhesus dreaming of Diomedes even as Diomedes killed him.[108] All Greeks who had heard or read Homer knew about the Gate of Ivory, through which, Penelope says, false dreams reach us (while the true ones emerge from the Gate of Horn).[109] The Goose Dream, which gave rise to Penelope's analysis, was truth-telling—but too obscure for her to understand it.

One can only extrapolate from Homer's attitude to those of his contemporaries in the most general way. The evidence pulls in both directions: Penelope's Goose Dream is of great structural importance in the *Odyssey,* preparing the audience if not Penelope for the *dénouement* that is to take

104. Cicero, *De natura deorum* i.18, but notice that an Epicurean is speaking (and he uses *somnia* to mean 'ravings' in i.42; cf. i.39). In *Att.* ix.13.6 *somniabam* means 'I was thinking confusedly of'. In vii.23.1 and *Luc.* 121, *somnia* are 'delusions'. Vergil, *Ecl.* viii. 108, Horace, *Epist.* ii.1.52, Seneca, *De const.* 11.1, *De prov.* 6.3, *De ben.* vii.10.4, Columella i.8.2, Quintilian, *Inst.* vi.2.30, Apuleius, *Met.* iii.22, use either the verb or the noun in roughly this sense.

105. *Il.* i.62–63.

106. The poet's only other reference to an *oneiropolos* (Il. v.150–152) involves his failure to foresee that his sons would be killed at Troy by Diomedes.

107. *Il.* ii.38. At ii.79–83 wise Nestor says that if Agamemnon's dream had been recounted by anyone else, 'we would have said that it was a falsehood and we would have turned our backs on it', and he noticeably avoids saying that it is true even coming from Agamemnon.

108. *Il.* x.496.

109. *Od.* xix.562–567.

place the following day, and hence we are compelled to think that the poet expected his patrons to find it believable. That also implies that they agreed in thinking that quite a number of dreams emerge from the Gate of Horn. Many archaic Greeks must have expected dreams to have some prophetic value, though of a highly uncertain kind.

But all three of the prophetic dreams in the *Odyssey* serve to help the hero, Athena's favourite, towards his triumphant ending—we are far indeed from ordinary life. Dream prophecy is absent from Hesiod and virtually all the rest of archaic Greek literature, and it is reasonable to conclude with Brelich that oneiromancy was less important to the Greeks of this time than some other forms of divination such as the Delphic and other oracles, and the condition of sacrificial victims.[110] For those who could not afford such things there was thunder and the flights of birds.

Fifth-century Athens

The Athenians are the only fifth-century Greeks about whom we can generalize in this respect. There is evidence from elsewhere that allows us to get a glimpse at least of what non-Athenians thought. But the Pre-Platonic philosophers whom we shall be considering in the next chapter give us little or no guidance as to prevailing Greek opinions about prophetic dreaming. Pindar, as we saw earlier, seems to have held that dreams were frequently meaningless,[111] while he also admits a prophetic dream in the legendary surroundings of ancient Troy.[112] That hardly allows us to say anything about the views of poets or of Thebans, let alone anyone else. We need a solid corpus of texts that interacted with great numbers of citizens.

Prometheus Bound sets us on the right path, at least for the 450s, and probably for a much longer period.[113] After the hero—whose name virtually means forethought—has told how he bestowed knowledge of medicine

---

110. Cf. Brelich 1966, 297. The significance of the reference to dreams in the Derveni papyrus (col. V, line 6) is wholly unclear.

111. *Ol.* i.28–36 also show him to have been to some degree sceptical about existing stories concerning the gods.

112. Hecuba dreamt of giving birth to a firebrand: *Paean* VIIIa Snell, lines 16–25. See also fr. 131.

113. Not by Aeschylus: West 1990, 51–72, etc.

on humankind, he passes on to divination, and first of all to dream-divination: 'I was the first to judge which dreams would turn into waking reality'.[114] Whatever the audience is supposed to feel about Prometheus, this must be understood as a major benefaction. But elsewhere in the same play dreams once again stand for the confused and the ineffectual.[115] Most of the audience probably supposed that occasional dreams could 'turn into reality'— only an expert could judge which ones, and a certain number of experts were on hand—but they also took it for granted that most dreams did not. Let us see whether this peremptory reading is consistent with the rest of the evidence.

In the second half of the century there were new religious ideas in circulation, and the tragic poets were sometimes willing to make them heard.[116] So we shall not shy away from differences of opinion. Virtually no one questioned the existence of the gods or their willingness to intervene, at least from time to time, in human affairs; all knew that certain oracles were reputed to have shown extraordinary sagacity on various occasions in the past, and the Delphic Oracle in particular retained great prestige; yet from about the middle of the fifth century a certain number of Greeks had shown an unprecedented inclination to seek secular explanations of all phenomena whatsoever. We shall consider this movement in Chapter IV; here it is enough to note that the tendency of the 'Presocratics' was sceptical in this matter. We have already mentioned Xenophanes.[117] Empedocles put forward the view that dreams are made up of our waking activities,[118] a view later echoed by a character in Herodotus. The 'materialist' Democritus considered some dreams to be truth-telling;[119] but he was probably the first person to attempt to reconcile this opinion with the view that the gods

114. [Aeschylus], *PV* 485–486. Van Lieshout 1980, 9, translates 'which portion of dreams of necessity comes to be true as dream-reality' (cf. 41–44), but this is an eccentricity.

115. Lines 448–450: early ignorant humans, who lacked the most elementary skills, were 'like the shapes of dreams'; see also 548.

116. Cf. Harris 2002, 173–174, and also Humphreys 2004 [1986], 54, though to my mind she simplifies the composition of the audience.

117. Above, p. 51.

118. 31 B 108. That this really was his meaning is argued in Chapter IV.

119. See Cicero, *De div.* i.5 (68 A 138 D-K) (with the parallels quoted by Pease). But he probably limited them to cases in which the dreamer 'gained telepathic knowledge of the intentions of persons who brought about' the events dreamt of (Bicknell 1970, 303).

were *not* responsible for the prophetic value of what was seen in the night.[120]

Aeschylus is likely to have been a traditionalist on the subject of dreams if any of the surviving dramatists were, and we have already noted his apparent interest in the subject, and also mentioned (in chapter I) the great epiphany dream in the *Eumenides* in which Clytemnestra appears to the Furies. Personages on the Aeschylean stage sometimes assume that dreams can have revelatory power, if interpreted correctly, and the viability of the drama depends on the audience's assent to this idea—that is, to the idea that Clytemnestra, for example, having dreamt of giving birth to a snake which then drew blood from her breast,[121] had received a truthtelling message (there seem to be experts present in Agamemnon's palace who can do the interpreting).[122] Queen Atossa's great dream in the *Persae* is in this respect a parallel.[123] These truth-telling dreams were experienced long ago or far away.

But Aeschylus' language sometimes also reveals a degree of dreamscepticism, shared with all or most of his Athenian citizen audience. Dreams are like old men, as we noted earlier. The poet's characters use more or less incidental language suggesting that in the real world dreams are meaningless muddles. When Menelaus dreams of Helen, she is in reality far away, for 'fine things' seen in dreams are delusions.[124] The ordinary thing to do with 'hard-to-interpret dreams' is to forget them, so the *Agamemnon* Chorus implies.[125] The Furies in the *Eumenides* dream that they are hunting

120. See Chapter IV.

121. *Choeph.* 32–41, 527–550.

122. *Choeph.* 37, with A. F. Garvie's n. There is no point in speculating here about how Stesichorus presented the dream in his lost *Oresteia* (for some discussion of fr. 42 Page see Garvie, 1986, xix–xxii).

123. Lines 176–230. She dreamt of two women, one Persian, the other Dorian, whom Xerxes harnessed to a chariot; the Dorian rebels, Xerxes falls. The Chorus advises the queen to pray that the plain meaning should go unfulfilled. Note that she had previously had many other dreams that were less clear, 176–179.

124. The Chorus in *Ag.* 420–426.

125. *Ag.* 980–984. Rousseau 1963, 113, concludes, against his own general theory, that the dream imagery in the *Agamemnon* 'mutes any suggestion of the veridical nature of dreams'; I would say rather that it suggests that Aeschylus located truth-telling dreams among the kings and queens of long ago and far way, while allowing that they too will often have had other dreams. 1218: in what respects are the children of Thyestes 'like the shapes of dreams'?

Orestes when all that they are doing is sleeping.[126] Clytemnestra invents a dream to mislead her husband.[127]

Clytemnestra goes too far. She would not be so rash as to announce the fall of Troy because of some dream,[128] but of course she is overcautious. Her great dream in the *Choephori* is, for the poet and his audience, authentic, even though her dream-interpreters failed to grasp its main significance. When she appears to the Furies in the *Eumenides,* she herself is a dream figure, passionately desiring to be accepted as authentic,[129] so that the Furies will awake and pursue the murderer. But dream prediction *in general* is scarcely vindicated. The topic was clearly under discussion. The earliest known Greek books about dreams, datable to the third quarter of the fifth century, were the work of Antiphon already mentioned, presumably written in Athens, and one by a certain Panyasis of Halicarnassus; they are both likely to have offered interpretations of dreams according to their content.[130] This was strikingly early in the history of Greek handbook literature[131]—which suggests the possibility that the need for them was strongly felt; but for all we know, Antiphon and Panyasis may have thought that they had to contend with growing scepticism.

We can say much more about another Halicarnassian, Herodotus, who certainly aimed to speak to an Athenian audience among others. He made

126. *Eum.* 131. Lines 104–105 tell us nothing about Aeschylus' thinking about dreams, since they are an interpolation (see A. H. Sommerstein's n. [1989]; but perhaps they come from elsewhere in the same poet's work).

127. *Ag.* 891–895. He may not have been deceived: cf. 918–920.

128. *Ag.* 269–277, esp. 275 ('I would not accept the impression, *doxa,* of a slumbering mind'). This remark shows her to have been 'vain and boastful' according to Rousseau 1963, 108.

129. See esp. *Eum.* 116.

130. On Antiphon see above, p. 138; there is no reason to follow Näf 2004, 47, in thinking that his book was a mainly theoretical-philosophical work. On Panyasis—not apparently the most famous person of that name—see Artemidorus i.2 end, i.64, ii.35. The Suda (s.v.) says that this Panyasis was younger than the other and wrote two books about dreams; it also calls him a *philosophos,* which again led Näf (ibid.) to say that this work was about the philosophical aspects of dreaming; that does not suit the Artemidoran evidence. The Suda's idea of a philosopher was wide enough to include, for example, both Alcibiades and the Druids. It is tempting to think that increased contact with Egypt, where dream-books had long been known (Del Corno 1966, 110), instigated fifth-century Greeks to write some too.

131. Harris 1989, 82. One Polemainetos possessed books about divination in the fifth century (Isocrates xix.45), probably about midcentury (cf. Pritchett 1979, 73).

it a leitmotif of his history that divinely predicted events are bound to come to pass, however much humans may struggle to prevent it. The dreams that he recounts (some fourteen in number)[132] all, in so far as they are predictions, come true, and in so far as they are instructions are eventually obeyed—with a single exception.[133] Xerxes' repeated dream, in which he was instructed not to cancel his expedition against the Greeks,[134] is not an exception, and we should not assume that Herodotus himself agreed with the naturalistic explanation of dreams offered by Xerxes' uncle Artabanus ('mostly', Artabanus says, 'dreams are 'shadows of what we have been thinking about during the day').[135] The willingness of fate or the gods to deceive Xerxes should not of course cause any surprise.[136] On one occasion, Herodotus says explicitly that a dream had an external origin: it was 'the *daimon*' that revealed to Cyrus his imminent death.[137]

Yet there *is* a discordant element in Herodotus' thinking about dreams:[138] Artabanus is after all wise and far-sighted, and hardly anyone in Herodotus' audience would, I suggest, have denied that ordinary everyday dreams occur just as Artabanus says that they do; in fact Herodotus *had* to include an explanation of this kind, or risk being thought of as credulous.[139] Further: all the dreams in Herodotus were dreamt by 'barbarians'[140] or by tyrants or

132. Counting Xerxes' dream as one, even though it was dreamt three times.

133. Obviously it does not follow, in spite of Frisch 1968, 61, that Herodotus thought that all dreams were important, or that they all came true. The exception: Sabacos the Ethiopian in ii.139 (on his dream cf. S. West 1987, 263–267). See further Harrison 2000, 132.

134. vii.12–19.

135. vii.16.β.2. By the criteria Artabanus himself sets out, the dream in question 'partakes of the divine' (vii.16.γ.1).

136. Harrison 2000, 136 n. 52.

137. i.210. Cf. De Jong 2006, 12.

138. Harrison 2000, 136, claims that the belief in the divine origin of dreams was 'not one projected back into a world of larger-than-life figures', but he depends for this on the views of Xenophon (for which see below); Harrison allows, however, that Herodotus thought that some dreams were 'blanks'.

139. And this was the logical place in the history to situate it, when the biggest decision of all is in the balance; see Harrison 2000, 132, on the importance of the location. But it is not plausible to suppose that Artabanus' opinion is introduced 'for the sole purpose of being contradicted' (135). He may even have thought that it was true about the majority of dreams (as suggested by van Lieshout 1980, 41).

140. The barbarian Nasamones practise divination by means of dream-incubation (iv.172), but that is probably not meant to show that it was a typically barbaric practice.

their family-members,[141] with a solitary exception that is not difficult to explain (the dream of Pericles' mother, Agariste, that she gave birth to a lion).[142] Such dreams belonged to a sinister world of lawless power,[143] and even there their value is limited, for they are usually misunderstood by the dreamers themselves. Thus the historian distances divine dreaming from daily experience, and adds to the grand, mythic and Homeric quality of his narrative. That is not to say that Herodotus' belief was 'literary', simply that this form of divination was not likely, in his view, to be much use in the here and now. That is also, I think, likely to have been the audience's prejudice and conclusion.

Nothing in the preserved plays of Sophocles or Euripides contradicts this hypothesis about the general Athenian view of truth-telling dreams. Truth-telling oracles and prophets are at the heart of Sophocles' work,[144] but humans usually misunderstand them. Dreams meanwhile receive very little attention until the late play *Electra*—Sophocles seems to have been much less interested in them than Aeschylus or Herodotus were, and it can reasonably be concluded that he did not believe that gods communicate intelligibly with mankind through dreams. Clytemnestra's dream in *Electra* does in fact offer an intelligible and true prediction,[145] which is understood well enough by all who hear of it, except apparently the dreamer herself. Prior versions of the story, and especially the *Oresteia,* made it impossible to dispense with this famous dream (which is not to argue that Sophocles would have wished to do so).[146] It represents in metaphorical form the victorious return of Orestes, and it causes the dreamer to send off her daugh-

141. Hipparchus, Hippias, Polycrates' daughter.

142. vi.131. Most probably this was a family legend of the Alcmaeonids, whom Herodotus certainly favoured. Agariste was also the grand-daughter of a tyrant.

143. Herodotus' admiration for the Persians in general does not prevent him from painting Xerxes in the darkest colours: Harris 2002, 231. For the hatred of tyrants in fifth-century Athens see Seaford 2008, 64.

144. Jouanna 1997.

145. *El.* 410–427: she dreamt that she slept with Agamemnon, who then planted a sceptre which grew into a tree overshadowing all Mycenae. Some scholars have found the dream ambiguous (e.g. Bächli 1954, 57), apparently for no better reason than that Clytemnestra, evidently in denial, says that it was (645—on the meaning of her words see Jebb's n.). The real-life audience will have understood the dream's reference to Orestes immediately.

146. The Oresteia was still well known more than forty years after its first production in 458 (cf. Harris 1989, 86–87). How much it is present in this play is disputed: Bowman

ter Chrysothemis to make an apotropaic libation, just as a well-to-do
Athenian matron might. Both Electra and the Chorus, women of Mycenae,
interpret the dream correctly, and even Clytemnestra is forced to admit
what it may mean. Electra suggests that Orestes himself had sent the
dream,[147] which separates the poet at least a little from what is supposed to
have been the conventional view, that truth-telling dreams came from the
gods. The Chorus pronounces that the dream will come true, and adds
that, if it does not, there are no true prophecies in dreams *or in oracles.*[148]
A little later Clytemnestra, in a remarkable phrase, asks Apollo to turn the
dream back on her enemies if it was a hostile one, for all the world as if it
had been sent by means of a magical spell.[149] Sophocles could in short still
make dramatic use of a well-known dream-story, and allows that humans
may understand a prophetic dream sent from the gods. But he did not suppose that even in mythical times the gods often sent informative messages
in the night.

As for Euripides, Aristophanes made fun of him because of his dream-
reporting scenes;[150] the implied criticism is interesting in itself, but it has
only a little to do with the dream-reports in the surviving plays. Two plays
in particular concern us here: *Hecuba* (produced about 424) and *Iphigeneia in Tauris* (about 413). *Hecuba* sets out from a dream or a pair of
dreams, from which the heroine learns that her son Polydorus and her
daughter Polyxena are in danger.[151] Whatever it was she saw, she does not
know how to interpret it,[152] but the worst happens—Polydorus is dead and

---

1997, 135 n. 11; I tend to agree with Winnington-Ingram 1980, 217–218, that it is very
much present.

147. *El.* 459–460. The Pythagoreans were supposed to have believed that dreams were
sent by the souls (of dead people) 'that are called *daimones* and heroes' (Diogenes Laertius viii.32 = *FVS* 58 B 1a).

148. *El.* 472–501; cf. Cederstrom 1971, 85. These words seem to hint at a partly sceptical audience.

149. *El.* 644–647. In the remaining 850 lines of the play the dream is barely heard of
again, only at 1389–1390 (it had played a larger part in the *Choephori*: Bowman 1997,
137). There is no need to discuss here the famous lines in Sophocles, *OT* 981–982, in
which Jocasta says that many mortals have dreamt of going to bed with their mothers, or
Acrisios fr. 65, in which the speaker assures a woman, probably with dramatic irony, that
frightening dreams 'grow mild' by daylight.

150. *Frogs* 1331–1363.

151. *Hec.* 30–31, 54, 68–97 (I cannot decide whether lines 90–91 are genuine), 703–711.

152. Lines 87–89.

Polyxena dies too, sacrificed by the victorious Greeks. The poet treats prophetic dreaming with complete solemnity throughout—but he has transported his audience to a long-lost world, and into a royal house.

In *Iphigeneia in Tauris*—set in that same world—Iphigeneia begins by reporting a dream,[153] which she misinterprets as proof that Orestes is dead;[154] the mistake must have been evident to the audience,[155] and a moment later Orestes appears on stage. Iphigeneia eventually realizes her error of interpretation:[156] 'farewell, deceptive dreams, it turns out that you were nothing'. Later still the Chorus explains, in mythological terms, why dreams are unreliable sources of information: Apollo competed with Earth, the mother of dreams, for the prerogative of true prophecy, and Zeus decided in Apollo's favour—'he wrested night-seen truth away from mortal men'.[157] Which is somewhat surprising in context, because the dream at the start of the play seems in fact, on the sort of interpretation a Greek is likely to have given it, to be coming true.[158]

Elsewhere in Euripides' work it is assumed that the dead can, if they wish, appear in the dreams of the living, and (in a satyr play) that dreams are futile.[159] I conclude that Euripides expected much if not all his audience to believe, while they were in the theatre, that sometimes in the past royal persons had dreamt revelatory dreams (otherwise no *Hecuba* and no tension at the start of *Iphigeneia in Tauris*), and to see nothing incredible in the thought that the dead may decide to visit the living in dreams; but on balance it is likely that he expected no discernible truth from dreams occurring in quotidian Athens.

153. *IT* 42–64: she dreamt that she was living in Argos when a night-time earthquake destroyed her house, except for one column, which then became a human being, whom she put to death, weeping the while. Dreaming recurs: 452–454, 518.

154. This belief continues to guide her actions (348).

155. Bächli 1954, 61.

156. 569. Orestes' comments that 'the *daimones* who are called wise are no more trustworthy *(apseudesteroi)* than winged dreams' (570–571) (because an oracle instructed him to kill his mother).

157. 1234–1282 (esp. 1275–1276).

158. Yet Euripides' ingenuity has not ended yet, and when King Thoas plans to capture the fugitive siblings the audience may once again worry how the good ending is going to be brought about; the answer is the sudden appearance of Athena.

159. *Alcestis* 354–357, *Heracles* 490–501; *Cyclops* 8–10. In *Orest.* 618, there would be a scornful reference to dreams if one read *oneirat'*, but C. W. Willink ad loc. must have been right to emend the word away.

Except in the anomalous *Rhesus*, all the dreaming in Athenian tragedy is done by women,[160] which may suggest that, in the poets' thinking, it went along with excesses of emotion (yet can one say that of Hecuba?). One investigator concluded that in tragedy 'very little faith' is expressed in the prophetic function of dreaming.[161] That is true, but the poets also, I think, express, in varying degrees, a lingering regret that the messages the gods occasionally send through dreams are almost always mysterious, and at the same time they make dramatic use of the audience's real willingness to suspend its disbelief.

Besides the key passage in *Prometheus Bound*, the most revealing fifth-century text of all is, I suggest, the scene in Aristophanes' *Knights* in which rival demagogues, the Paphlagonian and the Sausage-seller, compete in courting the People by means of dream prophecies:

> PA: But I've had a dream: I saw Athena herself pouring Health and Wealth over the People with a big ladle.
>
> SS: I swear I've had one too: I saw Athena herself coming from the acropolis and an owl was sitting on her helmet; then she poured a flask of ambrosia over your head, People, and a flask of garlic sauce over this fellow's.[162]

This is the climax of their rivalry, and for Aristophanes it is the final proof that they are vulgar charlatans. One might read this as a baseless libel, but it would be more plausible to suppose, as also when Aeschines similarly defamed Demosthenes (see below), that Athenian political orators sometimes did invoke meaningful dreams in real life, in the knowledge that some of their hearers would be impressed. Thucydides says that 'oracle-mongers and prophets *(manteis)*', whom he naturally despised, encouraged the Athenians to undertake the Sicilian Expedition—to act, in other words—and this probably included some dream-interpretation.[163] But one should also suppose, on the basis of the *Knights*, that another (larger?)

---

160. Cf. Hundt 1935, 42 n. 7.

161. Cederstrom 1971, 84.

162. Lines 1090–1095. Cf. N. D. Smith 1989, 149; but his observation that the poet 'never suggests that dream interpreters should be distrusted in general' gives entirely the wrong impression.

163. viii.1. But none of the prophecies in Plutarch *Nic.* 13 involved dreams.

group of citizens would look down on any such rhetorical tactic. It is therefore to be supposed that in the opening scene of the *Wasps,* when the slave Xanthias foresees that some unpleasant happening will follow his nasty dream,[164] some of the audience was expected to share his attitude while others will have seen it as a piece of amusing servile foolishness.

Later, in the *Frogs,* Aristophanes' Aeschylus demonstrates Euripides' triviality by means of a parody in which a poor woman takes fright on dreaming that her cockerel has been stolen.[165] Many thought that it was inappropriate to represent an ordinary poor woman on the tragic stage, and even more so to bother about her trivial dreams; but the attack only works if some Athenians did sometimes think that their dreams told the truth. In *Wealth,* Aristophanes shows little respect for the incubation practised at shrines of Asclepius—the priest covertly appropriates the food left on the altars[166]—but that does not exclude the strong possibility that many in the audience believed that the god sometimes appeared to the incubants in their dreams. This is not everyday medicine—Wealth was blind, and ordinary medicine could not possibly have helped him; one should not think of the Athenians hastening to incubation shrines every time their backs ached.

A recent writer claimed that in fifth-century Athens the upper classes paid more and more attention to dream-interpretation,[167] but the evidence for this does not hold up. It consists mostly of stories from Plutarch, who crammed dreams uncritically into his biographies (forty-five are retold 'in some detail', according to one count).[168] A dream, along with other signs,

---

164. Lines 23–24; 'don't worry', says his companion.

165. Lines 1331–1363.

166. Lines 676–683. Commentators have gone to great lengths to show that 'everything we hear of Asclepius tends to increase his glory' (A. H. Sommerstein in his commentary, p. 13; cf. Roos 1960, 77–87), but there is an element of mockery, notwithstanding the fact that the incubation procedure is described by the ill-behaved slave Carion (on whom see Olson 1989). Aristophanes' parodistic attitude towards certain other religious rituals (Humphreys 2004 [1986], 63) is relevant here.

167. Näf 2004, 47. There was still room, he thinks, for dream-prophecy to become continually more accepted in Hellenistic times (63).

168. Pritchett 1979, 96. Sometimes you can practically catch Plutarch in the act of improving a story, or choosing the more fantastic version. There was plenty of psychological warfare before the Battle of Leuctra (371 BC), but the better sources (Xenophon, *Hell.* vi.4, Diodorus Siculus xv.54) know nothing of the dream of Pelopidas which gives rise to

foretold the death of Cimon in the late 450s;[169] the story could be contemporary. But some of these stories are demonstrably apocryphal, and others are suspect—for example, a tale about a dream of Athena in which she told Pericles how to heal the injuries of an injured workman on the Propylaea looks like a later aetiological invention.[170] There are few facts here, still less trends.

There was a credulous tradition that survived anything that the sceptics could say, but it is hard to make out a trend in one direction or the other. We might hypothesize that for almost everyone most dreams were rubbish, but that an especially striking or frightening dream, above all if it occurred in a moment of crisis, would be suspected of conveying truth.

We may refer here to the thinking of Hippocratic doctors, even though the bulk of the texts belong to the very late fifth century or the fourth.[171] The Hippocratic writers were not in fact unanimous about this matter, but they are of very great importance for the subject of this chapter, since they initiated the notion that dreams could have important predictive value even if they had nothing directly to do with the gods. *On Regimen* begins its discussion of dreams by saying that 'anyone who correctly understands the signs that occur in sleep will find that they have great significance *(dunamin)* for everything'.[172] He expresses the view that certain dreams are of divine origin *(theia)* and may have significance for the state as well as for the individual, and he recommends—though apparently as something

---

an excellent story in Plutarch, *Pelop.* 21–22 (which Pritchett 99 should not have recounted as fact). As we shall see later, Plutarch was actually something of a sceptic about dreams.

169. *Cimon* 18.

170. *Per.* 13; P. A. Stadter's note [1989], shows how the story grew. Appropriately lurid stories were told about the death of Alcibiades, isolated with his hetaira in a Phrygian village, including details of an admonitory dream (Plutarch, *Alc.* 39; the sources are listed by Pease in his note on Cicero, *De div.* ii.143, the earliest writer to refer to this case); there is alas nothing here to tell us what Alcibiades or his contemporaries thought about dreams. Xenophon, *Hell.* iii.4.4, shows that the dream of Agesilaus in Plutarch, *Ages.* 6, is not contemporary: Bommelaer 1983. Plutarch, *Dem.* 29, has a probably apocryphal story about an admonitory dream the orator was supposed to have dreamt shortly before his suicide. When later centuries told tales about classical artists whose portraits of the gods were modelled on how they appeared in dreams, we may suspect a topos of Hellenistic or even Roman origin; Näf 2004, 53–54, gives cases but rightly suspects that they are the product of a later age.

171. Jouanna 1999 [1992], 373–416.

172. iv.86. The author of this treatise took a favourable view of divination *(mantike)* in general: i.12; contrast *De virginum morbis* viii.468 Littré.

of an afterthought[173]—that part of the correct response to some dreams is apotropaic prayer.[174]

But the same writer attributes most dreams to the body's condition, and with the exception just noted it is true to say that the 'references to divination in the Hippocratic treatises are critical and contemptuous'.[175] The author of *On the Sacred Disease* probably wrote that dreams are products of our brains.[176] The reason why a number of Hippocratic authors thought that dreams had some value or even great value in prognosis[177] was not that the gods had sent them or because of any other mysterious influence but because they arose from the patient's physical condition. The author of *Ancient Medicine* claims that if a man misses lunch, he will later on have 'wild and troubled' dreams;[178] nothing supernatural about that. In much later eras, some doctors were more accepting, as we shall see.

Ordinary and Extraordinary Athenians in the Fourth Century

We can move from what ordinary Athenians believed to what Plato and Aristotle thought (while keeping much about Aristotle for the next chapter). And in fact the philosophers provide some important evidence about ordinary men and women. Women, and men who are in danger or difficulty—so says the now elderly Plato, waxing indignant and rhetorical—are

173. See below, p. 246.

174. iv.87; iv.89 end, 90 end. The apparent inconsistency may be an indication that the work is a compilation (on this controversy see Cambiano 1980, 88); or perhaps the author later decided to make a concession to common opinion. My view is that the author saw no inconsistency.

175. Vlastos 1949, 286 n. 74; he cited *On Regimen* iv.87, *On the Regime in Acute Diseases* 8 [p. 39 Joly], *Prorrhetic* 2.1, and *On Diseases of Girls* [VIII p. 468 Littré].

176. Ch. 17 Jones = 14 Jouanna. In his 2003 edition Jouanna showed (pp. LXXIV–LXXXVII) that the MS (M) that reads *enhupnia* ('dreams') in this passage is at least as worthy of respect as the MS ([Gk] theta) that reads *agrhupniai* ('fits of sleeplessness'), and he prints *enhupnia*, which clearly gives a better sense.

177. *On Regimen* iii.71, iv.90; *Humours* 4; and see Chapter IV. Oberhelman 1983, 36, was in error when he used the latter passage to show that 'Hippocrates' accepted dream divination. His claim that 'nearly every ancient physician' 'accepted the validity of the curative directives revealed in god-sent dreams' is just the type of misleading generalization that this chapter aims to eliminate.

178. *Ancient Medicine* 10.

in the habit of engaging in all sorts of private religious practices, and we must stop them doing so.[179]

> And the terror they feel when they see apparitions, either in dreams or awake, or when they recall a whole series of visions, leads them to seek remedies for each of these visions, with the result that they found altars and shrines in open spaces or anywhere where such an incident has occurred, and fill every house and village with them.

In other words, a certain number of Athenians did such things. More soberly, Aristotle remarked at the beginning of his book *On Prophecy through Sleep* that 'all or many people presume that dreams have something significant about them' *(echein ti semeiodes).*[180] We may suppose that he meant some dreams, the interesting ones, not all dreams whatsoever.

How does this fit the other evidence? An Athenian might interpret a dream as requiring him to set up a fairly elaborate dedication to a 'hero'.[181] You might think of taking action in response to a very unpleasant dream. In Xenophon's *Symposium* Callias teases Charmides about his praise of poverty:[182] 'Do you actually pray then that you will never be rich, and if you have a good dream, do you make an apotropaic sacrifice?' In other words, an educated Athenian might think of making a sacrifice if he had a particularly evil-seeming dream. In the *Duskolos* of Menander an inauspicious-seeming dream of the god Pan leads a woman of exceptional means to order a sacrifice at a country shrine, in order to make 'the frightening thing turn out for the better'[183]—not perhaps a typical scene of Attic life, but quite probably a reflection of real fears. In the same author's *Shield*, on the other hand, dreams are a shorthand for illusions.[184]

Every time he dreams, says Theophrastus, the superstitious person asks the interpreter which god or goddess he should sacrifice to,[185] that is

179. *Laws* x.909e–910a.

180. 1.462b14–15. 'Presume', I think, rather than 'suppose' (D. Gallop), and 'something significant about them' rather than 'qualche significato' (L. Repici).

181. For a new example see Camp 2004, who lists parallels (133); the dedicant was evidently a successful shoe-maker with several employees. The date: second quarter of the fourth century.

182. iv.33.

183. Lines 402–455, esp. 418 (Pan has a special role in this play).

184. Lines 358–359.

185. *Char.* 16.11 Some are reluctant to translate *deisidaimon* simply as 'superstitious', but no single word serves better. On Theophrastus' conception of *deisidaimonia* see D. B. Martin 2004, ch. 3. Van Straten 1976, 14, was misguided to belittle this passage, but it only

to say *some* people *sometimes* asked for advice on this point.[186] (His dreams are among the boring things the talkative man insists on recounting to strangers.)[187]

Yet no Athenian pleader is known to have explained anyone's behaviour to the jurymen by reference to visions in the night,[188] and no Greek politician or general is known to have invoked a dream or a prophet's dream-interpretation as a reason for action or inaction—not even Xenophon,[189] even though, as we shall shortly see, he professed to believe that dreams could sometimes be genuine omens. When Aeschines said that his enemy Demosthenes, in a political speech, had recounted dreams (one dreamt by a Sicilian priestess and one of his own), he was trying to discredit him[190]— for dreams were not good proof; Demosthenes' published speeches contain no such stories, and it may all have been Aeschines' slander. Most probably, however, actual orators did occasionally exploit dream stories,[191]

---

criticizes extreme behaviour, not all belief in the predictive power of dreams. Those who refer to this text (e.g. Näf 2004, 48) frequently claim that Theophrastus regards it a superstitious to take any dream to an interpreter; not so. Presumably Theophrastus' monograph *On Sleep and Dreams* (Diogenes Laertius v.45) explained dreams naturalistically.

186. Another Peripatetic, Demetrius of Phalerum, is said by Artemidorus (ii.44) to have written five books on dreams that had come true, mostly about cures brought about by Serapis, but this seems likely to be erroneous (no such books are mentioned in Diogenes Laertius' list of his works; not that the list is complete—see Sollenberger 2000, 312). Cf. Del Corno 1969, 138–139. Demetrius wrote paeans in honour of Serapis after the god cured him of blindness in Alexandria (Diogenes Laertius v.76), and this may be the origin of Artemidorus' assertion, especially as Diogenes says that the paeans were still sung in his own time.

187. *Char.* 3.2.

188. Näf 2004, 53, says that references in Attic orators show that serious attention was paid to dreams in the public sphere, but his only evidence, the case of Euxenippus (to be discussed shortly), falls far short of proving this. Mikalson 1983, 48, is by contrast admirably precise: noting the absence of references to oracles, omens and prophets in the published speeches of Athenian litigants, he concludes: 'Either Athenians of the period did not regularly practise divination in their personal lives outside of matters of grave physical danger or religious uncertainty, or such practices lacked, to a certain extent, public respectability and acceptance'. He prefers the latter alternative.

189. Näf 2004, 47, supposes that the Lyceum at Athens was decorated with depictions of dreams, which results from using an obviously inferior text of Xenophon, *Anab.* vii.8.1 (the text probably said that Cleagoras painted 'wall-paintings' [*entoichia*] there, not 'dreams').

190. ii.10, iii.77 ('Zeus and Athena, the gods by whom he perjures himself by day—he says he talks to them by night and they tell him the future'), 219.

191. Parker 2005, 114, leaves this issue unresolved.

while excluding them from the more solemn and lasting medium of the written text.[192] In military affairs, purported dreams were occasionally useful for encouraging the troops, but they would not be relied on to the extent of influencing actual orders.[193]

To return briefly to Xenophon, whom we might think of, not without risk, as fairly typical of the educated Athenians of his generation (born about 430). He most definitely believed that the gods warn the people they want to warn by means of sacrifices, oracles, voices and also dreams, and that such warnings can be important in time of war.[194] The authoritative Cyrus is made to say that it is in sleep that humans foresee the future, and he himself receives a dream foretelling his death.[195] In the greatest crisis in the *Anabasis*, when the Greeks are far from home and have lost their leaders, Xenophon dreamt, so he says, that a thunderbolt fell on his father's house, which all caught fire; he awoke in fright, but

> he [he writes of himself in the third person] thought that in some respects the dream was a good one, because in the midst of his difficulties and dangers he had dreamed of a great light from Zeus; but in other respects he was alarmed by it. . . . But what kind of experience it is to have a dream like this can be seen from what happened after the dream.[196]

What happened afterwards was this: Xenophon decided that he should take command of one regiment of the Greek army, and persuaded it to elect him and to follow his advice, making some seven speeches,[197] some of them quite long, in which he makes no mention whatsoever of this dream—which suggests that it would not have done him any good with an assortment of Greek soldiers. We are, then, in something of a dilemma: did Xenophon feel the psychological effects of a real dream, or did he improve an actual dream in order to impress his readers? Somewhat later (but only

---

192. Thus Isocrates ix.21 ostentatiously leaves out the favourable dreams concerning the birth of King Evagoras, not because he disbelieves them, he says, but to free of any suspicion of inventing.

193. Cf. Pritchett 1979, 92–101.

194. *Hipparch.* ix.9. It is curious that dreams are absent from a similar list of methods of divine communication in *Mem.* i.1.3. For Xenophon's pious belief in nondream divination see Bowden 2004, 232–238, Burkert 2005, 41–42.

195. *Cyr.* viii.7.21 and 2 respectively.

196. *Anab.* iii.1.11–13. The last remark remains somewhat enigmatic.

197. *Anab.* iii.1–2.

on one other occasion in the *Anabasis*) Xenophon again reports a dream: he dreamt an auspicious dream before a difficult and contested river-crossing, and reported it to a fellow-officer; a favourable turn of events followed (two soldiers discovered a ford). He and his attendants then poured a libation and prayed to the gods for a successful crossing, which duly took place. In both these cases we might say that dreams contributed a little to morale and nothing to decision-making; they were also intended to impress the reader—Xenophon was among those whom the gods cared to help.

An intriguing incident occurred in Attica in the 330s: having reacquired the territory of Oropus, which included an important shrine of the healing god Amphiaraus, the Athenians found themselves having to determine whether a certain mountain in that territory could be exploited by their own citizens or belonged to the god. In order to decide this, they despatched three citizens to sleep in Amphiaraus' temple, in the expectation that he would reveal the answer to them in a dream. We know of all this because one of the sleepers, Euxenippus, was later impeached and had the orator Hypereides speak in his defence.[198] Apparently Euxenippus—who we happen to know was particularly attached to the Oropian shrine of Amphiaraus[199]—claimed to have dreamt an informative dream, but those whose interests were not served said that he was lying. What matters here is that the *demos* proposed to trust a dream in a matter of practical import;[200] what very much reduces the significance of that choice, on the other hand, is that Amphiaraus, like Asclepius, was an incubation deity who might be particularly expected to respond since his own property rights were in question.[201]

Which brings us back to the realm of medicine. When Plato wrote of the weak and those in danger, he was presumably thinking in part of the sick and infirm. Medicine was plainly an area in which dream-instructions might be severely needed. The fourth-century Attic evidence includes, besides Aristophanes' *Wealth*, reliefs from the Asklepieion of Piraeus

198. Hypereides iv (see esp. sec. 3—a dream is a trivial subject for an impeachment court—,14–18).

199. He made a dedication there to Hygieia (Good Health), *SEG* xv (1958), no. 291; unfortunately we do not know the relative chronology of these events.

200. The *demos* is specified in Hypereides iv.14.

201. Did the *demos* hope that all three of its emissaries would dream the same dream—or that an incubant had one chance in three of receiving a message (they could have sent say ten sleepers)?

Plate 9. Amphiaraos appearing to a sleeping Patient, who appears to be shown three times (the snake who licks him is the god's helper). Dedication by the patient Archinos, from the shrine of Amphiaraos, Oropus (Attica), first half of the fourth century BC. The inscription: *IG* II/III².4394. Athens, National Museum, inv.3369. Photo: Emile, Deutsches Archäologisches Institut, Athens.

(Plate 3, page 33) and the temple of Amphiaraus at Oropus (Plate 9),[202] good evidence that some at least among the men of property believed that the two gods in question communicated with them by sending dreams. And we also have to take into account the many who must have gone to such shrines and come away disappointed, though not necessarily disillu-

202. Guidorizzi 1988, pls. IX and VIII, Comella 2002, 73 and 132, Näf 2004, figs. 10 and 11.

203. Here we can turn on its head a remark sometimes attributed to Diogenes, who supposedly pointed out, with respect to the numerous dedications on Samothrace, that the many disappointed pilgrims were not represented (Diogenes Laertius vi.59); what matters

sioned.[203] The really rich epigraphical material comes not from Attica but from Epidaurus, which was Asclepius' capital. Two fourth-century *stelai* describe some forty-three incubation miracles, such as the ones quoted in Chapters I and II.[204] It is very striking that the pilgrims who experienced these cures came not only from nearby but from such relatively distant places as Torone and Thasos in the north and Lampsacos, Mytilene and Cnidos on the other side of the Aegean. Yet it is not easy to say how widely or deeply Athenians believed that Asclepius or Amphiaraus were willing to bring about helpful dreams; the analogy of Lourdes, the centre of a large industry, may be relevant. Few educated persons other than ecclesiastics can believe that it is the scene of constant miracles.

There is little evidence that fourth-century medical writers, even those—a minority, I would suppose—who thought that some dreams came from the gods (see above), believed in Asclepian incubation. And since the Hippocratic monographs mostly had a persuasive function, not just the ostensibly expository function of a modern scientific text—they were aimed partly at prospective pupils and clients, among others[205]—they could not depart very far from the presuppositions of their readers or hearers. The more knowledgeable kind of Athenian was not usually an innocent believer in Asclepian dreams.

After discussing the views of Plato and Aristotle, we are about to leave Athens and consider the wider Greek world in the brilliantly variegated Hellenistic age. Two almost mythical figures stand at its entrance, Diogenes of Sinope and Alexander of Macedon. Both of them, as it happens, have something to offer on the topic at hand. Diogenes—the ancient world's prime teller of inconvenient truths—knew what to think: 'To those who were excited about their dreams he would say that they did not care about what they did while awake, but got very busy about the things they imagined in their sleep'.[206] Let us suppose that this was Diogenes' authentic sentiment; if so, it will plainly serve as evidence that concern about dreams was quite general. As for Alexander, his opinions cannot be

---

for us is that they had hoped (and to be disappointed was not necessarily to be disillusioned).

204. Above, pp. 31, 108.

205. Cf. Lloyd 1992, 7.

206. Diogenes Laertius vi.43 (but he was not 'cynical', pace van Straten 1976, 14, which would suggest that his opinions were marginal—and that is not quite true).

known.[207] Plutarch's life naturally includes several dreams,[208] but the more sober account by Arrian recounts only one, which occurred when Alexander needed to encourage his troops during the difficult siege of Tyre: Heracles stretched out his hand and welcomed him into the city.[209] Alexander was a man of his age in that he had a favourite seer, Aristander of Telmessus.[210] And also in that there is little or no sign that as a man of intelligence he believed in predictive dreams. But when Alexander was dying, some of his courtiers passed the night in an incubation shrine to ask the god (whose identity is disputed) whether they should bring the king there; they were told to leave him where he was.[211] It was the kind of step a Macedonian officer might take in desperation.

Plato and Aristotle

What did Plato think? At first inspection, his views seem inconsistent (and not because of any chronological development). The fact that Cicero allows a speaker in *On Divination* to enroll Socrates and Plato among those who believed in the predictive power of certain dreams is not of great significance,[212] but Plato had in fact made no less a person than Diotima, not to mention Socrates, put trust in them: *daimones* bring messages from the gods.[213] In *Republic* IV, Socrates is shown using the word *enhupnion* to refer to a splendid ideal.[214] It was because of dreams as well as other kinds of

207. Näf 2004, 66.

208. Chs. 24, 26, 50.

209. *Anab.* ii.18. Bosworth ad loc. remarks that this dream 'seems to be a piece of contemporary propaganda (Alexander's ancestor yielding up the city)'.

210. Näf 2004, 64–65. Aristander leads Weber 1999, 13, to the conclusion that Alexander was 'fundamentally interested' in his dreams (sc. as being prophetic), but we know nothing of his interpreting dreams.

211. Arrian, *Anab.* vii.26, Plutarch, *Alex.* 76, etc.

212. *De div.* i.60–61, paraphrasing *Rep.* ix.571c–572b, but tendentiously making Plato say that it is easier to have veridical dreams than he really did; this of course suits the argument of the Quintus figure. In i.5 Cicero in his own person included 'all the Socratics' among those who accepted divination in general; but it is clear that he exaggerated the philosophers' support for divination, presumably to build up the opposition that his dialogue was planning to overcome. Ps.-Galen, *Hist.Philos.* 105 = Doxographi Graeci p. 639 Diels, similarly mispresents Plato's opinion.

213. 'And the man who is wise about such things is *daimonios*', inspired, *Symp.* 203a. Cf. Plato, *Tim.* 71de.

214. iv.443b: nothing less than the ideal state that embodies justice.

prophecy that Socrates persecuted the Athenians with questions.[215] Platonic dialogues sometimes make Socrates introduce dreams at climactic moments—in the *Theaetetus*, the *Symposium*, and the *Charmides*.[216] His aim may have been to add to the superhuman stature of the master's teaching. And this could be rationalized, as we shall see in a moment. One may suspect, however, that it was the historical Socrates whose practice is represented here, for at Athens it was not in fact particularly heroic to have meaningful dreams.

On the other hand, Plato seems to have thought that dream-content was influenced by diet,[217] he used a dream as a figure of speech for something subject to diverse interpretations *(amphisbetesimos)*[218] and he otherwise ranked dream-knowledge very low.[219] It is typical that in the *Politicus* the Eleatic Stranger says that he was not dreaming when he maintained that such-and-such, meaning that he was not wrong.[220] And while earlier writers had occasionally noticed that dreams sometimes seem to fulfil people's desires,[221] Plato is the earliest surviving writer to have elaborated the notion that (some) dreams are wish-fulfilments.[222]

There is no insoluble puzzle here,[223] for while most people's dreams are without value, in Plato's eyes, the dreams of the man or woman in whom the reasoning element is dominant can—thanks to the gods—yield important truths:[224]

215. *Apol.* 33c. This he took to be a divine order.

216. *Theaet.* 201d–202c, *Symp.* l.c., *Charm.* 173a (where he brings in the Gates of Horn and Ivory); see further Desjardins 1981, 110–112, according to whom 'the deliberate introduction [by Plato] of material as being the *content* of a dream is invariably significant . . . a "dream" represents a kind of divine or oracular statement which . . . is the vehicle of important, if riddling, truth' (110).

217. *Rep.* ix.571c–572b.

218. *Symp.* 175e.

219. See *Lys.* 218c, *Rep.* v.476c, vii.520c, *Tim.* 52bc, *Laws* xii.969b, *Theaet.* 158b, 190b, 208b, Phil. 65e. See further Vegléris 1982, 53. In *Meno* 85c (correct) opinions of uncertain origin are said to have arrived as in a dream.

220. *Pol.* 290b.

221. Homer, *Od.* xx.87. On [Hippocrates], *On Regimen* iv.93, see below, p. 245.

222. *Rep.* ix.571cd, *Tim.* 45d–46a. For some later parallels see Von Staden 1989, 306 n. 236.

223. Desjardins 1981 seems to me the best guide to this matter. See also Burnyeat 1970, Gallop 1971, Vegléris 1982, Rotondaro 1998.

224. Plato, *Rep.* ix.571d–572b (somewhat simplified). In Chapter I we met the dreams of Socrates described in the *Crito* and the *Phaedo*.

But when a man of healthy and self-controlled character, before he goes to sleep, has awakened his own reasoning faculty and given it its fill of excellent arguments and inquiries, and reached awareness of himself (?) *(sunnoia)* (his desires he has neither starved nor indulged, so that they sink to rest and don't plague the highest part of him. . ., but leave it to its endeavours to apprehend things still unknown to it, whether past, present or future . . .). . . . Thus he goes to rest . . . and in such a state he grasps the truth and is exempt from imagining lawless dreams.[225]

Years later, in the *Timaeus,* he gives a very different view, suitable to the Pythagorean who is made to express it:[226]

For our makers, remembering that their father had ordered them to make human beings as perfect as possible, rectified even the base element in us [the 'desiring' part], and gave it the power of prophecy so that it might have some apprehension of truth. And there is sufficient evidence that god gave this power to man's unthinking part; no one who is thinking properly can achieve inspired and true prophecy, but only when the power of our understanding is inhibited in sleep, or when he is in an abnormal condition owing to disease or divine inspiration. And it is the function of someone in his right mind to construe what is remembered of utterances made in dream or waking by those who have the gift of divine inspiration . . . and to discern in what way and for whom they are significant.

The contrast between these ideas and those expressed in the bulk of Plato's work is a complex problem which we can avoid confronting here,[227] for Plato's own assumptions and the views he attributes to Socrates are both reasonably clear.

The possibility that dreams could tell the truth seems to have puzzled Aristotle considerably.[228] Seeking for something that will serve as a paradigm of falseness *(pseudos),* one of the two things he lights on is dreams *(enhupnia):* they exist but they are not what they seem.[229] He maintains

---

225. It is unclear what 'grasping the truth' might mean here. Zeno then draws the 'logical' conclusion: if your dreams become less 'immoral', you are making moral progress (*SVF* fr. 234, vol. I p. 56).

226. *Tim.* 71d–72a.

227. For a recent account, dealing with this passage of the *Timaeus,* see Lorenz 2006, 100–101. See especially van Lieshout 1980, 103–142.

228. The best analysis is that of van der Eijk 2005, 186–193.

229. *Metaph.* iv.29.1024b23–24.

that it is difficult to reject predictive dreams because all or most people 'presume that they have something significant about them', but also difficult to believe in them.[230] He argues that most supposedly 'fulfilled' dreams are only fulfilled by coincidence; and most dreams are not fulfilled at all. In *On Prophecy through Sleep* he attempts to explain why some dreams come true,[231] his most emphatic point being that such dreams are not sent by gods. They could not be, since other animals dream too.[232] 'Nevertheless they are daemonic; for nature is daemonic not divine'.[233] Their daemonic origin is proved by the fact that quite commonplace people—whom the gods would not bother with, he thinks—have veridical dreams. For some people do have veridical dreams, and he sets out to describe the mental and psychological characteristics of such people.[234] His reasoning will be described and contextualized in much more detail in Chapter IV: the important point for now is that in his view some dreams are in fact correct predictions.

It is quite wrong incidentally to infer from the story about Aristotle and the dream of his friend Eudemus recounted by Cicero[235] that Aristotle was at one time inclined to think that dreams were inspired by the gods.[236] While Eudemus the Cypriot was visiting Pherae during the tyranny of Alexander, he fell desperately ill; he dreamt that a handsome young man told them that he would recover quickly, that Alexander would soon die, and that five years later he would return home. The first two predictions came true, and for the speaker in the *De divinatione* (for Aristotle too?) the third too, since when Eudemus died five years later in Sicily he could in a sense be said to have gone home. But Cicero probably had this story not directly from Aristotle, rather from a Stoic who used the story to suggest what no other source comes close to suggesting, that the great philosopher

---

230. *De div. per somnum* 1.462b12–16.

231. 2.463b12–464b6.

232. 2.463b12–13.

233. I suspect that Gallop 1996, 182, was mistaken when he concluded that the term *daimonion* does not 'carry any connotation of the "supernatural"' (except that a Greek would not contrast the *daimones* with 'nature'). Gallop suggests that the meaning is 'uncanny'.

234. It is not difficult to read Aristotle's views too rationalistically here: Gallop, author of a fine edition of this treatise, maintains that Aristotle argues that 'precognitive' dreams are 'no more than the long arm of coincidence' (p. 44). Repici 2003, 47–53, slips into the same error.

235. *De div.* i.53, our only source for this. See further Wardle 2006, 240.

236. So C. Lévy 1997, 325.

shared the commonest Stoic view about dream-divination (which was favourable).[237] And it is easy to see what the Aristotle of the *Parva Naturalia* would have said about the Eudemus story: it proves nothing, because the sick sometimes recover and tyrants are quite often assassinated—these were coincidences; as for the third 'fulfilment', it was merely a play on words.[238]

Nonetheless dreams may be useful. 'Even medical experts', says Aristotle, 'say that one should pay extremely close attention to dreams'[239]— potentially at least, they have diagnostic value, he appears to think. The approach is strictly physiological. But then the ground shifts. Sometimes we dream about actions we are going to perform.[240] And now we come to the mental and psychological characteristics of those who foresee things in dreams: some mad people *(ekstatikoi)* have this capacity. Friends are liable to have straight dreams about friends, and the *melancholikoi* (not melancholy people in a modern sense, but people with too much black bile who are therefore manic)[241] 'hit the target' (this may remind us of the passage in the *Timaeus* quoted above, even though it does not concern the *melancholikoi).*[242] The most skilful judge *(krites)* of dreams is the man who can see resemblances—which presupposes, apparently, that predictive dreams do occur. It should be emphasized, however, that Aristotle steadfastly maintains that *most* apparently truth-telling dreams are coincidences.[243]

Hellenistic Impressions

In 257 BC Apollonius, the 'finance minister' of King Ptolemy II Philadelphus, received a letter from one Zoilos of Aspendos, evidently an important person, telling him that Serapis had twice appeared to Zoilos in dreams telling him to build a temple for the god somewhere in the Ptolemaic do-

237. This tale has lead scholars far astray: for useful discussion see Repici 1991, van der Eijk 1994, 91–92. Aristotle's *Eudemus,* from which this story is sometimes said to derive, was in any case a dialogue, perhaps expressing diverse views.

238. Furthermore, it has been suggested that Aristotle's *Eudemus* 'is strongly modelled on . . . Socrates in Plato's *Phaedo*' (Bos 2003, 239).

239. *De div. per somnum* 1.463a5–6.

240. 1.463a21–31.

241. For this translation see below, p. 000.

242. He says the same in effect at *EE* viii.2.1248a39–40. Cf. van der Eijk 2005, 190, on the possible reasons why Aristotle thought this.

243. 1.463b1: the majority *(ta polla),* not just 'molti' (Repici, who elsewhere paraphrases 'in gran parte', p. 44).

main, and had punished him with successive illnesses for delaying; he now asked Apollonius to take the matter in hand.[244] 'Don't worry about the cost . . . for I shall join in taking charge of all this'. Dreamers could apparently claim very great authority in the Ptolemaic court (but we have no idea whether Apollonius cooperated).[245]

A recent writer was brave enough to generalize about Hellenistic beliefs about dreams: dream-prophecy, he claimed, had 'more and more effects'.[246] Another, though somewhat more cautious, still felt able to generalize.[247] The huge new territorial diffusion of the Greeks, and the non-Greek cultural influences that some of them felt as a result of this diffusion, challenge us to consider the evidence more systematically. What we must do, in default of any contemporary generalization, is to consider first those pieces of evidence that have some chance of reflecting a widespread view; then we can consider known dream-interpreters and individual religious gestures; and finally individual expressions of opinion, including those of the philosophers (but we may note at once the favour which most Stoics and even Peripatetics showed towards predictive dreams).

Greeks in this era sought healing and prophecy in a number of new places, such as the Serapaeum at Memphis. But whether this means that the 'average' Greek was more receptive to revelatory dreams than before is very hard to say. We should resist any assumption that Hellenistic Greeks were more religious than their predecessors.[248] We also need to take notice of the 'epigraphic habit', in other words we must not assume that more dedications inscribed on the orders of dreams necessarily means a strengthening of belief.

A source problem faces us at once: Plautus presents us with a world in which dream-interpretation is an everyday occurrence—much more than Menander does. The four dreams described in most detail in Plautus' comedies have plausibly been attributed by most scholars to his frequent models

244. *P.Cair.Zen.* I.59034. For further bibliography see Totti 1985, 160 (who reprints the text), and Weber 1998, 28 n. 23. The case is summarized by Bresciani 2005, 104–105.

245. We must also wonder, with Z. Stewart 1977, 544, how much this letter was inspired by personal ambition.

246. Näf 2004, 63. Does this mean more in 30 BC than in 323?

247. Weber 1998 reaches the vague conclusion that the dreams were interesting to all social groups in the Hellenistic world and gave rise to actions of very considerable consequence.

248. See Pakkanen 1996, 113. For a brief but balanced discussion of Hellenistic religiosity see Graf 1995.

Philemon and Diphilus, approximate contemporaries of Menander[249]—but are they a reflection of late-fourth-century Attic life or a dramatic convention, or both? Plautus' characters assume that anyone can learn to interpret dreams,[250] and also that dreams are commonly nonsense (see below). No conclusion is secure, except that New Comedy audiences were thoroughly familiar with the idea that ordinary people could sometimes have truth-telling dreams.

Hellenistic rulers from time to time attempted to exploit dream prophecies. Most of these stories concern dreams about Alexander of Macedon,[251] and in some cases they may indeed have been contemporary and hence useful indicators, to some extent, of the attitudes of their original audiences.[252] Eumenes of Cardia, for example, claimed that he had dreamt of Alexander (who had died some five years before) holding a council and giving orders; this helped the non-Macedonian Eumenes to raise his status among the Macedonian commanders (Plutarch names the two principal figures in question), and to some extent it worked.[253] But those who were to be impressed were quite far from being a cross-section of Greeks—and Greeks may indeed have thought that the Macedonians had been rather successfully hoodwinked. And when Hellenistic rulers got down to the serious business of warfare they showed themselves exceedingly *un*interested in dream-predictions.[254] Apart from Judah Maccabee and Mithridates VI of Pontus, neither of them Greeks, they also made rather little political use of dreams.[255]

The Ptolemies are the most intriguing case. We saw earlier how King Ptolemy Soter apparently used the authority of a dream to establish the cult of Serapis.[256] His great-grandson, Ptolemy IV Philopator, is known

249. For these passages, see below, p. 178.

250. Traill 2004, 123.

251. See the material gathered by Näf 2004, 68–72.

252. This may well be true of those stories that are known only from Plutarch, but these are very uncertain indicators of Hellenistic opinion. The plainly apocryphal dream-story about Seleucus I in Appian *Syr.* 56 must be Hellenistic—who after the fall of the Seleucid monarchy would have wanted to invent it?

253. Diodorus Siculus xviii.60–61, Nepos, *Eum.* 7, Plutarch, *Eum.* 13 (who actually says for once that Eumenes' actions were an exploitation of superstition, *deisidaimonia*), etc.

254. Weber 1999, 28.

255. Weber 1999, 29; but he separates politics and religion a little too much.

256. It is to be noted that Ptolemy consulted Egyptian priests as well as Greeks: see H. Heubner's note on Tacitus, *Hist.* iv.83 (pp. 191–192).

from a trilingual inscription, the Pithom Stele, to have dreamt before the Battle of Raphia (217) that the gods visited him, promising victory. His government commemorated this 'fact' in hieroglyphics, demotic Egyptian and Greek.[257] It may be suggested that the realm of the Ptolemies was particularly favourable to such a technique.[258]

A dream could be invoked to lend authority to a religious-political action on an ordinary Aegean island. Some time in the third century, when the ex-soldier Artemidorus of Perge set up an altar to Harmony (Homonoia) in a substantial sanctuary on the island of Thera, he said that he did so 'according to a dream';[259] no doubt his purpose was to seal the suppression of unrest that followed the Ptolemaic occupation of the place,[260] and the dream gave him extra religious authority. The Homonoia altar seems to have been the centrepiece of Artemidorus' building activities at this site.[261] Once again we happen to be in Ptolemaic territory.

Still in search of widespread opinions, we can try some literary texts, for example a genre poem to be found in the corpus of Theocritus. Two poor fishermen discuss a favourable dream, taking it for granted that one can learn to interpret dreams; but the moral is 'If you want a golden fish, go catch it, don't just dream about it'.[262] Even fishermen know that dreams are illusions—yet it is significant that this was thought to be worth saying.[263] Other literary practice is less relevant here, but we cannot ignore the fact

---

257. Weber 1999, 8–9. The inscription: Thissen 1966 (he lists the dreams attributed to previous kings of Egypt, 51–53). On Chrysermos, the physician and *exegetes* (seer) of Ptolemy VI, see Weber 27–28; he may have interpreted dreams.

258. *P. Goodspeed* 3 (= *Epistulae Privatae Graecae* ed. S. Witkowski, no. 30), a third-century letter from one Greek to another quoting a divine dream-description in demotic, suggests that Greeks in Egypt may have been encouraged by their surroundings to take dreams still more seriously.

259. *IG* XII.3 Suppl.1336.

260. As suggested by Wilamowitz; see Thériault 1996, 28, Weber 1998, 27. For Artemidorus' career see Chaniotis 2005, 153–154.

261. Graf 1995, 107–112.

262. Ps.-Theocritus 21; it should be noted that this poem has occasionally been given a Roman date. Learning: line 29. But there is some connection between what you have eaten and what you dream: lines 40–41. If you swore an oath in a dream, you did not really swear it: line 63. The moral: lines 63–67. Fishermen were by convention uneducated—did that make them suitable persons to think that a dream was worth discussing?

263. Herodas' *Mimiamb* VIII is an account of a dream, but will not support any relevant conclusion, the text being badly mutilated.

that Posidippus, Callimachus, Apollonius of Rhodes and Moschus all made use of the dream motif.[264]

The most cited evidence concerns religious centres such as Epidaurus and Memphis, which sometimes foretold the future as well as providing healing.[265] It seems to be precisely at religious centres that dream-interpreters flourished most, quite naturally. Thus it is at Memphis that we find the Cretan dream-interpreter's shingle mentioned before,[266] and other evidence concerns Delos.[267] How matters stood with such people in an ordinary Hellenistic city is another matter.

The temple of Serapis at Delos is the source for yet another dream-story, contained in the so-called Delian Serapis-aretalogy put up by the priest, another Apollonius. Apollonius was told by Serapis in a dream to build him a temple, and when people put obstacles in Apollonius' way Serapis appeared to him a second time.[268] But while this tells us something about Serapis cult, it hardly helps to settle our central problem.[269]

The priests of Athena at Lindos recorded her occasional epiphanies,[270] including one that took place during the great siege of Rhodes by Demetrius the Besieger in 305–304; she was understood to have given the sensible advice that Rhodes should invoke the help of King Ptolemy Soter.

Just as Zoilos and Artemidorus of Perge claimed to have received instructions in dreams, so did a number of others. Renberg shows clearly that it is in the second century BC that the number of Greek inscriptions reporting divine instructions in dreams becomes really noteworthy, but in his

264. For the first two see Chapter I; for Apollonius see Kessels 1982 (a fine discussion); for Moschus see *Europa* 1–27.

265. Miracle XLVI at Epidaurus, e.g., is about locating a treasure (*IG* IV².1.123). Near Nysa in the valley of the Maeander, says Strabo (xiv.649–650), there is a shrine of Pluto, with nearby a cave called the Charonion, where priests sleep and dream cures which they pass on to believers; 'and they often bring the sick into the cave and leave there . . . Sometimes the sick pay attention to their own dreams' while still making use of the priests. A full catalogue of such shrines is needed.

266. Also another *enhupniokrites* in 161 BC: *UPZ* I.84, line 79; he was a trader in textiles too, which suggests the limitations of the dream-interpreting business.

267. Above, p. 135. Some more evidence for dream-interpretation in Hellenistic Delos seems to emerge from the local writer Semos, *FGrH* 396 F 4. Dedications made there in obedience to dreams are also relevant: see below.

268. *IG* XI.4.1299.

269. Engelmann 1975, 2, claimed that Apollonius remained culturally Egyptian.

270. Above, p. 26.

view the increase merely corresponds to the overall production of Greek inscriptions[271]—so it can hardly be taken as an indication of a change in belief or in religious practice.

In the previous chapter we met the dream-descriptions of Ptolemaios son of Glaucias of the Memphis Serapaeum. What is also worth mentioning is that one of the other documents in this archive is a letter to Ptolemaios from his brother Apollonios expressing complete disillusionment with predictive dreams: 'we have failed, being misled by the gods and trusting dreams'.[272] This attitude is not generalizable either.

No writers, perhaps, had smaller audiences than the historians, but Timaeus and Polybius may nonetheless have been fairly representative of that large part of the Greek intelligentsia of their time that was not obsessed with religion. Polybius was, as one might expect, thoroughly hardnosed on this subject: he criticizes Timaeus for including in his history a great quantity of 'dreams, prodigies, incredible tales, and in short ignoble superstition and womanish love of the marvellous'.[273] Like most of what Polybius had to say about the man of Tauromenium, this was probably unfair: the 164 Jacoby fragments of Timaeus only contain one definite reference on his part to a dream.[274] Later Polybius reinforces this point of view—dreams are a waste of time for the historian.[275] He pours scorn on the idea that Scipio Africanus had been guided by 'dreams and omens' in building the Roman Empire (which obviously indicates that others had claimed exactly that),[276] and told with approval the story that Scipio encouraged his troops at New Carthage by telling them how Neptune ('Poseidon') had appeared in a dream and promised his help.[277] He also tells approvingly how, in order to be able to stand prematurely for the aedileship, Scipio lyingly told his mother that he had had a certain predictive

271. All this: Renberg 2003, 143.

272. *UPZ* I.70, recto, lines 27–30.

273. xii.24.5. He mentions some himself, Philip V's (v.108.5—a metaphor perhaps), as well as Scipio's.

274. *FGrH* 566 F 29. This fragment has generated a considerable bibliography: see Weber 1999, 9 n. 30. Other dreams in Hellenistic historians: Kragelund 2001, 53 n. 4.

275. xxxiii.21. More hostility towards dreaming: xii.12b.1, xviii.46.7 (paraphrased by Livy xxxiii.32.7). A bad conscience produces bad dreams: xviii.15.12–13.

276. x.2.9.

277. x.11.7. Polybius does not say in so many words that the dream was invented, but the implication is clear. See below on the meaning of this story for Roman thinking.

dream.[278] But there were also Hellenistic historians who appear to have re-counted certain dreams in a respectful fashion, as Silenus of Caleacte prob-ably did in the case of the dream of his hero Hannibal.[279] We must be intrigued by the fact that Polybius twice states or implies that women are particularly liable to believe stories about dreams—he writes that Scipio's mother exhibited 'womanly emotion' when her son told her about his dream, and hence was deceived.[280] This was something of a Hellenistic cliché. Polybius' older contemporary Agatharchides cites the Seleucid queen Stratonice as an example of foolish superstition because she obeyed a dream, with fatal results.[281]

As to the specific dream theories of the major schools of philosophy, we shall examine them in more detail in the next chapter; what is of concern here is whether they can help us to generalize about Hellenistic opinion. The Stoics, first of all: according to Cicero, the leading Stoics, starting with Zeno, had accepted 'almost all' forms of divination; Chrysippus had written a volume about dreams, apparently all or most of it about divination, and there can be no doubt that he believed that some dreams at least were truth-telling. Chrysippus did not blush to make use of stories about truth-telling dreams,[282] but he also engaged in some aprioristic reasoning: the gods must know the future, and we believe that they are benevolent towards mankind, therefore they must wish to provide us with information by some intelligible means (we have little notion how if at all he explained that dreams are generally not clear premonitions).[283] He found it very conven-ient to explain dreams that had 'gone wrong' by reverting to the method of interpretation by contraries that we have traced back to Antiphon.[284] But

278. x.4.

279. *FGrH* 175 F 2. The story is analysed by D'Arco 2002; for Livy's treatment see below.

280. x.4.7.

281. *FGrH* 86 F 20 (from Josephus).

282. One about the murderous inn-keeper of Megara, who was given away by a dream that told accurately of the recent past and the immediate future, *SVF* II.1204–1205; an-other about an egg that showed the whereabouts of a treasure in two colours, white and yellow, i.e. silver and gold, *SVF* II.1201–1202; he may have quoted many others.

283. This is an abbreviated paraphrase of Cicero, *De div.* i.82–83 = *SVF* II.1192. Cicero knew how to counter these arguments: ibid. ii.101–102, 104–106.

284. Cicero, *De div.* ii.144–145 = *SVF* II.1206. Van Lieshout 1980, 186, inferred from *De div.* i.60 ('At multa falsa. Immo obscura fortasse nobis') that the Stoics thought that all dreams were truth-telling; that may be correct, but if they had done so we would perhaps

the Stoics were not in full agreement with each other: Cicero says that while Panaetius did not dare to say that divination was vacuous, he expressed his doubts, *dubitare se dixit*[285] (he was, however, the only important Stoic to take this line).[286] From the more reliable Diogenes Laertius on the other hand we learn that Panaetius held all divination to be 'without foundation',[287] and it is plain that Cicero has understated Panaetius' scepticism,[288] just as he had that of Plato. Poseidonius, however, was a believer.[289]

Now, the interplay between received opinions and philosophy is as complicated in this period as in any other. Starting probably with Aristotle, philosophers had bit by bit changed their educational role—unless we attribute most of the initiative to educated men who were their students or readers.[290] From Menander to Cicero, the Hellenistic world was populated with nonphilosophers who had absorbed significant quantities of serious philosophy. It is most improbable that so many Stoic philosophers would have maintained their attitude towards dream-divination if it had not been widely accepted as at least an occasional phenomenon, and no doubt those who believed in it, like 'Quintus Cicero' in the *De divinatione*, took some comfort in the notion that they had a certain amount of philosophical opinion on their side. But even 'Quintus Cicero' rejected the Stoic doctrine of divination as too 'superstitious',[291] and neither the Stoics nor any other philosophers had a good record of persuading people that their doctrines should be acted upon—who, for instance, ever acted on the Stoic view that health—not to mention wealth—is an 'indifferent'?

You could also be a respected Peripatetic and believe in the possibility of dream-prophecy. This may apply to the early followers of Aristotle such as

---

have expected to hear more of it from some anti-Stoic polemicist (and Tertullian would probably have mentioned it in *De anima* 46).

285. Cicero, *De div.* i.6, cf. *Acad.Pr.* ii.107.

286. *Acad.Pr.* loc. cit.

287. Diogenes Laertius vii.149 (fr. 73 van Straaten), where the use of technical language makes one think that Diogenes was well-informed (see further Pease on Cicero, loc. cit.). Epiphanius, *De fide* ix.45, says something similar about Panaetius and this became fr. 68 van Straaten; but a glance at Epiphanius' descriptions of the views of other non-Christian philosophers is enough to show that his testimony is worthless. Alesse 1994, 234 n. 40, reviews what scholars have said about Panaetius' opinions.

288. So already Schmekel 1892, 191 n. 1.

289. Below, p. 269.

290. I discussed this change briefly in Harris 2002, 366.

291. *De div.* ii.100.

Dicaearchus[292] and Strato,[293] and it applies more definitely to Cicero's contemporary Cratippus.[294] No doubt there were a number of educated Hellenistic persons who would more or less have agreed with 'Quintus Cicero' when he said that he found the Peripatetic view more convincing than that of the Stoics. 'They think that there is in the minds of men a kind of oracle [*oraculum aliquod*] on the basis of which people foresee things that will happen in the future, if the soul . . . is relaxed by sleep and moves freely and easily'.[295] Cratippus held that the soul of man was of divine origin, and that part of it moved around outside the body during sleep. The kernel of his argument seems to have been that since dreams have sometimes predicted the truth (he listed cases), their divinatory capacity really exists.[296] Cicero has no difficulty demolishing this reasoning, but one may suspect that it had a wide appeal.[297]

In so far as we know the opinions on this subject of Plato's successors in the Academy, they are those of Carneades, who was sceptical about divination in general[298] and is often supposed to have been the main source of the ideas in the second, sceptical, book of Cicero's *On Divination*.

The Epicureans meanwhile offered a purely naturalistic view of dreams: both Epicurus himself and all his followers were thorough-going sceptics about dream-prediction, as indeed about all forms of divination.[299] It so happens that we possess a work by one of Epicurus' disciples, Polystratus' *On Irrational Contempt of Common Opinions*, which specifies that there is no reason to be disturbed by dreams—but implicitly recognizes that many

---

292. In fact the evidence is not very clear in this case: Cicero (*De div.* i.5) says that Dicaearchus, who excluded other kinds of divination, left standing ('reliquit') dreams and mad inspiration (cf. i.113, ii.100); the other sources (edited once by F. Wehrli, and now by D. C. Mirhady) are not much use. For discussion see Dodds 1951, 134 n. 117, Del Corno 1969, 161–163, Sharples 2000, 163–173.

293. He wrote a book about dreams (Diogenes Laertius v.59, Tertullian, *De anima* 46), but little is known of its contents (it seems to have been unknown to Cicero), and he may have been as sceptical as Aristotle. Cf. Del Corno 1969, 145–146.

294. For whose views see Del Corno 1969, 76–77, 158–160.

295. *De div.* ii.100.

296. i.70–71 (cf. ii.107). He is said to have claimed that 'innumerable' prophecies had come true, and very many of these must have been dream-prophecies.

297. It should be mentioned, however, that Cratippus' view of this matter left very few traces outside Cicero.

298. *De div.* ii.9–10.

299. See Pease on Cicero, *De div.* i.5 (p. 55), R. D. Brown on Lucretius iv.1239.

people are in fact disturbed by them.[300] The question remains open, how much influence the Epicureans had in Hellenistic Greece (their influence in the Latin world is a separate question).

Perhaps we can only end this section with Hellenistic impressions, not conclusions. Two points seem most worth reiterating: a disproportionate amount of the evidence for Hellenistic confidence in the truthfulness of dreams comes from the kingdom of the Ptolemies[301] and from actual sanctuaries elsewhere (sanctuaries which sometimes had a widely scattered clientele); and elsewhere it is hard to find much sign of firm belief except in the rarefied atmosphere of Zeno's Stoa.

Predictive Dreams in the Context of Greek Divination

How does all this fit into the history of classical 'divination' in general, given all the other means that existed of obtaining revelations? In most people's eyes, dream-interpretation seems not to have been the most reliable method of doing so; sacrifices and oracles were better.[302] But it would be a mistake to think that there was a clear hierarchy. On occasion, dreams could be important: they could provoke fear and apotropaic action, fear in particular that some evil event was impending; they might resolve a medical or religious crisis with specific guidance that a sacrifice could not supply, and without the great effort that was needed to send to Delphi.[303] They could be useful in other ways too, to convince doubtful hearers, since there was a general suspicion that dreams might tell the truth, and whereas an oracle or a sacrifice was rather public, a dreamer, at least one with prestige, could not be proved to be lying.

Since we have found it hard to distinguish levels and types of belief from one Greek milieu to another, the task of explaining belief may be entirely beyond us. Working against belief, perhaps, was the argumentative and sceptical, though generally not antireligious, atmosphere of fifth- and fourth-

300. Chs. 1, 2, 8 Indelli (with the latter's comm., pp. 149–151).

301. But the Greeks seem to have brought incubation prophecy with them to Egypt, they did not discover it there; cf. Dunand 1997, 72–74.

302. Orators never question the veracity of oracles. On the superiority of oracles to dreams in the eyes of the fourth-century Athenians see Mikalson 1983, 39–40.

303. For the superior authority of the Delphic Oracle see for instance Plato, *Rep.* iv.427bc. [Aeschylus], *PV* 658–672, seems to imply this. See also above, n. 49. But Delphi came to be less consulted by Athens after 479: Parker 2005, ch.5.

century Athens, which certainly spilled over to some extent into the rest of the Greek world. Working in its favour, I suggest, was the labour of those who presided over, or otherwise benefited from, the incubation shrines of Asclepius, Amphiaraus and Serapis. And clearly the Ptolemaic court considered that dream-reports were an effective way of influencing many of their subjects, both in Egypt and elsewhere.

The sources give the impression that there was a crescendo of interest in the fourth century, though it would not be hard to argue that the impression derives from the survival of an unusually large quantity of appropriate source material. If there was such a crescendo, one would like to be able to relate it to other developments of various kinds. Is it possible that fourth-century Athenians or Greeks, more than their predecessors or successors, believed in the benevolence of the gods?

The Roman Republic down to Sulla

The Roman social elite did not in this era have any serious degree of faith in the predictive value of dreams, which consequently did not enter into the public religion of the state, except on rare occasions. But its members recognized that there was a certain amount of popular belief, and did their best to exploit that belief when it was possible to do so (in some emergency or other).[304]

Rome's first historian, the senator Fabius Pictor, described a dream dreamt by Aeneas. Our immediate sources for this, Diodorus and Cicero, both recognize that the story belongs to mythical times—which is not to say that they thought it was untrue, still less that Fabius did (his actual words are not preserved).[305] But of course it tells nothing about what they expected in their own times. Fabius also recounted a dream-story that was

304. In my view, the class distinction is primary. One scholar proposes that 'a *private* person could consult an interpreter . . . of dreams, raise a dedication "on account of a dream", be miraculously healed and perhaps even obtain divine advice, but such practices had no natural place in the conduct of *public* business' (Kragelund 2001, 80), a reasonable formulation that is weakened by the vagueness of the word 'natural'. In my view there is virtually no reason to suppose that elite Roman males prior to Sulla did any of the things listed in the first part of the sentence just quoted.

305. Diodorus Siculus vii.5 (Fabius fr. 4 Peter = 5 Chassignet); Cicero, *De div.* i.43 (fr. 3 Peter = 3 Chassignet). In fact the dreams are different. Dionysius of Halicarnassus i.56 gives a version of the Diodorus story as a variant, without mentioning Fabius.

probably already popular and certainly was so later. It told of a dream dreamt three times by a peasant, in the time of a Latin war, in other words long ago: he was told that the Ludi Maximi, which had just been celebrated for the first time, were defective and should be repeated, but he was too humble to approach the Senate until he had been severely punished by a divine power; eventually the Senate decided that his dream was authentic and had the games repeated.[306] For Roman taste, this was an excellent tale—but once again about the remote past.[307]

Other stories can be somewhat informative about the era of the second-century or 'Sullan' annalists who transmitted them. Thus the heroic P. Decius Mus (consul in 340), was supposed to have had a dream before his famous *devotio* (though as Kragelund has pointed out, there had to be a sacrifice to confirm it that the dream was telling the truth).[308]

Scipio Africanus and some of his connections are at the centre of a some-what problematical group of dream stories. Polybius tells one about Scipio in his youth and his election to the aedileship: to deflect his mother's disap-proval of his presenting himself as a candidate in the same year as his older brother, he invented for her a dream to the effect that the brothers would both be victorious—and she, 'just like a woman', believed in the dream.[309] Roman men of the senatorial class may have thought it was womanly to take any serious notice of a dream (or they may have projected on to women their own half-belief). Another Polybian story about Scipio Africanus' deceit may bring us a little nearer to Romans in general: at a crucial mo-ment in the siege of New Carthage, Scipio encouraged his troops by telling them that the god Neptune had appeared to him in a dream and assured

---

306. Cicero, *De div.* i.55 (*somnio comprobato*) (fr. 15 Peter = 19 Chassignet); see also Livy ii.36.1, and parallels (more than a dozen versions are known: Kragelund 2001, 77). Cn. Gellius and Coelius Antipater also told the story (Cicero, loc. cit.).

307. The story about Numerius Suffustius of Praeneste in Cicero, *De div.* ii.85, suggests that 'epiphany' dreams had a fairly old tradition behind them in central Italy. The story about the Sabine Valesius and the origin of the Secular Games recounted by Valerius Max-imus ii.4.5 (see also Zosimus ii.1–7), which includes a dream of an unidentified god, points in the same direction.

308. Livy viii.6.11 (with Kragelund 2001, 79–80); Cicero *De div.* i.51 omits this detail, perhaps because it would not have suited Quintus' argument. Kragelund 87 also points out in useful detail how few dreams there are in Livy and in Plutarch's lives of Romans who lived before the first century BC.

309. Polybius x.4–5. The story contains various factual errors (see Walbank's comm.).

him of victory;[310] whatever his own attitude was, he must have been convinced that his men, in these circumstances at least, would be impressed, and presumably some of them were. He often used dreams in working on the multitude in Rome itself.[311] When the older Scipios had fallen in battle in Spain in 211, their command was taken over by an officer named L. Marcius, probably a *tribunus militum:* before a certain battle he told his soldiers that he received advice from the Scipios in dreams.[312] We may suppose that he shared the technique of Africanus. All this struck Polybius and probably Livy as so much manipulation, and on balance they are likely to have been right. For over a century, no other member of the Roman aristocracy followed Africanus' example in this respect, which suggests that his peers largely disapproved.[313]

Official Roman religion had little room for dream-predictions,[314] and dreams did not appear, as far as we know, among the hundreds of officially recorded *prodigia;* if the *pontifex maximus* had bad dreams no one seems to have been especially interested. Cicero, however, asserts in *On Divination* that 'relatively serious dreams that have seemed to be relevant to public affairs have not been neglected by the Senate'.[315] Yet he gives only one example (and the only one we can add from all of our other sources is the story of the unfortunate *rusticus*).[316] The case Cicero mentions here occurred during the Social War: the Senate instructed one of the consuls of the year 90 BC to repair a particular temple because of a dream reported by Caecilia Metella, the daughter of a consular; her social rank no doubt

310. Polybius x.11.7–8.

311. Livy xxvi.19.3–4. As to whether Livy used Polybius, directly or indirectly, in this book, see P. Jal's comm., pp. x–xiii.

312. Livy xxv.38.5: 'Scipiones me ambo dies noctesque curis insomniisque agitant et excitant saepe somno . . .'. Kragelund 2001, 82 n. 86, establishes that the reference is to dreams not a waking vision. In his view (83), 'it is plausible' that this story 'featured in the early historians'; Marcius' very obscurity argues in favour of the story's being contemporary.

313. Cf. Kragelund 2001, 86.

314. The definition of it ascribed to Cotta in Cicero, *De natura deorum* iii.5, which was meant to be conservative, permits 'the warnings given by the interpreters of the Sibyl and by the *haruspices* because of portents and monsters', and evidently excluded *coniectores*.

315. 'Nec vero somnia graviora, si quae ad rem publicam pertinere visa sunt, a summo consilio neglecta sunt', *De div.* i.4.

316. The lack of other examples seems more significant to me now than when I wrote 2003, 25.

made some difference, and—most important of all—the state happened to be in dire crisis because of the rebellion of the Italian allies.[317]

The second-century annalists had told some dream stories, none of them set in recent times, but the historian Sisenna, a little later, was categorical: while other kinds of portents are genuine, dreams are not to be believed.[318] In the same general period, as part of his attack on the superstitious, Lucilius says that 'they' (but it is not clear exactly who he is referring to) believe made-up dreams to be true (his criticism may have been limited in various ways).[319]

It was a different matter for a poet: Ennius' *Annals* introduce the dream of Ilia, daughter of Aeneas, concerning no lesser a theme than the foundation of Rome,[320] and we have to suppose that the broad credibility of such a story—set in the remote mythic past—was accepted by most of his hearers and readers. When Ennius claimed authority because of a dream about Homer,[321] he no doubt expected his public to be impressed. But when a character in one of his plays says, in a context we cannot identify, that some dreams are true, but it is not necessary that all should be—'aliquot somnia vera, sed omnia non necesse est'[322]—we really have no clue as to whether that was the poet's opinion; at most it shows that some people in Ennian

317. There had been many other portents: Kragelund 2001, 56. The supposed content of Metella's dream: Obsequens 55. On her strong character see Kragelund 63–64. For an incident that took place in the crisis autumn 105 see Granius Licinianus xxxiii.22 (p. 13 Flemisch, p. 11 Criniti) (some married women contributed money for sacrifices after dreaming a dream in common). Kragelund 88 hypothesizes that in the very late second century BC Roman opinion was shifting towards willingness to view a dream as an official *prodigium,* but the 105 incident does not establish that.

318. Cicero, *De div.* i.99 = fr. 5 Peter: 'quod . . . somnium Sisenna cum disputavisset mirifice ad verbum cum re convenisse, tum insolenter, credo ab Epicureo aliquo inductus, disputat somniis credere non oportere. Idem contra ostenta nihil disputat . . .'. ('Quintus' speaking of course). Kragelund 2001, 90–91 argues that Sisenna's hostility was 'constitutional' rather than philosophical, and others have had like suspicions; but Cicero implies that the basis of the historian's view was indeed philosophical; and why not?

319. Lines 487–488 Marx: 'sic isti somnia ficta / vera putant', with Lachmann's emendation of the impossible *omnia ficta* (for the reading see O'Hara 1987). Here and in Lucretius i.104 *somnia fingere* seems to mean 'to interpret dreams misleadingly'.

320. Book 1, lines 34–50 Skutsch.

321. Book 1, lines 2–11, Skutsch. See above, p. 26.

322. Cicero, *De div.* ii.127 = *Fab.* 429 Vahlen. The exact form of this line need not concern us.

Rome thought that sometimes dreams came true.[323] Accius, two generations later, made much of a predictive dream in his play *Brutus:* the dreamer
was Tarquinius Superbus, an antihero to be set on a level with the great figures of Greek myth; and Accius knew that some dreams consisted of the
day's leavings.[324]

But there were paid dream-interpreters at Rome, as we have seen. Some
other clear evidence for popular belief is the very fact that Scipio Africanus
was to some extent able to manipulate that belief. And there is evidence
that in the second century BC sick people far outside the social elite sometimes turned to an incubation shrine, for at the Latin colony of Fregellae
(culturally somewhat distinct from Rome), which was destroyed by Rome
in 125 BC, it is quite likely that the shrine of Aesculapius was the scene of
incubation dreaming.[325] There may have been a fairly widespread 'healing
belief' in the whole region.

Does Plautus offer us any further understanding of popular belief? As
we have already seen, the dream scenes in Plautus' plays almost certainly
imitate Greek models; but Roman dramatists had public roles, and their
religious and psychological presuppositions could not deviate very far from
those of respectable citizens. It is of some consequence therefore that
every time a dream is recounted in detail in a play of Plautus, there is an element of burlesque or of the comically undignified: in the *Curculio* Cappa-
dox the pimp, who is due for discomfiture at the end of the play, dreams
that Aesculapius sits far away from him, clearly a bad sign;[326] in the *Merca-
tor* the hero's father, a classic *senex comicus,* has dreamt the plot of the play,
with the characters represented as goats and a monkey;[327] in the *Miles*

323. A speaker in Ennius' *Telamo* seems to have included dream-interpreters in his denunciation of 'superstitious prophets and shameless soothsayers' (Cicero, *De div.* i.132 =
fr. cxxxiv Jocelyn), even though it is not clear where Cicero ends and the paraphrase of Ennius begins ('Telamo clearly denounced all classes [of diviners]', Jocelyn p. 397), but that
does not help us with the problem at hand.

324. Brutus frr. 1–2 (pp. 237–238 Dangel): 'quae in vita usurpant homines, cogitant, cu-
rant vident . . . ea si cui in somno accidit, minus mirum est . . .', says the Seer, but that
does not prevent him interpreting Tarquin's dream as a danger signal.

325. Degrassi 1986, 151; the scepticism of Renberg 2006, 113–114, seems in this case
exaggerated, given Asclepius' wide fame as an incubation deity.

326. Lines 246–273. Cf. Renberg 2006, 108–109.

327. Lines 225–254.

Gloriosus the whore tells an invented and misleading dream, from the best of motives.[328]

Greek influence, mounting steadily during the second century, probably pulled Roman thinking in different directions. Inscriptions from Delos and elsewhere in the Greek world suggest that Romans were beginning to learn some new dream-practices, in particular the practice of making a dedication in obedience to a divine dream.[329] On the other hand there is scarcely any reason to think that Hellenistic Greeks outside the world of the Ptolemies trusted dreams more than ordinary Romans did. And Epicurean scepticism was about to open the eyes of the Italian literate classes.

We come back to Sulla, the man who is supposed to have written in the dedication of his memoirs to Lucullus that orders given in dreams by the *daimonion* were 'the most secure things'.[330] The question to resolve here is not the nature of the man's own conviction, but what effects he had on other Romans by telling them about his dreams. The best attested Sullan dream was mentioned in an inscription described by Appian: Sulla made a dedication to Aphrodite because he had seen her in a dream armed, leading the host and fighting with the arms of Ares. This dedication he seems to have made at Aphrodisias in Caria.[331] What we most need to know—and probably cannot know—is whether Sulla's dream of the Cappadocian goddess Ma-Bellona, a dream known to us only from Plutarch and dated by him to 88 (that crucial year of subversive violence) was actually publicized by him at that time. The goddess, 'whether she was Semele or Athena or Bellona' (Plutarch), handed him a thunderbolt and helped him to strike down his enemies (who at that moment were Romans).[332] This story is probably authentic, in the sense that Sulla himself spoke of it, and it is rea-

328. Lines 380–396 (see esp. Mazzoli 1995). In *Rudens* 593–612 we hear of another animal dream, which enigmatically informs the sleeper about something that has in fact just happened.

329. Seven cases from Delos: *I. Délos* 2109, 2113, 2346, 2355, 2437, 2443, and Bruneau 1970, 223 (Renberg 2003, no. 166), with the comments of Renberg 201–202. It would be interesting if an epigrapher could narrow the dating within the period 166 to 67; all we know is that 2355 must be later than 92. A similar case from Clazomenae (*IGSK* II.518; Renberg no. 380) might be second-century.

330. Above, p. 128.

331. Appian, *BC* i.97.453–455.

332. Plutarch, *Sull.* 9. Kragelund 2001, 92–93, discusses whether this came from Sulla's autobiography, hesitating more than I would. See further H. Behr 1993, 74–76.

sonable to guess that he spoke of it to some of his troops (few members of the senatorial or equestrian orders are likely to have been sympathetic).[333] All this may also have applied to a story about a later dream of Sulla's in which the younger C. Marius, with whom Sulla was about to do battle, was warned by his late father not to fight on that particular day.[334] It is probable in fact that Sulla was at least to some degree personally convinced of the truthfulness of his own dreams: he added to his memoirs an account of a dream which he dreamt shortly before his death.[335] Generations later, Sulla was remembered as having made *exceptional* political use of his alleged dreams, and of religion more generally.[336] Since he was able to defeat the Mariani and the Cinnani we must suppose that this helped him to convince his troops that he would conquer; it seems very doubtful, however, that he expected members of the social elite to believe that any of his dreams really came from the gods.

Lucretius, Cicero, and the Late Republic

If Sulla made a vigorous attempt to exercise influence by exploiting his real or alleged dreams, he may not have been fighting an easy battle as far as the

333. Which is not to exclude that Sulla later on directed this story to the higher ranks of society. It was evidently the origin of the real and imitation gems depicting the Ma-Bellona dream (for the material see among others Vollenweider 1958–1959, who thought that they were mass-produced from 88 onwards). Behr 1993, 105 was probably both right and wrong to say that Sulla's religious assumptions were those of his contemporaries: right for the soldiers, wrong for senators. The coin-type of 44 BC (Crawford 480/1) that is some-times thought to allude to this dream really cannot do so (Kragelund 2001, 94 n. 119) and would not in any case help with the question at hand.

334. Plutarch, *Sull.* 28 (82 BC).

335. Plutarch, *Sull.* 37. But this detail is not given by Appian (*BC* i.105.492), who was presumably referring to the same dream. The twenty-two books of Sulla's memoirs, in Greek, were of course intended for a fairly exclusive public.

336. Valerius Maximus i.2.3, Frontinus, *Strat.* i.11.11 (the latter may allude to dream stories). Kragelund 94 writes that an army commander now required 'a new kind of polit-ical charisma', and that applies to Sulla and to Sertorius (the latter also used dream-trickery: Plutarch, *Sert.* 11, 20; Gellius xv.22). Lucullus too once made use of a dream-story, Plutarch says (*Luc.* 12). But while Pompey and Caesar showed some imagination in ap-pealing to their soldiers, they are not known to have resorted to this method. The story told in Plutarch, *Pomp.* 23 and *Crass.* 12 has an eccentric ring to it, but it appears to show that (in 70) you could speak in a *contio* about dreaming of Jupiter. In the civil wars after 44, Oc-tavian showed himself to be Sulla's heir in this as in other respects.

educated elite was concerned.[337] The late Republic saw no change in the public importance of dreams: try to imagine Cicero relying on the evidence of a dream in a political or in a forensic speech—it cannot be done. What about other Romans?

We should not, to start with, dismiss the Epicureans too readily: after all, Cicero, not at all their best friend philosophically, said that they 'conquered all of Italy'.[338] Lucretius' view, typically Epicurean as far as we know, was that dreams are partly reflections of the subject's waking preoccupations, partly (and very commonly) anxiety-dreams and partly erotic wish-fulfilments.[339] Dreams for him are among the weapons of superstition.[340] It is incidentally not correct to suppose that the Epicurean sympathizer Philodemus held that dreams were messages from the gods.[341]

Yet Cicero hints that some of his contemporaries did turn for cures to Aesculapius and Serapis, and accepts that doctors can tell from dreams whether a patient is 'full or empty'.[342] He also reveals in passing that by this date Romans too sometimes made dedications because dreams had instructed them to do so (but the fact that we have no clear epigraphical evidence of this until Augustan times suggests that it was not really common).[343]

Cicero himself, though he detested Epicurean philosophy, was nonethe-

---

337. For scholars who believe(d) that the first-century elite was sceptical about divination see Beard 1986, 33 (setting up an opponent).

338. *Tusc.Disp.* iv.7.

339. iv.962–1019, 1020–1025, 1030–1036, respectively. See also iii.316. Which is not to suppose that the Epicureans were always in agreement with one another (cf. Harris 2002, 102). For the view that Lucretius should be judged an eclectic on this topic see Schrijvers 1980.

340. i.102–106, where, Bailey notwithstanding, I take *somnia* to mean dreams in a literal sense. Other important passages: iv.455–461, v.1169–1182.

341. As claimed by Brillante 1991, 31, on the basis of *De pietate* 92, lines 12–15 (as edited by T. Gomperz, *Philodem: Ueber die Frömmigkeit* [Leipzig, 1866], p. 43), where even if Gomperz's text is right it is a matter of Homer's (supposed) opinion, not that of Philodemus. Philodemus' sceptical view seems to be indicated by line 1450 Obbink.

342. *De div.* ii.123, 142 (Näf 2004, 85, probably exaggerates the significance of the latter passage).

343. *De domo* 140, a fantastic moment of bravado in which he compares Clodius to a barbarian pirate—who after sacking a temple might be expected to consecrate 'aram aliquam in litore deserto somniis stimulatus aut religione aliqua'. The deserted shore gives the whole passage a strongly literary ring. The lack of epigraphical corroboration can mostly, but not entirely, be attributed to the fact that a relatively small number of Latin in-

less beyond any reasonable doubt a dream-sceptic, at least by the time he wrote *On Divination* (45–44 BC). This is proved by the fact that he assigns the sceptical role to himself in that dialogue (whereas he often leaves himself out), while assigning the more credulous view to Quintus, and by the fact that the sceptical view is stated second, the standard capping position which ancient rhetoric gave to what was viewed as the stronger argument (this consideration is virtually sufficient on its own to indicate Cicero's opinion).[344] It is certainly of some significance that in Book I he gave ample space to a moderately 'favourable' argument, even though he answered it in II—in other words, he thought that the case was worth stating,[345] even though he knew that at Rome dreams had never had the degree of official acceptance afforded to some other means of divination.

Attempts to show that Book II of *On Divination* does not represent Cicero's views, or does not mainly mean what it seems to mean, are to be firmly rejected.[346] This is not one of the subjects on which it was difficult

---

scriptions survives from republican times even in Italy (Kragelund 2001, 81 n. 83, thinks that this silence is 'probably accidental'). *CIL* I^2 998, a fragmentary dedication by a freedman, may be an exception. The lost inscription *CIL* I^2 1423 (= XIV 23) cannot be used here (pace Weber 2005–2006, 80); since Dessau (*CIL* xiv p. 3) it has been seen as imperial.

344. See Leonhardt 1999, 25–31.

345. He could hardly deny it, since it was known that in earlier years he had taken at least one dream as an encouraging prediction—a dream about Marius he experienced as he was going into exile in 58 (*De div.* i.59; his later explanation: ii.140). Evidently he did not have to defend the fact that he had used the imaginary dream of Scipio in *De republica*. That Quintus is represented as retreating from most kinds of divination (*De div.* ii.100) confirms, if confirmation is necessary, that Marcus really did favour the sceptical view.

346. Beard 1986. *De natura deorum* i.10, where Cicero says that his own opinions are off the agenda, is largely irrelevant (*pace* Beard 35), since in that work Cicero does not in fact put much argumentation in his own mouth. According to Beard 43, the character of Marcus in *De div.* 'highlights the underlying problems in reconciling traditional Roman practice and the Greek philosophical theory', but in the first place there was no great contradiction with respect to dreams (as I hope to have shown), and if there is anything in *De div.* II which is merely formal, it is the nod towards the believers (see the text). See further Wardle 2006. Schofield 1986 is more moderate, admitting that Marcus 'inclines towards' the sceptical view of divination (61). The source of all this trouble is perhaps that Cicero really was ambivalent about some other types of divination (cf. Schofield 56–57). For a critique of Beard and Schofield see Timpanaro 1994, 257–264. In Timpanaro's view, Cicero did not write the first book to defend divination, 'ma per mostrarne la mancanza di fondamenti razionali, per preparare il terreno alla sua confutazione' (260); that, however, seems too simple. The theory of Cancik 1999, 173, that Cicero was only sceptical about dreams

for Cicero and his contemporaries to reconcile philosophical arguments
with the institutions of traditional Roman religion, for although dreams
sometimes had religious importance ascribed to them in late-republican
Rome, they had a far from major role. Critics have made much out of the
fact that after resoundingly denouncing dream-divination at the climax of
the book ('Explodatur igitur haec quoque somniorum divinatio pariter cum
ceteris. . . . Multum enim et nobismet ipsis et nostris profuturi videbamur,
si eam funditus sustulissemus', etc.),[347] Cicero seems to retreat a little.[348]
But this is merely a polite nod in the direction of Quintus (and perhaps the
moderate Stoics whose case he had presented): the Academy does not put
forward its own *iudicium,* but it approves what seems closest to the truth.
The hearers are free to make up their own minds—which does not imply
that Cicero himself has not decided what to think. He after all states quite
bluntly that divination 'does not exist'.[349]

More important than Cicero's own views, for present purposes, is his estimate of contemporary opinion:[350]

> How many people are there who obey dreams or understand them or re-
> member them? What a lot of people there are, on the other hand, who treat
> them with disdain and think that believing in them is a superstition of silly
> old women! . . . most dreams are ignored or at least disregarded.

This judgement is socially limited, but it cannot be discarded as testimony
about the contemporary Roman elite—all the less so if Cicero was more
neutral than appears to have been the case.

There were certainly diverse views—why otherwise would Cicero have
written *On Divination?* A friend of his who was an expert on divination,
P. Nigidius Figulus, is said to have written a book about dreams,[351] and it is

---

because that was the tradition of official Roman religion does not need refutation. For another mis-statement of Cicero's views see Le Goff 1985, 200.

347. ii.148–149.

348. ii.150: 'Cum autem proprium sit Academiae iudicium suum nullum interponere,
ea probare quae simillima veri videantur, conferre causas, et quid in quamque sententiam
dici possit expromere, nulla adhibita sua auctoritate iudicium audientium relinquere inte-
grum ac liberum'; but this does not outweigh the lengthy denunciation which has gone before.

349. *De div.* ii.8.

350. ii.125.

351. Lydus, *De ost.* 45 = fr. 82 Swoboda.

not likely to have been sceptical in outlook. This, however, is the only attested Latin work of dream-interpretation from classical times[352]—a fact of considerable significance. And taken together, the available testimony suggests that the educated, even the moderately educated, did not, in ordinary circumstances, expect dreams to tell them anything. Caesar's commentaries are dream-free and it is hard to imagine him telling his soldiers dream stories about gods before joining battle.[353] The Temple of Aesculapius in Rome, founded in 291, did not become an incubation shrine under the Republic,[354] whatever happened at Fregellae. In moments of very high tension, however, such as a crucial moment in a civil war, those who were by temperament more impressionable (Octavian, but not Caesar) might feel strong emotions, especially fear, because of the dreams which they to some extent believed to be significant. Some people were also inclined to believe that particularly dramatic events, such as the assassination of Caesar, must have been foretold in dreams.

Incubation and the Doctors

Trust in 'incubation' under the Roman Empire is a complex question that spans the periods and social classes that will be discussed in the remainder of this chapter, or at least seems to. First of all, it was largely though not exclusively a phenomenon of the Greek world and of Egypt. In the former, incubation shrines were quite numerous. Literary and subliterary texts of the first to fourth centuries from time to time mention incubation shrines in the present tense,[355] or recount miracles that have taken place in them.[356] The great majority of incubants sought cures, though some brought non-

352. Del Corno 1969, xi.

353. Appian, *Lib.* 136.645–646, tells of a dream Caesar dreamt during the Thapsus campaign which served to justify refounding the city of Carthage; it is possible that Caesar himself was the ultimate source, but Appian is the only writer to mention the story.

354. According to Renberg 2006, 112–113, it did not do so even in imperial times, but this is not the majority view: Miller 1994, 114–115, Wacht 1998, 194.

355. Pausanias i.34.4 (Oropus), Philostratus, *Vita Ap.* iv.11 (Pergamum), Iamblichus, *De mysteriis* iii.3.

356. Rufus of Ephesus ap. Oribasius, *Collectiones Medicae* xlv.30.11–13 (Oribasius ed. Raeder III p. 192), Plutarch, *De defectu oraculorum* 45 (*Mor.* 434d–f); for the experience of the fourth-century philosopher Plutarch see the Suda s.v. Domninus.

medical questions too.[357] Literary and epigraphical texts quite often refer to cures provided by Asclepius, without always showing explicitly that incubation was involved.[358]

The well-to-do, such as Aelius Aristides[359] and those with moderate resources both underwent incubation.[360] In Severan times, Alexander of Aphrodisias wrote that 'almost all men have recourse to him [Asclepius], where he is most fully manifested',[361] which suggests that incubation really was very popular. While some doctors seem to have cooperated,[362] other and probably more prestigious ones were hostile[363]—but the authority of doctors was generally weaker than it is in a modern society. One may suspect that the incubants who felt trust or hope were for the most part the exceptionally superstitious and those—not a negligible number—who were in desperate medical straits. But it is likely that from the mid-second century on, in his own cultural area, Asclepius was even more widely revered than before.[364]

357. See Plutarch's story about the oracle of Mopsus referred to in the preceding note.

358. See for instance Philostratus, *VS* ii.25 (Pergamum), *IG* II^2.4514 (Athens, second century), Libanius, *Or.* i.143.

359. For an incubation that he experienced at Pergamum see *Or.* xlviii.28–35; another rich incubant there: Galen, *Subfiguratio empirica* 10 (Deichgräber 1930, 78). Caracalla went there too, for the same reason: Herodian iv.8.3. M. Iulius Apellas, who dedicated *SIG*^{3} 1170 (often reproduced elsewhere: see Girone 1998, no. II.4) at Epidaurus about 160 AD, was clearly well-to-do (and cf. Girone II.5 from Epidaurus and IV.2 from Pergamum).

360. *IGUR* 148 (a set of four texts from the Tiber island: Girone V.2a–d) seems to concern very ordinary folk. These were probably all incubations, though there is no explicit evidence of that.

361. *De Fato* 32, trans. R. W. Sharples.

362. In truth, evidence of this is not very abundant (cf. Riethmüller 2005, I, 389–390). The references to Aelius Aristides given by Behr 1968, 170, to show that 'some doctors . . . did not balk at administering his [Asclepius'] prescriptions' fail to do so. Saying that a certain doctor 'yielded to the god' (Aelius Aristides, *Or.* xlvii.57) is hardly evidence for cooperation. The fact that doctors sometimes made dedications to Asclepius in precincts where incubation was practised (e.g. Samama 2003, no. 187) is scarcely decisive either.

363. As we shall see, the Roman doctors whose books have survived were, down to the time of Soranus, more or less negative about dreams as sources of therapeutic advice (which admittedly does not formally exclude the possibility that they thought that Asclepian incubation might work); Galen was a degree more pious. Some of Asclepius' prescriptions were in fact astonishing: Miller 1994, 115.

364. Cf. Nock 1950, 48.

Augustus to the Flavians

Since it is a tenable hypothesis at least that the attitude of the educated inhabitants of the Roman Empire underwent a detectable change about 100 AD,[365] let us provisionally separate the two periods. This is not to claim that in either period there was a single 'Roman conception of the dream',[366] simply that practices and beliefs may well have evolved. At last we have, in any case, an ample body of material, at least by ancient-historical standards. We are also attempting to deal with, to say the least, an ample number of different milieux. When Dio Chrysostom, probably some time in the 70s,[367] addressed the people of Alexandria, he asserted that the god Serapis showed them his power 'almost daily' through oracles and dreams,[368] whatever that implied.[369] Yet we should probably assume that Alexandria was somewhat *a*typical of the Greek world in this respect.

How then did the inhabitants of the early Roman Empire react to their dreams? The senior Pliny posed the problem in Vespasian's time (and we are naturally tempted to place him near the middle of the spectrum as far as educated opinion on dreams is concerned). Having asserted that small children do indeed dream, he stated the problem of predictive dreams in these terms:[370]

---

365. Harris 2003, 31. It is an error to suppose that Roman imperial times shared a single 'dream theory' (Miller 1994, 38; she attributes the theory to 'late antiquity', a period she apparently starts in the late Republic [9]!). I can make no sense out of her statement (65) that 'most of the [Roman-period] theorists of dreams agreed that dream-speech was divine speech' (Who is a theorist? What is dream-speech?).

366. Veyne 1987, 384, was rightly at pains to disprove that there was a single concept. As he remarks, belief and scepticism do not advance and retreat like trench-warfare armies. He further maintains that 'most often, the Romans thought about dreams as we do, but certain types of dreams were not treated with the indifference which was accorded to most dreams'. He compares Roman attitudes towards dreams to our attitude towards *lapsus—some* are significant.

367. I follow the dating of C. P. Jones 1978, 134.

368. xxxii.12.

369. Perhaps no more than that in emergencies of one kind or another the Alexandrians went more frequently to sleep in a holy shrine than people of other cities that did not possess one as famous as the Alexandrian Serapaeum. His claim also fits his hope of making the Alexandrians more pious.

370. *NH* x.211.

It is a major question in life [*magnus hic in vita locus*], and one well supplied with conflicting evidence, whether there are cases of prior knowledge which the mind experiences in sleep [*utrumne sint aliqua praescita animi quiescentis*], and how they occur, or whether it is a matter of chance like most things. If the two sides were to be argued from particular instances, they would undoubtedly come out equal.

It is pretty well agreed, he says, that dreams dreamt in certain physical conditions are empty, but sleep is simply the retreat of the mind into its innermost self. He seems to lean slightly towards scepticism (rather like Aristotle, he cannot find the mechanism that would explain predictive dreams), but he allows that there are plenty of apparent cases of foreknowledge.[371] He is not above stating firmly that a god had recently provided a cure for rabies by causing the mother of a praetorian guardsman to dream of it.[372] A precious stone found in Bactria, if you sleep with it beneath your head, provides 'visa nocturna' like an oracle;[373] almost equally distant is another stone from Ethiopia, which 'is promised to give *praedivina somnia*'.[374]

Let us consider first emperors and courtiers, then senators and the rest of the well-to-do, then the 'learned professions', then the 'middle classes';[375] the opinions of the poor we can scarcely more than glimpse.

---

371. This text alone is enough to dispose of the comment of Miller 1994, 9, that 'the question of divination's rationality did not seem to most late-antique [i.e. Roman-period] thinkers to be a question worthy of debate. Cicero was the major exception' (dreams were her subject here). For Pliny's religious views see Beagon 1992, ch. 3.

372. *NH* xxv.16–18. A man who went blind while dreaming that he was doing so: vii.166 (this was a story about one of Sulla's ancestors, and it may well have derived from Sulla's autobiography: see R. G. Lewis 1991, 513, Kragelund 2001, 88 n. 105). Lysander, while he was besieging Athens, was told in a dream to permit the burial of Sophocles: vii.109. And we recall Pliny's willingness to write the history of the German Wars in twenty books because of an epiphany dream (Plin. *Ep.* iii.5.4).

373. *NH* xxxvii.160.

374. xxxvii.167; here Pliny holds back (Önnerfors 1976, 354), as he also does in xxii.44 and xxxvi.97.

375. Some will disapprove of this term, but see Harris 1988 (and I hope to return to the subject). I intend to refer to those who lived consistently in some comfort though outside the social elite (Pompeii makes the existence of such a social stratum quite obvious). The significance of the term is of course different in a modern context.

Emperors and Courtiers

It is plainly false to say that most Roman emperors based major decisions on their dreams.[376] It is a more delicate question to decide how much they or their agents made 'propagandistic' use of dream-predictions. Augustus wrote that at the Battle of Philippi he owed his life to having heeded a warning that came from a dream dreamt by his doctor M. Artorius Asclepiades.[377] This became part of a useful wider story to the effect that Fortune was on Octavian's side. But Augustus, and his ten immediate successors too, set us a difficult problem: Suetonius, Dio and others provide us with many dreams that might have served Augustus' propagandistic purposes, but we know that both these writers were very fond of recounting dreams, so how many such stories should we think of as contemporary? In some cases (dreams about Octavian attributed to Catulus and Cicero)[378] it is hard to think that they can have had much resonance when Catulus and Cicero had long been dead—so these stories at least are probably early.

Augustus, says the well-informed but somewhat unscrupulous Suetonius, 'did not neglect his own dreams or other people's dreams about himself'.[379] What did this mean in practice? On an important occasion, he followed Asclepiades' highly convenient advice. A dream about Iuppiter Capitolinus led him to add some bells to the temple of Iuppiter Tonans.[380] Suetonius also says that one day a year, in obedience to a dream, he pretended to be a beggar, a story that scholars have understandably but needlessly doubted.[381] All this amounts to very little for a man who was accounted rather superstitious by his contemporaries: no sign, for example,

376. As claimed by Frenschkowski and Morgenthaler 2002, 31.

377. This story appeared in Augustus' *De vita sua* (fr. 10 Peter) according to Plutarch, *Brut.* 41, who is to be believed on this point. Other early sources: Velleius Paterculus ii.70, Valerius Maximus i.7.1.

378. Suetonius, *DA* 94.13–14, etc. For commentary see Vigourt 2001, 401–404.

379. *DA* 91.1. One notes the slight distortion that is involved in paraphrasing this statement with the words 'besonders traumgläubig' (Weber 2000, 325); the same author (298) concludes from Suetonius' statement that every spring Augustus dreamt dreams that were 'terrifying and empty and false' that they aroused real emotions; I would need better evidence than this that Augustus ever felt any emotion (other than occasionally, anger). The rest of this paragraph is based on the same chapter of Suetonius.

380. And in obedience to another dream he gave a statue of Apollo back to the Ephesians (Pliny, *NH* xxxiv.58). See further Vigourt 276–277—'signs' seldom led to specific actions.

381. Weber 2000, 325–327 gives ample bibliography.

that Augustus ever dedicated a temple in accordance with a dream, or underwent (during any of his numerous illnesses) any medical treatment recommended in a dream.[382]

Early emperors tried to restrict the activities of seers and astrologers[383]—which suggests that somewhere in the political class, fairly evidently among senators and equestrians, prophecies might be expected to have a disturbing effect. In the year 47 the emperor Claudius had two Roman knights, brothers, put to death, on the pretext that one of them had allegedly dreamt a dream (though it was not agreed what he had dreamt) that predicted something extremely negative about the emperor.[384] This meant that a Roman consular prosecutor could solemnly employ such a pretext before the Senate without provoking laughter—but of course there was no laughter, because authority was in the hands of a sanguinary tyrant. Nothing like this had ever happened before in the classical world. The fact that this pretext was used can hardly be doubted, whatever we may think of Suetonius' stories about Claudius' willingness to execute people for treasonous dreaming.[385] His contemporaries, however, regarded Claudius as at best eccentric, and the discontented no doubt spread and improved the story of the emperor's paranoia.

A lunatic was in charge. That is the message of a bizarre story that Tacitus recounts about the reign of Nero (in fact he gives it considerable prominence).[386] One Caesellius Bassus, a man 'of Punic origin and confused

382. Valerius Maximus, who would clearly have liked to include more stories about Augustan dreams, cf. i.7.1–2, had to content himself with the one about Asclepiades.

383. Suetonius, *DA* 31.1: Augustus burnt more than two thousand books of prophecies on a single occasion; see also Tacitus, *Ann.* ii.32.

384. Tacitus, *Ann.* xi.4; the real reason was that they had allowed the disgraced Poppaea Sabina (the most beautiful woman of her generation: *Ann.* xiii.45) and her lover Mnester to meet in their house, he credibly says; it would have been embarrassing to admit this. When Tacitus says that a dream destroyed them, he is obviously not forgetting that the dream was a pretext (thus Näf 2004, 97, makes Tacitus more dream-credulous in this case than he really was).

385. Suetonius, *Claud.* 37, retails two stories of this kind, one about anonymous litigants, the other about the plot of Messallina and Narcissus which led to the killing of the consular Ap. Iunius Silanus in 42 (another version in Dio lx.14) (they both told Claudius that they had dreamt that Silanus had assassinated him). Suetonius qualifies this story as merely a tale ('ferunt'), but claims that Claudius recounted the whole matter to the Senate.

386. *Ann.* xvi.1–3, in other words at the beginning of the second half of his history of the reign of Nero.

mind', dreamt that there was a cavern full of treasure on his African estates.[387] He was so confident about the dream that, without bothering to identify the cavern, he sailed from Africa to Rome, where he convinced the emperor; Nero accordingly expected new revenue and spent still more extravagantly. Later, before the disappointed and desperate Caesellius committed suicide, he expressed surprise, claiming that his dreams had never before been false (if that is what happened). Tacitus calls Caesellius insane and implies that Nero was too. Yet though the narrative is exquisitely literary,[388] we may come away with a Julio-Claudian fact—there were some very credulous people at court.[389]

After Fortune appeared in a dream to Galba and complained that he had deprived her of an offering, he rushed off to Tusculum to placate her—so says Suetonius, offering a long list of bad omens.[390] It *might* be true, but it is very unlikely.[391] That in any case was the end, for the time being. The Flavians used real or invented dreams as propaganda,[392] but as far as we know took no notice of what they really dreamt.[393]

Senators and the Well-to-do in General

Pliny's dilemma presumably affected the whole upper order of society, except for those who were under Epicurean influence. I will argue that such people were sometimes quite attentive to their dreams—more so than their modern equivalents—but that they only acted on them in somewhat exceptional cases.

---

387. A long-established dream subject: Herodotus v.92, Cicero, *De div.* ii.134, Sallust, *Hist.* iii.109, etc.

388. The reminiscence of Vergil's Dido, another dreamer, is merely one element.

389. Syme (1958, 523) said of Tacitus' *Annals* that 'not until the later books do the prodigia become a regular entry. It would be fanciful to discover a sceptical historian's relapse into antiquated credulities'. An easy explanation is that the central figures, Claudius and Nero, and possibly but not necessarily some of their entourages, were indeed more credulous than their predecessors.

390. *Galba* 18.

391. Neither Plutarch nor Cassius Dio mentions this incident.

392. E.g. Suetonius, *Vesp.* 7.

393. The dream auguring Vespasian's triumph in Suetonius, *Vesp.* 5 could presumably not have been made public at the time it is supposed to have been dreamt. For some further discussion see Weber 2000, 190–192. It is reasonably clear that Vespasian really did set some store by portents.

A young aristocrat, Libo Drusus, was prevailed on by a senatorial friend to entertain ambitions of imperial power; Drusus frequented Chaldaeans, mages and interpreters of dreams.[394] We learn both that there were professional dream-interpreters (though they are not heard of again at Rome for another eighty years), and that only a man without brains would consult them.[395] Drusus killed himself. The *mathematici* and *magi,* and no doubt some dream-interpreters too, were now in trouble: two were executed and the rest expelled from Italy.[396]

Serious men might make stories out of their dreams. That must ultimately be how Tacitus knew that the general A. Caecina had had a horrid dream the night before a battle in Germany—in which he confounded the dream by winning.[397] As for the dream of Germanicus we met in Chapter I,[398] it was presumably a timely invention to encourage the troops.

At Canopus in Egypt, says Strabo,[399] the temple of Serapis is so effective at delivering cures that 'even the most respected men' *(kai tous ellogimotatous andras)* have confidence in it *(pisteuein)* and undergo incubation. Normally, it seems, Greek men of such standing would not have much confidence even in a famed site of incubation (and that fits the epigraphical evidence).[400] (Incubation shrines do not in any case seem to have existed on any significant scale in the western empire.)[401] Strabo himself seems to be a dream-sceptic: faced with a story about a dream supposedly dreamt by Alexander of Macedon in which the latter had found a cure for the wounded Ptolemy, he replaced it with a naturalistic explanation.[402] And in his language, dream-like notions *(enhupniodeis hupolepseis)* are misleading fantasies.[403]

---

394. *Ann.* ii.27 (16 AD).

395. 'Improvidum et facilem inanibus', Tacitus; 'tam stolidus quam nobilis', Seneca, *Ep.* 70.10.

396. *Ann.* ii.32. We do not seem to hear of *coniectores* in the first century until they appear in Quintilian, *Inst.* iii.6.30, v.7.36 (but cf. Suetonius, *Nero* 6).

397. *Ann.* i.65.4.

398. P. 44.

399. xvii.801.

400. Was it of any significance that by the time Pausanias saw the shrine of Asclepius at Epidaurus the famous tablets recording incubation cures had apparently been suffering some neglect (ii.27.3)?

401. For the western evidence see Wacht 1998, 194–195, Weber 2005–2006, 66, and, more sceptically, Renberg 2006.

402. *eikos,* xv.733.

403. xv.713.

Seneca's Stoicism might theoretically have inclined him to defend predic-tive dreams. In fact he largely avoids the subject,[404] but his once having writ-ten a dialogue *De superstitione* may suggest that he took a sceptical view.[405] The wise man passes over insults as though they were 'the delusive appear-ances of dreams and nocturnal visions which have nothing in them that is sub-stantial and true'.[406] We are not authorized to count him, or Tacitus either for that matter, as representative of their class. But a little later Epictetus will con-firm to us that while Greek opinion in general was becoming more credulous about dreams, the Stoics were moving in the opposite direction; after a posi-tively sarcastic chapter about divination in general, the philosopher proposes that no one really sleeps in a temple to find out the origin of his ill fortune.[407]

That Plutarch was a pious adherent of the traditional religion and its prac-tices will be disputed by no one (his literary life began in the period we are discussing and continued into the next one; we may as well discuss him here).[408] Does this include in his case belief in predictive dreams? The ev-idence seems to be somewhat contradictory, and has led to the hypothesis that the early work *De superstitione* expressed a more sceptical view than he would have endorsed later.[409] A full discussion would bulk too large here, all the more so since I consider that recent accounts have probably under-estimated his scepticism[410] and a lengthy argument would need to be ex-pounded.[411] (My view, be it noted, has the essential characteristic of making Plutarch reasonably consistent with the views of the philosopher he most admired, Plato[412]—at least as I interpreted them earlier in this chapter.)

404. The Chorus in *HF* 1070–1071 assumes that some dreams are true, some false. The one dream described at length in the tragedies is Andromache's dream of Hector in *Troad.* 439–460. In *NQ* ii.32 it is better to read 'omina', with Gronovius (followed by Hine) rather than the manuscripts' 'somnia'; the latter would mean that Seneca regarded dreams as the main alternative to entrails in Etruscan and Roman divination, which is false. The dream attributed to Seneca in Suetonius, *Nero* 7, must be apocryphal.

405. On its contents see Attridge 1978, 67–68.

406. *De const.* 11.1. Cf. *De prov.* 6.3: 'longo fallacique somnio'. *Ep.* 102.1 does not im-ply a different view.

407. Epictetus ii.7, ii.16.17 (that appears to be his meaning).

408. On his social standing and wealth see C. P. Jones 1971, 13–64.

409. Brenk 1987, 260. Froidefond 1987, 228, argues against the view that Plutarch grew less 'rationalistic' as he grew older; see also Erbse 1952.

410. E.g. Brenk 1987, 322–327, Näf 2004, 104–105.

411. For some prior comments see p. 113.

412. For Plutarch's relationship to the various forms of Platonism alive in his time see Froidefond 1987.

On the only occasion when the Boeotian grandee addressed part of this question explicitly in his own person, he treats trust in such dreams as a mark of superstition, at length and with some emphasis:[413] superstitious people, when they wake up after a nightmare, 'do not despise them or make mock of them, nor do they realize that there was nothing true in what disturbed them, but trying to escape the shadow of a harmless delusion, they make fools of themselves while they are awake,' entrusting themselves to charlatans and engaging in absurd rituals.[414] (How seriously we should take this as evidence that some of Plutarch's social equals were superstitious in this fashion is a somewhat open question.) Bad dreams cause fear as a result of superstition, he says elsewhere.[415] None of this excludes the possibility that some dreams may be truth-telling,[416] but the tone is sceptical. Even in his lives, which are constellated with dream-descriptions (forty-five or fifty-three, depending on whether you count the ones that are described briefly), he sometimes admits that a dream was fraudulent or likely to be nonsense.[417] He also thought that eating too many fish heads can cause nightmares.[418]

Two or possibly three factors have made Plutarch seem less sceptical in this regard than he really was. One is that he was pious enough to point out at length, in his dialogue *On the Disappearance of Oracles*, that the decline of oracles was neither complete nor evidence of the indifference of the gods. His brother Lamprias, who *might* be speaking on his behalf in that

413. *De superstitione* 3 = *Mor.* 165e–166c. It has sometimes been argued that *De superstitione* is not really Plutarch's work, but for no good reason (see D. B. Martin 2004, 104–105).

414. But it is inaccurate to say that here Plutarch 'severely criticizes those who are too prone to believe in the oracular significance of their dreams', as asserted by S.-V. Teodorsson on Plutarch, *Quaest.conv.* ii.3 = *Mor.* 635e.

415. *De virtute* 2 = *Mor.* 100f. But a little bit of superstition was harmless: in *Quaest.conv.* ii.3 = *Mor.* 635e he writes that he had given up eggs because of a recurrent dream (S.-V. Teodorsson ad loc. writes that Plutarch shows a 'somewhat ambivalent attitude towards the significance of dreams').

416. Cf. *De sera numinis vindicta* 28 (*Mor.* 566c).

417. In *Eum.* 13 he describes Eumenes' use of an obviously invented dream for political purposes as an application of superstition. In *Cicero* 2 he says that a dream of Cicero's nurse about the baby's future greatness, 'which looks like nonsense', turned out to be true. But *Lys.* 20 does not (contrary to Weber 1999, 9 n. 28) show his scepticism; it simply reflects the scepticism of many of Lysander's contemporaries as to whether he had really dreamt this dream.

418. *Quomodo adulescens* 1 = *Mor.* 15b.

dialogue, claims that souls, because of their capacity for memory, 'often blossom and shine out both in dreams *(enhupnia)* and sometimes in the hour of death';[419] and near the end of the dialogue, Lamprias seems to adopt a partially Aristotelian view to the effect that people of 'melancholic' temperament 'often' know the future from their dreams, 'so it seems'.[420] Truth-telling dreams do occur, but they tend to be unclear.[421]

The second factor is simply that Plutarch loved telling good stories, and he certainly expected most of the readers of his lives and his essays to consume dream-fulfilment stories with pleasure.[422] A speaker in *On the Disappearance of Oracles* tells how a Roman governor of Cilicia who held Epicurean opinions—a harsh and ill-natured fellow—attempted to discredit the famous local Oracle of Mopsus. He sent a freedman there with a sealed tablet to sleep in the shrine. A superhuman figure appeared in the freedman's dream, uttering one word, 'Black'. The governor was amazed, because what he had written in the tablet was 'Shall I sacrifice a white bull or a black one?' The Epicureans were confounded—serve them right— and the governor became a devotee of Mopsus.[423]

A third factor, which is banal enough, is that scholars have sometimes assumed that speakers in Plutarch's dialogues speak straightforwardly for the author.[424]

✧   ✧   ✧

419. *De defectu oraculorum* 40 = *Mor.* 432c. But as Brenk remarks (1987, 322), 'we do not have to believe that Plutarch himself believed every detail of [Lamprias'] theory'.

420. *De defectu oraculorum* 50 = *Mor.* 437f.

421. Hence his description of the *kuphi* of the Isiacs (*De Iside et Osiride* 80 = *Mor.* 383e–384a), a complex aromatic that had the effect of 'brightening and making clearer the faculty of the imagination that is receptive of *oneiroi*', is plainly a description of something desirable.

422. Dreams made good stories: *De recta ratione audiendi* 3 = *Mor.* 39a. See Pelling 1997, 199, for the suspicion that Plutarch himself sometimes 'introduced' the dreams he recounts in his biographies.

423. *De defectu oraculorum* 45 (*Mor.* 434d–f). He was plainly pleased to represent the Epicureans' discomfiture.

424. *Amatorius* 19 = *Mor.* 764f is sometimes thought to contradict the statement in *De superstitione* (e.g. Brenk 1987, 260). In that very complex dialogue, Plutarch's father is apparently made to say that the soul's real period of wakefulness is in the other world; when the soul arrives in this world, it is by means of dreams *(enhupnia)* that it 'greets and is as-

To complete this picture, made up partly of civilized indifference, partly of philosophical puzzlement, partly of fear and conviction and partly of literary tradition, we may refer to a monument to Priapus erected at Tibur by a wealthy imperial freedman, Iulius Agathemerus. The exuberant and highly sexed inscription that went with it seems to mock a convention of ordinary folk—for Agathemerus made the dedication 'somnio monitus', instructed in a dream. In so far as there is any evidence of date for this text, it points to the first century AD rather than the second.[425]

The Learned Professions

Ancient physicians must often have found themselves more or less flummoxed by the cases before them.[426] But their tradition had since Hippocratic times been sceptical about dreams as superhuman sources of guidance; at the same time, some of them at least understood dreams as possible indicators of the patient's physical condition. This was the view taken by Rufus of Ephesus, a leading physician of Flavian date. He considered that dreams could be symptomatic of malfunctioning 'humours'. 'I am altogether convinced', he wrote, 'that dream-images signifying either good things or bad for a person occur according to the humours in the body'.[427] He says that if

tonished by that which is most beautiful and most divine'. The speaker then quotes an unidentified poet: 'about it there pour delightful but treacherous dreams' (*doloenta oneira*). Aside from textual difficulties, this passage, though it shows some sympathy for a point of view quite different from the more sceptical one Plutarch sometimes expresses, is far from showing that he had changed his mind. Even less material is the passage in *Septem Sapientium Convivium* 15 (= *Mor.* 159a), according to which dreaming is 'our most ancient form of divination': the speaker is Diocles, a seer of ancient times who is dining with the Seven Sages.

425. *CIL* XIV.3565. See Kragelund 1989, 447–448, for the humour, and Buchheit 1962, 72, on the metrical argument in favour of a first-century date.

426. There were no corporate professions in a modern sense, but the category is easy to recognize: we can count all those who earned income by using a large body of knowledge initially acquired when they were young.

427. *Medical Questions* 5.33 (p. 8 in the Teubner ed. by H. Gärtner), which admittedly implies that some physicians took a different view. The physician should ask about the patient's dreams, 'because he can draw conclusions *even* from such evidence' (5.28). It is true that in a long passage of Rufus about the determination of humours which is quoted in Oribasius' *Medical Collections* there is a single account of a patient who received advice from Asclepius in an incubation-dream he experienced at Pergamum (xlv.30.11–13 = III p. 192 Raeder [*CMG* VI, 2, 1]; the passage is quoted, out of context, and translated in

the athlete Myron of Ephesus had had an intelligent trainer the trainer would have taken notice of a dream in which the athlete spent the whole night in a black pond,[428] but the divine does not come into this. The well-preserved medical writers of the Roman Empire prior to Galen, that is to say Celsus, Aretaeus of Cappadocia[429] and Soranus, most certainly did not depend for diagnoses or treatments on dreams. Those who claim that ancient physicians all believed in prophetic dreams never attempt to explain this fact. Dioscorides, the great ancient expert on *materia medica,* naturally identifies certain plants as causes of bad dreams,[430] which suggests an altogether naturalistic approach.

Let us now turn to the profession of poetry, and above all to Vergil. Dreams are notably absent from his earlier works,[431] quite probably because of Epicurean influence, but there are more dreams in the *Aeneid* than there are in Homer. Anchises appears in dreams to redirect his son; the river-god Tiberinus sends Aeneas to see Evander.[432] At a vital moment, when Aeneas is in Crete, the Trojan Penates appear to him by night to tell him to go to Italy[433]—but here, intriguingly, the poet emphasizes that he was awake,[434] as if to eliminate the delusiveness that might have attached to a dream. Nonetheless the *Aeneid* contains about a dozen descriptions of 'true' dreams.[435]

When Vergil reworks the Homeric theme of the Gates of Horn and Ivory,[436] he seems to be speaking for himself:

> sunt geminae Somni portae, quarum altera fertur
> cornea, qua veris facilis datur exitus umbris,

Edelstein and Edelstein I, 238–239). The god's reply was unhelpful, and Rufus' interest is in what happened after the epileptic patient subsequently experienced a quartan fever.

428. *Medical Questions* 5.29–30. He briefly describes two other cases (cf. Oberhelman 1993, 138).

429. Aretaeus' date is controversial; some think that he was Galen's contemporary, but an earlier date seems to me more likely (cf. Kudlien 1967, 103: mid–first century).

430. ii.105, 107, 146, v.6.

431. Cf. *Ecl.* viii.108: 'credimus? an qui amant ipsi sibi somnia fingunt?' Servius says that this was a proverb. See further Kragelund 1989, 442 n. 45.

432. iv.351–353, v.722–745; viii.26–67.

433. *Aen.* iii.147–171.

434. He was in bed—'nec sopor illud erat, sed coram adgnoscere voltus/ velatasque comas praesentiaque ora videbar', iii.173–174. Cf. Veyne 1987, 389.

435. See Steiner 1952, also Bouquet 2001, 19–53, and Walde 2001, 261–311.

436. *Aen.* vi.893–896. Horace, *Odes* iii.27.41, which was presumably written earlier, also refers to them.

> altera candenti perfecta nitens elephanto,
> sed falsa ad caelum mittunt insomnia manes.[437]

We should notice that true dreams are not called dreams at all but shades, *umbrae,* almost as if true dreams were for the poet a quite difficult concept.[438] The *falsa insomnia* might be nonsense dreams, or misleading dreams such as the one that brought about Palinurus' shipwreck.[439] But true dreams, like the anger of Juno, must in some sense be taken seriously by the poet and his audience, otherwise the whole work threatens to disintegrate. Furthermore, it was through these four lines about the Gates of Horn and Ivory that Vergil chose to deliver the poem's sharpest shock—the exit of Aeneas and the Sibyl through the Gate of Ivory[440]—for a shock they are on any interpretation.

False dreams as well as true are part of the world of the *Aeneid.* The phantom Aeneas who deceives Turnus in *Aeneid* X is like the things 'quae sopitos deludunt somnia sensus' (present tense).[441] The *Aeneid* in short presents dreams that came true in solemn mythical-historical times, others that were deceptive; it expects nothing from dreams in the here-and-now. In so far as its influence was felt—and in a sense it was felt very widely—the poem will have transmitted both messages but above all perhaps the message of caution expressed at the end of Book VI.

Seeking to emulate the great writers of epic, both Greek and Latin, Vergil committed himself heavily to the credibility of certain dreams (and was resoundingly vindicated). His successors were more or less obliged to create their own variations.[442]

437. 'The gates of sleep are a pair. One of them is said to be made of horn, and by that one true shades are easily able to leave. The other is made of shining white ivory, but it is the way that the spirits of the dead send false dreams to the world above'.

438. Cf. Steiner 1952, 90–91. Though this is perhaps natural, given that several *Aeneid* dreams are apparitions of the dead, Hector in Book II and Anchises in Book IV. Earlier on, as Aeneas and the Sibyl are approaching the underworld, they encounter the elm tree where ('so they say') empty dreams, *somnia vana,* live under every leaf (lines 282–284). Nothing is said about where in the underworld true dreams might live, and the passage seems to hint that most dreams are fallacious.

439. *Aen.* v.840–846.

440. vi.898. Miller 1994, 26, absurdly says that Vergil made a 'mistake' about Homer's passage on the gates of dreams.

441. x.642: 'the dreams that dupe our sleeping senses'.

442. Stoicism perhaps encouraged Lucan to include four dreams in the *Pharsalia,* though as we have seen Seneca, the poet's Stoic uncle, was probably sceptical. The Lucan

A great deal depended on literary genre. Historians of this time were probably well advised to keep dream-predictions somewhat on the margins. Some scholars have argued that Livy was altogether sceptical about dreams,[443] as would be appropriate for an admirer of Polybius. Scipio Africanus, he says, was always inventing dreams to tell to the *multitudo* (a reminiscence of Polybius),[444] and the famous dream Hannibal dreamt before invading Italy was ultimately misleading.[445] The dreams dreamt by the heroic consuls of 340 BC are qualified by the word 'dicitur', 'it is said'.[446] Livy would probably not have told the story of Latinius' dream[447] if it had belonged to much more recent times. At the most, he was content to leave certain cases open.[448] There is no sign of personal confidence in the premonitory dream. The best-preserved Greek historian of the period, Dionysius of Halicarnassus (apart from Josephus), seems a degree less sceptical: he is not Herodotean in this respect, but he is not Polybian either. He tells the story of Latinius as the defeat of a sceptic,[449] and allows room for heaven-sent dreams in archaic Latium;[450] but delusions are dreams *(oneirata)*,[451] and Dionysius considers that he has to *explain* why King Pyrrhus believed an inauspicious dream (he had had a bad dream before that had been followed by a disaster).[452] When Q. Curtius approached the history of

---

references are i.185–194, iii.8–35, vii.7–24 (with speculations as to why Pompey dreamt an enjoyable dream the night before Pharsalus), 764–786 (both Caesar and his soldiers dream, an ingenious idea). For dreams in other silver-Latin epics see Näf 2004, 94.

443. See the bibliography given in Levene 1993, 16 (this is not his position, however).

444. xxvi.19.3–4. Davies 2004, 128, should not therefore have cited the claims that Scipio makes about his dreams in xxvi.41.18 as evidence that Livy was a believer.

445. The dream: xxi.22.6–9 ('fama est . . .'). Levene 1993, 46, points out that the dream does not promise Hannibal ultimate victory, but it certainly (in the story) encouraged him. I disagree with the judgement of Pelling (1997, 204) that here we are 'in a world like that of Herodotus'. For sources and bibliography on this dream see Weber 1999, 24 n. 78, D'Arco 2002.

446. For 'dicitur' see viii.6.9 (ignored by Pelling 202), with Oakley's n. Davies 2004, 128, is in error here too.

447. ii.36.

448. When Livy writes (xliii.13) that people 'now' do not generally believe that the gods send portents, he may imply that they did not much believe in truth-telling dreams either.

449. *Ant.Rom.* vii.68–69, 73.

450. i.57; iii.67.3 and v.54.2 are also relevant.

451. vi.7.5.

452. xx.12. Josephus considered that he had to defend the inclusion of a dream in his *Antiquities* (*AJ* xvii.354), even though the dream was a rather credible one.

Alexander of Macedon, he encountered many dream-stories (we can read them in Plutarch's life); as we have already seen, he retained only one. So when we read that the great Drusus ordered the elder Pliny, in a dream, to write the history of his German wars,[453] we may not only detect a literary tradition but an elegant way of disguising an act of self-ingratiation (Claudius, the current emperor, was Drusus' son).

Did early imperial orators introduce dream-stories as evidence? From Quintilian, it looks as if it sometimes happened,[454] but we have too little evidence to judge. The lofty Ciceronian tradition was against it, and there was always the risk of antagonizing Epicurean judges. The elder Seneca recommended against it—'it is ridiculous to make a point that cannot be proved false'—and gently mocked Iunius Otho, a senatorial orator of some fame, who had published four books of *colores* that contained so many dreams that they were called 'the books of Antiphon'.[455] But the gap between teachers and *controversiae* on the one side and the real world of the courtroom on the other was notoriously wide. And every orator worthy of the name knew how to refute an argument based on the providence of the gods as manifested in dreams.[456]

Valerius Maximus is not to be confused with a historian. The author of *facta et dicta memorabilia,* a collection of exemplary stories, is writing in a wholly uncritical genre and is almost of necessity the enemy of scepticism. He recounts eight Roman and ten foreign examples of interesting dreams.[457] Some are stories that others had rejected.[458] In any case Valerius should be seen as the extreme of Roman credulity in this era.

The last author to consider in this section is Petronius, the historian's great temptation—for we are tempted to see him as a commentator on 'real life'.[459] I shall not attempt to resolve here the question of Petronius'

453. Pliny, *Ep.* iii.5.

454. *Inst.* v.7.35. According to Kragelund, 'as evidence dreams carried little weight, but some would use them as ornament *(color)*' (2001, 91 n. 115).

455. *Contr.* ii.1.33; cf. vii.7.15.

456. See Seneca, *Suas.* 4.4, with Kragelund 1991, 262.

457. i.7; there are others elsewhere, e.g. ii.4.5.

458. The story in i.7.3 was treated sceptically in Cicero, *De div.* ii.136, and subjected to the word 'dicitur' in Livy. The stories in Valerius Maximus i.7.4 and 6 had also been dismissed in Cicero, loc. cit.

459. I reserve the Greek novelists for the moment, even though it could be maintained that Xenophon of Ephesus, probably the earliest of them and quite probably a first-

personal opinions about this or any other subject, except to say that I believe Kragelund to have demonstrated that Petronius was not committed to the doctrines of Epicurus.[460] In my opinion, he in fact makes fun of Epicurean dogma about dreaming. The latter possibility arises because of the splendid scene in which Lichas and Tryphaena dream—correctly, in fact—that Giton is on board their ship, only to have Eumolpus attempt to mislead them by invoking Epicurus: 'that shows you', says he, 'that Epicurus was a divine man, for in the cleverest way he showed up that kind of illusion'.[461] It is certainly tempting, however, to think that Petronius was a dream-sceptic: one of his characters rates *interpretations* of dreams as worthless stuff, on the level of broken glass,[462] and Fragment 30, like Lucretius, puts forward the theory that dreams correspond to our waking preoccupations; this passage specifically denies that they are sent by the gods. But we cannot even say for certain that Petronius or his readers were very much intrigued by dreams, since they appear in generous numbers in almost all ancient novels.[463]

The 'Middle Classes'

Some dreams are truthful, some are false: the *Aeneid* reinforced the lesson for anyone who had been to a Latin-speaking school for a few years (in other words, a smallish minority). But there is no literary access to the middle classes. It would only be a long shot to trust the Lives of Aesop, probably productions of the first century AD. In one of them, 'Aesop' explains in rough-and-ready mythological terms why some dreams are true and others false.[464] He also implies that it is only brainless women who pay heed to what they dream.[465]

---

century writer, supports the argument that scepticism about predictive dreams was then quite strong in the social elite.

460. Kragelund 1989, 449–450.

461. *Sat.* 104. Kragelund 1989, 440–443, attempts to avoid this conclusion by pointing out that the dreams of Lichas and Tryphaena were in fact quasi-Epicurean wish-fulfilments; the fact remains that they quickly proved to be true, as Epicurean doctrine said they only could by chance. Cf. Habermehl 2006, 389.

462. *Sat.* 10 (*vitrea fracta*). See further *Sat.* 128.

463. On the *Satyrica* as a novel see among others Kragelund 1989, 437. For another Petronian dream see *Sat.* 17.7 (reading *somnio*), with Kragelund 1989, 445–446.

464. *Vita G*, 33. It was a matter of competition with Apollo, as in *Iphigeneia in Tauris*.

465. *Vita G*, 29–30.

Much the best evidence about the attitudes of the middle classes seems to come from the inscriptions, which we have already mentioned several times, alluding to divine instructions delivered in dreams. All those responsible for such dedications were in this period from outside the upper social elite, though some of them were certainly people of some means and some education. The dedicants presumably expected that the community in general would react to their dedications with respect, or at least without derision, and this may be especially true in those cases in which the dedication was unconnected with any shrine of a god such as Serapis or Asclepius who was known to make frequent use of dream-communication.[466]

The great majority of Latin *visu/iussu* dedications date from the second and third centuries, as Renberg observes. He argues, however, that the production of such inscriptions reflects the expansion of the Latin 'epigraphic habit' first described by Mrozek and MacMullen.[467] And whereas Romans of earlier times made dedications to deities without specifying whether dreams were involved, freedmen and easterners (plus a few others) spread the custom in Italy and nearby in the first century AD;[468] after 100 it spread to inhabitants of the western empire of many different national origins.[469] In short, there is on this view, no change in religious practice,[470] a somewhat misleading conclusion, since dedicants were now bold enough to mention that they had in person received divine epiphanies and/or instructions.

But what is most fascinating here is that while the production of Latin inscriptions of this kind does not seem to increase after 100 *relative to the overall production of inscriptions*, in the Greek world things do change at about that date. Greek inscriptions alluding to the appearances of gods in dreams are, on my reading of Renberg's catalogue, at least six times as common in the second century AD as in the first (of course there are innumerable dating problems—but also quite a lot of inscriptions with precise internal dates). This cannot mainly be because of a change in the Greek epigraphic habit.

---

466. Cf. Weber 2005–2006, 78–80.

467. Renberg 2003, 158, 207; Mrozek 1973, MacMullen 1982; see further Mouritsen 2005.

468. Renberg 2003, 205–206. The earliest specific date for an *ex visu* inscription is 51, *ILS* 4375 (Rome; no. 685 in Renberg's catalogue).

469. Renberg 2003, 210.

470. Renberg 2003, 207.

What does all this mean? This body of material seldom if ever refers to predictive dreams. Yet belief in and trust in dreams is certainly involved. A mild and somewhat alien increase in belief and trust may be hypothesized for the Latin-speaking zones in the first century AD. What happened there after 100 is quite curious and will be discussed below.

When people with chronic diseases despair of normal medicine, says a speaker in one of Plutarch's dialogues, they turn to expiations, amulets and dreams.[471] It is, from his perspective, a counsel of desperation for the few.

A Victory for Religion? 100–250 AD

The Sceptic philosopher and doctor Sextus Empiricus, by contrast, writing towards the end of the second century, includes among 'things which are believed in by all men' divination, divine inspiration, astrology and 'prediction by means of *oneiroi*'.[472] This did not mean that everyone believed that all dreams were revealing: Tertullian counts it as an eccentricity of the people of Telmessus that they supposedly entertained some such belief.[473] But if Sextus Empiricus—who presumably had mainly Greeks in mind[474]— was right, there had been a significant change in attitude since the first century. And moderns sometimes go beyond these sources: thus an expert on Artemidorus once wrote, for example, that in the age of the Antonine emperors 'most men [he means people, I take it] considered their dream-experiences . . . prophetic'.[475]

It is a fairly old idea that there was a reaction towards stronger religious feelings in the Roman Empire of the second century, and although the idea has sometimes taken strange forms and received strange explanations there

---

471. *De facie quae in orbe lunae* 1 = *Mor.* 920b. Cf. Diodorus Siculus xxxi.43. The speaker is Lamprias, whom we mentioned earlier; in fact he is not unsympathetic to such persons.

472. *Adv.Math.* ix (= *Adv.phys.* i).132. Such a universal conviction is this, he claims, that it guarantees the existence of the gods, without whom there could be no prophecy. Obviously the point is polemical.

473. *De anima* 46.3: 'nulla somnia evacuant, imbecillitatem coniectationis incusant'. They were sometimes supposed to have invented oneiromancy (Tatian, *Oratio* 1.1).

474. Though he spent some of his life in Rome.

475. Pack 1955, 280.

is much to be said for it.[476] Changing views about predictive dreams may fit such a hypothesis quite well.[477]

But how much of change was there? It might give us pause that the partisan but very experienced dream-interpreter Artemidorus knew that some people held views sharply different from his own. 'I have been afraid', he writes, 'of the adverse criticism of those . . . who believe there is no such thing as divination or as providence of the gods. . . . from the superabundance of examples, I am able . . . to prove the truth of my assertions comprehensively and clearly'.[478] Evidently he did not suppose that he was operating in a world in which everyone agreed with him. Even the paid oneiromancers must generally have avoided the trap of claiming that *all* dreams had predictive force—Artemidorus himself regarded a lot of dreams as rubbish[479] and was well aware that some were simply erotic wish-fulfilments.[480]

The significance of Artemidorus in all this is not in fact clear. We can hardly say in any detail who he catered to, apart perhaps from those who were particularly superstitious or particularly vulnerable to the vagaries of fate (politicians, the sick, owners of small vineyards . . .). He must have had a considerable number of more or less convinced informants, and there must have been a measure of popular appeal in his general approach.[481] A

476. Cf. Geffcken 1978 [1920], ch. 1, Drachmann 1922, 120–122, and, more recently, Veyne 1986. Yet it is not at all certain that the volume of interest in Epicureanism declined (see below).

477. Cf. Dulaey 1973, 30–31.

478. I prooem. This passage may give the impression that Artemidorus thought that truth-telling dreams came from the gods; but he appears not to have been of this opinion (see the next chapter).

479. V prooem.: 'it was difficult and laborious to attempt to gather together only those dreams that were worth recording—for it is very easy and takes no time at all to record a large number of random dreams'.

480. i.78 p. 88 lines 12–15.

481. No doubt Pomeroy 1991 was right to suppose that Artemidoran interpretation had some popular appeal. Bowersock's suggestion (1994, 97–98) that 'prediction was . . . of far more importance to the upper strata of society than the lower' is scarcely persuasive. You could meet petty fortune-tellers in any *agora* (cf. Artemidorus i prooem. p. 2.14). See Weber 1999, 224–225, who, however, struggles relentlessly to overstate the size of Artemidorus' likely readership. The misconception that Artemidorus was 'widely used': Hunt 1989, 87; cf. Oberhelman 1997, 56.

recent attempt to place him in a more precise cultural context implies, however, that his imagined reader is likely to have come from western Asia Minor, like the author himself.[482] It is also likely, in any case, that his *Onei-rocritica* will mainly have come mostly into the hands of the few rich people who could afford such a book, and into those of professional diviners such as Artemidorus' son, to whom part of it was addressed.[483]

The continuance of the old education and the old philosophical schools no doubt limited the speed at which opinion changed. Yet we shall find some of the exponents of the Second Sophistic among those most inclined to trust their dreams. I will proceed by rereviewing the strata of Roman society that we considered in their first-century manifestations.

Emperors and Courtiers

The imperial court may regularly have disseminated stories of dreams designed to strengthen the emperor's reputation, but the sources for this are never contemporary until Septimius Severus.[484] How strongly the emperors felt any personal interest in dreams is seldom clear until we come to Marcus; a number of stories are told concerning Hadrian and dreams, but they tell us more about the age (see below) than about the individual or his immediate circle.

Marcus, like an orthodox Stoic, asserts that 'the gods help humans in all sorts of ways, through dreams [they come first] and through prophecies,

482. Bowersock 2004, 61–62, demonstrates the regional tinge in Artemidorus' Greek.

483. The logic of Roman literacy and book-distribution, combined with the (non)evidence of the papyri, points in that direction. Artemidorus says that he wrote so as not to 'waste' his wisdom (iv prooem.), and Books I–III evidently circulated among experts (ibid., p. 237.18); IV–V, on the other hand, were written for his homonymous son, with explicit instructions to keep them to himself (ibid., p. 238.2–6), which he apparently did not mean literally (see v prooem. p. 301.15).

484. Two cases concern Trajan, Suetonius, *Dom.* 23.2, but since this refers to the emperors, plural, who would succeed him, we may think it belongs to the reign of Hadrian. The dream said by Dio lxviii.5.1 to have been dreamt by Trajan may be contemporary, but Dio is hardly to be trusted on this point. The same applies to the dream of Hadrian (the night before he became emperor!) in lxix.2.1 (there is no reason to think that he included many if any dreams in his autobiography, though that is possible—cf. Weber 2000, 124 n. 172—and indeed if he had done so, we would have heard more about them; the book was known to Dio, Syme 1991, 398). Dio lxxi = lxxii.36.1 and SHA, *Marcus* 5, describe a favourable dream Marcus is supposed to have dreamt in 138.

with regard to the things they quarrel about'.[485] It is all the more striking that the only dreams he refers to are some that gave him medical advice.[486] Fronto also, it appears, took medical advice from a dream on at least one occasion.[487] If Marcus allowed dreams to influence any other area of his life, he was altogether reticent about it, but he allowed Galen not to accompany him on his German campaign when the latter offered the transparent excuse that Asclepius, in a dream, had instructed him to stay behind.[488]

In the summer of 193 Cassius Dio was a young senator on the make, a praetor designate, while Septimius Severus was a fresh usurper far from secure in his new position. Dio composed a little book in which he described the dreams and portents which showed that Septimius was destined to become emperor; he made it public and sent a copy to the emperor, who showed his favour by writing Dio 'many complimentary things' that same evening.[489] What is most important here is that the six dreams Dio lists must have been described or invented by Septimius himself or possibly by someone in his entourage, and must have been thought of as useful propaganda.[490] Septimius had an equestrian statue of himself set up in the Forum Romanum on the spot where, in a supposed dream, he had seen Pertinax's horse throw him and acknowledge its new master.[491] And there is other evidence that Septimius' confidence in dreams was not a pretence:

485. *To Himself* ix.27 (the exact meaning of the last phrase is not certain, but the standard translation by A. Farquharson cannot be right). Fronto's attitude was similar, *Ad M.Caes.* iii.9.1.

486. i.17.20. Motschmann 2002, 41, erroneously speaks of a single occasion. As to how such commands were to be understood to work cf. v.8.1.

487. Artemidorus iv.22.

488. Galen, *De libris propriis* 2 = XIX.18–19K.

489. lxxii = lxxiii.23 ('publishing' will mean that he sent copies to the men of power). The dreams and portents are listed in lxxiv = lxxv.3. On the chronology of these events see Millar 1964, 29.

490. His dreams were as follows. (1) He was suckled by a she-wolf, like Romulus. (2) Marcus Aurelius' wife Faustina prepared his wedding chamber in the Temple of Venus near the imperial palace. (3) Water flowed from his hand. (4) The whole Roman Empire saluted him. (5) He played on the whole world like a musical instrument. (6) A horse threw Pertinax in the forum and Septimius mounted it. Weber 2000, 76–77, makes unnecessary difficulties over the evident origin of these real or supposed dreams. He also lists the other sources (203–210).

491. Herodian ii.9.4–6, who claims to have this from Septimius' autobiography. He also says (9.3) that 'these things are believed to be honest and true when they turn out well'. In ii.15.6 he makes a derogatory comment about the historians and poets who had written at

he put the very powerful Plautianus to death partly because of a dream he dreamt the night before Plautianus was accused (unless this was only gossip);[492] and the Senate had to discuss a treasonous dream dreamt by the nurse of one of its members (he had already been condemned).[493]

The son and heir Caracalla demonstrated his devotion to the sanctuary of Asclepius at Pergamum, which he visited in the winter of 214–215.[494] By this time, he seems to have been obsessed with seers and soothsayers.[495] He also showed his favour to Apollo Grannus, a Celtic deity in whose sanctuaries incubation may have been practised, and to Serapis.[496] Thus both father and son placed some trust in their dreams.

Subversive divination had attracted hostile attention from the emperors since the beginning, but it is only with the Severans that the evidence for legislation against dreamers becomes fairly explicit: 'those who pronounce or bandy about or knowingly invent things under the pretext that they are doing so "on the instructions of the gods" must by no means go unpunished'— so Ulpian.[497] The government was now much more exercised over these matters.

Senators and the Well-to-do in General

The value of Pliny's letters is that in this as in many other respects they show how a senator wished to be seen, and perhaps what a senator without philosophical interests actually thought. He seems to reflect a milieu in which dream-predictions are, sometimes at least, rather readily believed. Negative dreams may require precautions.[498] When he recounts his uncle's dream about Drusus, he gives no hint that the former might have been well-advised to make up his own mind before embarking on writing a

---

length about the numerous signs of divine favour Septimius was supposed to have received.

492. Herodian's fairly detailed account says nothing of this dream.

493. Dio lxxvi = lxxvii.3 and 8.

494. Herodian iv.8.3 explicitly says that the emperor wanted to make use of 'the treatments of Asclepius' and that while at the sanctuary 'he had his fill of dreams'.

495. iv.12.3.

496. Fowden 2005, 546–547.

497. VII De officio proconsulis, in Mosaicarum et Romanarum Legum Collatio xv.2.6 (FIRA II, p. 580).

498. On the case of Suetonius' lawsuit, see above p. 132.

twenty-book history.[499] Yet he professes some doubt about the predictive value of a dream dreamt by one of his freedmen, afterwards echoed by a slave's dream: did it mean something or not?[500]

Among Pliny's correspondents, Suetonius reads as something of a believer, Tacitus much less so. Admittedly both had to conform to the rules of their respective literary genres, and neither the profusion of dreams in Suetonius' lives,[501] nor the occasional irony on the part of Tacitus, is a cause for surprise. But even Tacitus sometimes appears to tell a dream-story with a straight face: we met Germanicus' propitious dream in Chapter I.[502]

The wealthy and highly educated friend Aelius Aristides was clearly part of a very substantial group of Greeks and others who sought medical help from their dreams, but some of his friends criticized him for acting on his dreams so much, and he portrays his doctors as having been sceptical about the advice his dreams gave him on the subject of what was apparently his gravest illness, his 'tumour'.[503] His initial reaction to that illness had been to turn to ordinary doctors; it was only when they despaired that he turned to dreams,[504] perhaps rather as modern patients suffering from terminal cancer sometimes turn to 'alternative medicine'. It is certain in any case that Aristides very firmly believed in his own dreams. But he will not have extended this to the whole of mankind: it was Asclepius' favour that brought him his steady supply of unconscious truth. We may suppose that Aristides was not unique in this respect: the Cilician sophist (P. Anteius) Antiochus, member of a consular family, 'used to spend very many nights in the temple of Asclepius' in his native Aegae, both because of the dreams he had there and because of the conversations he had with Asclepius while awake.[505] Philostratus, incidentally, did not think that Aelius Aristides' de-

499. *Ep.* iii.5.4. Similarly he recounts a premonitory dream about death as a straightforward fact, v.5.5–6.

500. *Ep.* vii.27.12–16.

501. *DJ* 7, *DA* 94, *Tib.* 74, *Cal.* 50 (nothing predictive here) and 57, *Claud.* 37, *Nero* 46, *Galba* 4, *Otho* 7, *Vesp.* 5, *Dom.* 23.

502. *Annals* xii.13 (the hunting dreams of the Parthian priests of 'Hercules'), on the other hand, seems to be simply an exotic detail of no particular consequence, inserted to relieve a military narrative (which happens not to be at all tedious).

503. *Orat.* xlvii.63; 62 and 67. It is not clear what was wrong with him (see C. A. Behr's n. 89 in his translation of this work [1981]).

504. See Behr 1968, 22, and cf. Festugière 1954, 99–100. Compare what is said about the role of Imhotep/Imouthes/Asclepius in *P.Oxy.* xi.1381, lines 53–56 (second century).

505. Philostratus, *VS* ii.3 p. 568.

votion to dreaming of Asclepius was remarkable enough to be worth mentioning in the biographical sketch he wrote, even though he knew the *Sacred Tales*.

There continued to be wealthy Epicureans in midcentury, and they continued to deny that dreams were sent by the gods: Diogenes of Oenoanda is quite specific.[506] We have ample evidence in the pages of Galen, Lucian, Tertullian, Aelian and Origen, among others, that Epicureanism continued to have influence at least down to Severan times[507]—but here we are straying outside the uppermost order.

Inside or outside the senatorial order, it would be hard to find any other wealthy Roman after Tacitus who expressed scepticism about revelatory dreams. That is not by any means to claim that Aelius Aristides or Cassius Dio was typical, or to deny that most sensible people went about their lives undisturbed by dreams, but there does seems to have been a certain shift. It is almost impossible to imagine that a senator of say a hundred years earlier than Cassius Dio could have approached a hard-headed general in the manner in which Dio approached Septimius Severus. And that was only part of Dio's known experience with dreams: the goddess Tyche (Fortune) appeared to him regularly, he says.[508] Other passages make it clear that he believed or professed to believe that some dreams came true.[509] He once dreamt a dream in which Septimius predicted that he, Dio, would write the history of Caracalla,[510] and he dreamt, thanks to the *daimonion* he says, the clever ending of his entire mammoth history.[511] Unlike Tacitus, he is never known to have dismissed a dream as untrue.[512]

The epigraphical record also helps: M. Antonius Polemon, a rich sophist

---

506. Fragment 9 Smith (*The Epicurean Inscription,* ed. M. F. Smith, 1993), col. VI, lines 6–11. The date is hardly likely to be later than the middle of the second century: cf. Smith, pp. 39–48.

507. Cf. Ferguson and Hershbell 1990.

508. lxxii = lxxiii.23.4.

509. The dream-oracle of Mallos, lxxii = lxxiii.7.1–2; a dream of the 'priest of Jupiter', i.e. the flamen Dialis, lxxv.8.2.

510. lxxviii = lxxix.10.1–2.

511. lxxx.5.3. He quoted the *Iliad* (xi.163–164): 'Hector Zeus saved from the spears and the dust and the slaughter and the blood and the uproar'.

512. Freyburger-Galland 1999, 533, implies that ancient historical writers in general thought premonitory dreams were important, which is of course false. Her article amply documents Dio's obsession. Arrian too reached consular rank, but I postpone him till the next section.

closely connected at one time to the imperial court, dedicated a statue of Demosthenes in the sanctuary of Asclepius at Pergamum because he had been told to do so in a dream.[513] This would have been about midcentury. Some time after 180, a senator and *pontifex* in Rome, Q. Pompeius Falco Sosius Priscus, made a dedication to his late distinguished great-grandfather Q. Pompeius Sosius Priscus (*consul ordinarius* in 149), 'instructed to do so by a dream'.[514]

The Learned Professions

Authoritative dreams seem to have gained respectability among second-century physicians. Galen provides the main evidence, and it is plain that he expected his sentiments to seem reasonable to many though not all other members of his profession (there were marked differences of opinion, as we shall see). Here I will speak about the degree of trust Galen seems to have placed in dreams, while in the next chapter I shall say more about the intellectual context of his ideas. A physician of a generation or so earlier, Soranus, shows that taking notice of dreams was for him an ordinary part of female superstition (to be avoided in a children's nurse).[515] The contradiction with Galen's views is not formal, but there nonetheless seems to have been a change.

It may be useful to distinguish between Galen's attitude towards dreams in his actual medical practice, his more general attitude towards dreams, and his belief in the efficacy of incubation shrines. As we saw in Chapter I, he had actually become a physician because of dreams dreamt by his father Nicon. A dream (*enhupnion*) featuring the *Demiourgos* himself instructed him to expand a section of *On the Uses of Parts* concerning that 'most divine organ', the eye.[516] He seems to have believed in divination more generally,[517] but

513. *Die Inschriften des Asklepieions*, ed. C. Habicht (Altertümer von Pergamon VIII.3), no. 33. The dream may have been a pure invention, an excuse for claiming a link with Demosthenes. Polemo showed his great self-esteem by using only that name (as Habicht remarks).

514. *ILS* 1006; this seems to be the earliest known inscription of this type to be erected by a senator.

515. *Gyn.* i.3.

516. III.812K; cf. Nutton 2004, 279. At the same time, he excuses himself for writing at such length.

517. *In Hippocratis de Acutorum Victu Librum* (also in i.15 = XV.441-442K (also in *CMG* V.9.1 pp. 128–129 Helmreich).

not surprisingly he will not have anything to do with drugs that are used for dream-sending.[518] None of this seems especially remarkable in its context.

How far in fact did Galen rely on dreams in his medical practice? The fact that he was led into the profession by his father's dreams does not necessarily mean that 'dreams are fully incorporated into [his] medical science'.[519]

The short essay called *About Diagnosis from Dreams* that appears in the Galenic corpus I treat here as a compilation based on his authentic work.[520] It maintains that dreams indicate the condition of the body's humours or other bodily conditions; but there is nothing fantastic about this ('some who were about to sweat critically seemed [in dreams] to be bathing or swimming in hot water'), and while he asserts that there are genuine prophetic dreams he says that they are hard to tell from those of physical origin. In other words, he does not go very far here.[521] The lost treatise we know that he wrote about dreams[522] may possibly have gone further.

The main reason for thinking so is a well-known passage in his treatise *De curandi ratione per venae sectionem:*[523]

---

518. *De simplicium medicamentorum temperamentis ac facultatibus* x.1 = XII.251K.

519. The phrase is from Oberhelman 1983, 37.

520. VI.832–835K. Demuth 1972, 71, judges it to be Byzantine; Guidorizzi 1973 also sees it as a compilation. It is no longer accurate, as far as I can tell, to say that it is 'generally considered' spurious (Lloyd 1987, 31 n. 95). There is an English translation in Oberhelman 1983, and another by L. Pearcy at www.medicinaantiqua.org.uk/tr_GalDreams .html. Neither translation is felicitous (for a translation of one section of the treatise see Chapter IV). I previously thought that the treatise was probably too mechanistic and simple-minded to be Galen's genuine work (Harris 2003, 23), but I now think that these qualities are the result of excerpting genuine works. Some sentences coincide with sentences in Galen, *Comm. in Hipp. Epid.* I (see *CMG* V.10.1 p. 108 Wenkebach) (according to Guidorizzi 98, they both derive from another [lost] work of Galen's). There is nothing in *About Diagnosis from Dreams* that contradicts any known belief of Galen's, and the work is preserved in several MSS together with summaries of authentic work of Galen (Guidorizzi 99). Cf. also Oberhelman 1993, 139–141.

521. His most revealing comment concerns a man who dreamt that one of his legs turned to stone. The people Galen calls the experts said that this dream concerned his slaves, but in fact the leg in question became paralysed, 'which none of us expected' (VI.834K).

522. *De fac. nat.* i.12 (II.29 K): 'This school [the Epicureans] despises dreams, omens, portents, and the whole of astrology, subjects which we have dealt with at greater length in another work'.

523. Ch. 23 = XI.314K. I have largely followed the translation of von Staden 2003, 21.

I shall now indicate to you how I was stirred to practise the cutting of an artery. Urged on by some dreams I had, two of which were vivid, I reached for the artery in the space between the index finger and the thumb of the right hand, and I let the blood flow until it stopped spontaneously, as the dream had commanded. Not quite a whole *litra* [about a quarter of a litre] flowed out. Instantly a long-standing pain ceased that had been pressing most against the part where the liver meets the diaphragm. This then happened to me in my youth.

Perhaps Galen would not have done this in later life, perhaps he would not have done it to a patient, but the story is patently true and it displays a degree of trust in dreams that few if any leading physicians had displayed in preceding centuries.[524] And he certainly did not suppose that such a narrative would in itself harm his professional reputation. There were in any case limits to Galen's confidence in the medical value of dreams: he criticized Empiricist doctors for sometimes allowing their dreams to determine their treatments.[525]

Galen appears to have believed that he was especially favoured, without saying that any god, such as Asclepius, was responsible. Von Staden has argued that the form of this belief was trust in his own *daimon,* reminiscent of Socrates' *daimon.*[526]

Galen also thought that patients often received sound advice at the great sanctuaries. In the passage just quoted he mentions a worshipper of Asclepius at Pergamum who underwent a similar successful treatment, 'having come to it in a dream' (in the god's sanctuary?).[527] In another case, Asclepius, cured a patient of elephantiasis (though no dream is mentioned).[528] All this may receive some confirmation from an Arabic fragment of his lost *Commentary on the Oath of Hippocrates,* which says that 'we find an innumerably large number of people to whom their cure came from god, some (obtaining it) through Serapis, and others through Asclepius in the city of Epidaurus, the city of Cos, and the city of Pergamon—the last mentioned

---

524. In another case, a fellow doctor dreamt that Galen's proposed treatment was the right one: *De methodo medendi* xiv.8 = X.972K. Von Staden 2003, 24, lucidly distinguishes Galen's attitude from that of the leading physicians of earlier times.

525. Kudlien 1981, 121, referring to *De methodo medendi* iii.2 (X.164K), *De sectis* 2 (II.66–67K), *De compositione medicamentorum* i.1 (XIII.366K).

526. Von Staden 2003.

527. XI.315K; see von Staden 2003, 22–23.

528. *De morborum differentiis* 9 = VI. 869K.

one being my own city.'[529] But there remain substantial doubts about the accuracy of this quotation, which may overstate Galen's trust in dreams.[530]

To sum up, Galen had a quite profound belief in the authenticity of some apparently divine dreams, especially when they occurred in a shrine of Asclepius, and he was willing to put an almost unprecedented trust in the advice dreams gave about medical treatments—though he never quite reveals how far he was willing to go in this respect. The general conclusion is plain enough: second-century doctors to some degree diverged from the Hippocratic tradition in the direction of trusting the treatments they thought their dreams recommended to them.

Is it possible to generalize about second-century historians? Were Cassius Dio's predecessors on the way to becoming enthusiasts for predictive dreams? Both Arrian and Appian do occasionally admit such dreams, but as noted earlier Arrian only describes a single dream that he attributes to Alexander. One of the signs of divine influence over Alexander's life, he says, was that various people dreamt dreams prophesying his death.[531] None of this amounts to very much for a life so surrounded by fables, and the sceptical attitude of Arrian's teacher Epictetus may have had some effect here; but it did not prevent Arrian from telling Hadrian that he found convincing the story of the Black Sea mariners that they received navigational instructions in their dreams from Achilles.[532] As for Appian, he includes dreams at a greater pace, and without apparent reserve.[533]

The opinions of the novelists, on the other hand, are largely hidden from us: contrary to what is sometimes implied, they do not speak to us directly on this subject. 'The *daimonion* often tells mortals the future by night', says Achilles Tatius,[534] but it is the hero speaking. They all played on the convention that dreams could be truth-telling in one way or another, but the

529. Quoted by the thirteenth-century medical historian Ibn Abî Uṣaybi'ah, in Rosenthal 1956, 60 (fr. 1c).

530. Cf. Kudlien 1981, 119. The trouble is that the preceding sentence states (in Rosenthal's translation) that 'people in general bear witness to the fact that it was God who gave them the craft of medicine through inspiration in dreams and visions delivering them from severe diseases'. However Nutton 2004, 279, takes the whole passage to be authentic.

531. vii.30.

532. If, that is to say, the *Periplous Maris Euxini* is his genuine work; Achilles: ch. 34.

533. In one case at least, the silence of other sources may be significant: *Lib.* 136. Other cases: *Lib.* 1, *Syr.* 56, *Mithr.* 9, 27, 83, *BC* i.97, i.105, ii.68 (misunderstood), ii.115, iv.110.

534. i.3.

convention was already there when such texts first appear. The characters in all the five preserved Greek novels quite often take dreams to be super-human admonitions, inevitably, we may say.[535] An actor in a novel will oc-casionally make a pejorative remark about dreams—Heliodorus' Cnemon, for instance, treats fussing about the meaning of dreams as a waste of time.[536] The characters commonly draw erroneous conclusions from their own and others' dreams,[537] and Shadi Bartsch has shown how, for instance, Achilles Tatius and Heliodorus employ mistaken interpretations of dreams and oracles to forward their narratives.[538] When the authorial voice is audible, it is coolly detached: 'he explained the dream in this way, his desire inter-preting it for him thus'[539]—which is a long way of course from saying that the dream could easily have been nonsense.

In all these circumstances, we would be astonished if the lengthy biog-raphy of a holy hero did *not* make him into an expert on dream inter-pretation, favoured by the higher powers with significant dreams (see Chapter I on the *Shepherd* of Hermas, for example). Philostratus' biogra-phy of Apollonius of Tyana fulfils our expectations—but even here there are complexities, including the overarching question whether we prefer to call Philostratus' book a novel.[540] A dream summoned Apollonius to visit Crete, and another converted a doubter to Apollonius' cause.[541] Once, at least, a dream comes true.[542] The chief Indian gymnosophist cryptically but not unreasonably warns Apollonius against dreams 'that lift you off the earth'.[543] We will not worry that dreams can provide cowards with ex-cuses.[544] But it is part of Apollonius' omniscience that when he visited the shrine of Asclepius at Pergamum he suggested to some of the suppliants 'what they should do to obtain favourable dreams'—quite improper tres-

535. See in general Said 1997.

536. ii.16.6. Cf. Chariton ii.5.7, iii.1.4.

537. E.g. Chariton iii.7.4–5, Heliodorus i.16.3–4, i.18.5. Cf. Heliodorus ii.36.2.

538. Bartsch 1989, 85–94. Cf. Longus i.7–8, iii.27–29, iv.34. In the view of Bowersock 1994, 89, Achilles Tatius, Chariton and Xenophon of Ephesus were uninterested in predic-tive dreams, only in epiphany dreams and those that reflected psychological states.

539. Heliodorus i.19.1.

540. Following Bowersock 1969, 5, and earlier Eduard Meyer; almost a novel, in the judgement of Bowie 1978, 1664 n. 42.

541. *V.Ap.* iv.34, viii.31.

542. viii.12.

543. vi.10.

544. iv.37.

passing, one might think.[545] The book is after all, at the very least, novelistic—
and from time to time ironical. Are we being teased, as Apollonius is said
to have teased his companion Damis? Early on, in Mesopotamia, a god
constructed a dream for him in which he saw some fish marooned on dry
land—they lamented like humans and asked the assistance of a passing dol-
phin; Apollonius was not frightened by this (as an ordinary person would
have been?), and understood what it meant. But to give Damis a shock, he
told him that the dream foretold something bad. Damis swallowed the bait,
but Apollonius laughed. 'You have not become a philosopher yet if you are
afraid of this'. He explains that they are near to territory settled by Greeks
from Eretria 500 years before, and that the gods wanted him to tend to
their needs and perhaps to those of all the Greeks stranded in that region.[546]
Later, Apollonius states that 'the faculty of divination by dreams' is 'the
most divine [*theiotaton*] of human faculties'.[547] There can be little doubt
that this was the opinion of Philostratus, and that it was widely diffused in
Severan times, probably more so than in the past.

The 'Middle Classes'

As we saw, the evidence of religious dedications shows that in the Greek-
speaking population references to instructions received in dreams became
far commoner in the second century than the first. This appears to be roughly
contemporary with a shift towards greater trust in dreams on the part of some
members of the social and intellectual elites (so far, at least it has not been
possible to establish which social group, if any, led the way). Acceptance was
in any case widespread: in one Greek case at least, a whole town council set
up an altar to the 'Holy and Just' in obedience to a dream, presumably dreamt
by some authoritative local citizen.[548] 'Many people', according to Origen,
'have had revelations in their dreams telling them what to do'.[549]

545. iv.11.

546. i.23.

547. ii.37: Apollonius makes this remark to the King of the Indians, in the course of recommending his own mantic capacities on the grounds that he drinks water not wine.

548. This was at Nicopolis ad Istrum in Lower Moesia: *IGRR* I.568 (Renberg 2003,
no. 273); cf. MacMullen 1981, 60. This piece of evidence is of course a fortuitous survival.
The date: late second century (Renberg).

549. *Contra Celsum* i.66. It may be that *IGUR* 148, a Greek inscription from Rome
recording prescriptions Asclepius (apparently) gave to individual patients in their sleep, is
characteristic of its date, the early third century.

In the Latin-speaking population, however, the increase in the number of dream-dictated dedications is at first matched if not outstripped by the growth in the epigraphic habit. After the reign of Hadrian they become steadily commoner in relationship to the general production of inscriptions (there is an apparent reversal during the reign of Septimius Severus, but it may be a statistical illusion). It is indeed remarkable that in the period 235–251 AD, when economic and other conditions sharply reduced general epigraphic production, there are so many of them.[550] This seems to mean that trust in dream-instructions grew stronger. It also explodes the superficially reasonable theory that the popularity of dream-ordered dedications was a sign of prosperity.[551] If we are to understand the phenomenon, we would need to test the apparent truth that in the Latin-speaking world the trend we are describing came, socially speaking, from the top downwards, at first from people like the elder Pliny and Suetonius (and their readers), later from the Severan court and its satellites.

It would be difficult to document any thorough-going dream-sceptic in the period 150 to 250.[552] Dream experiences are sometimes spoken of by the sceptical wit Lucian as unreal,[553] or as fraudulent,[554] but they are seldom treated as meaningless or as mere wish-fulfilments.[555] The sensible Celsus, in his attack on Christianity, could point it out as a fact that Asclepius had often appeared in dreams and assert that the god must therefore be real.[556] When Tertullian, who thought that most dreams were sent by demons,

550. A religious dedication on the Aventine in 244 'iussu numinis': *ILS* 4320, etc., Renberg 2003, no. 704; another of the same year from near Aquileia '[visu?] moniti', *CIL* V.8237, etc., Renberg no. 848; another from Apulum in Dacia under the Gordians, 'ex iussu dei', *IDR* III.5.31, etc., Renberg no. 904; another from Noricum in 240 'ex visu', Renberg no. 970; etc.

551. For this notion see Weber 2005–2006, 92.

552. Tertullian, *De anima* 46, still saw Epicurus as a major opponent on the subject of dreams.

553. Lucian, *Timon* 41. Lucian's tour-de-force on the subject of dreams is to be found in his *Vera Historia*, where he describes his visit to the Island of Dreams (ii.32–35): there are four gates, not just the Homeric two (one is of iron, another ceramic). Sleep, the king of the island, has two deputies, Anxiety, son of Futility, and Wealth the son of Fantasy (loose translations). The dreams are very hospitable. The epiphany dream in *The Scythian* 2 is probably part of a playful invention (Gorrini 2003).

554. Id., *Alexander* 49.

555. For straightforward romantic and sexual wish-fulfilments see Chariton v.5.5, Longus ii.10.

556. Origen, *Contra Celsum* iii.24.

nonetheless remarked that that 'the majority of people, almost, learn about god through dreams', he is referring to Christians and non-Christians alike,[557] and seems to refer to what he considers a standard experience.

Thus Sextus Empiricus, quoted at the beginning of this section, seems to have been roughly right to say that prediction by means of dreams was in his time 'believed in by all men'. There were always exceptions, it is true—and, as throughout this chapter, we cannot help feeling the absence of useful testimony about the beliefs of 'the woman working with her husband in the fields of the island of Chios'.[558]

What Dreams Were Good for under the Roman Empire

For many things certainly: they could provide a cure, they could give warning of death or danger, they could provide excuses (excuses for having written too much, for refusing to serve with the army—but only a Galen could get away with that), they could occasionally be used to encourage troops, or to establish the special status of a leader, political, military or religious. They might even bring back one's dead husband.[559] They could change a person's religious outlook. They could improve stories by moving the action forward or by illuminating an individual's character (Caesellius Bassus' dream, as told by Tacitus, was a powerful commentary on Nero). They also provided opportunities for ingenuity, wit and learning. No one, on the other hand, thought that they revealed what was taking place in the dreamers' unconscious.

What was the status of dream divination under the Roman Empire with respect to other divinatory practices? A full answer would require a separate volume, but we can risk a hypothetical answer. Artemidorus is a prejudiced witness (as well as being necessarily limited by time and place), but he may reveal more than he meant to. Among those who are worthy of credence when they appear in dreams are prophets (*manteis*)

> but only those prophets who are not deceitful or false. For everything else that the Pythagoreans say, and the physiognomists and the prophets who

---

557. *De anima* 47 ('maior paene vis hominum ex visionibus deum discunt', where *visiones* must mean dreams, since they are the subject of this whole portion of his book). Cf. Minucius Felix, *Oct.* vii.6 ('per quietem deos vidimus, audimus, agnoscimus').

558. See above, n. 17.

559. *ILS* 8006.

interpret dice or cheese or sieves or forms or the palms of hands or dishes or the dead, all this must be regarded as false and without foundation. For that is the nature of their techniques, and they do not have even the slightest knowledge of divination. . . . The only things that are true are the utterances of those who sacrifice, those who interpret the flight of birds, astrologers, observers of bizarre phenomena, dream interpreters, and soothsayers who examine livers. And I will treat mathematical horoscope-casters later.[560]

To a great extent this seems to be a normal Graeco-Roman hierarchy. But whereas it would be hard to find anyone except an Epicurean or a Christian who would have questioned the reliability of sacrificial victims, many questioned the reliability of dreams. And whereas we may imagine that cheese-prophets were not much in demand, there was always a demand for palm-readers as for dream-interpreters. Further research might reveal whether where the latter really fitted into what we might regard as the middle band of seers, those who had a real clientele but also generated a great deal of disbelief.

Late Antiquity

In this penultimate section I hope to show how ideas about the truth-content of dreams evolved in late antiquity, taking that to mean for present purposes the approximate period 250 to 450 (by which time the main lines of mediaeval thinking may already have been set, though I shall not insist on this possibility). But how to create some order out of the large amount of available material? The obvious and usual path is to juxtapose Christian ideas, whatever those were exactly, to traditional ideas—whatever those were. But these two sets of ideas are for various reasons too amorphous to permit a clear analysis. Nor can we easily use the social categories we used in the previous section—they too have become more amorphous.[561] Instead of all this, I will offer a set of five interconnected propositions.

560. ii.69. He does not seem to return to horoscopes in the surviving book.
561. There also looms the question whether we can sensibly deal with trust in dreams without also discussing prophecy and all late-antique thinking about the world of the gods. It would be relevant to ask for example whether the god of the Christians was more punitive and less benevolent to mankind than the traditional gods, and if so whether this was compensated for by the benevolence of the Christian angels and saints (but Christian controversialists often asserted that the old gods were described by their own worshippers as vengeful and malicious: Tatian, *Orat.* 21, Arnobius vii.42). Shulman and Stroumsa 1999, 5,

(1) *The Christian tradition prior to 250 had been ambivalent about dreams,* not in the sense that there were two different views, but in the sense that there were many. See the prior discussion in Chapter I. The ambivalence seems to be very early (and it was already there in Jewish tradition),[562] for the nativity narrative of Matthew includes between three and five dreams, as we saw in Chapter I, while Luke's contains none at all (and only Pilate's wife dreams elsewhere in the canonical Gospels). But there are four dreams dreamt by Paul in Acts, and while the author implies that a waking vision is somehow superior to a dream, he shows no embarrassment about reporting dreams of divine origin.[563]

In fact Christian doubts about significant dreams have sometimes been rather overstated, and it would not be unreasonable to suppose that after about 200 at least their views moved closer to those of the rest of the population. And as we have already seen, the Christians had particular motives for making use of dream stories: among other things, they lent power to narratives of conversion,[564] and they might serve to strengthen the courage of martyrs.[565] On the other hand, none of this necessarily led ordinary Christians to expect that they might receive dreams of divine origin in the ordinary course of their religious lives. Christians made few if any epigraphical dedications because of instructions received in dreams;[566] but that is hardly surprising in a time when the sect was still outlawed. The commentary on the Book of Daniel attributed to Hippolytus, a third-century text designed to calm expectations that the end of the world was coming, denounces the head of a church in Pontus who trusted his repeated dreams *rather than scripture.*[567]

---

associate 'revealed' religion with limited man-god contacts, including divine dreams; but the point is that Christianity aspired to monopolize/regulate such contacts. In the endless bibliography I have found Le Goff 1985, Lane Fox 1986 and Gramaglia 1989 especially instructive; but what follows diverges from each of these accounts.

562. On Israelite divination see most recently Noegel 2007, 113–123.

563. 16:9, 18:9, 23:11, 27:23–26. In 12:9 the author distinguishes between a real (*alethes*) angel and a *horama* (in his language, a dream). The book contains in fact more waking visions than dreams.

564. Origen, *Contra Celsum* i.46—but Origen expects the pagans to mock this claim. And see above, p. 71.

565. Le Goff 1985, 186–188.

566. Weber 2005–2006, 93.

567. *Comm. in Danielem* iv.19. The quotation in Le Goff 189 is inaccurate.

'Christians were especially wary of the validity of dreaming', it has been said.[568] That may in fact be going too far. Tatian, who laid heavy emphasis on the activities of evil demons, also thought nonetheless that the (pagan) Telmessians had discovered prophecy through dreams.[569] In Tertullian's eyes most dreams come from demons but even pagans may sometimes have truth-telling dreams (no need to repeat what was said about him earlier).[570] One of the sermons falsely attributed to Clement of Rome (but actually written in the third century), says that while we cannot be sure which dreams to trust, even the pagans often see truth-telling dreams.[571] Some 'gnostics' at least, the Valentinians, considered that dreams were an important means of communication between god and man.[572] 'Heretics' might be described as magicians and more specifically as 'dream-senders',[573] but dream-sending was never a mainstream practice, so that distancing oneself from it did not mean that one was a dream-sceptic. One would not baptize an *oneirokrites*,[574] logically enough, since he was in practice a rival. But that did not exclude the possibility that a dream might well be true.[575]

Down to the mid–third century the most significant Christian figure who clearly trusted his own dreams and was not embarrassed to say so was Cyprian bishop of Carthage, who speaks for instance of being warned of

568. Lane Fox 1986, 391.

569. *Orat. ad Graecos* 16–20 and 1, respectively. The date is between 165 and 172 according to M. Marcovich (his edition, p. 3).

570. *De anima* 47 (by the time he wrote this, Tertullian was a Montanist, and that no doubt affected his views about dreams: Le Goff 1985, 190–193).

571. Ps.-Clement, *Hom.* 17.14–15 (third ed. by B. Rehm, Berlin, 1992, pp. 236–237). And this attitude continues: see *Les Miracles de Sainte Thècle*, ed. G. Dagron, praef. (mid–fifth century).

572. Le Goff 1985, 189–190.

573. Irenaeus, *Adv.haer.* i.20.2, 23.4. As Miller 1994, 65, observes, 'dream, demon, and magic formed a convenient unholy triad . . . my angel is your demon, just as my (true) revelation is your (false) dream'. See further Le Goff 1985, 189, who, however, is too inclined to revert to the model of a single 'orthodox church' in the midst of curious bands of heretics.

574. Hippolytus, *Trad.* 16; cf. Clement of Alexandria, *Protr.* 2.11.2.

575. If we were to follow the most recent editors of the *Acts of John*, we would be faced with a Christian tract of c. 150–200 in which the hero worries about whether certain of his dreams come from god or the devil (ch. 21): see *Acta Iohannis* ed. E. Junod and J.-D. Kaestli (*CC-SA* 1.167; see 2.700 for the date). But in my opinion this work not only resembles a novel, it *is* (a fragment of) a novel, and probably of later date. That naturally does not deprive it of interest!

imminent repression by 'frequent and persistent dreams' *(ostensiones)*.[576]
No doubt, however, he regarded such communications as a special privilege.

(2) *In late antiquity many secular men of power thought that dream-
stories and dream-interpretations could affect people's opinions in important ways.* Constantine revived an old practice in encouraging his soldiers
with a dream-story on the morning of the Battle of Saxa Rubra, though putting a new symbol on the shields was an original idea.[577] We may or may not
want to believe that he himself was the source of the story of the dream
that told him where to build Constantinople, a dream in which god himself
appeared.[578] A little later (355), Julian's panegyric on Constantius II seems
to show that the rise to power of such a new emperor was normally accompanied by dream-stories as well as other positive portents, but also that a
man of Julian's standing would avoid talking about them in detail in such an
oration—that was work for poets.[579] He himself claimed to have dreamt an
epiphany dream the night before he had himself proclaimed emperor (see
Chapter I). His ambition had been inflamed by portents and dreams that
indicated that Constantius did not have long to live.[580]

What the men of power themselves thought about dreams is seldom if
ever known in detail, but their attitude towards dream-interpreters, from
time to time severe, suggests in any case that belief of some kind was widespread. 'Let the obsession with divination be abolished for good', says an
edict of Constantius.[581] That persons of some consideration in the mid-
fourth century believed in the predictive force of dreams is confirmed by
the fact that when Constantius added to the already very long series of

---

576. *Ep.* 57 (*CSEL* 3.2.651); cf. *Ep.* 16 and 39, with Gramaglia 1989, 544.

577. Harris 2005a.

578. As stated by Sozomen, *Hist.Eccl.* ii.3.3. The emperor had started building the city
at Troy.

579. *Oration* 1.10b: 'As for voices and prophecies and dreams *(opseis tas en tois hup-
nois)* and the rest of the things that people like to chatter about when a man has achieved
such brilliant and conspicuous success, such as Cyrus, Romulus, Alexander of Macedon,
and so on, I willingly pass them by; for they are part of the responsibility of the poets'.

580. Ammianus Marcellinus xxi.1.6. In *Letter* 14 Bidez-Cumont (4 Wright) of 358–359
Julian described to his friend Oribasius a dream that clearly portended that he would succeed Constantius, concluding ambiguously 'god knows what it means'. In *Oration* viii.248a
one seems to hear the voice of a dream-sceptic.

581. *C.Th.* ix.16.4 ('sileat omnibus perpetuo divinandi curiositas').

imperial measures against divination, he for the first time specifically included the use of dreams.[582]

> If any magician . . . or soothsayer or seer or certainly augur or even astrologer [*mathematicus*] should be apprehended in my retinue [*comitatus*] or that of the Caesar either concealing some art of divination by describing dreams or practising any similar art, he is not to escape execution or torture by virtue of his rank.[583]

Before long, the emperor set up a court at Scythopolis in Palestine to hear charges of treason against persons from the principal cities in the eastern empire.[584] It was exceedingly dangerous in the upper orders to be suspected of practising divination, as we know from both Ammianus and Libanius.[585] (But what is equally interesting is Ammianus' approval of strict investigation and torture to protect the person of the emperor;[586] he himself was a convinced believer in the truthfulness of dreams, as we shall shortly see.)

(3) *Ecclesiastics were especially eager to delegitimize threatening uses of dreams and to arrogate to themselves the right to decide which dreams came from god and which from evil demons.* Third- and fourth-century Christian theologians generally supposed that dreams did sometimes tell the truth, in the sense that they allowed authentic contact with god. Dream-stories had become an important part of narratives about the casualties of the persecutions, such as Perpetua.[587] They served more and more purposes, as we saw in Chapter I.

The leaders of the official church were heartily opposed to all forms of divination (the small Council of Ancyra in 314 already punished those who

582. *C.Th.* ix.16.6.

583. C. Pharr translates 'narrandis somniis' as 'interpreting dreams', and presumably that is what the legislator actually meant.

584. Sandwell 2005, 115.

585. Ammianus Marcellinus xix.12.14–15. In *Or.* xviii.131 Libanius also spoke of Constantius' reign as a time when 'charges of magic and murder' were used as a way to seize peoples' fortunes. However, Ammianus 'may be exaggerating' (Syme 1968, 33). In *Or.* i.239–240 he refers to a former student who courted 'danger' by talking too much about his dreams.

586. xix.12.17.

587. See also the *Passio Sanctorum Mariani et Iacobi* 6, 7, 8, 10, another African text probably written in the second half of the third century (cf. Musurillo 1972, xxxiv).

practised it),[588] which suggests above all that they feared that their flock might easily be misled. The attempt to outlaw divination continued, and the dreams the Christian authorities approved of, while they might tell of a happy after-life or indicate that death was near, did not otherwise predict the future, unlike a large proportion of the truth-telling dreams of the past.[589]

We reviewed in Chapter I much of the evidence for the Christian acceptance and use of prophetic and instructive dreams. Jerome asserted that revelatory dreams were only available to the saints and the servants of god,[590] but in practice the authorities also held that 'heretics' and evil-doers might receive admonitory dreams too.[591] The ample dossier on Augustine roundly contradicts the view that he became less and less trusting towards predictive dreams.[592] Indeed the readiness with which prominent ecclesiastics recounted edifying dream-stories must have made it difficult to rein in private enthusiasts. A council held at Carthage in 401 attempted to counteract what has been called 'a sort of epidemic of dreams'.[593] And certain dream-stories now figured largely in the official religion: when Santa Maria Maggiore was decorated with mosaics in the fifth century, the subjects included the Old Testament dream of Joseph.[594]

---

588. Canon 23 (see G. D. Mansi, *Sacrorum Conciliorum Nova et Amplissima Collectio* II [Florence, 1759]).

589. So at least Le Goff 1985, 197. But what the saints provide, according to *Les Miracles de Sainte Thècle*, ed. G. Dagron, praef., is cures and *thespismata*, oracular sayings.

590. *In Hierem.* 4.59 (*CC-SL* 74.225). Cf. *Ep.* 22.16. But even they had to be careful: *In Rufinum* i.31 shows Jerome defending himself with characteristic rhetorical skill against Rufinus' charge that he had paid attention to dreams—of course, he says, we all know that dreams are not to be believed. But Rufinus' complaint was not that Jerome's Cicero dream was untrue or inappropriate but that he had failed to keep his promise to abstain from 'secular' authors (*Apologia contra Hieronymum* ii.6–7 = *CC-SL* 20.87–88).

591. Yet it is wholly false to say that for the Christians 'all dreams are significant' (Le Goff 1985, 194).

592. As alleged by Le Goff 1985, 200–203. On the contrary, Augustine seems to move from a fairly sceptical view in *De quantitate animae* xxxiii.71 (387 AD) to a moderate position in *De Genesi ad litteram* xii.18 (393 AD; there are true dreams and false) to the acceptance of fantastic dream stories in *De cura pro mortuis* of 421 (see Chapter I) and in *De civitate Dei* of 413–427 (references below). See further Brown 1967, 413–414.

593. Gramaglia 1989, 506, quoting Canon 83, as above, p. 75. Some have suspected, perhaps rightly, that African Christians were especially interested in their dreams: Le Goff 199.

594. Cecchelli 1956.

As we also saw in Chapter I, incubation was such a deeply engrained practice that it survived the superimposition of Christianity. What is not clear is whether in quantitative terms it was as important in, say, the fifth century as it had been in the second.[595] It would be easy to suppose that the thinly veiled 'paganism' of the whole practice meant that it was not allowed to flourish. In reality, it flourished widely in its Christian guise. Augustine tells an extraordinary story of a kind of dreamless Christian incubation that took place at a church at Uzalis where the supposed relics of the martyr Stephen had been installed: in 424 two Christians, brother and sister, who had come all the way from Cappadocia, guided by epiphany dreams, was cured of chronic trembling;[596] other cures were effected there too.[597]

(4) *For the first time, some educated persons, both traditionalist and Christian, maintained that all dreams are meaningful if properly understood.* We know of no earlier Greek or Roman who believed this,[598] but rather suddenly, in the course of a decade or two, two ostensibly quite different personalities, the soldier and historian Ammianus Marcellinus and the Neoplatonist 'Christian' Synesius of Cyrene, author of a substantial essay on dreaming, take the extreme position. 'The truthfulness of dreams would be accepted and beyond doubt if those who interpret them did not make mistakes', says Ammianus.[599] In other places too Ammianus shows clear sympathy with Neoplatonist opinions: there is in fact a whole theology behind the doctrine just quoted.[600] 'Not even a tyrant could forbid us

595. Edelstein and Edelstein 1945, II, 255–257, chronicle the stages in the decline that the cult of Asclepius suffered from the mid–third century onwards.

596. Paulus, the brother, after praying at the *martyrium*, 'dormienti simillimus iacuit . . . et ecce surrexit' (*De civ. Dei* xxii.8.22; his own description is quoted in Augustine, *Sermo* 322, PL 38.1443–1444). The fact that nothing is said about dreaming as distinct from sleeping suggest a wish to differentiate the event from non-Christian incubation miracles. On Christian incubation, see above, p. 75.

597. Of the twenty-two healing miracles described by Augustine, *De civ. Dei* xxii.8, as evidence that miracles still happen, seven involved dreams in one way or another.

598. For the possibly Stoic origins of this view see above, p. 17; on the eccentric Telmessians, p. 202. But Vigourt 2001, 163, who seems to find this sentiment in first-century writers, is in error.

599. Ammianus xxi.1.12: 'somniorum autem rata fides et indubitabilis foret, ni ratiocinantes coniectura fallerentur'. He follows this with an apparently bogus reference to Aristotle. See also xiv.11.17–18.

600. Matthews 1989, 428–429, making use of Szidat 1982.

to dream', says Synesius.[601] This form of divination is available to all, and it is what provides humans with useful warnings but above all with hope. Humans would give up on life, because of its numerous miseries, if Prometheus had not taught the interpretation of dreams. It is merely human weakness (*astheneia*) that prevents them from always knowing what their meaning may be: Penelope was quite wrong, he says, to divide dreams into true and false, she should have made them all pass through the Gate of Horn.[602] But the books on dream-interpretation are ridiculous and of little use: we must each do it for ourselves, writing dream-diaries.[603] Naturally he wrote his dream monograph on instructions received in a dream.[604]

(5) *There was a further increase in trust in dreams.* Ammianus' attitude is in itself quite striking, and he reports a relatively new attitude on the part of others. An imperial official named Mercurius was a leading informer after the suppression of the Caesar Gallus in 354: he was known as the 'Count of Dreams'

> because . . . he would often insert himself into banquets and other gatherings, and if anyone had told a friend that he had seen something in a dream . . . , he would give it a worse colour by his poisonous arts and pour it into the waiting ears of the emperor.[605]

In consequence, he says, people would scarcely admit that they had been to sleep. But the important point is that all persons of high rank assumed that their dreams might be politically significant. It seems characteristic of the times that Pappus of Alexandria, a much-respected mathematician of Constantine's time, had written a book on *Oneirocritica*.[606] Libanius too, in

---

601. *De insomniis* 12 end.

602. *De insomniis* 13. And since Penelope fails to interpret her truth-telling Goose Dream, Synesius is able to claim that Homer agreed with him. Synesius' extreme position is not to be explained by a wish to thwart political rivals (Bregman 1982, 147), but I suppose by his personal temperament and the religious thinking of his time.

603. *De insomniis* 17–18, 20.

604. *Ep.* 154.

605. xv.3.3–6. The mixed metaphor is in the original. For Mercurius see *PLRE* I, s.v. no.1. For further evidence on the importance now attributed to dreams at this social level see xv.6.2.

606. Suda s.v. (his chronology is controversial). Two centuries later the philosopher Damascius claimed that the Alexandrians almost all have such good dreams that they 'even now' call them 'oracles' (*Vita Isidori* 12, p. 14 Zintzen).

the next generation, showed that he expected his readers to regard dream-based predictions as entirely respectable. He tells the readers of his auto-biography of a dream which he interpreted to mean that he would prevail in a lawsuit (which he did);[607] and over a period of several years he consulted the shrine of Asclepius at Aegae, usually, it seems, through intermediaries.[608] A city-councillor at Antioch about 385 was in the habit of telling people about his deceptive dreams and making jokes about them, but this became dangerous to him and even to his hearers, and he might have been sentenced to death.[609] It is clear at least that most upper-class Antiochenes knew that a significant number of their fellow citizens felt that dreams had predictive value. Shortly after the events just referred to Libanius had a dream that he took to be a sign of 'spells, incantations, and the hostility of sorcerers', which he thought came true when he discovered a dead chameleon (intended as an instrument of hostile magic) in his classroom.[610]

A Conclusion

A perhaps unexpectedly complex history has emerged. Different kinds of Greeks and Romans reacted to their dreams, and to the dreams of others, in different ways. Life and literature diverged, and many a story was told about remote times and places that would not have been credited if they had been told about the person in the next house. It also seems probable that the weight of opinion shifted from time to time.

The concept of a 'truthful' dream is itself too simple to serve our purposes perfectly, partly because dreams were often understood not as revelations but as instructions, partly because a dream was widely considered to have been an accurate premonition if it was followed by a positive or negative turn of events as the case might be. Belief, trust, confidence are also complicated ideas, and in the case of dreams we find a few people who profess at least to believe that they are all meaningful, a great number of people who believe or half-believe stories they had heard about truth-

607. *Or.* i.67.

608. *Ep.* 706–708, 1300, *Or.* i.143.

609. *Or.* i.239–241. The dreams were *kibdeloi,* not 'silly' (A. F. Norman) but just deceptive; they 'promised things that did not come to pass'.

610. *Or.* i. 245–250. He dreamt that he saw two boys sacrificed and one of their bodies put in the temple of Zeus. He protested against the sacrilege and was told that in the evening the body would be buried.

telling dreams and are frightened by a bad dream and even take some apotropaic countermeasure, others still who take very few dreams as revelatory but see no reason why there should not be an occasional exception. It is in any case highly misleading to say that the people of Graeco-Roman antiquity, during their waking lives, took what they had seen in their dreams for reality.[611]

Greeks and Romans rarely made serious decisions on the basis of dreams, more often they were alarmed by them, or mystified or encouraged. Their practical reactions, prior at least to the arrival of Christianity, would at most amount to consulting an expert and possibly making a libation or performing some other gesture; I suppose that very many people did this at least once or twice in their lives. The kind of dream that was most likely to lead to action of some kind was probably the medical dream, especially but not only if it were dreamt at the shrine of a god.

Throughout antiquity the inducing and interpretation of dreams sometimes formed part of what we may call 'organized religion' (meaning by this simply a system of religious practices that provides priests or magicians or others with a livelihood). The practitioners and supporters of certain religious cults, especially but not only those of Asclepius and Serapis, let it be known that a particular god had appeared in dreams with significant messages, or had sent significant messages. Practitioners of magic in Greek-speaking Egypt, and no doubt elsewhere, made regular use of dream-prediction.[612]

Dream-revelations that turned out to be true—or in some cases either tricking or even false—continued to have enough credibility throughout antiquity to be a recurrent literary theme—but not to the same degree in all genres. And there was enormous individual variation. The most intriguing case is undoubtedly Vergil—probably under Epicurean influence as a young man, writing for a public that probably troubled little about its own dreams (Suetonius on Augustus notwithstanding), yet staking a huge sum in the *Aeneid* on the artistic success of a whole series of dream narratives.

Opinion shifted from time to time. There can be no greater error than to suppose that archaic Greek opinion put deep trust in dreams: the Gate of Ivory was always open. On the other hand we should suppose that most Greeks prior to the emergence of the great questioning of conventional re-

---

611. As claimed by Liatsi 2003, 8.
612. E.g. *PGM* V.488, VI.47. See further Miller 1994, 120–122.

ligion that began with Xenophanes took it for granted that if the gods wished to communicate with humans, especially important humans, they might do so by means of dreams. This belief came to be questioned in the fifth century, so that opinion was divided: as far as the highly educated are concerned we might set Herodotus at one extreme, Thucydides at the other. But belief in dreams was now rationalized as well as questioned (see *Prometheus Bound*). And a little later, with the early Hippocratics, a new way of extracting information from dreams had gained ground—they could be seen as symptoms of a person's physical condition.

Even after we have made allowances for the varying character of the source material from one century to another, fourth-century BC Athenians seem to have been a degree more receptive than those who lived in the period c. 450 to 400. Stoic influence might have helped to carry this trend forward into the Hellenistic world, but in this era we meet another kind of possibly important distinction: much of the evidence for belief in meaningful dreams comes from the empire of the Ptolemies.

In republican Rome, the social elite always seems to have been relatively though not rigidly sceptical about revelatory dreams, while some of the evidence suggest that ordinary Romans were a degree more susceptible, especially in times of unusual fear. Yet the social elite did not deny that the gods sometimes sent meaningful dreams, and this accepting attitude was reflected in the literature that they produced and encouraged. The counterforce, in the late Republic, was philosophical.

I have set out the case for supposing that after very roughly 100 AD there was a marked change in attitude, detectable in various different milieux, both among the members of what I have called the learned professions in Italy and elsewhere (Galen is an important case), among ordinary Greeks, and eventually in both the imperial court and the senatorial order. Sextus Empiricus was probably right to think that most of his contemporaries believed in prediction by means of dreams. But we must consider exactly what that means: there is still very little evidence that dreams led directly to practical consequences, but there can be no doubt that dreams sometimes, for example, changed people's religious convictions. In late antiquity, the most important change may be said to have been a certain gain in intellectual respectability for belief in dreams, attributable in the first place to the general retreat of scepticism and religious moderation among the most educated (who by the time of Augustine had had a very different education from that of 300 years earlier).

These temporal variations challenge us to devise explanations. The Roman Empire is always too plural and variegated a place to permit explanations of cultural changes as amorphous as the ones we have been examining. At most we may be able to get the rulers and the learned into focus. Three factors seem to stand out, though they are all circumscribed by reservations. Dodds's 'age of anxiety' was a great mistake, at least for the times before the plague under Marcus Aurelius, and one characteristic that Galen and Aelius Aristides and a number of their contemporaries have in common is a marked confidence that the gods or a god would come to their aid (but was this more true of them than it would have been of their counterparts 100 years earlier?). Secondly, there seems to have been a decline in the familiarity of the elite with the classic works of philosophy, at first a gradual decline, after the mid–third century a precipitous one; and though the great philosophers had been somewhat divided on the subject of dreams, most of them, apart from the Old Stoa, had at least admitted elements of scepticism. Finally, and most problematical of all, is the possibility that as the older education weakened, more credulous ideas came in from the poor and uneducated, who, throughout this long chapter, have been the great unknowable.

IV

Naturalistic Explanations

Introduction

What do dreams mean? What should we do about them? Where do they come from? These, for most ancient populations, were sometimes pressing questions, both in life, especially religious life, and in literature. We have seen how Greek and Roman populations attempted to respond to them, both in the form of assumptions and in the form of more or less articulated answers. But there was also, as we have seen from time to time, a philosophical approach—the ancestor of the scientific approach invented, as far as dreams are concerned, in the nineteenth century[1]—which sought to explain, on a more theoretical level, what dreaming was about. Why do we dream? Why do dreams take the forms that they do? Are they perhaps entirely internal, entirely inside us? Can we classify them? Some extremely incisive Greek (and occasionally Roman) minds wrestled with these and related problems. In this final chapter I consider how philosophers, or rather those philosophers who took a naturalistic approach, dealt with this slippery matter.

One way of understanding dreams was to suppose that they were sent by gods, but from an early date some Greeks found that this was at best an incomplete answer. What first led people to seek for *other* explanations can only be conjectured. We might suspect that the false inferences suggested by so many dreams were always part of the trouble—and the *oneiropoloi* were bound to give the wrong answer fairly often—but that problem was

---

1. Hobson 1988, 23–51, sketches nineteenth-century scientific thinking on this subject.

not new in the sixth or fifth century, when naturalistic theories begin to emerge. In any case Homer's audience had accepted, without difficulty we must suppose, that the gods could send false dreams as well as true ones. We want to know what other impulses may have led to naturalistic inquiry—by which I mean inquiry that pays systematic attention to the phenomena and seeks more understanding than simply attributing dreams to the intervention of a god, inquiry that presupposes that human experiences *follow patterns* and can be explained without reference to superhuman powers.[2]

It would be possible to articulate this inquiry around the five preserved texts that seem to be most important:

(1) Pseudo-Hippocrates' *On Regimen* (in particular its last section, chapters 86–93)

(2) Aristotle's three short pieces *On Sleeping and Waking, On Dreams* and *On Prophecy through Sleep* (which are in fact a unity)[3]

(3) Lucretius' main discussion of dreams (in *On the Nature of Things* Book IV)—taken as a more or less orthodox exposition of Epicurean teaching on this topic

(4) Cicero, *On Divination*

(5) And, somewhat incongruously, the dream-book of Artemidorus of Daldis.

Understanding these texts properly is essential. But the method followed here will be quite different, for the argument will be that each of the writers in question, our anonymous Hippocratic doctor, Aristotle, Epicurus, Lucretius, Cicero, and Artemidorus, depended heavily on his predecessors

---

2. When referring to the intellectual activities of the ancients, I have avoided the term 'science' and its cognates as much as possible, mainly because of the gulf between the meaning of 'scientific knowledge' and its nearest Greek equivalent, *episteme* (see Sharples 2005, 1–3). This may well seem excessively punctilious, and I am not sure that it was the correct decision. I use the words 'rational' and 'rationality' with caution, not because of the exaggerated and, if I may say so, innocent relativism exemplified, in a medical context, by Horstmanshoff and Stol 2004, 4–7 (one wonders whether they really doubt that modern medicine is more effective than what preceded it; those of us whose lives have been saved by it will tend not to agree): these authors slipped from questioning whether Greek medicine was 'rational' to questioning whether the category exists. The point is rather that the most intelligent ancients always continued to argue, more or less intensely, about the best methods of drawing conclusions about the natural world, and given that there was never a scientific revolution we should therefore be very slow to blame people who said things that are in a sense absurd.

3. On this question see Gallop 1996, 118, Repici 2003, 10–11.

and needs to be fitted into a continuous history. For part of the purpose here is to ask whether ancient investigation of dreaming can help us to understand more generally how the Greeks and Romans developed new ideas about the natural world, taking into account both 'external' factors (the society around the people in question) and 'internal' ones (the existing ideas to which they reacted).[4]

In *The Road since Structure* Thomas Kuhn describes how as a young scientist he had occasion to study Aristotle's *Physics,* and how he abruptly realized some of the intellectual differences between Aristotle's mental world and the Newtonian world in which he had grown up.[5] We shall be equally far from modern questions and modern methods. Yet there were some formidably powerful intellects in antiquity that concerned themselves, occasionally, with the intricacies of the phenomenon of dreaming. What exactly was their achievement and what were its limits?

We have been brought up not to write progressive or teleological history, and to contextualize our studies of past thinking about the natural world. But we want explanations too, even if they have to be quite speculative. Can we discover why ancient thinkers about dreaming moved from phase to phase, how they interacted with each other's ideas,[6] and why they ceased to find out more?[7] In all this, we shall keep in mind that dreams are a peculiar subject—inaccessible and always of very debatable importance.

The reader will already be aware that this investigation will constantly be dependent on lost and fragmentary texts whose significance is obscure and contested. And it is not only texts that matter: it so happens that the earliest text that mentions the monsters we sometimes see in dreams is the Hippocratic *On Regimen* (*allomorpha somata*—bodies that have abnormal forms)[8]—with one exception, which we encountered earlier, the opening scene of Aristophanes' *Wasps.* Now it is as plain as could be that neither writer 'discovered' *allomorpha somata*—everyone already knew about them. And often, in fact normally, we do not know who initiated an explanation or

4. Yet this dichotomy is too simple, for we need to take account of such factors as generalized religious scepticism which are not purely external or internal.

5. Kuhn 2000, 15–20.

6. Cf. Kuhn 1970 [1962], 3.

7. This last phrase may alarm those who think that we should never be judgemental about the intellectual achievements of other cultures, but that is in the end an antihistorical position too. There were fools and dullards in antiquity too, and some of them wrote books. There were also brilliant investigators who found certain problems intractable.

8. iv.93.

an argument.[9] The main purpose of the present chapter is to trace a sequence of arguments,[10] but it is just the sequence that it is often impossible to establish.

The ramifications are quite challenging. Some of them are obvious: opinions about dreams were often linked not only to people's opinions about the gods and divination, but in the case of men of wisdom to their opinions about physics and metaphysics, about physiology and about human nature more widely. Others are perhaps less obvious: how honest were ancient controversialists in representing each other's opinions? To grasp this problem, it is enough to review the 'fragments' and 'testimonia' of Democritus, an important figure in this story, and to notice how much of the evidence comes from those who were more or less passionately his opponents.[11]

How much, and how accurately, did ancient thinkers on this subject even *know* each other's opinions, given the persisting semioral nature of Greek and Roman culture and the stratospheric cost of books?[12] Plato and Aristotle, we may suppose, knew virtually all of what they needed to know about their predecessors, but by the second century AD the ancients, like us though in a very different way, were suffering from information overkill, which at some point gave way to an even worse phenomenon, the actual disappearance of important books.

The Origins of Naturalistic Thinking about Dreams

No teleological history then. But the history of science differs from all or most other history fields—since people do sometimes make scientific discoveries. The point is not to award marks to defenceless figures from the past, especially in a field such as dreaming in which modern progress has

9. The problem persists throughout this chapter. Who, for instance, is to say which idea first attested in Lucretius was originally put into circulation by the largely lost Democritus? Besides Democritus, the worst sufferers, among theorists of dreaming, are in my opinion probably Xenophanes, Empedocles, Epicurus, and Herophilus; possibly Theophrastus too.

10. Holowchak 2002, the only existing account, is deficient. Lloyd 1987, a wider study, is very useful, but the following account diverges from his tendency to treat the sources, at least from Hippocrates to Galen, achronically.

11. See the edition of Taylor 1999 and Morel 2002 on the way Aristotle represented Democritus in his *Parva Naturalia*.

12. On the effects of these factors on the transmission of Greek medical knowledge cf. Nutton 2004, 3–4.

generally been so limping and uncertain; but that should not prevent us from at least distinguishing perceptive comments from mere flim-flam. 'S'abstenir de juger, c'est s'exclure de toute histoire des sciences digne de ce nom', wrote a historian of Greek medicine.[13] To speak of 'judging' brings in unwanted overtones, but we must not throw away our compasses.

In so far as scholars have evaluated ancient writing on the subject of dreams, they seem to have given the palm of honour to Aristotle ('the dawn of the science of dreams'), for it was he, so it is widely thought, who first entirely denied the existence of prophetic dreams and tried to analyse dreaming by naturalistic methods. For once, the received doctrine may be more true than false, and it would be very easy to argue that Aristotle's essays about dreams are in fact part of a much wider 'paradigm shift' that he almost single-handedly created (though not of course without help from forerunners). But this is *not* in the end a progressive story, for dusk followed dawn relatively soon, and no one later than the first century BC had any new naturalistic idea of any substance about dreaming. Yet where does that leave Artemidorus, who collected and ordered endless material, largely excluded the gods from his explanation of it, and might be thought to be as 'scientific' as anyone else?[14]

How then did naturalistic thinking about dreams begin? It is now generally understood that the early Greek philosophers, those of the sixth and fifth centuries, did not set out to discredit religion as such, but 'to gain a correct apprehension of the divine'[15] in addition to investigating certain aspects of the natural world. Nature, their original subject, included the divine, so they thought.[16] Nonetheless they offered explanations of the physical phenomena that were at least partly secular. And while they at first concerned themselves with cosmology and physics and only later turned their attention to investigating humankind, the new theology of scientific thinkers often tended, from the sixth century on, to undermine prophecy, including prophecy based on dreams.[17] It seems broadly correct to say that Heraclitus and later on Democritus 'recognized that such familiar physio-

13. Joly 1980, 293.

14. According to Blum 1936, 81, the 'most conspicuous feature' of his book 'is perhaps its reasonable character' (but he goes on to write of its 'pseudo-scientific spirit').

15. A phrase from Lloyd 1987, 47, though his application of it is rather different.

16. See for instance Vlastos 1949, 282–283.

17. See Chapters I and III.

logical phenomena as locomotion, nutrition, perception, and reproduction require explanation'.[18]

There was another intellectual tradition highly relevant to the understanding of dreams, the medical tradition. Exactly how separate medicine was from philosophy in the first half of the fifth century BC, it is hard to say.[19] Certain figures, such as Empedocles, were probably well informed about both kinds of thinking.[20] It clearly will not do in any case to suppose that 'rational' medicine emerged abruptly in the late fifth century in the time of the historical Hippocrates,[21] and recent scholarship has sometimes acknowledged this. Hippocrates himself no doubt contributed greatly, but his predecessors must gradually have accumulated both techniques and information (even the Homeric doctors hardly started from nothing). It seems a virtual certainty (whatever we think about the roots of 'incubation') that doctors had sometimes considered the possible significance of dreams for their patients' health long before our earliest evidence of this in the decades around 400 BC. The strictly secular contents of the Hippocratic book *On the Nature of Man*—apparently written by Hippocrates' son-in-law Polybus—may reflect an already fairly old tradition.[22]

Whereas the previous chapters in this book have mainly analysed cultural conventions and religious attitudes, we shall be concerned here with a set of intellectual changes. It scarcely needs to be noted that these changes

18. Mayr 1982, 86. He continued as follows: 'What strikes the modern student as strange is the fact that they thought they could provide such explanation merely by concentrated thinking', without experiments.

19. This separation is perhaps somewhat overstated by Lloyd 2002; see Laks 2006, 55–81. [Hippocrates], *Ancient Medicine* 20, shows that at least some early Hippocratics believed in their own separateness (and superiority): 'I hold that all that has been written about nature by sophists or by doctors pertains less to medicine than it does to the art of drawing [*graphike*]. I also hold that clear knowledge about nature can come from no other source but medicine'. This passage, well known because it contains a little earlier the first known use of the word *philosophia*, is usefully discussed by Laks 71–73 (who translates *graphike* as 'painting').

20. Cf. Nutton 2004, 46–47.

21. In [Aeschylus], *PV* 477–483 Prometheus claims to have given pharmacy to mankind, and then goes on to the passage, discussed in Chapter III, in which he claims to have told them how to know which dreams would come true; critical thought in both fields seems to go together in some way.

22. On this text see Nutton 2004, 84–86. On its authorship and date (last decade of the fifth century?) see Jouanna 1999 [1992], 400. The case was first made by Goody and Watt 1968 and modified and elaborated in Goody 1977 and 1986.

were certainly rooted in material conditions and social practices. But can we identify these conditions and practices in any useful way?

The 'semioral' aspect of classical Greek culture has already made an appearance. There should, I think, be little hesitation in accepting in a modified form the now very familiar notion, originated by Jack Goody above all, that the Greek adaptation of Phoenician script and its subsequent diffusion had a crucial effect, from the sixth century onwards, in all areas of intellectual disagreement.[23] This is not the occasion to discuss theories of this kind in all their aspects, but certain points need to be emphasized. Accepting such a theory need not involve any underestimation of the intellectual achievements of Ancient Near Eastern cultures,[24] but that comparison requires us to set out as exactly as possible what the east-Aegean Greeks and, later on, western Greeks gained, in the intellectual sphere, from the diffusion of literacy. This in turn suggests that we need a credible model of this diffusion—something that has often been lacking in the scholarly literature, even in recent times.[25]

It gradually became easier to recall or learn, and scrutinize, exactly what men of wisdom had already thought, and it probably became more and more indispensable for those with intellectual ambitions to take account of their predecessors.

But we must avoid exaggerating the role of the diffusion of literacy at the expense of other factors.[26] Spreading literacy was not sufficient by itself to produce the Greek philosophical or medical revolutions. No such revolutions occurred when writing first came to non-Greek Italy—to take one example out of many. When a society first becomes somewhat literate, that is to say when people outside a specialized corps of scribes start to find that writing is seriously useful, it does not of necessity start *questioning* its received opinions,[27] and conversely some ancient and anthropological

23. But it should be noted that some well-informed scholars resist this hypothesis, e.g, Kahn 2003, 141 (without, however, presenting a full case). For a statement of the objections see Thomas 1992, 16–20.

24. In particular we may doubt whether the spread of alphabetic literacy was as revolutionary in mathematics as in some other fields; see Lloyd 1987, 73–78.

25. My version, which did not attempt a full discussion of the question now at issue: Harris 1989, 45–64.

26. Still less can we assent to the claim that 'the textualisation of mythological material [a different phenomenon from the promiscuous diffusion of literacy] led . . . to criticism' (Morgan 2000, 24). But this author's overall account (24–29) is balanced.

27. A point already made by Bremmer 1982, 48–49; cf. Harris 1989, 40–42.

societies—but not many—have achieved extraordinary intellectual feats without the aid of writing. And as Lloyd has remarked, a canonical text can have the opposite effect, stifling criticism not stimulating it.[28]

For intellectual progress to be made, various other conditions were necessary,[29] most notably, I would suppose, (1) greater leisure for speculation[30]—explicable at least in part by increased Greek wealth—and (2) a growing and self-conscious tradition of relative freedom,[31] including freedom of speech.[32] In addition, a wide range of rewards awaited those who were inventive, and many people knew this.

In recent times a new and ingenious theory has proposed that the diffusion of coinage in archaic Greece gave a vital stimulus to the development of philosophical ways of thinking.[33] Without judging this theory, one may suggest that it is symptomatic of a problem which cannot be solved because of sheer lack of evidence. Another recent study considered the polemics of some of the major figures—Xenophanes, Heraclitus and Empedocles.[34] It emerges from that material not that written texts were unimportant in 'Presocratic' polemics, but rather that the sources do not reveal to us whether they were or not. The same applies to the at least equally polemical or perhaps even more polemical world of the late-fifth-century doctors.[35] To a very great extent the impact of the written word on the development of sixth- and fifth-century Greek thought is a matter of inference.

28. Lloyd 2003, 4–5 (see also Harris 1989, 39). But few Greeks were ever in a position to stifle philosophical criticism, and Homer was criticized shortly after he became canonical if not indeed before.

29. See Bremmer 1982, 50.

30. Aristotle saw the importance of this factor, *Metaph.* i.1.16.981b (it does not matter whether he was right to think that the Egyptian priests made progress in mathematics because they had nothing much else to take up their time). Cf. Guthrie 1962–1981, I.30–31.

31. Cf. among other texts Hippocrates, *Airs, Waters, Places* 16 and 23, where, however, the focus is on the warlike and aggressive qualities of the free.

32. See esp. Lloyd 1987, 81, and 1990. Cf. Laks 2001, 134–135, who suggests that the most important factor at the origin of Greek science, besides literacy, was the habit of political and judiciary debate (see also Lloyd 1987, 78–108, Morgan 2000, 26).

33. Seaford 2004.

34. Gemelli Marciano 2002.

35. For their polemics see among others Cambiano 1992, 544, 547–548 (commenting on the awareness of the effects of the written word on the part of some of the Hippocratic writers), Nutton 2004, 63–66, 85–86.

Dreams and dreaming may have seemed quite unimportant problems to many Greeks, but both were not only extremely puzzling and in need of practical assessment (did they tell the truth?), they more or less forced themselves on to anyone who wished to understand such vital matters as the behaviour of the gods and the health of the human body.

The Preplatonic Philosophers

The first philosopher who is known to have shown an interest in dreams is Heraclitus, but no one has been able to propose any secure reconstruction of how he explained them,[36] and the doxographical tradition knew of no large dream theory of his. Nowhere, in fact, in the fragments of his work, do we encounter 'the common terminology for dream . . . and the act of dreaming'.[37] According to Sextus Empiricus, Heraclitus held that a major difference between waking experience and sleeping is that in sleep we are forgetful,[38] but that does not carry us very far towards a general theory. When he said that 'that which appears to all in common is trustworthy (for it is perceived by the common and divine reason), but that which affects one person alone is, for the opposite cause, untrustworthy',[39] he probably had dreams in mind among other things. He also asserted that sleepers resort to their own private worlds,[40] which seems to justify seeing him as a sceptic about prophetic dreams. But we can scarcely take this any further.

We can get a much better handle, as far as this subject is concerned, on the ideas of Empedocles. The furious condition of current Empedocles scholarship should not be allowed to obscure this, and there is no need to decide whether he deserves to be called a philosopher, a magician, or both.

36. Notwithstanding heroic efforts by among others van Lieshout 1980, 67–85, Brillante 1986, 10–25, Schofield 1991, and the modern editors of the fragments.

37. Van Lieshout 1980, 67.

38. *Adv.math.* vii.129, 132 = 22 A 16, B 1 D-K (= fr. 1 Marcovich); not that the meaning of the text is clear. On the authenticity of this information see Brillante 1986, 11 n. 5.

39. *Adv.math.* vii.131 = 22 A 16 = 116 Marcovich (who, however, considers the quotation inauthentic).

40. 22 B 89 = 24 Marcovich. What he seems to say is that 'for those who are awake there is a single common universe, whereas in sleep each person turns away into <his> own, private <universe>' (so T. M. Robinson). Does this mean that dreams are internally generated or simply that they cannot be observed by others?

A learned late-antique commentator on Aristotle, John Philoponus, tells us that a phrase Aristotle quoted from Empedocles referred to dreaming, even though Aristotle himself did not say so. Philoponus asserts that Empedocles, 'speaking about the differences between dreams [*oneiraton*], says that imaginings at night [*nukterinai phantasiai*] arise from one's activities [*energemata*] by day; this imagining he calls "thinking" in the passage "whence they also always think differently [*to phronein alloia*, if that is what the expression means]"'.[41] Now, Empedocles cannot have used the word *energema*, which is Hellenistic and cannot in any case go into hexameters, the metre in which he invariably framed his doctrines. But it is exceedingly unlikely that Philoponus was in error in claiming that Empedocles, parts at least of whose poetry he knew well,[42] was here referring to dreams. Aristotle in no way hinted that that was so, but there was no call for him to do so in either of the contexts in which he quotes this line.[43]

Furthermore an opinion such as the one quoted above fits quite easily with Empedocles' known opinion that sensations come to us through 'effluences' from physical objects.[44] Empedocles was said, plausibly enough, to have been an admirer of Xenophanes,[45] who altogether denied that divina-

41. John Philoponus, *In Aristotelis de anima libros commentaria* (*CAG* XV) p. 486, lines 13–16, commenting on *De anima* iii.3.427a4 (cf. Empedocles 31 B 108 D-K, fr. 534 Bollack; Wright 1981, 236, appears very dubious that Empedocles formed any such thought, and Inwood 1992 ignores the matter). (It does not seem important here to enter the controversy as to which commentator wrote the commentary on the third book: see Blumenthal 1996, 61–65). The commentary of Simplicius or Pseudo-Simplicius on the same passage of the *De anima* (*CAG* XI) also brings in dreams (p. 202, line 31), but does not attribute any statement about them to Empedocles.

42. See the *index nominum* in *CAG* XV; he quotes some thirteen lines. His knowledge did not, however, come near to rivalling that of Simplicius.

43. Cf. J. Bollack's note (vol. III of his edition, p. 459). Aristotle, *Metaph.* iv.1009b21, quotes the Empedocles passage more fully; it seems to mean 'as much as they change into a different nature, so much do they also continually have different thoughts'. In 1942 Verdenius (20–21) could brush aside Philoponus more easily than most would now. His suggestion that the word *paristatai* led to this interpretation was quite feeble. He is unfortunately followed by Kingsley 1995, 284 n. 22.

44. Aristotle, *De sensu* 2.438a4–5 (but this was not his consistent view), with Wright 1981, 242–243; and see 31 B 89 = fr. 73 Wright = fr. 88 Inwood.

45. Diogenes Laertius viii.56 (his source was Hermippus, whom he evidently trusted more than most of his sources, rightly or wrongly; cf. Mejer 1978, 32). The story was a 'fabrication' according to Bollansée 1999, 453 n. 15. A number of scholars have explored the points of intellectual contact between the two, for instance Morgan 2000, 58–62.

tion was possible,[46] and it would be reasonable to think that this influence—probably not in fact personal—helped to free the younger man (he was about two generations younger) from traditional notions about dreams so that he was able to fit them into his philosophy of sensation. It was suggested earlier that Xenophanes' scepticism about prophetic dreams may well have helped to start him on the path of naturalistic inquiry. This is not to say that he desired to undertake scientific research in anything remotely like a modern sense.

As far as Empedocles is concerned, it is plain that his philosophical activity has sometimes been cast in excessively modern terms, and the Hippocratic text *On Ancient Medicine*, which named him as the archetypal philosopher, held that he was too impressionistic to give a good account of nature.[47] But Aristotle refers to him more than to any other philosopher except Plato,[48] and Empedocles did not earn this respect by means of mystification. According to one scholar, 'his repudiation of divination, and his related demythologized cosmology, constitute a departure from earlier ways of thinking that is justly thought of as revolutionary';[49] that may be going too far, but there is nothing implausible about his having adopted a rationalizing explanation of dreaming.

There is further confirmation. Previous scholars have observed that the Hippocratic work *On Winds*,[50] in the section that concerns changes in the blood, owes a debt to Empedocles.[51] When therefore he writes that as blood changes, so thinking *(phronesis)* also changes, 'once the blood grows cold . . . the eyes close, thinking is altered [*alloioutai*], and other representations install themselves, which we call dreams', we may suppose that he is echoing the Empedoclean passage later referred to by Philoponus.[52]

As far as we can tell from our fragmentary evidence, Empedocles was at the origin of naturalistic endeavours in this field, a position of some histor-

46. Cicero, *De div.* i.5.

47. Ch. 20. For the text see the edition of J. Jouanna 1990.

48. And notice how much attention he receives in a programmatic passage such as *De sensu* 2.437b–438a.

49. Lesher 1978, 16–17.

50. Ch. 14.2. For the text see once again Jouanna 1988.

51. For other allusions to Empedocles in this text see Jouanna 1988, 28–29, with references to the earlier literature.

52. Van Lieshout 1980, 41, thus appears to have been in error when he claimed that the earliest formulation of a 'day's residue' theory is provided by Herodotus' Artabanus.

ical importance. The theory of 'the day's residue' may be crude, but at least it depends more than any earlier theory on at least a modicum of observation. We have ample evidence that Empedocles attempted to explain other psychological phenomena in a naturalistic fashion.[53] It is quite likely that he deserves credit for first formulating a theory that dreams are generated internally (as we have seen, however, Homer himself might well have found such a theory acceptable). His philosophical successor in this respect was Democritus, but we may possibly be able to trace some influence of Empedocles' thinking in Herodotus too (and we should not forget that Herodotus was also for a time a western Greek).[54] What Herodotus' Artabanus is made to say is that most dreams show us things we have been thinking about during the day (he does not exclude divine dreams altogether), and hence it was to be expected that Xerxes, busy during the previous days with his army's expedition, should have dreamt about it.[55] This might have been an eccentric opinion, but more probably an opinion of this kind was common currency at Thurii and Athens at the time when Herodotus was composing his history.

Gradually, we may suppose, some Greeks came to see nature as a sphere distinct from the world of the gods and daemons. Fairly early in the fifth century the concepts *phue* and *phusis* were probably extended to individual humans,[56] and before the beginning of the Peloponnesian War the philosopher Diogenes of Apollonia and perhaps Democritus had written books entitled *On the Nature of Man*.[57] The tendency of the age, at least in Athens, was towards secular explanation of human behaviour.[58] It was also the time when Protagoras expressed his scepticism about the existence of the gods,[59] arousing interest rather than universal derision, and when, as

53. Cf. Hankinson 1991, 199.

54. We considered in the previous chapter whether Herodotus is likely to have shared the naturalistic explanation of dreams that he attributes to Artabanus (probably not).

55. vii.16.β.2.

56. Cf. Guthrie 1962–1981, II, 351–352.

57. 64 A 4 and 68 A 33 D-K (on what may have been contained in the latter work and related Democritean treatises see Leszl 2007, 30–31, 45).

58. Cf. Harris 2002, 357. One result was accusations of atheism. On Thucydides' participation in this tendency see among others Solmsen 1975, 141–147.

59. For discussion see Burkert 1985 [1977], 313, Schiappa 1991, 141–153. The exact chronology of these events is notoriously elusive.

we now know, Prodicus—who may also have written a book about human nature—went even further and denied that they existed at all.[60]

Democritus believed that dreams could in some instances foretell the future, but he seems to have been the first person who set out to explain this without recourse to the traditional kind of divine intervention.[61] More than five hundred years later the Epicurean preacher Diogenes of Oenoanda wrote that Democritus' opinion was that dreams were sent by the gods, but that was probably a polemical distortion.[62] In Democritus' view, the minds of the sleeping 'are struck by external and extraneous vision';[63] dreams are attributable to 'images and effluences [*aporroiai*]'.[64] Plutarch supplies more details, and shows how Democritus answered the question that previous philosophers had left unanswered, how images [*eidola*] that flow from physical objects get into our sleeping minds.[65] Images penetrate the body through the pores, and when they 'rise up' they make us see things in our sleep; such images are especially given off by living beings 'because of their restlessness and their warmth'.

> They also pick up images of each person's psychic motions, desires, habits, and emotions, and when, together with these images, they collide with people,

60. For his book about the nature of man see 84 B 4 D-K (from Galen). For Prodicus as an atheist see the papyrus fragment *P.Herc.* 1428 fr. 19 in the version of Henrichs 1975 (see esp. 107–109). Are we sure we believe this? Prodicus is a shadowy figure.

61. For the opposing view see Brillante 1991, 75. But he should not have used the passage that I am about to quote as evidence that Democritus took the view that the gods brought about predictive dreams.

62. See Warren 2007, 99, on Epicurean polemic as a cause of the obscurity, to us, of Democritus' views about the gods. For Diogenes see fr. 9.III.6–8 Smith (1993) and fr. 43. The sources cited by Morel 1996, 297 n. 185, to show that Diogenes was right may suggest that Democritus thought that dreams were themselves divine, but not that they were 'sent by the gods' in any normal sense. Diogenes also very probably misrepresented Aristotle and his followers (fr. 5.I.13–II.8) (Smith's defence, 1993, 128–130, is largely special pleading, but he cites prior discussions). In both cases his motive was probably polemical (though some older scholars thought that he was a philosophical ignoramus).

63. Cicero, *De div.* ii.120 (68 A 137 D-K): 'Utrum igitur censemus dormientium animos . . . an, ut Democritus censet, externa et adventicia visione pulsari? Sive enim sic est sive illo modo, videri possunt permulta somniantibus falsa pro veris'.

64. Aristotle, *De div. per somnum* 2. 464a5–6; D-K failed to include this passage in the fragments of Democritus: see II p. 422 (*Nachträge*), Taylor 1999, 126. Democritus wrote a book *About Images or Foreknowledge* (Diogenes Laertius ix.47).

65. *Quaest.conv.* viii.10 (*Mor.* 734f–735c) = 68 A 77 D-K.

they talk as if they were alive, and tell those who receive them the opinions, words, and actions of those who emitted them, provided that when they arrive they preserve the images articulated and distinct.[66]

Diogenes of Oenoanda may or may not be reporting fairly—as a matter of fact, I doubt that he is[67]—when he attributes to Democritus the view that the images we receive in sleep 'are sentient and rational and really talk to us'.[68]

Democritus was not an atheist, but he did have an unusual, and according to more conventional ancients such as Cicero confused, set of ideas about the gods: he sometimes said that the gods were 'animate images which do us good or harm',[69] which suggests that when people dreamt of the gods the gods were playing an active role, but these images were not even immortal.[70] He seems to have been the first person to have argued that humans of old derived from such images the idea that (a) god exists,[71] a point of view later developed by the Epicureans.

Democritus was intent on finding an explanation of dreams that was naturalistic not theological. It is fairly plain that he did not think that they were sent by any conventional kind of god.[72] Yet a good deal remains unclear in this matter, for the philosopher is reported to have 'prayed' to encounter only 'propitious *eidola*',[73] which implies that divine beings of some kind could choose whether to send propitious or unpropitious dreams.

66. Mostly as translated by Taylor 1999, 127. Democritus deserves credit for appreciating that the *vivacity* of dream images was one of the things that needed to be explained, but I wonder whether he and indeed many of his successors (not Lucretius, however) were somewhat influenced by the epiphany dream—in other words, he may sometimes have thought of the typical dream as a dream about one person or object, whereas we tend to think of dreams as episodes centred around ourselves.

67. See n. 62.

68. Fr. 10.V.10–14, essentially in Smith's translation.

69. *De natura deorum* i.120 = 68 A 74.

70. Democritus' theology has given rise to extensive controversy; see most recently Taylor 1999, 211–216, Warren 2007, 97–99.

71. Sextus Empiricus, *Adv.math.* iii.19 = 68 B 166 D-K.

72. Cicero, *De natura deorum* i.29.

73. Plutarch, *De defectu* 17 = *Mor.* 419a (omitted by D-K: see Taylor 140); Sextus Empiricus, *Adv.math.* ix.19 = 68 B 166 D-K. Diels-Kranz translated *eucheto* as 'wünschte', 'wished for', but the word usually involves the gods. I would rather take *eucheto* as ironical than suppose that Democritus thought that the gods choose which dreams to send us. It is

These views expressed by Empedocles and Democritus were a success story, in the sense that they had shown, with reservations that in each case it is hard to define, that dreaming could be understood on a purely human plane. That did not mean that every educated Greek in the future would think like that, but at least it gave those who were temperamentally not likely to turn to divine explanations some support for their point of view. It was a negative victory, however: the nagging questions about dreams— what do they mean? why do we dream?—remained unanswered. And if the gods were out of the picture, these questions lost much of their urgency.

'Hippocratic' Doctors

At least ten of the surviving Hippocratic treatises have something to say about dreaming, but only one, *On Regimen*, develops any detailed thinking on the subject. It seems to be atypical of the Hippocratic corpus, in that it allows that *some* dreams are of divine origin—whereas it is clear that around 400 BC most medical writers saw dreams in largely naturalistic terms.[74] If we are unwilling to give the title to Empedocles, it is to an anonymous Hippocratic doctor that we should give the credit for first theorizing that dreams are produced internally.

The Hippocratics variously thought of bad dreams as negative events in themselves, or as symptoms, or as signs of illnesses to come (prodromic symptoms, in other words).[75] Some evidently gave more importance to

---

also to be noted that in ix.21 Sextus distorts Aristotle's views about dreaming; in both cases, he was trying to make older philosophers more like the Stoics than they really were.

74. See Chapter III. *On Regimen* is now generally dated to the early fourth century, though in the past it has sometimes been dated after 350 (for a conspectus of opinion see Holowchak 2001, 387 n. 12).

75. These distinctions cannot always be applied. But for bad dreams as an evil in themselves see *Ancient Medicine* 10, *On Diseases of Girls*, *On Internal Pathologies (peri ton entos pathon)* 48 (usually called *Internal Affections*), *On Regimen* iv.88 (Book IV is sometimes called *Dreams*); for dreams as symptoms see *Epidemics* i.23 Jones ('the kind of dream and when they were dreamt'), *Humours* 4, *Prorrhetic* i.5, *On Diseases* ii.72, *On Sevens* 45 [IX p. 460 Littré] (this could be a much later treatise—cf. Jouanna 1999 [1992], 412–413); for dreams as signs of illnesses to come see *On Regimen* iii.71. It is misguided to say that the Hippocratic writers 'followed' the classification of dreams first known to us from Artemidorus half a millennium later (Oberhelman 1987, 49).

dreams than others (and in the case histories in *Epidemics* dreams do not make many appearances), but no one denied that dreams had real diagnostic value. Wet dreams are simply natural events that have a physical explanation.[76] However there is no sign of systematic investigation of dreaming, with one large exception.[77]

That exception is the last section of the treatise on dietetics—an important subject in Hippocratic medicine—*On Regimen*.[78] Some dreams, the author thinks, are divine,[79] while others have somatic causes.[80] Of all the Hippocratics, this writer in general gave most space to the actions of the gods—he is 'the most explicit when it comes to assigning a role to the gods . . . in the maintaining of health', as van der Eijk remarks, yet 'this role is rather limited'.[81] Dreams are not diagnostic, but through them the soul (*psuche*)[82] gives advance warning of ill health.[83]

The author makes a strenuous effort to explain:

> When the body is awake, the soul is subordinate to it and its attention is divided among many things. It is not in command of itself, but assigns some of itself to each faculty of the body, to hearing, sight, touch, and walking, and to acts of the whole body; but the mind [*dianoia*] does not enjoy inde-

76. *Generation* 1.3.

77. Unless we also want to count *On Internal Pathologies* 48, which says that victims of a particular form of insanity suffer from bad dreams that correspond to their actions in sleep and to the things they say in their sleep.

78. Note the editions of Joly (1967), and Joly and Byl (1984). *On Regimen* has a good deal of internal coherence, and is probably to be seen as a unity (though some good scholars have doubted this): see Diller 1959. The fact that he only introduces the gods in Book IV is probably a consequence of the specific subject-matter. The author's emphasis on *pro-diagnosis* (i.2) seems to lead logically to his interest in dreams (yet his initial preview does not mention them); and there seems to be connection between his micro-macrocosmic theory (i.10) and his views about dreams (Jouanna 1998).

79. iv.87. Avoiding the words *oneiros* and *oneirata* in favour of *enhupnion,* as is the almost unvarying custom of the Hippocratic corpus, and the absolutely unvarying practice of Aristotle, probably indicates a wish to keep the gods out of the matter (cf. Frère 1983, 34).

80. iv.71, 86, 88–93.

81. Van der Eijk 2004b, 189.

82. Modern readers may be put off by this word and may find it easier to follow the author's thought if they substitute 'mind' or 'brain', thought those are not of course exact translations.

83. iv.87 (it is not clear whether he thinks that the 'soul' can foresee some things independently of the gods), 90.

pendence. But whenever the body is at rest, the soul—being set in motion and awake[84]—administers its own household and performs all the acts of the body by itself. For the sleeping body has no perception, but the soul, being awake, has cognizance of everything—it sees what is visible, hears what is audible, walks, touches, suffers,[85] ponders, all in its narrow space.[86] All the functions of both body and soul are performed during sleep by the soul.[87]

Developing ideas about the *psuche* now made it possible to suppose that it operated independently in this fashion.[88]

But the author has more to say about what causes dreaming. Dreams may be caused by *merimna,* that is care or anxiety,[89] while dreams of eating or drinking one's usual diet are apparently taken to be signs of hunger—a simple form of wish-fulfilment.[90] He knows furthermore that the 'day's residue' may be present: 'such dreams as repeat during the night a person's daytime actions or thoughts (intentions?) just as they were done or intended by day in a normal act.'[91] He observes that dreams sometimes 'contradict daily affairs', forming a *tarache* (disorder or confusion),[92]—which must be a reference to what is commonly referred to by dream-experts as bizarreness. As noted above, he also mentions the 'bodies in strange forms', *allomorpha somata,* that we may see in dreams: 'they frighten a person, and indicate a surfeit of unusual foods, a secretion [*apokrisin*], a discharge of bile [?] [*choleran*] and a dangerous illness' (he proceeds to recommend treatment).[93] The author has in short paid attention to the phenomena. (It is of course perfectly possible, even likely, that earlier authors had anticipated his descriptions in every respect.)

84. The text is somewhat in doubt here.

85. *lupeetai* includes the idea of psychic as well as physical pain (cf. Harris 2002, 343).

86. Here I use the text of Joly.

87. iv.86.

88. Cf. Harris 2002, 347.

89. iv.89.

90. iv.93, reading *epithumien* with Littré and Joly 1967 for the highly improbable *athumien* of the MSS. The phrase *psuches epithumien* is drawn from six lines lower. Homer, as we have seen, already knew of wish-fulfilment dreams.

91. iv.88 (the phrase 'in a normal act' has caused difficulty). See also iv.93 ('whenever in one's sleep one thinks that one is eating or drinking one's usual food or drink . . .').

92. iv.88–89.

93. iv.93; cf. iii.71.

This was not an abstract inquiry: for the reasons already mentioned, our author thought that dreams could have practical value and should lead to the proper reaction. 'Whoever knows how to interpret [*krinein*] them [*tauta*] correctly knows a great part of wisdom'.[94] The experts, who recommend apotropaic prayer, have nothing else to recommend ('praying is good', he adds, but one must also help oneself).[95] The author himself advises prayer in some cases, apparently as something of an afterthought,[96] but above all he advises physical treatment, dietary changes and exercise,[97] sometimes arbitrarily—so it seems—matching regimens to improbable dreams in manic detail.[98] (He is obsessed by dreams about heavenly bodies and weather,[99] in consequence of his theory of correspondences between the cosmos and the human body.)[100]

His classification is the earliest one we know of that goes beyond Penelope's true dreams and false. Nondivine dreams are categorized by content, as follows:[101]

Ch. 88:　activities of the daytime (they may be repeated or they may be 'opposed'), strife about such activities.

Ch. 89:　the sun, moon, sky and stars, 'pure and bright' or the opposite; receiving things, pure or otherwise, from the gods;[102] rain.

94. iv.86 end (not 'qui sait juger cela correctement', Joly; W. H. S. Jones is also wrong).
95. iv.87.
96. iv.89 end: he names the gods to pray to in the event of positive dreams (the Sun, Zeus of Heaven, Zeus Protector of the Home, Athena Protector of the Home, Hermes, Apollo), and those to pray to avert negative ones (Earth and the Heroes); 90 end: a phrase recommending in certain circumstances prayer to Earth, Hermes and the Heroes. In the case of other dreams he refuses to give an opinion about prayer: 88.2. The last sentence of the treatise (93 end) mentions the help the gods gave the author in his research. Martin 2004, 47, claims that religious advice is mixed 'indiscriminately' with medical advice in *Regimen* IV; not so, on a more careful reading.
97. iv.88–93.
98. Joly 1960, 168–178, however, attempted to show that the author's thinking was systematic.
99. iv.89.
100. Cf. Jouanna 1998.
101. This is simply a summary. Cf. van der Eijk 2004b, 199, for a slightly different presentation, to which I am indebted. On lists in early Greek medical prose cf. Humphreys 1996, 8–9.
102. Enigmatic in the original, but the item is included in a list of 'celestial' topics.

Ch. 90:   seeing and hearing what is on the earth;
          walking and running well;
          thriving and well-watered land;
          the opposite of the above;
          sight, hearing and limbs that are impaired;
          rough sea, earthquake, flood.
Ch. 91:   clothes.
Ch. 92:   the dead;
          receiving things from them or losing things to them.
Ch. 93:   *allomorpha somata;*
          eating and drinking;
          usual things;
          frightening things;
          fighting, being tied up;
          difficult movements, crossing rivers;
          soldiers, enemies, monsters.

In accordance with the microcosmic doctrine he had set out earlier, the author gives regimen instruction for each category of dream.[103] The reasoning is by analogy and not empirical.[104] If you dream of clothes that are too big or too small, it is not good; in the one case you should eat less, in the other more.[105] If you dream certain kinds of dreams about the dead, it is 'not favourable' *(ouk epitedeion):* you should 'purge them away' by going for runs and walks (probably the advice I would give), taking an emetic and then following a soft and light diet.[106] Dreams are 'good', 'not good', 'not favourable', 'pathological', 'dangerous', and threaten a wide variety of physical consequences.

The author (or some prototype of this catalogue) was the first to mention anxiety dreams, and the first to trace different kinds of dream to diet, another notion with a lengthy future. And his efforts were at least in part nat-

103. For discussion see van der Eijk 2004b, 199–203.

104. Holowchak 2001, 395. Yet it is true that the author had a relatively strong taste for observation (Bourgey 1953, 125). Elsewhere Hippocratic writers sometimes emphasize the empirical nature of their methods, e.g. *Epidemics* i.23 Jones. But whereas other Hippocratic texts show some impulse towards assessing if not measuring probability (see the fascinating discussion in Di Benedetto 1986, 126–142), the author of this text seems uninterested.

105. iv.91.

106. iv.92.

uralistic, while at the same time they coincided neatly with his professional lore and interests. And he deserves some credit for excluding all speculation about the 'humours'.[107]

What then is the relationship between this text and what came before and afterwards?[108] The author refers at the outset to those who have written about regimen before—there were many of them, he says—but as is normal in Hippocratic writings he does not name them. There are dream-interpreters, who as far as medically significant dreams are concerned are sometimes right and sometimes wrong, and do not understand why this is the case.[109] Did he in fact draw on existing dream-books written by non-physicians? The parallels between his views and those of Artemidorus[110] should not lead us to this conclusion[111] (in part they result from Artemidorus' own respect for physicians—see below), though no doubt it is true that in the early fourth century one could have one foot in the camp of the *iatroi* and the other in that of the *oneiropoloi*.

It was long ago suggested that this text also drew somehow on Babylonian sources,[112] and as we saw earlier there was considerable interest in dream divination both in Mesopotamia and among the Hittites. If *On Regimen* ultimately derives in part from non-Greek sources, it is evident that the intermediaries are likely to have been fairly numerous and that they may have made large adjustments. Mesopotamia had a large literature of dream omens, and it is quite likely that some of it filtered into contiguous cultures. A recent and detailed assessment describes both similarities and differences:[113] some of the dream subjects are the same as those listed above, but on the other hand what Babylonian dreams portend is frequently prosperity or the opposite, only sometimes a medical consequence. If there was any naturalistic Mesopotamian theorizing about dreams, it has been

---

107. Contrary to the statement of Guidorizzi 1988, 88, they play no significant part.

108. Lloyd 1987, 37: this text 'draws heavily on, and at points is merely a rationalisation of, popular beliefs'. But he also notes the author's ambition to improve on traditional accounts.

109. iv.88.

110. Fredrich 1899, 206–217.

111. Holowchak 2001, 388 n. 15, notwithstanding. In so far as his arguments have any weight, they merely cast doubt on the unity of *On Regimen*.

112. Capelle 1925, esp. 381–387.

113. Van der Eijk 2004, 206–215. For a specific similarity between a Babylonian handbook and the Hippocratic *De morbis* (diagnosis partly by reference to dreams of the dead) see Geller 2004, 43.

lost to us.[114] I conclude that in this case the debt probably exists but is not large.

After *On Regimen*, doctors took the study of dreams no further, in spite of the fact that the Hippocratic tradition was progressive in spirit and well aware that knowledge could be extended by research.[115] We can hardly say that the execution of Socrates 'halted scientific progress',[116] as far as medicine was concerned. The easy explanation is that in practice physicians eventually realized that dreams were seldom much use, but it is also possible that the growing popularity of incubation shrines, from the time of the Peloponnesian War onwards, meant that relying on dreams came to be associated with a rival form of medicine (it was only much later, I think, that 'rational' medicine and the incubation shrines cooperated).[117] It is true that there is no *overt* hostility on the Hippocratic side,[118] but doctors found themselves in a delicate position—they could not possibly speak ill of Asclepius himself. The fragments of the next major medical writer after the Hippocratics, Diocles of Carystus,[119] are relatively abundant on the subject of dietetics,[120] yet there is no sign anywhere in the surviving testimony that

114. Cf. Butler 1998, esp. 24.

115. See for example *Ancient Medicine* 8 and 12. See also Jouanna 1999 [1992], 238–239, who, however, points out that some other Hippocratic authors consider that medical knowledge is already complete (*Places in Man* 46, *The Art* 8). This complacency undoubtedly had some negative effects.

116. Janko 2002–2003, 18.

117. Plato, *Phaedr.* 270c, calls Hippocrates one of the Asclepiadae, and we know that doctors made dedications to Asclepius in classical Athens (see Aleshire 1989, 65–66, Nutton 2004, 111, Gorrini 2005, 143–145). Nutton ch. 7 is at pains to deny that there was any hostility between doctors and incubation shrines in classical Greece, but I know of no doctor's dedication from an incubation shrine that is earlier than the Roman period. In Hellenistic Cos, the medical centre par excellence, there seems to have been at least some degree of separation between the Asclepieion and the doctors (see Sherwin-White 1978, 275–278). The texts cited by Gorrini 146 fail to support her contention that 'physicians themselves allow their patients to go to the temple', though in Roman times they obviously did so. I doubt that physicians often encouraged their patients to undergo incubation at any period.

118. Jouanna 1999 [1992], 202, who summarizes very well the whole problem of this competition, or noncompetition (195–203).

119. His chronology is disputed: see among others van der Eijk 2000–2001, II, xxxi–xxxiv. He falls between the Hippocratic writings and Herophilus, but whether before, at the same time as, or after Aristotle is indeterminate.

120. I pp. 282–385 van der Eijk.

he took the slightest professional interest in dreams. Is that an accident? One might guess that he in fact disagreed with the Hippocratic *On Regimen* on this subject.[121]

Back to Plato

Plato made liberal use of images of dreaming,[122] but it is scarcely surprising, given his concerns and opinions, that he did not confront the whole subject directly and in detail. As we saw in the previous chapter, he considered that a small number of exceptional persons, including Socrates, enjoyed the privilege of dreaming veridical dreams, thanks to the gods. Ordinary dreaming on the other hand was a mass of illusions. Nonetheless he made a number of observations that are of significance in the present context. (I shall restrict these comments to those that are naturalistic in nature, leaving mostly aside the metaphysical aspect of his psychology.)

What is best known about Plato's comments is his identification of wish-fulfilment dreams in Book IX of the *Republic*. Discussing the 'tyrannical' character, he tells us that excessive eating and drinking leads us to dream that we are fulfilling our basest desires, letting the lusting *epithumetikon* part of the soul have its way, for there is in each of us a terrible, bestial and lawless type of desire, even in some of us who appear to be well-behaved (*metrioi*), which 'reveals itself particularly in dreams'.[123] A man of good character on the other hand has no such dreams, for the rational element in his soul stays awake as the rest sleeps.[124]

Where do these thoughts come from, and what is novel? The Hippocratics had already, in all probability, put forward some ideas on the relationship between dreams and diet (even if *On Regimen* is later than the *Republic*, which is not impossible). What Plato has to say beyond this connection includes a measure of penetrating observation of experience (including no

121. For the likelihood that he knew the Hippocratic treatise (there is no certainty about it) see van der Eijk 2005, 75.

122. Burnyeat 1970, 103, Brillante 1996. He was also in some respects an alert observer of dreams: he knew, for instance, that they could include absurd transformations: single objects suddenly become numerous, small ones huge—*Parmenides* 164d (cf. van Lieshout 1980, 105). The view that we dream about our waking preoccupations is echoed in *Theaet.* 173d.

123. *Rep.* ix.571c–572b; cf. 574e. Rotondaro 1998, 119, argues that the tyrannical man's life is represented as being as illusory as a dream.

124. *Rep.* ix. 571d–572a.

doubt his own), and a measure, ironically enough, of wish-fulfilment. No one had previously captured the wish-fulfilment dream—which was already known to Homer—quite so explicitly, though we may suppose that most Greek wish-fulfilment dreams were neither terrible nor bestial nor perhaps even lawless. It was Platonic psychology, equipped with its tripartite view of the psyche—a very useful notion, be it said, at that stage of psychological inquiry—that enabled Plato and his readers to face the fact that some dreams seem to articulate forbidden wishes. Thus the philosopher creates a much wider view of the psychological causation of dreams than we have met in any previous writer; but it is also a more moralistic view.[125] How much Plato wishes that the wicked had lawless dreams and the virtuous had truth-telling ones! We have to wait for Christian theologians before we can find anyone else so firmly in the grip of ideology that he can believe that it is really so, but the presumption was probably widespread that the pious were more likely to receive true dreams than others were.[126] (To some extent, however, Plato admits that it is a matter of degree: the virtuous man is the *least likely* to see the one kind of dream and the *most likely* to see the other.)[127] But two elements fail to fit together perfectly—eating and drinking, and moral character. Presumably the tyrannical man is most likely to overindulge, but what if he takes an evening off from his excesses?

In the previous chapter we briefly took into account that puzzling work of Plato's, the *Timaeus*, quoting one of the pair of passages in which he has something to say about dreams.[128] The gods, the Pythagorean Timaeus is made to say, have made it possible for inspired people to have prophetic dreams. The liver is the essential organ.

Earlier in the dialogue, he had explained dreams in different terms. Vision, according to this account, partly depends on a kind of fire in our eyes; when we are asleep, the gods bring it about that our eyelids confine the force of this fire, which

> dissolves [disperses? *diachei*] and levels [*homalunei*] the internal motions; this leads to calm [*hesuchia*], and when this calm is profound, sleep comes

125. Cf. van Lieshout 1980, 112.

126. 'It would be terrible if the same divine signs appeared to the pious and to the wicked', said a fourth-century orator (Lycurgus, *Leocr.* 93).

127. *Rep.* ix.572a end.

128. Slaveva-Griffin 2005 provides a survey of the different ways in which this dialogue has been read in recent years.

with little dreaming [*brachuoneiros*], but when larger motions remain, visions [*phantasmata*] corresponding in quality and number to the type and location of the remaining motions are formed internally, and are remembered as external when we wake.[129]

There are a number of mysteries in this highly frustrating passage.[130] For one thing, 'Timaeus' seems to be saying that all dreams are in some sense internal,[131] but one cannot be confident that he thereby excluded divine-message dreams.[132] Nor is it revealed why he thinks, as he apparently does, that we are better off with as few dreams as possible,[133] and it would be even more curious if what he meant was we are better off with dreams that are short.[134]

There was no fruitful line of investigation here. What Plato puts into Timaeus' mouth on this subject, as the latter expounds the creation of the world, is not the result of naturalistic thinking or observation,[135] but of an inspired mythical attempt to explain how the Demiurge's creation is constructed. That was Plato's intellectual taste.

Aristotle Uncertain

Aristotle, on the other hand, has sometimes been portrayed as the originator of the science of dreams.[136] Naturally he built on the work of his predecessors.[137] More recently, in any case, van der Eijk has argued that while

129. *Tim.* 45b–46a; the quotation is from 45e–46a. The original of the last phrase seems ambiguous; for a review of possible translations see Holowchak 2002, 36 n. 9.

130. Cf., among the relatively recent literature, Rotondaro 1998, 29–70, esp. 46. Can the two passages in fact be reconciled? Holowchak 2002, 25–37 attempts to show that they can.

131. As Heraclitus also seems to have said (above, p. 237).

132. In fact 41a strongly suggests that he did not.

133. In *Apol.* 40c–e Socrates argues that we are happier when we do not dream.

134. As Rotondaro thinks (1998, 55).

135. Sassi 2005, 145, does not justify her claim that 'Timaeus' gives 'unprecedented attention to the prior tradition of investigating nature', though others have written similarly.

136. Frère 1983. 'It is Aristotle who definitively turns his back on a predictive interpretation of dreams', Sassi 2001 [1988], 142 n. 6. Both judgements are on the target but not bull's-eyes. Compare the acid comments of van der Eijk 1994, 11.

137. It seems very probable, though it cannot be proved decisively, that he knew *On Regimen* IV directly: see van der Eijk 1994, 279, and 2005, 198.

Aristotle records a considerable number of apparently empirical observations about dreaming—whether they are really his own or drawn for example from other writers—his reasoning on the subject is of a particular kind and not to be confused with the procedures that we recognize as scientific.[138] To this we shall shortly return.

Before discussing Aristotle's thinking in some detail, however, I will summarize what the pre-Aristotelians achieved. The four nontraditional ideas that stand out—apart from the god-excluding approach which Aristotle probably inherited from Democritus—are (1) the Empedoclean theory that dreams 'arise from one's activities by day', (2) the notion that dreams take place entirely *within* the individual, and (3) that they are connected with the individual's physical condition, and (Plato) with his personality. Democritus meanwhile had attempted to explain (4) how particular images came to be in the individual's consciousness. Each of these claims makes its appearance, in one way or another, in the group of three treatises— *On Sleep and Waking, On Dreams* and *On Prophecy through Sleep*—which make up part of Aristotle's *Parva Naturalia.*[139]

We need not, I think, concern ourselves at length with the possibility that there was an earlier and different Aristotelian view of dreams before the main texts in the *Parva Naturalia.*[140] The most intriguing piece of evidence, apart from the story about Aristotle's student Eudemus which we discussed in the previous chapter, is an apparent fragment of his lost work *On Philosophy,* in which, according to Sextus Empiricus, he took up Democritus' notion that humans get their ideas of the gods from dreams (from other sources too, he says).[141] Here he also accepts the notion that we can have prophetic dreams.[142]

138. Van der Eijk 2005, 181–182.

139. Least prominent perhaps is notion (2). See *De div. per somnum* 1.463a23–27 ('when we are going to act, or are acting, or have acted, we are frequently engaged in these actions, and do them, in easy-to-interpret dreams'). Cf. *Problems* xxx.14.957a23–24, though that is probably a post-Aristotelian work.

140. Frère 1983, 28–29, and others. The relative chronology of the *Parva Naturalia* and the *De anima* does not have to be settled here.

141. Fr. 12a Ross = Sextus Empiricus, *Adv.math.* iii.20–23.

142. According to *Protrepticus* fr. 9 Ross (55 Rose), all dreams are false. This should lead us to doubt whether this section of the source, Iamblichus, *Protr.* 8, is really Aristotelian; and even Düring, who ardently believed that Iamblichus was here drawing on Aristotle, admitted that there were others sources too (see his 1993 edition, p. 12). The

But his detailed discussion is to be found in the three treatises just
named. Here he sets out his questions about dreaming as follows (I have
given them numbers for ease of reference):[143]

> (1) we must ask what a dream is [which turns out to mean how they come
> about], and (2) from what cause sleepers sometimes dream but sometimes
> do not. Or (3) is it the case that sleepers always dream [i.e. that all sleepers
> dream] but <some of them> do not remember, and (4) if this is so, why does
> it happen? And (5) is it or is it not possible to foresee the future <in
> dreams>,[144] and if so, in what way? And (6) is it possible to foresee only hu-
> man actions, or also things for which the superhuman [*to daimonion*] is re-
> sponsible and that happen by nature or by chance?[145]

Questions (2), (3), by extension (4), and (6) appear to be new. It will be
seen at once that Aristotle goes beyond questions about the content of
dreams, though he shows some interest in that too, to questions about the
whole phenomenon of dreaming. He does not, be it noted, raise the question of the 'function' of dreaming,[146] at least not in any normal sense, for
quite apart from the evolutionary freight that that term carries, Aristotle is
not asking what purpose dreaming in general might serve; this is confirmed
by the answers he gives.

Aristotle provides these answers, sometimes quite elliptically, in *On
Dreams* and *On Prophecy through Sleep*. In summary, they are as follows:

(1) Dreams are the work of our senses, but in their imagining capacity;
they result from the survival of perceptions from the time when we were
awake.[147] These residual perceptions are carried by the blood to the heart,
which is the organ of perception, and they become visible to it, because the
senses are asleep; sometimes these residual perceptions get muddled up

---

'fragment' is not admitted to the edition of Aristotle's *Protrepticus* by G. Schneeweiss
(2005).

143. *On Sleep* 1.453b17–24. It would take an undue amount of space to dispute other
scholars' comprehension of these questions and their answers, but I have indicated significant divergences from the invaluable accounts of Repici 2003 and van der Eijk 2005.

144. Thus he does not discuss whether they can give information about the present or
the past.

145. Question 6 does not seem to receive a direct answer, but the implied answer seems
to be positive (cf. Gallop 1996, 119).

146. As claimed by Flanagan 2000, 35–36. See Gallop 1996, 28–38. The question is certainly not raised 'in every ancient text' (Flanagan 36).

147. Freud 1954 [1900], 2, seems to misrepresent 462a.

en route.[148] (2) Not dreaming, except in small children (who do not dream at all), is a consequence of the internal movement produced by eating.[149] (3) and (4) Some people really do not dream, because of a congenital 'abundance of [internal] motion', which may, however, be altered by age.[150]

(5) and (6) There are reasons both for and against believing in dream foresight, but we cannot trace prophetic dreams to gods, for a god would send such dreams to the best and wisest people (Plato had at one time maintained that this really happened),[151] whereas all sorts of people dream, and animals too;[152] and apart from the gods there is no other reasonable explanation. But dreams can be *causes* of future events or *signs* of them (and hence they can permit foresight). For this reason the 'most discerning' physicians, *ton iatron hoi charientes*, say that one should pay very close attention to dreams.[153] But many dreams seem to be coincidences, especially those that are outlandish *(huperbata)* or have origins outside the dreamer such as dreams of naval battles or far-off events.[154]

So far, a reasonably tidy and consistent point of view. Dreams, Aristotle continues, are not divine, but they are *daimonion*, superhuman, 'for nature is superhuman but not divine'.[155] Proof that they are not divine? Quite ordinary humans are good at seeing into the future *(prooratikoi)* and have easily understandable dreams *(euthuoneiroi)*.[156] These are people who are

---

148. *On Dreams* 1.458a33–3.462a31. He offers a detailed explanation of why we perceive these remembered images as moving, including his image of the notorious red mirrors, and of how it is possible for the senses to be deceived, 459b23–460b27.

149. *On Dreams* 3.461a8–25.

150. 3.462a31–b11.

151. *De div. per somnum* 1.462b21–22.

152. On this point: *De div. per somnum* 2.463b12; cf. *Hist.An.* iv.10.537b13. For the notion that animals dream, which recurs in Lucretius and Pliny, see Schrijvers 1980, 143–144.

153. *De div. per somnum* 1.463a5. For this translation see Lloyd 1987, 34; there have been many others. 'I medici più raffinati' (Repici 2003, 169) gets the meaning well.

154. All this: *De div. per somnum* 1.462b12–463b11.

155. 2.463b14–15. On the meaning of *daimonion* in this text see esp. van der Eijk 2005, 191.

156. I interpret this word thus, since a little later (2.464b7) our author says that 'anyone can interpret *euthuoneiriai*'. Van der Eijk 1994 translates 'zu klaren Träumen geneigt'. These are presumably thought of as including (most) epiphany dreams. Others translate *euthuoneiroi* as '[having] vivid dreams' (Hett), '[having] direct dream-vision' (whatever that means) (Gallop), or '[avendo] sogni lineari' (also obscure) (Repici). Martínez 2000, 58, considers that it means 'ce qui voit en songe ce que doit vraiment arriver'.

talkative and 'manic'[157]—the reason being that they 'experience many movements of every kind'.[158] Without much warning, we seem after all to be in a world in which dreams really do have some predictive potential. And Aristotle presents a physical theory to account for this potential, and for the 'fact' that it is not the wisest people but ordinary people, and especially 'some of the insane', who have this capacity.[159] Furthermore there are more skilled and less skilled dream-interpreters, whence it follows that there are predictive dreams.[160]

We are faced in fact with a dilemma.[161] We can either agree with the commentators who claim that Aristotle is simply speaking about people who *seem* to have veridical dreams, fortuitously.[162] Or we can accept what the text seems to say, namely that some correct dream predictions are not entirely coincidental. It should be obvious that the latter view is preferable.

The last part of *On Prophecy through Sleep*, which is perhaps even more difficult, begins as follows:[163]

> As for dreams that do not have origins of the kind we have described, but origins that are bizarre either in time, place or size,[164] or are not like this but do not have their origins within the dreamer—unless the prediction is a coincidence, such dreams <we should explain> in the following manner rather than as Democritus does (the latter attributes them to images and emanations).

157. This seems to be the best word for translating *melancholikoi*—those who are full of black bile: see Harris 2002, 16–17. It is quite misleading to translate it with 'melancholic', as even van der Eijk does (2005, 181). There is a textual problem in 463b16–18 (cf. Gallop 1996, 110), but in any case Aristotle confirms a little later that he thinks that the 'manic' are good at dreaming the future (464a32–24). In *Eud.Eth.* viii.2.1248a35–40 too he asserts that the *melancholikoi* are *euthuoneiroi*.

158. 2.463b19.

159. 2.463b13–464b5.

160. 2. 464b5–16.

161. Properly recognized only by van der Eijk 2005, 201–205.

162. This seems to be the view of Gallop 1996, 163 (cf. 43–48), and Repici 2003, 48.

163. 463b31–464a6. In my discussion of this passage I leave aside a number of subsidiary problems.

164. How can the *origins* (*archai*) of dreams be 'alien' or 'extravagant' (*huperorias*) in time or place or size? In default of a better suggestion I suppose that Aristotle is referring to *dreams* that have such characteristics. Van der Eijk paraphrases as follows (1994, 306): 'Es gibt Fälle von Vorhersehen der Zukunft durch Träume, bei denen . . . die Ursache der Verwirklichung ihres Inhalts ausserhalb des Bereichs des Träumenden liegt, entweder in Zeit, Raum oder Umfang . . .'. That makes good sense (see his 307–308 for a fuller discussion)—but it is not what the text actually says.

He proceeds to unveil his physical theory: some sort of movement, like the movements of water or air, passes from objects to the human mind (here he mentions Democritus' 'images' and 'effluences'), and they are especially perceptible at night when the air is less disturbed. They make an impression on the minds of ordinary people because these are 'deserted and void'.[165]

As van der Eijk remarks, 'very little is left' by now of Aristotle's '*a priori* assumption that sleep is an incapacitation of the sensitive part of the soul'.[166] So we are faced not only with a contradiction about the existence of predictive dreams, but about how dreams work. Kahn and van der Eijk have pointed out in fact that Aristotle sometimes arrives at conclusions that contradict his earlier ones without taking note of the fact, and that is the case here. 'In his work on sleep and dreams, as in his biological works at large, [Aristotle] sometimes shows himself an improviser of *ad hoc* explanations, constantly prepared to adapt his theories to what the phenomena suggest', gently referring to this as a 'lack of systematicity'.[167]

But in this case it looks as if what Aristotle was belatedly taking account of was not the phenomena but Democritus, who appears for the first time in the passage just quoted. And this leads us to the wider question how Aristotle reacted to previous theorizers about dreaming. He saw (correctly) that the earlier opinions most in need of consideration were those of Democritus and 'the most discerning' of the physicians.[168] With regard to the latter, the opinion he attributes to them is that 'one should pay careful attention to dreams',[169] which as we have seen was the opinion of many Hippocratic doctors (though some would have said that a modicum of attention was enough). For Aristotle, obviously counting himself as one of those who 'are pursuing a theoretical inquiry',[170] it was important to understand *why* this was so, the answer being that dreams could be signs or causes of future events.

As for Democritus, it is hard for us to judge, without the actual text of his work, how fairly or thoroughly Aristotle treated his theory about dreams. Similarly the incoherences in Aristotle's own work are open to various

---

165. 2.464a6–24.

166. Van der Eijk 2005, 202.

167. Ibid., 203, alluding to Kahn 1979 [1966], 7.

168. Repici 2003, 11, complains in a modern fashion that Aristotle does not refer more fully to earlier theorists.

169. *De div. per somnum* 1.463a4–6.

170. 1.463a7–8, trans. Gallop.

possible explanations. One view is that he simply thought that dreams were unimportant: they 'do not have any cognitive or moral significance and do not contribute in any way to the full realisation of human virtues'.[171] Up to a point, this is clearly correct, but he also seems to have found some of the problems that dreams raise tantalizingly difficult: at the end of *On Prophecy through Sleep*, he was still struggling to understand.

And a good deal of empirical observation, not necessarily of course by Aristotle himself, fed into his opinions.[172] In *On Dreams* his main empirical—or apparently empirical—statements are these:[173]

(1) We often have thoughts while we are seeing dream images (458b11, 18–19)[174]

(2) Going to sleep immediately after eating, one does not dream (461a10–13)

(3) Very young children do not dream at all (461a10–13);[175]

(4) *Melancholikoi*, that is to say manic people, and drunks and those suffering from fever have disturbed and monstrous and [?] incoherent dreams (461a21–23)[176]

(5) 'When the blood has subsided' [i.e., in the early morning], dreams are coherent [?] (461a25–27)[177]

(6) 'One seems to be two' (461b3)

(7) While dreaming, we are sometimes aware that we are dreaming (the 'lucid dream') (462a2–8)

171. Van der Eijk 2005, 204, referring in particular to *De div. per somnum* 463b12–18.

172. For a nice round declaration of the principle that *logoi*, theories, must give way to the observed facts *(aisthesis)* see *Gen.An.* iii.10.760b28–33.

173. This account differs from that of van der Eijk 2005, but there is no pressing need to discuss the divergences.

174. 'What we think in dreaming of X is distinct from our dream', Gallop 1996, 138. Was Aristotle influenced here by 'lucid' dreaming in the technical sense?

175. In *Hist.An.* iv.10.537b13–16, he specifies that dreaming usually begins at the age of four or five. Modern opinion is divided about this: Strauch and Meier 1996, 182–184, favour Aristotle, Stoddard et al. 1996, 25, disagree. Elsewhere in fact Aristotle says that small children do dream but do not remember their dreams: *Hist.An.* vii.10.587b10, *Gen.An.* v.1.779a12–13.

176. Reading *eiromena* ('coherent') in lines 22 and 27; see van der Eijk 1994b, 220 (not convinced), Gallop 1996, 98.

177. I leave aside the textual problem. Cf. van der Eijk 1994b, 222, and 2005, 181 ('dreams occur in a later stage of sleep').

(8) One sometimes sees dream-images at transitional moments of falling asleep and waking (462a10–11)[178]

(9) While asleep, one may faintly see and hear things in one's vicinity, and even answer questions, but these are not real dreams (462a17–29)

(10) Many have never dreamt, while others first do so late in life (462b1–11).

If we leave aside the definitional question raised by 9, only 2 seems to be definitely false, while 1, 3, 6, 7, 8, 9 and 10 are correct. Almost all of these points appear to be original. Van der Eijk has argued that Aristotle here mentions empirical data 'in the course of [his] theoretical argument . . . in order to support or clarify opinions and presuppositions which [he] already seems to take for granted'.[179] That may be exaggerated, and we should be wary of a model of scientific thinking that denies any role to theory or to preconceived ideas. How Aristotle actually reached his conclusions is largely hidden from us.

Turning to *On Prophecy through Sleep*, we can again summarize Aristotle's main empirical claims:[180]

(11) Dreams that come true happen to average people *(tois tuchoisi)* (462b20–22, 464a18–20)[181]

(12) Some people do foresee events that will take place at the ends of the earth (462b24–26)

(13) When one is asleep, weak sensations appear strong (slight noises appear as thunder, etc.) (463a11–18)[182]

(14) Our future, present or past actions often appear in readily understandable dreams *(euthuoneiria)* (463a21–25)

178. This, he says, happens to some young people even when their eyes are wide open while it is dark and they are in bed.

179. Van der Eijk 2005, 182. 'The general impression one gets is that empirical evidence is primarily mentioned when it suits the argument—and if not, it is either ignored or explained away in a questionable manner'. But Philip van der Eijk states (by letter) that what he was concerned with here was 'how the argument is presented in the text'.

180. Van der Eijk 2005, 186–188, gives a different version.

181. And see below, item 16.

182. Van der Eijk 2005, 199–201, points out that Aristotle is here tracing dreams to sensations during sleep, whereas earlier he had traced them to sensations left over from *before* sleep.

(15) Not only humans but some animals dream (463b12);[183]

(16) Very ordinary people have dreams that come true: they are the garrulous and the 'melancholic', who have highly various dreams (463b15–18)[184]

(17) Many dreams do not come true (463b22–23)

(18) (Returning to 16) those who have prophetic dreams are some of the insane *(ekstatikoi)*, or alternatively the 'melancholics' (464a24–27, 32)[185]

(19) Some people tend to have readily intelligible dreams (464a27)

(20) And this is especially true when people dream about those who are familiar to them (464a27–32)

(21) Some interpreters of dreams are more skilled *(technikos)* than others (464b5–7).

These observations are more debatable—they seem in fact to be a mixture of more or less learned conjectures without an adequate empirical base (11, 12, 14, 16, 18, 19, 20, 21) and correct observations or inferences (13, 15, 17), of which two (13, 15) appear to be original.

Perspectives change. '[Aristotle's] whole approach to the problem is scientific, not religious; and one may in fact doubt whether in this matter modern science has advanced very far beyond him', wrote Dodds, for whom Freud represented science.[186] More recent scholars, while generally agreeing that 'his works on sleep and dreams are without any doubt the most intelligent extant treatment of the subject in classical literature',[187] have delivered more nuanced verdicts. His strength resides in 'the shrewd and original questions he asks'. His attempts at empirical inquiry are of a premodern kind, and his optimism about his own achievement inevitably seems exaggerated.[188] It should be added that in spite of the obstacles in his path, Aristotle seems to have been able to go beyond his predecessors (certainly far beyond what was generally believed in the wider culture—

183. Hence dreams cannot be god-sent.

184. I.e. they have many 'shots' and consequently more 'hits' (463b18–22).

185. Van der Eijk 2005, 188 (cf. 1994, 321) does not convince me that *ekstatikoi* here means 'prone to anger', a concept which Aristotle knew very well how to express.

186. Dodds 1951, 120. Bourgey, in the same period, could still be forcibly struck by the modernity of Aristotle's writing on this subject (1955, 32, 95). The second half of Dodds's opinion is repeated by Holowchak 1996, 422.

187. Van der Eijk 2005, 205.

188. Ibid.

and here we shall not forget the noteworthy level of confidence in divine dreams that prevailed among Aristotle's contemporaries), and he also rescued empirical investigation from the dungeon to which Plato professedly wished to condemn it.

What questions about dreaming could Aristotle have answered even with the most refined methods that were available to him? If he had less respect for the opinions of other humans, he might have excluded the predictive dream more decisively, as Cicero did. But without the habit of counting or rigorously assessing probability,[189] and with only the most rudimentary knowledge of neurology, his prospects of further advance were slight. And so his ancient successors found. Dodds said of them that they 'certainly' did not make any further advances on this subject.[190] Is that in fact correct? Aristotle's own school does not indeed seem to have moved forward. Theophrastus, his successor, tried, since he wrote a book *On Sleep and Dreams*,[191] but the fact that, as far as is known, it made no impact whatsoever on later thinkers[192] suggests that it lacked originality.

The Epicureans

Did the Hellenistic schools of philosophy, so creative in other respects, propound any important new naturalistic ideas about dreams? And did Hellenistic doctors achieve anything in this area? The authors we are interested in are once again, in almost all cases, fragmentary or indeed entirely lost. Take the case of the Epicureans—the only philosophical school that is of major interest here: most of our evidence comes from the great poem of Lucretius (some from Epicurus himself, some from Cicero, Diogenes of Oenoanda and Sextus Empiricus), and we may wonder whether Epicurus' own views, let alone those of the other founding fathers of Epicureanism, can be reconstructed (it was realized long ago that the Epicureans sometimes disagreed with each other, sometimes quite fiercely).

189. Cf. Hankinson 1998, 289.

190. Dodds 1951, 121.

191. See fr. 328, 11a and 11b in the edition of W. W. Fortenbaugh et al. Some thoroughly unconvincing mediaeval 'fragments' are given as nos. 342–344; see Huby 1999, 13, 92–93.

192. Sedley 1998, 183, argued that Epicurus accessed Peripatetic ideas through the writings of Theophrastus, but there is, as far as I can tell, no sign in the existing evidence of independent Theophrastan thinking on this particular topic.

Epicurus himself certainly had something to say about dreaming. His *Letter to Herodotus* shows that his theory of sensation took account of dreams.[193] It is not to be forgotten that he wrote *About Nature* in no fewer than thirty-seven books.[194] And in establishing his theology, which was simultaneously respectful of the gods and intent on demonstrating that they took no interest in human affairs, he could not have avoided asserting that dreams are never messages from the immortals.[195] His 'Letter to his Mother', quoted by Diogenes of Oenoanda, may possibly not be from the master's own hand (in my view the positive arguments outweigh the negative ones).[196] The text is fragmentary indeed, but according to a plausible reconstruction, it says in part:

> [But if you examine the whole matter carefully, you will learn that] the images of persons who are not present are of precisely the same kind as those of persons who are present. For although the images are perceived not by the senses, but by the mind, they have the same power . . . Therefore, with regard to these matters, mother, [be of good heart: do not reckon] the visions [of us to be bad].

It is evident that the author is attempting to reassure the recipient about the insignificance of her dreams.

To judge from Lucretius and from Diogenes too, dreaming was an important subject for Epicurean philosophers, both because so many people believed that the gods sent dreams or even appeared in them, but also because they so readily gave rise to fear.[197] Lucretius held that the main reason why religious observance had originally spread—that great historical disaster—was because people dreamt of the gods.[198] No doubt the essential doctrine was always that 'dreams do not have a divine nature or

193. Sec. 51.

194. Diogenes Laertius x.27 and 30. For a new edition of the Herculaneum papyrus containing Book XXXIV, which concerned among other things dreams, see Leone 2002; but it seems to be too fragmentary to deepen our knowledge of Epicurus' thinking on the subject.

195. Kragelund 1989, 441.

196. Fr. 125 Smith, in his translation (1993, 414). For the controversy over the letter's authenticity see Smith 1993, 555–558, and 2003, 126–127. What follows is part of Smith's translation; the words in square brackets are conjectural.

197. The most helpful accounts of Epicurean thinking on this subject are Schrijvers 1980, Kragelund 1989.

198. v.1161–1182 (note *magis* in line 1171).

prophetic power, but come about because of the incidence of images [*ei-dola*]'.[199]

That sounds very much like Democritus, especially if we free Democritus from the confusion spread by Diogenes of Oenoanda (see above). The only way we can find out, with a reasonable chance of success, whether Epicurus' naturalistic understanding of dreams diverged from that of Democritus is by looking close at Lucretius Book IV (and we may be encouraged here by Sedley's argument that Lucretius' deep respect for his Epicurean predecessors 'focused more narrowly on Epicurus himself than [Epicurean] school practice in his day expected').[200] As for other writers with whom Epicurus might theoretically have debated, there is no specific trace of the works of Aristotle we have just considered. But to make matters more complicated, a recent scholar, Sedley again, has argued that Lucretius' poem shows a strong influence from Empedocles[201]—and as we shall see, it may contain an echo of the older poet's thinking about dreams.

What Lucretius teaches about the mechanisms by which we dream is unfortunately brief. Physical objects, he says, give off images (*simulacra*, his commonest translation of Greek *eidola*), while other images come into being spontaneously; these very tenuous *simulacra* move swiftly around all over the place, and sometimes combine (so that we see centaurs, even though they do not exist).[202] These *simulacra* easily enter the mind (*animus*), as distinct from the eyes, while we are asleep, because they 'assail' it so much (*lacessunt . . . adeo*).[203] As to the reason why the *simulacra* move so much in our dreams—they seem to dance and play—well, that is because different images present themselves at subliminal speed, and give the impression of movement (*tanta est mobilitas et rerum copia tanta*).[204] This clever, effectively cinematographic, answer clearly reflects some careful thinking about vision.

How much then do these doctrines differ from those of Democritus? Fortunately Plutarch tells us, at least in outline, in a passage that was partly

---

199. *Gnom.Vat.* 24 (p. 145 Arrighetti).

200. Sedley 1998, 67.

201. Ibid., ch. 1.

202. iv.724–748. He turns explicitly to sleep and dreams only at 757, but I take it that the talk of centaurs and so on from 732 onwards refers to things seen in dreams.

203. iv.747–761. And because our senses and memory are occluded or resting, we cannot tell true images from false ones.

204. iv.768–817, with Schrijvers 1980, 140–141. The line quoted is 799.

quoted earlier in this chapter,[205] which happens to represent precisely the point where, according to Plutarch or rather a character in his dialogue, Epicurus diverged from Democritus. In brief, he agreed with him that tenuous films of *eidola* are given off by physical objects, including people, but rejected his notion that the *eidola* also 'pick up', and include in dreams, 'images of each person's psychic motions, desires, habits, and emotions'.[206] Accepting the latter idea might have led Epicurus closer to the supposition, which he could not possibly accept, that dreams might convey truths. But this refusal of his cannot be counted as a naturalistic advance—it was a matter of presuppositions.

Lucretius' other concern is with the actual content of dreams, and in particular with their typology. (Here one may suspect that the evident personal affinity between Lucretius' fantastic imagination, often centred on animals, and the world of dreams, has made his account rather different from anything that Epicurus may have written on this topic.) This was in fact a very important matter to get right, because if we are ever going to explain dreams thoroughly we must account for their content as well as for the biological and neurological mechanisms.

Lucretius' claim that we dream of our waking obsessions[207] was, as we have seen, far from new. But his typology is rather impressive, since he knows not only of the day's residue but of wish-fulfilment and anxiety dreams, giving a better account of both than any previous author.[208] He was also the first analytic writer to refer at any length, to transformation dreams, though these had been identified long before:

> it sometimes happens that the image that follows is of a different kind: what was a woman before seems to have changed into a man in our very hands, or different faces and ages succeed each other. But sleep and forgetfulness see to it that we are not surprised.[209]

He nicely catches the dreamer's characteristic frustration: 'a thirsty man [in a dream] sits down besides a stream or a pleasant spring, and gulps almost

205. P. 241.

206. *Quaest.Conv.* viii.10 (*Mor.* 735ab).

207. iv.962–999.

208. For wish-fulfilment dreams see iii.115–116, iv.984 (reading *voluptas*, not *voluntas*: Kragelund 1989, 440 n. 28), 1024–1025, 1030–1036; on anxiety dreams see esp. 1020–1025.

209. iv.818-822.

the whole river down his throat'.[210] This is the first of a set of three kinds of dream of physiological origin—thirst dreams, the bed-wetting dreams of children, followed by the wet dreams of youth.[211]

Not that Lucretius is an entirely perfect observer. We are so struck by the force of his introductory comments,[212] 'And whatever a man is obsessed with almost, whatever matters we have previously have spent our time on, so that the mind was especially exerted in that pursuit, in our sleep we mostly seem to encounter the same things'—generals dream of battles and so on—that we overlook the fact that this old opinion (first heard in Herodotus) is pretty much false. Few of us, I think, dream about the books we are writing.

Other Hellenistic Voices

The other Hellenistic voice most worth listening to on the subject of dreams, from a naturalistic perspective, may be that of the medical scientist Herophilus of Alexandria (we shall return later to philosophers). Herophilus was a giant in his field—some would say a monster, since he probably cut open the bodies of prisoners condemned to death—whose stature was not widely appreciated until the 1989 monograph of Von Staden. But we only know a little about his opinions about dreams and how he justified them.

> Herophilus says that some dreams are inspired by a god [*theopneustous*] and arise by necessity, while others are natural [*phusikous*] and arise when the soul forms for itself an image [-*eidolo*-] of what is to its own advantage and of what will happen next; and still others are mixed [?][213] and arise independently [or spontaneously?][214] according to the impact of the images,

---

210. iv.1024–1025. It is not clear whether this dreamer is really thirsty or simply dreams it.

211. iv.1026–1036. On the structure of this passage see R. D. Brown's commentary (1987, 171); he also gives (172–173) a useful catalogue of other ancient references to wet dreams. Aristotle thought that females as well as males experienced such dreams (*Hist.An.* x.6.637b25–27), and nothing excludes the possibility that Lucretius thought so too.

212. iv.962–965.

213. Translating *sugkramatikous*. Cf. Brillante 1990b, 81. But the reading may well be wrong, and several scholars have tried to emend it.

214. 'ek tou automatou': cf. the discussions of this phrase by Schrijvers 1977, 20–21, Brillante 84.

whenever we see what we wish, as happens in the case of those who in their sleep possess the women they are in love with.[215]

So says an unidentified later author. It is a puzzling text in various ways. We need not be surprised that Herophilus, unlike some of the Hippocratic doctors, gave a role to the gods in this matter, and we can probably take it that his second category of dreams consists of certain kinds of warning dream—though this is expressed oddly ('*its* own advantage').[216] But why is the third category, exemplified by heterosexual male sexual wish-fulfilments, said to be 'mixed'? They can hardly be a mixture of the divinely inspired and the natural. What he probably meant, I think, was that the third type had elements of involuntariness, like the first category ('by necessity') and elements of voluntariness like the second ('forms for itself'). But is this a summary of Herophilus' whole classificatory system? If so, it is something of a disappointment.

Herophilus has received credit for having 'launched a remarkably rich Hellenistic and patristic tradition of dream theory',[217] but that is not justified. In fact it cannot be shown that Herophilus exercised any influence at all on theorizing about dreams (no writer of any importance ever refers or alludes to this thinking on the subject),[218] except possibly in so far as he introduced a brief classification. But earlier authors, including the *On Regimen* writer and Plato, had already asserted that dreams had several different causes, and Herophilus therefore deserves no prize for his 'some . . . others . . . others. . .'.[219] When Poseidonius later divided dreams into three types, they were quite different ones.[220] Nor is any later writer, not even

---

215. Ps.-Plutarch, *Placita* 5 (*Mor.* 904f) = T226b in Von Staden's edition. I have followed his text, with the reservation noted. I have borrowed much of his translation, but also made significant changes.

216. And here there is yet another textual problem.

217. Von Staden 1989, 307–308.

218. Von Staden himself points out (1989, 449) that none of Herophilus' own followers is known to have taken up the topic.

219. It was observed long ago (Marx 1838, 88–99; cf. Schrijvers 1977, 17) that Herophilus was fond of tripartite divisions; so was Plato.

220. According to Von Staden (308–309), two of Poseidonius' categories (to which we shall return shortly) are very close to those of Herophilus, but the two authors are not even classifying the same things—Poseidonius is speaking of ways in which *the gods* bring about dreams. Poseidonius' classification was reused, with some alterations, by Philo (*De somniis* i.1–2, ii.1).

Tertullian, who referred to him in his *On the Soul,* known to have taken over Herophilus' categories.

The latter's significance in this story seems to be quite other. Herophilus made anatomical discoveries of great importance, but as far as dreams were concerned he had hardly any method that could help him to discover anything, and no incentive to carry out the sort of detailed observations that doctors and *phusikoi* knew how to conduct, for it is probable that few if any doctors of the fourth or third centuries thought that dreams were likely to help them greatly with the actual conduct of medicine.[221] If Herophilus said, as he probably did, that dreams become more trustworthy from the beginning of January,[222] it is hardly likely that he based the comment on systematic observation.

Let us turn briefly to the Stoics. They were as a group perhaps the most religious philosophers of the ancient world, but that did not mean that they were uninterested in the natural world; there was a Stoic physics, in a sense, described in all the text-books. And dreams were of some serious concern to them, above all because Stoicism had to fit prophetic dreams into the case it made in favour of divination more generally. Zeno did not write at any length on divination,[223] but Chrysippus wrote books about prophecy and one about dreams.[224] There is no sign, however, that any Stoic before the first century BC, when dealing with dreams, went beyond theological statements and anecdote-collection.[225] In fact they seem to have taken the line that they had no need to explain *why* predictive dreams came true.[226] It is not altogether surprising that the acute Panaetius was dissatisfied and probably, as we saw in Chapter III, rejected all divination.

221. Cf. Vlastos 1949, 286–287.

222. Ioannes Lydus, *De mensibus* iv.135 = T226d Von Staden. Herophilus cannot of course have used the month-name January.

223. Cicero says that 'Zeno in suis commentariis quasi semina quaedam sparsisset, et ea Cleanthes paulo uberiora fecisset' (*De div.* i.6). Fr. 234 shows that Zeno was impressed by what Plato had written about the dreams of the man of virtue (cf. C. Lévy 1997, 334).

224. Cicero, *De div.* i.6. Yet we have no reason to think that he was 'obsessed' with the subject, as Walde says (2001, 29).

225. According to Schofield 1986, 52, 'it sounds as though Chrysippus' *On Dreams* consisted largely of an explanation of divinatory dreams whose significance he then explained', referring to Cicero, *De div.* i.39, ii.144.

226. Cicero, *De div.* i. 35: 'non enim me deus ista scire sed his tantum modo uti voluit', referring to dreams among other things. And see sec. 85. For the Stoics, divination 'is a logical derivation from the hypotheses of their natural philosophy' (Kidd I 1988, 436).

Table 2. Tripartite Classifications of Dreams

Herophilus	Poseidonius	Tertullian
Inspired by god and occur by necessity.	When gods speak directly to the sleeper.	Sent by god.
Natural, occurring when the soul forms for itself an image of what is to its own advantage and of what will happen next.	When the *animus* independently foresees things because it is linked to the gods.	Arise from the dreamer's *anima*, 'as a result of paying attention to surrounding circumstances'.
Mixed, occurring independently according to the impact of the images, whenever we see what we wish.	Because the air is full of immortal souls, in which there are 'marks of truth'.	The majority of dreams are sent by *daemonia*.*

In fact Tertullian briefly separates off a *fourth* category (*De anima* 47.4), those dreams that are 'unexpected and uninterpretable and indescribable' and are to be ascribed to a state of *ecstasis* (unreason? see J. H. Waszink's commentary, 1947).

De anima 47.1 (cf. 57.5). Why *daemonia* rather than his usual *daemones*?

Not even Poseidonius added to the naturalistic understanding of dreams,[227] though he brought nature into the matter as well as the gods.[228] He may possibly have been the first to suggest that dreams that seem to be false are in fact simply difficult to understand.[229] All that Poseidonius is actually known to have said about the process of dreaming amounts to the claim that when the *animus* is most free of the body, a human is most like a god and therefore capable of 'perceiving' things that it otherwise cannot see.[230]

There is one more strand of Hellenistic thought worth considering here, the so-called new Academy, represented for us by Cicero. We do not expect from him any original contribution to the naturalistic explanation of dreaming, but in order to bolster his rejection of all dream divination he had at least to offer an opinion about the nature of dreaming.[231] His main inspiration was Carneades,[232] who, however, wrote nothing himself and was known to later generations largely through the writings of the Hellenized Carthaginian Clitomachus.

Cicero's view of the mechanism of dreaming is supposedly modelled on Aristotle's:[233]

the *animus*, even when at rest, can never be free of agitation and movement. When, because the body is at rest, it cannot use the limbs or the

227. Pease's view (1920–1923, 60) was that Chrysippus 'systematized' Stoic thought about divination and Poseidonius merely 'transmitted' it.

228. For his theological account see *De div.* i.64 = fr. 108 E-K (there are three ways that the gods bring about human dreams, (1) when the *animus* independently foresees things because it is linked to the gods, (2) because the air is full of immortal souls, in which there are 'marks of truth', and (3) when the gods speak directly to the sleeper cf. above, p. 58. But there was divination based on 'fate', and that which was natural: Cicero, *De div.* i.125 = fr. 107, i.129 = fr. 110.

229. Cicero, *De div.* i.60 (cf. 24–25, 118), commonly but without sufficient grounds believed to be Poseidonian; the passage is not admitted as a fragment in the edition of E-K. This was a notion easy for Cicero to push aside (*De div.* ii.127), since it conflicted with the orthodox opinion that the gods were fundamentally benevolent to mankind. As we saw in Ch. III, the idea that all dreams are really true did not reappear until the late fourth century. A little later in the Stoic exposition we are told that when the body is asleep, the *animus* remembers the past and has divinatory powers, but no more than that (i.63).

230. *De div.* i.129 (not part of fr. 110).

231. I have already explained (Chapter III) my reasons for adhering to the majority view that Book II represents Cicero's own views.

232. Cf. *De div.* ii.150.

233. ii.128. This is restated in 139–140.

senses, it happens upon varied and unpredictable visions made-up from the surviving remains, as Aristotle says, of the things which it has done or thought while awake. The confusion of these remains sometimes produces dreams that are bizarre.

And this corresponds quite closely to what Aristotle had written.[234] Against Democritus, he argues that dreams cannot be dependent on effluences from people or things, because we sometimes dream of things we have never seen, such as the walls of Babylon or the face of Homer.[235]

But Cicero's great achievement in this area—which may in large part have been the achievement of Carneades or Clitomachus (it would be a pleasant irony if it was a Carthaginian who played the central role in producing the finest classical discussion of this topic)—was his review and analysis of the evidence for predictive dreams. He did even better than Aristotle because he reviewed the cases.[236] He in fact saw that the *number* of cases in which diviners got things right was a crucial issue (and he attributes the same position to the Stoicizing 'Quintus').[237]

The Reasons for a Failure

The failure of the ancients to find out anything more about dreaming was overdetermined. The study of 'nature' lost its initial impetus, and the intellectual barriers were insuperable. Faced with the natural world, Greeks did not ignore what they could observe, but their reasoning always strongly tended to be deductive.[238] And while there was a kind of scientific community among physicians, it was very attenuated by post-Scientific-Revolution standards, and it barely served for 'inhibiting some inquiries', 'stimulating others' and 'evaluating their results';[239] still less was this the case among *phusikoi* more generally. By late Hellenistic times at least, the stultifying

234. See esp. *De insomniis* 3.461a21–25 and *De div. per somn.* 1.463a22–31; van der Eijk 1993, 228.

235. ii.138–139.

236. Esp. ii.134–142.

237. *De div.* i.23, ii.52–53, 121. See Hankinson 1998, 289, who should not, however, have said that Cicero was making use of 'a statistically significant level of accuracy'.

238. And in these circumstances 'finding good-looking principles that can be claimed to be self-evident is extremely difficult' (Lloyd 2005, 120).

239. Lloyd 1983, 117.

effect of authority, embodied in written texts, was doing its inevitable harm. Notoriously, no one who was devoted to the human sciences felt the urge to experiment or to consider the phenomena statistically.[240] The value of investigating the phenomenon of dreaming was not in any case at all clear, as has already been noted. Both the believers and the sceptics and those who fell somewhere between the two extremes already had ample ammunition by the third century BC, and the physicians do not for a long time seem to have been deeply interested in dreams as symptoms or as a basis for a diagnosis.

To illustrate this intellectual ossification, I shall briefly describe three exceptional minds of the two-generational span 150 to 210 AD, minds that were to varying degrees much concerned with things seen in the night: Galen, Artemidorus,[241] and Tertullian.

A Note on Galen

Galen is in a sense a disappointment on this subject, certainly for anyone who has studied any of his best achievements. Here is a modern logician's verdict on his work overall:

> Galen's science is jejune, his conceptual equipment is imprecise, his therapies are usually vague and sometimes silly. That is to say, he was practising medicine at a time when basic science was too primitive to support the art. But his method is in all respects admirable. He grasps the importance of argument—and of rigour and formality in argument.[242]

This judgement only just stops short of anachronism, but its last two sentences seem well justified. Consequently we might have hoped, having heard from Galen that some dreams indicate the condition of the body's humours or other bodily conditions,[243] to learn from him how widely this

---

240. It is evident, however, that there was some discussion of mathematical probability in medical circles: Galen, *On Medical Experience* 15–17 (Walzer 1944).

241. Artemidorus was probably somewhat older than Galen, who appears to refer to him in *In Hippocratis de acutorum victu librum* i.15 = XV.444K (*CMG* V.9.1 p. 129 Helmreich), written in the period 176–179. Bowersock 2004, however, has now argued that we should move Artemidorus down to Severan times, and this cannot be excluded.

242. Barnes 1991, 102.

243. Above, p. 210.

principle can be applied. In what circumstances can a prognosis coming from dreams be relied upon? Not always, presumably. (We also, I suppose, want to know how probable Galen considered it that incubation in a shrine of Asclepius would result in a cure, but that is a kind of question that no one could have asked until the nineteenth century.) Admittedly it is hard to be fair to a work such as *About Diagnosis from Dreams* that survives in a probably crude summary.

This, according to the said summary, is how Galen saw the problems to be solved:

> But since the soul in sleep does not form dream images simply on the basis of the dispositions of the body, but also out of our habitual day-time actions, while other <dreams> originate in thoughts we have had <while awake>, and in yet others, finally, the soul predicts future events—for this too is demonstrated by experience [*peira*]—*the discernment (diagnosis) of dreams that emanate from the body is difficult.* For if it were simply necessary to distinguish them from <dreams derived from> the things we do and think during the day, it would not be at all difficult to think that whatever dreams are not of our <waking> actions and thoughts have their source in the body. But since we concede that some dreams are prophetic, *it is not easy to say how these dreams are to be distinguished from those which originate in the body.*[244]

He proceeds to illustrate the difficulty with a pair of cases. A man dreamt that one of his legs turned to stone. The people whom Galen, without irony it is to be presumed, describes as being 'good at such things' said, in Artemidoran fashion, that the dream concerned his slaves.[245] But in fact the leg in question became paralysed, 'which none of us expected'.[246] Here it is not enough to say that Galen's 'methods of interpretation were the same as those of the diviners and popular interpreters', because Galen clearly thought that he had learned something about the nature of dreaming from this mistake.[247] He then gives a series of examples of dreams corresponding to conditions of the dreamer's body, and ends with the long familiar conclusion that 'whatever sick people see or imagine they are do-

---

244. *De dignotione ex insomniis* 4 (VI.833K).
245. Cf. Artemidorus i.48.
246. *De dignotione* 5 (VI.834K).
247. Oberhelman 1987, 53, writing, however, of ancient medical writers in general.

ing in their dreams will often indicate to us the lack or excess or the quality of their humours.'[248] But of course he sees no need to enlarge on or justify that 'often'.

What Does a Swallow Mean?

Artemidorus of Daldis seems at first inspection the most credulous Greek who ever lived, assuring his readers that—to take a random example out of thousands—'a swallow [seen in a dream] is good in regard to work and business, to music, and above all to marriage. For she signifies that the dreamer's wife will be faithful and a good housekeeper, and usually that she will be Greek and musically inclined'.[249] But his case is made interestingly complex by his evident ambition,[250] by his mania for classification, by his insistence on the empirical basis of his work, and also by his rejection of supernatural explanations of the great majority of truth-telling dreams.

Artemidorus frequently claims that *peira,* actual experience, has shown the validity of his interpretations. But his interest is all in the experience that will prove his case, not in the explanation of the phenomenon of dreaming. There were plenty of potential critics around,[251] and Artemidorus' self-esteem and probably his livelihood were at stake. There was no common ground. His motives were a normal mixture of altruism and personal ambition, but there was no living and no reputation to be made in imperial Asia Minor by carefully balancing alternatives in the manner of Aristotle. Artemidorus was not operating within any kind of scientific community (none in fact existed outside the medical profession). He mentions Aristotle's treatise on dream prediction, but only to say that he will not raise the problem, as Aristotle had, whether dreams come from god or are produced internally,[252] and there is no sign and little likelihood that he knew Aristotle's work directly. None of the other opinions about dreams put for-

248. *De dignotione* 8 (VI.835K). For the opinion cf. the physicians referred to in Cicero, *De div.* ii.142.

249. ii.66, p. 191.

250. But I see no reason to think that his aim was 'to make dream interpretation acceptable to [the] high culture' (Price 1986, 31). He certainly does not admit to any such aim.

251. i.praef.

252. i.6, p. 16.

ward by philosophers or physicians over a period of six hundred years rates a mention.[253] One scholar has even written of his 'sovereign indifference to centuries of investigation on the formative mechanisms of dreams and the causes of their prophetic characteristics'.[254]

But he is not in fact hostile to medical knowledge, and he considers it worthwhile to claim that remedies genuinely suggested in dreams are 'entirely proper from a medical point of view and [do] not contradict medical expertise'.[255] He recommends his son to study medicine, because it will help him to avoid giving mistaken dream-interpretations (yet Artemidorus does not apparently expect to *learn* anything from physicians about dreaming).

His account of the origins of nonprophetic dreams is as follows:[256]

> some of the passions [*pathe*] naturally run up to and draw themselves up beside the soul, and so bring about *oneirogmoi* [normally wet dreams, but here perhaps a wider class of dreams]. For example, the lover necessarily dreams that he is with the boy he has a passion for, the frightened man dreams of what he fears, and again the hungry man dreams of eating and the thirsty one of drinking, and yet again the person who has stuffed himself with food dreams of vomiting or choking.

The first sentence in this quotation embodies what seems to be a new notion about the formation about dreams, but is evidently no more than a rewording of ideas that go back to the fourth century BC.

But what role did Artemidorus assign to the gods in producing dreams? Opinion has been somewhat divided about this.[257] Having announced at the outset that he will not investigate the issue, he says quite explicitly in the supplementary book he wrote for his son, that 'dreams [*oneiroi*] are

253. His notion that 'people who live a virtuous upright life do not have *enhupnia* [non-predictive dreams, in his vocabulary] or any other irrational fantasies . . . , for their *psuche* is not muddled by fears or expectations, but rather they control the pleasure of their bodies . . . [such dreams] to not appear to a man of virtue' (iv.praef., p. 239) goes back to Plato, but he may not have known that or cared.

254. Del Corno 1988 [1975], xxxiii.

255. iv.22, p. 257.

256. i.1, p. 3. Current translations distort this passage.

257. Price concluded that Artemidorus was deeply uncertain about this question (1986, 16–17). Walde 1999, 127, on the other hand refers to his 'highly secularized approach'.

works of the soul, *psuche,* and are not caused by anything outside'.[258] 'I use the word "god-sent"', he had written earlier, 'in the same way that we customarily call all unforeseen things "god-sent"',[259] in other words without any belief in divine agency. Nothing suggests that he is in general irreligious (nor is there any hint of sympathy with the Epicureans), though he seems to have an ambiguous attitude towards Serapis,[260] whom he must have known of as an incubation deity. The only divine dreams occur when the gods themselves appear in epiphany dreams, in which they always, he says, tell the truth, though sometimes in a riddling fashion;[261] even in these cases he does not in fact state that the gods are responsible. A god-fearing Greek assumed that if you asked a god about your 'present concerns',[262] you might get an answer in your dreams; 'but the way in which the prophecy should be given, one must leave up to the god, or to one's own mind'.[263] When people pray for cures at the great incubation shrines such as Pergamum and Alexandria, it is the gods who send the prescriptions (*suntagai*) that are recommended in dreams.[264] But the doctrine of an internal origin—for most dreams—is never contradicted.

Artemidorus' most interesting intellectual link has been pointed out by Blum and Price: he applied to dreams something very like the method of one of the three schools of contemporary medical thought, the so-called

258. iv.59, p. 284. Cf. iii.22, p. 213, iv.27, p. 261. Hence White 1975, 7, is simply in error when he writes that Artemidorus 'cautiously avoids the question of [*sic*] whether dreams are sent by the gods'.

259. i.6 end, p. 16, virtually repeated in iv.3, p. 247.

260. v.94; cf. ii.39, Del Corno 1966, 116.

261. iv.71, p. 292; see also ii.69, p. 195.

262. iv.2, p. 246; 'the things one is worried about', iv.2 end, p. 247. It is in the context of these prayers that he makes the remark that causes Price difficulty: 'for the god, or whatever else it is that causes a person to dream, presents to the dreamer's soul, which is by its very nature prophetic, dreams which correspond to future events' (his translation, slightly adapted) (iv.2). The gods *can* appear in dreams, and evidently they often do so at incubation shrines (see further on in the text), but elsewhere this is not the normal occurrence.

263. iv.2 end, p. 247. The last phrase seems to show Artemidorus doubting whether the gods were ever responsible for particular dreams, and he passes on to the phrase just cited according to which 'god-sent' dreams are merely a *façon de parler.*

264. iv.22, pp. 255–257. The force of the remark about the gods in iv.63 (a less than lucid chapter) is I think that those who offer dream-interpretations too recondite for Artemidorus' taste insult the gods by suggesting that the gods have made the world so hard to understand.

Empiricists.[265] The three main elements in Empiricist methodology, (1) transmitted experience or tradition, (2) reasoning by similarity, and (3) experience,[266] are also the main elements in the methodology of Artemidorus. He makes frequent use of the technical terminology, and there can be no doubt that even though the Empiricist tradition was old and may have been followed by some of Artemidorus' predecessors, he made conscious use of it.[267] This sympathy of his was in fact quite natural: it exempted him from paying attention to logic and probability, important considerations in the eyes of the rival Rationalist/Dogmatic school, and risky territory for a dream-interpreter (Aristotle and others had reasoned predictive dreams out of existence or come close to doing so). And it is evident that even Galen, who was more receptive to dreams that many previous physicians had been, and was partially in sympathy with the Empiricists,[268] thought that their reliance on dreams went too far. Some medicines have been discovered as a result of dreams, they said; 'blatant nonsense', says Galen.[269]

It would not make much sense to blame Artemidorus for his failure to achieve something he had no interest in achieving—a naturalistic understanding of the mechanisms of dreaming. But it is worth taking one more look at his use of 'experience', for that may strike a modern reader as the most promising of the methods he prepared to use.[270] He collects the evidence in a convenient place, the catalogue of ninety-five dreams in his final

265. Blum 1936, 88–91; Price 1986, 24–28. The three Greek terms are *historia, metabasis tou homoiou* ('transition by way of the similar', von Staden 1982, 82) and *peira* or *teresis.*

266. Von Staden, 1982, 82, adds some other elements: the Empiricists believed that 'the search for hidden causes . . . is useless, and hence that anatomy and physiology, along with dissection, should be banished from *ars medica*. . . . transmitted experience [was] understood as a passive reception of experiential traditions. . . . hypothesis formation and verification by experimentation . . . are ruled out firmly'.

267. There seems to be no explicit illusion, however; none was noted in the collection of 'fragments' by Deichgräber 1930.

268. Frede 1985, xxxi.

269. Deichgräber 1930, 149, lines 21–27 = *Method of Healing* iii.2 = X.164K. Similarly in Deichgräber 150, lines 11–15 = *On the Composition of Medicines by Type* i.1 = XIII.366K. See further von Staden 2003, 19.

270. It is all too easy to say that Artemidorus engaged in 'careful observation of the real world' (Kilborne 1987, 183), but that is a false inference from the sheer compendiousness of his work.

book. Why did this collection of evidence not lead Artemidorus to the conclusion that dreams only 'come true' by coincidence? One might say, 'because he ignored logic and probability';[271] I would rather say that it was because, like the Jack Altman we met in Chapter III, he did not really ask the question—for he already knew its answer.

A Complete Halt

As far as naturalistic explanations of dreaming were concerned, there was no way forward. The writings of Tertullian will help us to understand why. In spite of his professed antiintellectualism,[272] *On the Soul* contains one of the most learned of all classical discussions of dreaming. We dream, he says, because though the body sleeps the soul does not; but dreams are illusions, and the fact that they stir emotions in us shows that while we are asleep we are 'not in our senses'. What we imagine ourselves doing in sleep is of no consequence: 'we shall no more be punished for dreaming of illicit sex than we shall be crowned for dreaming of being martyred'.[273] Nonetheless god does send dreams that foretell the future—the Epicureans, he says, are wrong about this. To demonstrate this he does just what we expect an ancient writer to do—he takes stories from historians, or rather perhaps from a slightly earlier writer, Hermippus of Beirut, who in turn had gathered them from historians.[274] Other dreams come from demons, he says, others come in some way from the soul itself.[275] Yet others come to those who are in a state of unreason.[276]

There are two more questions: how do certain physical circumstances, such as the season and fasting, influence dreams, and are there people who

271. Cf. Sassi 2001, 185–186. She draws a good comparison between dream-interpretation and physiognomics, but when she writes that Artemidorus 'evades the true nature of the problem' (185), I wish to reply that his 'problem' was a problem of persuasion not discovery.

272. Lloyd 2003, 233–234, quotes his famous phrase 'What has Athens to do with Jerusalem?' (*De praescriptione haereticorum* 7), where he continues 'we have no need for curiosity after Jesus Christ, nor of research [*inquisitio*] after the gospel'.

273. 45.4.

274. 46.4–9, 11. Cf. J. H. Waszink's comm., p. 488.

275. 46.12–47.3. For earlier Christians who had said that dreams were sent by demons see above, p. 69. Pagan thinking about *daimones* in this period is summarized by I. G. Kidd on Poseidonius I fr. 108 (1988, 431).

276. 47.4.

do not dream at all? He answers both on the basis of his reading, but also with some attention to experience. Some people had suggested that you would have more veridical dreams if you abstained from various foodstuffs—well, I sleep while fasting, he says, and when I do I do not seem to dream at all.[277] As for those who think that young children do not dream, they should pay attention to their tremors and nods and smiles as they sleep and realize that their *animae* are in motion.[278]

✿   ✿   ✿

Synesius and Augustine, two centuries later, were still capable of reasoning about how dreams work on the basis of their own experience,[279] and the intelligence of some of their observations is not in question: what had long been marginalized, if not lost, was a tradition of naturalistic inquiry. Not that we should judge the ancients harshly, as far as understanding dreams is concerned, since it was not until the nineteenth century that the subject began to stir again, and the nineteenth century culminated in a fantasy explanation, the 'latent dream' (more of a centaur than a quark). And we still have a great deal to learn.

277. 48.3.
278. 49.1.
279. Synesius evidently refers to his own experience in *De insomniis* 19, and he advocates (17–18, 20) the keeping of a dream diary.

Conclusions

How did Greeks and Romans experience their dreams, and what did they make of their experience? By way of partial answers, what this book proposes can be summarized as follows.

In the introduction we saw how contemporary specialists describe some of the principal aspects of the phenomenon of dreaming, in particular the characteristic bizarreness of dreams. The point here was not to assume that nothing has changed—on the contrary we must be alert for possible differences—but to establish as clearly as possible the contours of the phenomenon that ancient writers were attempting to describe or make use of.

One important difference between Greek and Roman ways of representing dreams and our own is that the ancients rather frequently tell us of dreams in which a single authoritative figure dominates, conveying instructions or information—the 'epiphany' dream (Chapter I). Did the Greeks and Romans really dream in this fashion, or was it in effect nothing more or less than a narrative convention? A convention it certainly was, and the needs that the convention served, in story-telling both secular and religious, can be traced through the ages. The dreamer and/or the narrator could not only lay claim to superior instructions or information: epiphany dreams explained human actions and also conveyed prestige. The convention also reflects a world in which almost everyone supposed that gods and other superhuman figures sometimes took an interest in the affairs of individual humans, or at least certain outstanding humans. In view of all this, it should not come as a surprise that the epiphany dream stayed alive, indeed flourished, in Christian late antiquity and apparently throughout the Middle

Ages, finally expiring, as far as the European world is concerned, on the eve of the Enlightenment. Outside that world, it still lived on in the twentieth century.

On balance it is likely that the Greeks and Romans, and their successors too, did from time to time dream such dreams, or at least dreams of approximately this character. We can scarcely guess when this ceased to be true—in the late Middle Ages, I would suppose. We can on the other hand detect quite well when the convention weakened and disappeared: in short, the Renaissance weakened some of its foundations, and the spreading secularization of the sixteenth and seventeenth centuries gradually made such descriptions seem hopelessly implausible.

What the dreamer or the purportedly factual reporter describes may be accurate, or it may be convention or invention, or any mixture of these elements (Chapter II). Any student of the classical world who holds that dreams, sometimes at least, have hidden meanings of profound significance for the personality of the dreamer must necessarily wonder whether we can ever know what Greek or Roman people actually dreamt. But those who do not think that dreams are significant also have good reason to enquire, and not only because some authoritative scholars have from time to time accepted particular ancient dream-reports as true and even generalized about the content of actual ancient dreams: ancient conventions and inventions are also worth attending to.

Having established some detailed criteria for distinguishing genuine dreams from invented or distorted ones, we were able to put a number of ancient dream-reports to the test. The answer is not always a neat and tidy 'true' or 'false'—Perpetua and Aelius Aristides are left hanging to some extent. The latter, however, for all his egotism, emerges as a rare and relatively convincing informant. Our search for actual ancient dreams also I think brought out, or rather helped to confirm, some important aspects of Greek and Roman mental and discursive practices. Inventing or improving facts is normal human habit, but antiquity knew even fewer restraints than the modern world does. We also have a specific advantage when it comes to recounting dreams: we have much greater tolerance for the disjointed and the inconclusive. The new privileging of the dream that began in 1900 with the publication of the *Traumdeutung* may have made it easier for modern people to describe what they have seen in their sleep, as well as midwifing an entire modern aesthetic of the disjointed that we are familiar with from Fellini, Pinter and countless lesser figures.

One reason why dreams were so much worth inventing and distorting in classical antiquity was of course the common belief that they sometimes 'came true' (Chapter III). Such a belief was all the easier in antiquity because a dream was frequently counted as truth-telling even if it had only the vaguest or most obscure or tricking of similarities to some subsequent event. 'Belief', at all events, is a problematic concept: in particular, belief in dreams was highly unstable, and belief taken as a propensity to action was much more likely to lead to an apotropaic gesture than to a decision with practical consequences. Throughout antiquity there existed persons who claimed special expertise in dream-interpretation and attracted paying customers, but it is still more significant that the Greek and Latin languages both use words for 'dream' as metaphors for illusions and nonsense. The expectation of truth was quite restricted.

It is in fact quite wrong to suppose that a sceptical attitude towards the predictive value of dreams was restricted to a small number of eccentric philosophers. The evidence first becomes reasonably clear in fifth- and fourth-century Athens. Most people appear to have believed that dreams could sometimes reveal something, and might react to an especially striking or frightening one, but would not decide anything of importance because of what they had dreamt. There were experts who could tell you the significance of a dream, but other forms of divination were regarded as surer. A politician might speak of what he had dreamt, but risked being scorned by many of his hearers if he did so. At the same time, Herodotus could expect his hearers to believe that certain kinds of historical characters had experienced veridical dreams, and even more significantly Plato *added to* Socrates' stature by describing his dreams. Many must have supposed that Asclepius or Amphiaraus might bring a dream to someone who passed the night in his shrine. But such a supposition coexisted with a widespread assumption that the ordinary dreams of ordinary people, while they might occasionally portend good or evil, were never a reliable guide to life's real problems.

The Hellenistic evidence likewise reveals complex and somewhat unstable attitudes. The weight of this evidence suggests that most Greeks were prepared to believe in at least the occasional story of a dream come true, in the sense set out above. The educated debated the subject, or rather contradicted one another as to whether dreams could be veridical by more than coincidence; it may be that both the positive and the negative view came to be stated in stronger terms than before. Those whose religious fervour was lively enough to get them to travel to a centre such as Epidaurus or Delos were receptive. In most of the Hellenistic world, on the other hand, dream predictions could scarcely enter into the serious world of marriage, money and war. The partial exception—the region which gives rise to a disproportionate amount of the evidence that people believed in dreams—is the realm of the Ptolemies.

As for the Roman Republic, there is a certain amount of evidence for popular belief in predictive dreams, but it is probably restricted to times of exceptional crisis or stress. The social elite was not systematically sceptical—not at least until some of its members began to be affected by the doctrines of Epicurus—but it shows few signs of expecting truth in this quarter. When Sulla attempted to make political capital out of his dreams, some of his soldiers were probably impressed, but not his social equals. When the Quintus figure presents the case in favour of divination, including dream-divination, in Cicero's *De divinatione,* he does so on the basis of a newly amalgamated Graeco-Roman tradition. Even he does not go as far as the Stoics had gone.

Dream divination was perhaps not in very vigorous health at the beginning of the principate, which would make Vergil's quite intense use of the tradition even more intriguing. It is in any case plain that from Augustan times down to roughly the end of the first century AD, opinion was deeply divided in both the Latin world and the Greek. The more hard-headed took very little notice in their everyday lives, but almost anyone might occasionally be impressed by a dream; and one thing was new, namely that an exceedingly dream-credulous individual, a Claudius or a Nero, could come to supreme power.

A change occurred in the decades around 100. There were still dream-sceptical Greeks in the second century, but while the evidence is to some degree contradictory (Sextus Empiricus and Artemidorus effectively point in opposing directions, for the latter tells us about contemporary scepticism), they seem to be battling against a widespread supposition that some dreams portend the future. In the Latin world, the change may have come more slowly (so the epigraphical evidence suggests), but a certain change is definitely in evidence by the time of the accession of Septimius Severus.

Christian attitudes towards predictive dreams were at first decidedly mixed, and in the third century certain inhibitions remained: the proper view was still that dreams might easily come from evil demons and that only a privileged few could expect to receive divine guidance in this way. Yet dreams were accounted a common basis for conversion. By the fourth century, at all events, many secular men of power thought that dream-stories and dream-interpretations could affect people's opinions, and consequently took steps to use such stories and to control them. The growing trust in dreams was also reflected in the eagerness of ecclesiastics to delegitimize threatening uses of dreams and to assume the right to decide which dreams came from god and which from evil demons. In the same generation both a religious traditionalist—Ammianus—and a Christian (if he was a Christian at the time)—Synesius—took the virtually unprecedented view that not simply some but *all* dreams are meaningful.

So far, we were concerned with the Greeks and Romans at large. Finally we turned to the minority who thought naturalistically, without, however, detaching them from their social, religious or literary contexts. We attempted to understand how Greek and Roman quasi-scientific thinking about dreaming developed. As far as we can tell, it was Empedocles who was at the origin of this endeavour. His theory of 'the day's residue' depended more than any known earlier theory on at least a modicum of observation. Democritus subsequently tried to explain in a naturalistic fashion how particular images, some of them foretelling the future, came to be in the individual's consciousness.

The other major source of naturalistic ideas about dreams was Hippocratic medicine, which struggled hard to correlate dreams with illnesses, physical and otherwise. Homer was aware that dreams could be caused by anxiety, and that they could be wish-fulfilments: it was the Hippocratics, however, who seem to have made such ideas explicit. The author of *On Regimen* was the first, as far as we know, to have made a systematic attempt to correlate dreams to the dreamer's diet and physical condition and thus the first to have categorized dreams in detail. He did so largely according to the themes that were identified as the main subject of the dream (weather, clothes, the dead . . .). Thus by the early fourth century BC there had been some careful attention to the phenomena of dreaming, some classification, and some accumulation of thought on the subject. After *On Regimen,* however, doctors seem to have become less interested in the diagnostic value of dreams; indeed no one had a strong motive for investigating them naturalistically, and it was only the inextinguishable curiosity of Aristotle that produced a further advance. Plato's empirical or quasi-empirical contribution, apart from some assertions attributed to Timaeus, was mainly limited to the claim that, in effect, the quality of our dreams corresponds to the dominance of the lusting or the rational element in our souls.

Aristotle asked new questions and added a host of observations that are not attested before. His new questions concerned the incidence of dreaming and its possible explanation, and he set out more elaborately the question whether, in what circumstances and by what mechanisms dreams may sometimes foretell the future. The problem of predictive dreams Aristotle found so difficult that it led him into something very close to self-contradiction. But two things stand out, his attention to his predecessors and also (it is no paradox) his close attention to the phenomena. Very few of his empirical observations are false, and some of them are acute—he takes note for instance of the fact that we sometimes dream while half-awake.

Could ancient investigators of dreaming take the subject any further? Aristotle left the question of predictive dreams in some confusion, but the Epicureans took up the cudgels, resolutely rejecting the idea. They did so, however, because of a general view of the relations between gods and mortals, and because of their desire to eliminate irrational fears, rather than because of any investigation of the phenomena. It was, paradoxically, the Academic philosophers known to us through Cicero's *On Divination* who seem to have reviewed the actual evidence for dream-divination and shown that it was wanting. And the semiretired politician's essay was itself one of the high points of ancient thinking in this area.

Lucretius' contribution was superb description and a typology that built on others but surpasses anything formulated previously. However there was not much else to be achieved in ancient conditions, even by those who applied plenty of intelligence to the matter. Galen was moderately interested in the diagnostic use of dreams, but was evidently also frustrated by his not being able to see any practical way of telling the dreams that indicated malfunctioning humours or other medical conditions from those that did not.

Artemidorus illustrates another perennial difficulty. I have called him credulous, but he was also a man of a certain erudition who knew something about the medical science of his time. He accumulated and classified an enormous quantity of material. Yet he took no notice, at least in his writings, of what the sceptics had been writing for centuries about the implausibility of dream prediction. There was no debate. Tertullian, similarly, was erudite on the subject of dreams, and took some notice of his own experience, but knew by a priori reasoning what to think.

The dreams that we dream do not require anything of us. We may make use of them in a variety of ways, or we may reduce them—perhaps the best procedure—to curious personal stories. The Greeks and Romans faced the same dilemma. They had one great advantage over us, namely that dream stories could still be the material of great poetry and of great story-telling (think of Herodotus and the dream of Xerxes); this potential gradually diminished, but even a late author such as Heliodorus, if clever enough, could tap into it. As to understanding what, if anything, dreams may mean, Greeks and Romans had many difficulties in their way. From the point of view of the normally religious Greek or Roman (of course their religiosity came in many different shapes and sizes) the experience could be exalting or encouraging but must most of the time have been frustrating—if one supposed that dreams came 'from Zeus' or some other divine source, it was still hard to understand what their significance might be. Professionals existed but their track record was necessarily poor. The descriptive and analytic achievement was far from contemptible, however. Indeed it stands comparison with what has been written in modern times rather well. Physiology is largely a modern science (even though microscope-less Greek anatomy is sometimes impressive), and the physiology of dreaming has advanced enormously in the last half century. But—as we saw at the outset— the problems we encounter in understanding the content of our dreams and even in describing them are still intense.

Bibliography

Adams, K. 'Voices in My Dream: Children's Interpretation of Auditory Messages in Divine Dreams'. *Dreaming* 15 (2005), 195–204.

Aers, D. 'Interpreting Dreams: Reflections on Freud, Milton, and Chaucer'. In Brown 1999, 84–98.

Aleshire, S. B. *The Athenian Asklepieion: the People, their Dedications and the Inventories.* Amsterdam, 1989.

Alesse, F. *Panezio di Rodi e la tradizione stoica.* Naples, 1994.

Alföldi, A. *The Conversion of Constantine and Pagan Rome*, trans. H. Mattingly. Oxford, 1948.

Amat, J. *Songes et visions: L'au-delà dans la littérature latine tardive.* Paris, 1985.

Amat, J. 'L'Authenticité des songes de la Passion de Perpétue et de Félicité'. *Augustinianum* 29 (1989), 177–191.

Amat, J. (ed.). *Passion de Perpétue et de Félicité, suivi des Actes.* Paris, 1996.

Antin, P. 'Autour du songe de Saint-Jérôme'. *Revue des Etudes Latines* 41 (1963), 350–377.

Antrobus, J. S., and M. Bertini (eds.). *The Neuropsychology of Sleep and Dreaming.* Hillsdale, N.J., 1992.

Armstrong, N., and L. Tennenhouse. 'The Interior Difference: a Brief Genealogy of Dreams, 1650–1717, *Eighteenth-Century Studies* 23 (1989–1990), 458–478.

Arnold, J. H. *Belief and Unbelief in Medieval Europe.* London, 2005.

Arkin, A. M., J. S. Antrobus, and S. J. Ellman (eds.). *The Mind in Sleep: Psychology and Psychophysiology.* New York, 1978.

Aserinsky, E., and N. Kleitman. 'Regularly Occurring Periods of Eye Motility, and Concomitant Phenomena, during Sleep'. *Science* 118 (1953), 273–274.

Athanassiadi, P., 'Dreams, Therapy and Freelance Divination: The Testimony of Iamblichus'. *JRS* 83 (1993), 115–130.

Attridge, H. W. 'The Philosophical Critique of Religion under the Early Empire'. In *ANRW* II.16.1 (1978), 45–78.

Austin, C., and G. Bastianini (eds.). *Posidippi Pellaei opera quae supersunt omnia.* Milan, 2002.

Austin, J. L. *Sense and Sensibilia.* Oxford, 1962.

Bächli, E. *Die künstlerische Funktion von Orakelsprüchen, Weissagungen, Träume usw. in der griechischen Tragödie.* Zürich, 1954.

Bailey, C. (ed.). *Lucretius: De rerum natura,* 3 vols. Oxford, 1947.

Baldelli, I. 'Visione, immaginazione e fantasia nelle *Vita Nuova*'. In Gregory 1985, 1–10.

Barasch, M. *Icon: Studies in the History of an Idea.* New York, 1992.

Barnes, J. 'Galen on Logic and Therapy'. In F. Kudlien and R. J. Durling (eds.), *Galen's Method of Healing.* Leiden, 1991. 50–102.

Barrett, D. 'Through a Glass Darkly: Images of the Dead in Dreams'. *Omega* 24 (1991–1992), 97–108.

Barrett, D. (ed.) *Trauma and Dreams.* Cambridge, Mass., 1996.

Bartelink, G. J. M. 'Träume und Visionen in den Dialogen Gregors des Grossen'. In Lardinois 2006, 80–93.

Bartsch, S. *Decoding the Ancient Novel.* Princeton, 1989.

Beagon, M. *Roman Nature: The Thought of Pliny the Elder.* Oxford, 1992.

Beard, M. 'Cicero and Divination: The Formation of a Latin Discourse'. *JRS* 76 (1986), 33–46.

Beard, M., J. North, and S. Price. *Religions of Rome,* 2 vols. Cambridge, 1998.

Beaulieu-Prévost, D., and A. Zadra. 'Dream Recall Frequency and Attitude towards Dreams: A Reinterpretation of the Relation'. *Personality and Individual Differences* 38 (2005), 919–927.

Behr, C. A. *Aelius Aristides and the Sacred Tales.* Amsterdam, 1968.

Behr, C. A. *P. Aelius Aristides: The Complete Works,* 2 vols. Leiden, 1981, 1986.

Behr, H. *Die Selbstdarstellung Sullas.* Frankfurt am Main, 1993.

Belicki, K. 'Recalling Dreams: An Examination of Daily Variation and Individual Differences'. In Gackenbach 1986, 187–206.

Berglund, A.-I. *Zulu Thought-patterns and Symbolism*. Uppsala, 1976.

Berlin, N. R. 'Dreams in Roman Epic: The Hermeneutics of a Narrative Technique'. Diss., Michigan, 1994.

Betz, H.-D. *The Greek Magical Papyri in Translation, Including the Demotic Spells*. Chicago, 1986.

Bicknell, P. J. 'Democritus' Parapsychology Again'. *Revue des Etudes Grecques* 83 (1970), 301–304.

Bieler, L. 'Σκιᾶς ὄναρ ἄνθρωπος', *Wiener Studien* 51 (1933), 143–145.

Björck, G. 'ΟΝΑΡ ΙΔΕΙΝ: De la perception de rêve chez les anciens'. *Eranos* 44 (1946), 306–314.

Blagrove, M. 'Dreams Have Meaning but No Function'. *BBS* 23 (2000), 910–911.

Blasius, A., and B. U. Schipper (eds.). *Apokalyptik und Ägypten: Eine kritische Analyse der relevanten Texte aus dem griechisch-römischen Ägypten*. Leuven, 2002.

Blinkenberg, C. *Lindos: Fouilles et Recherches 1902–1914* II. Berlin and Copenhagen, 1941.

Bloch, M. E. F. *How We Think They Think: Anthropological Approaches to Cognition, Memory, and Literacy*. Boulder, Colo., 1998.

Blum, C. *Studies in the Dream-book of Artemidorus*. Uppsala, 1936.

Blumenthal, H. J. *Aristotle and Neoplatonism in Late Antiquity: Interpretations of the 'De anima.'* London, 1996.

Bogen, S. *Träumen und Erzählen: Selbstreflexion der Bildkunst vor 1300*. Munich, 2001.

Bokdam, S. 'La forme du 'songe' dans la poésie religieuse au seizième siècle'. In Charpentier 1990, 137–149.

Bolgar, R. R. *The Classical Heritage and Its Beneficiaries*. Cambridge, 1954.

Bollack, J. (ed.). *Empédocle*, 4 vols. Paris, 1965–1969.

Bollansée, J. *Hermippus of Smyrna*. (FGrH IVA, 3) Leiden, 1999.

Bolognini, S. Introduction to Bolognini (ed.), *Il sogno cento anni dopo*. Turin, 2000, 17–25.

Bommelaer, J.-F. 'Le songe d'Agésilas: Un mythe ou le rêve d'un mythe?' *Ktema* 8 (1983), 19–26.

Boriaud, J.-Y. 'La place du *Traité des Songes* dans la tradition onirocratique. Le problème de l'image onirique: L'*idolum* et la *visio*'. In M.

Baldi and G. Canziani (eds.), *Girolamo Cardano: Le opere, le fonti, la vita.* Milan, 1999, 215–225.

Borret, M. (ed.). *Origène: Contre Celse,* 4 vols. Paris, 1967–1976.

Bos, A. P. *The Soul and the Instrumental Body: A Reinterpretation of Aristotle's Philosophy of Living Nature.* Leiden, 2003.

Botman, H. I., and H. F. Crovitz. 'Dream Reports and Autobiographical Memory'. *Imagination, Cognition and Personality* 9 (1989–1990), 213–224.

Bouché-Leclercq, A. *Histoire de la divination dans l'antiquité,* 2 vols. Paris, 1879–1880.

Bouquet, J. *Le songe dans l'épopée latine d'Ennius à Claudien.* Brussels, 2001.

Bourgey, L. *Observation et expérience chez les médecins de la Collection Hippocratique.* Paris, 1953.

Bourgey, L. *Observation et expérience chez Aristote.* Paris, 1955.

Bourguignon, E. E. 'Dreams and Dream Interpretation in Haiti'. *American Anthropologist* 56 (1954), 262–268.

Bowden, H. 'Xenophon and the Scientific Study of Religion'. In C. Tuplin (ed.), *Xenophon and His World.* Stuttgart, 2004, 229–246.

Bowersock, G. W. *Greek Sophists in the Roman Empire.* Oxford, 1969.

Bowersock, G. W. *Fiction as History: Nero to Julian.* Berkeley, 1994.

Bowersock, G. W. 'Artemidorus and the Second Sophistic'. In B. E. Borg (ed.), *Paideia: The World of the Second Sophistic.* Berlin and New York, 2004, 53–63.

Bowie, E. L. 'Apollonius of Tyana: Tradition and Reality'. In *ANRW* II.16.2 (1978), 1652–1699.

Bowman, L. 'Klytaimnestra's Dream in Sophokles' Elektra'. *Phoenix* 51 (1997), 131–151.

Brakke, D. 'The Problematization of Nocturnal Emissions in Early Christian Syria, Egypt, and Gaul'. *Journal of Early Christian Studies* 3 (1995), 419–460.

Brancacci, A., and P. M. Morel (eds.). *Democritus: Science, the Arts, and the Care of the Soul.* Leiden, 2007.

Bregman, J. *Synesius of Cyrene: Philosopher-Bishop.* Berkeley, 1982.

Brelich, A. 'The Place of Dreams in the Religious World Concept of the Greeks'. In G. E. von Grunebaum and R. Caillois (eds.), *The Dream and Human Societies.* Berkeley and Los Angeles, 1966, 293–301.

Bremmer, J. N. 'Literacy and the Origins and Limitations of Greek Atheism'. In den Boeft and Kessels 1982, 43–55.

Bremmer, J. N. 'The Passion of Perpetua and the Development of Early
Christian Afterlife'. *Nederlands Theologisch Tijdschrift* 54 (2000), 97–111.

Bremmer, J. N. 'Perpetua and Her Diary: Authenticity, Family and Visions'. In W. Ameling (ed.), *Märtyrer und Märtyrerakten*. Stuttgart,
2002, 77–120.

Bremmer, J. N. 'The Vision of Constantine'. In Lardinois et al. 2006,
57–79 (2006a).

Bremmer, J. N. Rev. of P. Habermehl, *Bryn Mawr Classical Review*
(2006), (2006b).

Brenk, F. E. 'An Imperial Heritage: The Religious Spirit of Plutarch of
Chaironeia'. In *ANRW* II.36.1 (1987), 248–349.

Bresciani, E. *La porta dei sogni: Interpreti e sognatori nell'Egitto antico.*
Turin, 2005.

Brillante, C. 'Il sogno nella riflessione dei presocratici'. *Materiali e Discussioni* 16 (1986), 9–53. Repr. in Brillante 1991, 55–94.

Brillante, C. 'Metamorfosi di un'immagine: Le statue animate e il sogno'.
In Guidorizzi 1988, 17–33. Repr. in Brillante 1991, 95–111.

Brillante, C. 'Scene oniriche nei poemi omerici'. *Materiali e Discussioni*
24 (1990), 31–45 (1990a).

Brillante, C. 'L'interpretazione dei sogni nel sistema di Erofilo'. In
Mélanges Pierre Lévêque IV. Paris, 1990, 79–87 (1990b).

Brillante, C. *Studi sulla rappresentazione del sogno nella Grecia antica.*
Palermo, 1991.

Brillante, C. 'La realtà del sogno da Omero a Platone'. *Quaderni Urbinati
di Cultura Classica* 53 (1996), 7–26.

Brosseder, C. *Im Bann der Sterne: Caspar Peucer, Philipp Melanchthon
und andere Wittenberger Astrologen.* Berlin, 2004.

Brown, P. *Augustine of Hippo.* Berkeley, 1967.

Brown, P. (ed.). *Reading Dreams. The Interpretation of Dreams from
Chaucer to Shakespeare.* Oxford, 1999.

Brown, R. D. *Lucretius on Sex and Love: A Commentary on 'De rerum
natura' IV, 1030–1287.* Columbia Studies in the Classical Tradition 15.
Leiden, 1987.

Browne, A. 'Girolamo Cardano's *Somniorum Synesiorum libri IIII*'. *Bibliothèque d'Humanisme et Renaissance: Travaux et Documents* 41
(1979), 123–135.

Brubaker, L. *Vision and Meaning in Ninth-century Byzantium: Image as Exegesis in the Homilies of Gregory of Nazianzus*. Cambridge, 1999.

Bruneau, P. *Recherches sur les cultes de Délos à l'époque hellénistique et à l'époque impériale* Paris, 1970.

Buchheit, V. *Studien zum Corpus Priapeorum*. Munich, 1962.

Budd, S., 'The Shark behind the Sofa: Recent Developments in the Theory of Dreams', in D. Pick and L. Roper (eds.), *Dreams and History*, London, 2004, 253–269.

Bulkeley, K. (ed.). *Dreams: A Reader on Religious, Cultural, and Psychological Dimensions of Dreaming*. New York, 2001.

Burke, P. 'L'histoire sociale des rêves'. *Annales ESC* 28 (1973), 329–342.

Burkert, W. *Greek Religion: Archaic and Classical*, trans. J. Raffan, Oxford, 1985. (Original ed.: *Griechische Religion der archaischen und klassischen Epoche*, Stuttgart, 1977.)

Burkert, W. 'Signs, Commands, and Knowledge: Ancient Divination between Enigma and Epiphany', in Johnston and Struck 2005, 29–49.

Burnyeat, M. F. 'The Material and Sources of Plato's Dream'. *Phronesis* 15 (1970), 101–122.

Busink, R., and D. Kuiken. 'Identifying Types of Impactful Dreams: A Replication'. *Dreaming* 6 (1996), 97–119.

Butler, S. A. L. *Mesopotamian Conceptions of Dreams and Dream Rituals*. Münster, 1998.

Butler, S. F., and R. Watson. 'Individual Differences in Memory for Dreams: The Role of Cognitive Skills'. *Perceptual and Motor Skills* 61 (1985), 823–828.

Buxton, R. (ed.). *From Myth to Reason? Studies in the Development of Greek Thought*. Oxford, 1999.

Cambiano, G. 'Une interprétation 'matérialiste' des rêves: Du Régime IV'. In Grmek 1980, 87–96.

Cambiano, G. 'La nascita dei trattati e dei manuali'. In G. Cambiano, L. Canfora and D. Lanza (eds.), *Lo spazio letterario della Grecia antica* I, 1. Rome, 1992, 525–553.

Camp, J. 'Athenian Cobblers and Heroes', in S. Keay and S. Moser (eds.), *Greek Art in View. Essays in Honour of Brian Sparkes*, Oxford, 2004, 129–137.

Cancik, H. '*Idolum* and *imago:* Roman Dreams and Dream Theories'. In Shulman and Stroumsa 1999, 169–188.

Capelle, W. 'Älteste Spuren der Astrologie bei den Griechen'. *Hermes* 60 (1925), 373–395.

Cartwright, R. 'How and Why the Brain Makes Dreams: A Report Card on Current Research on Dreaming'. *BBS* 23 (2000), 914–916.

Cartwright, R., and B. Lerner. 'Empathy, Need to Change, and Improvement with Psychotherapy'. *Journal of Consulting and Clinical Psychology* 27 (1963), 138–144.

Cartwright, R. D. 'Dreams and Adaptation to Divorce', in Barrett 1996, 179–185.

Carty, C. M. 'The Role of Gunzo's Dream in the Building of Cluny III'. *Gesta* 27 (1988), 113–123.

Casati, R. 'Dreaming'. In *Routledge Encyclopedia of Philosophy*. www.rep.routledge.com/article/V010/ (1998).

Castelli, E. A. *Martyrdom and Memory: Early Christian Culture Making.* New York, 2004.

Cecchelli, C. *I mosaici della basilica di S. Maria Maggiore.* Turin, 1956.

Cederstrom, E. R. *Smikroi Logoi: A Study of the Nature and Function of Dreams in Greek Tragedy.* Bryn Mawr, Pa., 1971.

Chaniotis, A. *War in the Hellenistic World.* Oxford, 2005.

Charpentier, F. (ed.). *Le songe à la Renaissance.* Saint-Etienne, 1990.

Chevalier, U. *Répertoire des sources historiques du Moyen Âge*, 2 vols. Paris, 1903–1907.

Cipolli, C., and D. Poli. 'Story Structure in Verbal Reports of Mental Sleep Experience after Awakening in REM Sleep'. *Sleep* 15 (1992), 133–142.

Cohen, D. B. *Sleep and Dreaming: Origins, Nature and Functions.* New York, 1979.

Comella, A. *I rilievi votivi greci di periodo arcaico e classico.* Bari, 2002.

Cooper, R. 'Bibliographie d'ouvrages sur le songe jusqu'en 1600'. In Charpentier 1990, 255–271 (1990a).

Cooper, R. 'Deux médecins royaux onirocritiques: Jehan Thibault et Auger Ferrier'. In Charpentier 1990, 53–60 (1990b).

Coopland, G. W. *Nicolas Oresme and the Astrologers: A Study of His 'Livre de Divinacions'* Cambridge, Mass., 1952.

Craighill Handy, E. S. 'Dreaming in Relation to Spirit Kindred and Sickness in Hawaii', in *Essays in Anthropology Presented to A. L. Kroeber,* Berkeley, 1936, 119–127.

Crapanzano, V. 'Saints, Jnun, and Dreams: An Essay in Moroccan Ethnopsychology'. *Psychiatry* 38 (1975), 145–159.

Crapanzano, V. 'The Betwixt and Between of the Dream'. In B. Schnepel (ed.), *Hundert Jahre 'Die Traumdeutung'*. Cologne, 2001, 236–259.

Crawford, P. 'Women's Dreams in Early Modern England'. *History Workshop Journal* 49 (2000), 129–141.

Crépin, A. (ed.). *Bède le Vénérable: Histoire ecclésiastique du peuple anglais,* 3 vols. Paris, 2005.

Crick, F., and G. Mitchison. 'The Function of Dream Sleep'. *Nature* 304 (1983), 111–114.

Dagron, G. (ed.). *Vie et miracles de Sainte Thècle.* Brussels, 1978.

Dagron, G. 'Rêver de dieu et parler de soi: Le rêve et son interpretation d'après les sources byzantines'. In Gregory 1985, 37–55.

D'Arco, I. 'Il sogno premonitorio di Annibale e il pericolo delle Alpi'. *Quaderni di Storia* 55 (2002), 145–162.

Davies, J. P. *Rome's Religious History.* Cambridge, 2004.

Degrassi, D. 'Il culto di Esculapio in Italia centrale durante il periodo repubblicano'. In F. Coarelli (ed.), *Fregellae 2: Il santuario di Esculapio.* Rome, 1986, 145–152.

Deichgräber, K. *Die griechische Empirikerschule: Sammlung der Fragmente und Darstellung der Lehre.* Berlin, 1930.

De Jong, I. J. F. 'Herodotus and the Dream of Cambyses'. In Lardinois et al. 2006, 1–17.

Del Corno, D. 'Contributi papirologici allo studio dell'onirocritica'. In *Atti del XI Congresso Internazionale di Papirologia.* Milan, 1966, 109–117.

Del Corno, D. (ed.). *Graecorum de re onirocritica scriptorum reliquiae.* Varese and Milan, 1969.

Del Corno, D. 'C'è del metodo in questa follia: Artemidoro'. In Guidorizzi 1988, 147–159. Repr. from his translation of Artemidorus. Milan, 1975.

Del Corno, D. 'Dreams and their Interpretation in Ancient Greece'. *Bulletin of the Institute of Classical Studies* 29 (1982), 55–62.

Dement, W. 'Dream Recall and Eye Movements during Sleep in Schizophrenics and Normals'. *Journal of Nervous and Mental Disease* 122 (1955), 263–269.

Dement, W. C., E. Kahn and H. P. Roffwarg. 'The Influence of the Laboratory Situation on the Dreams of the Experimental Subject'. *Journal of Nervous and Mental Disease* 140 (1965), 119–131.

Dement, W., and N. Kleitman. 'The Relation of Eye Movements during Sleep to Dream Activity: An Objective Method for the Study of Dreaming'. *Journal of Experimental Psychology* 53 (1957), 339–346.

Demuth, G. *Ps.-Galeni De dignotione ex insomniis.* Göttingen, 1972.

den Boeft, J., and A. H. M. Kessels (eds.). *Studies in Honour of H. L. W. Nelson.* Utrecht, 1982.

Dentan, R. K. 'Ethnographic Considerations of the Cross Cultural Study of Dreams'. In Gackenbach (ed.), 1986, 317–358.

Deremble-Mannes, C. 'Die Traumwelt der Legenden in den Glasmalereien von Chartres'. In Paravicini Bagliani and Stabile 1989, 41–54.

Desjardins, R. 'The Horns of Dilemma: Dreaming and Waking Vision in the *Theaetetus*'. *Ancient Philosophy* 1 (1981), 109–126.

Devereux, G. *Dreams in Greek Tragedy.* Oxford, 1976.

Di Benedetto, V. *Il medico e la malattia: La scienza di Ippocrate.* Turin, 1986.

Diller, H. 'Der innere Zusammenhang der hippokratischen Schrift De victu'. *Hermes* 87 (1959), 39–56. Repr. in his *Kleine Schriften zur antiken Medizin.* Berlin, 1973, 71–88.

Dinzelbacher, P. *Vision und Visionsliteratur im Mittelalter.* Stuttgart, 1981.

Dinzelbacher, P. 'Der Traum Kaiser Karls IV'. In Paravicini Bagliani and Stabile 1989, 161–170.

Dodds, E. R. *The Greeks and the Irrational.* Berkeley and Los Angeles, 1951.

Dodds, E. R. *Pagans and Christians in an Age of Anxiety.* Cambridge, 1968.

Dodds, E. R. 'Supernormal Phenomena in Classical Antiquity'. In *The Ancient Concept of Progress and Other Essays on Greek Literature and Belief.* Oxford, 1973, 156–210.

Dolbeau, F. Untitled note. *Revue des Etudes Augustiniennes* 42 (1996), 312–313.

Domhoff, G. W. 'Needed: A New Theory'. *BBS* 23 (2000), 928–930.

Domhoff, G. W. *The Scientific Study of Dreams.* Washington, D.C., 2003.

Dorandi, T. 'Il "Diario" dei sogni di Elio Aristide: Per una interpretazione del primo *Discorso Sacro* (47 Keil)'. *Segno e Testo* 3 (2005), 51–69.

Drachmann, A. B. *Atheism in Pagan Antiquity.* London, 1922.

Düring, I. *Der Protreptikos des Aristoteles,* 2nd ed. Frankfurt, 1993.

Dulaey, M. *Le rêve dans la vie et la pensée de Saint-Augustin.* Paris, 1973.

Dunand, F. 'La consultation oraculaire en Égypte tardive: L'oracle de Bès à Abydos'. In Heintz 1997, 65–84.

Dunbar, N. (ed.). *Aristophanes: Birds.* Oxford, 1995.

Dutton, P. E. *The Politics of Dreaming in the Carolingian Empire.* Lincoln, Nebraska, 1994.

Dyson, G. W. 'Leonta tekein'. *CQ* 23 (1929), 186–195.

Easterling, P. E., and J. V. Muir (eds.) *Greek Religion and Society.* Cambridge, 1985.

Edelstein, E. J., and L. Edelstein. *Asclepius: A Collection and Interpretation of the Testimonies,* 2 vols. Baltimore, 1945.

Eisenstadt, S. N. (ed.). *The Origins and Diversity of Axial Age Civilizations.* Albany, NY, 1986.

Ellman, S. J., and J. S. Antrobus (eds.). *The Mind in Sleep: Psychology and Psychophysiology* (2nd ed.). New York, 1991.

Engelmann, H. *The Delian Aretalogy of Sarapis.* Leiden, 1975.

Erbse, H. 'Plutarchs Schrift ΠΕΡΙ ΔΕΙΣΙΔΑΙΜΟΝΙΑΣ.' *Hermes* 80 (1952), 296–314.

Everson, S. (ed.). *Psychology.* Companions to Ancient Thought 2. Cambridge, 1991.

Fabrega, H., and D. B. Silver. *Illness and Shamanistic Curing in Zinacantan: An Ethnomedical Analysis.* Stanford, 1973.

Farrell, J. *Latin Language and Latin Culture: From Ancient to Modern Times.* Cambridge, 2001.

Feeney, D. *Literature and Religion at Rome: Cultures, Contexts, and Beliefs.* Cambridge, 1998.

Ferguson, J., and J. P. Hershbell. 'Epicureanism under the Roman Empire'. In *ANRW* II.36.4 (1990), 2258–2327.

Festugière, A.-J. *Personal Religion among the Greeks.* Berkeley and Los Angeles, 1954.

Fichtner, G. *Corpus Galenicum: Verzeichnis der galenischen und pseudogalenischen Schriften.* Tübingen, 1985.

Flanagan, O. *Dreaming.* Oxford, 2000.

Flower, M. A. *The Seer in Classical Greece.* Berkeley, 2008.

Fontaine, J. (ed.). *Sulpice-Sévère: Vie de Saint-Martin,* 3 vols. Paris, 1967–1969.

Fontenrose, J. E. *The Delphic Oracle.* Berkeley, 1978.

Fortenbaugh, W. W., et al. (eds.). *Theophrastus of Eresus: Sources for his Life, Writings, Thought, and Influence,* 7 vols. Leiden, 1992–2007.

Fosse, M. J., R. Fosse, J. A. Hobson and R. J. Stickgold. 'Dreaming and Episodic Memory: A Functional Dissociation?' *Journal of Cognitive Neuroscience* 15 (2003), 1–9.

Fosshage, J. L. 'New Vistas in Dream Interpretation'. In M. L. Gluckman and S. L. Warner (eds.), *Dreams in New Perspective: The Royal Road Revisited.* New York, 1986, 23–43.

Fosshage, J. L., and C. A. Loew (eds.). *Dream Interpretation: A Comparative Study,* rev. ed. New York, 1986.

Foulkes, D. *Dreaming: A Cognitive-Psychological Analysis.* Hillsdale, N.J., 1985.

Foulkes, D. 'Dream Research, 1953–1993'. *Sleep* 19 (1996), 609–624.

Fowden, G. 'The Individual and the Gods'. In *Cambridge Ancient History,* 2nd ed. Cambridge, 2005, 12:538–552.

Fraenkel, E. *Aeschylus: Agamemnon,* 3 vols. Oxford, 1950.

Frankfurter, D. 'Voices, Books, and Dreams: The Diversification of Divination Media in Late Antique Egypt'. In Johnston and Struck 2005, 233–254.

Franzini, C. 'Sleep, Dreaming, and Brain Activation'. *BBS* 23 (2000), 939–940.

Frede, M. (ed.). *Galen, Three Treatises on the Nature of Science.* Indianapolis, 1985.

Fredrich, C. *Hippokratische Untersuchungen.* Berlin, 1899.

Frenschkowski, M. 'Traum und Traumdeutung im Matthäus-evangelium'. *Jahrbuch für Antike und Christentum* 41 (1998), 5–47.

Frenschkowski, M., and C. Morgenthaler. 'Traum'. *Theologische Realencyclopädie* 34 (2002), 28–50.

Frère, J. 'L'aurore de la science des rêves: Aristote'. *Ktema* 8 (1983), 27–37.

Freud, S. *The Interpretation of Dreams,* trans. J. Strachey. London, 1954. Original ed.: *Die Traumdeutung.* Leipzig and Vienna, 1900.

Freud, S. 'The Antithetical Meaning of Primal Words'. In *Standard Edition.* London, 1957, 11.153–161. Originally 'Über den Gegensinn der

Urworte'. *Jahrbuch für Psychoanalystische und Psychopathologische Forschungen* 2 (1910), 179–184.

Freud, S. 'Remarks on the Theory and Practice of Dream Interpretation', (1923). In *Standard Edition*. London, 1961, 19:109–121 (1923a).

Freud, S. 'The Ego and the Id' (1923). In *Standard Edition*. London, 1961, 19:3–66 (1923b).

Freud, S. *Introductory Lectures on Psychoanalysis*. Lecture XI, in *Standard Edition* 15. London, 1963, 170–183. Originally *Vorlesungen zur Einführing in die Psychoanalyse*. Leipzig and Vienna, 1916–1917.

Freyburger-Galland, M.-L. 'Les rêves chez Dion Cassius'. *Revue des Études Anciennes* 101 (1999), 533–545.

Fridh, A. *Le problème de la Passion des Saintes Perpétue et Félicité*. Gothenberg, 1968.

Frisch, P. *Die Träume bei Herodot*. Meisenheim am Glan, 1968.

Froidefond, C. 'Plutarche et le platonisme'. In *ANRW* II.36.1 (1987), 184–233.

Gackenbach, J. (ed.). *Sleep and Dreams: A Sourcebook*. New York and London, 1986.

Gallop, D. 'Dreaming and Waking in Plato'. In J. Anton and G. L. Kustas (eds.), *Essays in Ancient Greek Philosophy*. Albany, N.Y., 1971, 187–201.

Gallop, D. *Aristotle on Sleep and Dreams*, 2nd ed. Warminster, 1996.

Garvie, A. F. (ed.). *Aeschylus: Choephori*. Oxford, 1986.

Gauger, J.-D. 'Der "Traum des Nektanebos". Die griechische Fassung'. In Blasius and Schipper 2002, 189–219.

Geffcken, J. *The Last Days of Greco-Roman Paganism*, trans. S. MacCormack. Amsterdam, 1978. Original ed.: *Der Ausgang des griechisch-römischen Heidentums*. Heidelberg, 1920.

Geller, M. J. 'West Meets East: Early Greek and Babylonian Diagnosis'. In Hortsmannshoff and Stol 2004, 11–61.

Gemelli Marciano, M. L. 'Le contexte culturel des Présocratiques: Adversaires et destinataires'. In Laks and Louguet 2002, 83–114.

Gigli, D. 'Stile e linguaggio onirico nei "Discorsi sacri" di Elio Aristide'. *Cultura e scuola* 61–62 (1977), 214–224.

Girone, M. IAMATA: *Guarigioni miracolose di Asclepio in testi epigrafici*. Bari, 1998.

Gladigow, B. 'Epiphanie, Statuette, Kultbild: Griechische Gottesvorstellungen im Wechsel von Kontext und Medium'. *Visible Religion* 7 (1990), 98–121.

Gnuse, R. 'Dream Genre in the Matthean Infancy Narratives'. *Novum Testamentum* 32 (1990), 97–120.

Gnuse, R. K. *Dreams and Dream Reports in the Writings of Josephus.* Leiden, 1996.

Gollnick, J. T. *The Religious Dreamworld of Apuleius' Metamorphoses.* Waterloo, Ontario, 1999.

Goodenough, D. R. 'Dream Recall: History and Current Status of the Field'. In Arkin et al. 1978, 113–140. Repr. in Ellman and Antrobus 1991, 143–171.

Goody, J. *The Domestication of the Savage Mind.* Cambridge, 1977.

Goody, J. *The Logic of Writing and the Organization of Society.* Cambridge, 1986.

Goody, J., and I. Watt. 'The Consequences of Literacy'. In Goody (ed.), *Literacy in Traditional Societies.* Cambridge, 1968, 27–68.

Gordon, R. 'Fear of Freedom? Selective Continuity in Religion during the Hellenistic Period'. *Didaskalos* 4 (1972), 48–60.

Gordon, R. 'Reporting the Marvellous: Private Divination in the Greek Magical Papyri'. In P. Schäfer and H. G. Kippenberg (eds.), *Envisioning Magic.* Leiden, 1997, 65–92.

Gorrini, M. E. 'Eroi salutari della Grecia continentale tra istanze politiche ed universali'. *Annali di archeologia e storia antica* [Università di Napoli 'L'Orientale'] 9–10 (2002–2003), 163–196.

Gorrini, M. E. 'Toxaris, *ho xenos iatros*'. *Athenaeum* 91 (2003), 435–443.

Gorrini, M. E. 'The Hippocratic Impact on Healing Cults: The Archaeological Evidence in Attica'. In P. van der Eijk (ed.), *Hippocrates in Context: Papers Read at the XIth International Hippocrates Colloquium.* Leiden, 2005, 135–156.

Gould, J. 'On Making Sense of Greek Religion'. In Easterling and Muir 1985, 1–33.

Gould, S. J., and R. C. Lewontin. 'The Spandrels of San Marco and the Panglossian Paradigm: A Critique of the Adaptationist Programme'. *Proceedings of the Royal Society of London, Series B* 205 (1979), 581–598.

Goyne, J. 'Arthurian Dreams and Medieval Dream Theory'. *Medieval Perspectives* 12 (1997), 79–89.

Graf, F. 'Bemerkungen zur bürgerlichen Religiosität im Zeitalter des Hellenismus'. In M. Wörrle and P. Zanker (eds.), *Stadtbild und Bürgerbild im Hellenismus.* Munich, 1995, 102–114.

Grafton, A. T. *Cardano's Cosmos: The Worlds and Works of a Renais-sance Astrologer.* Cambridge, Mass., 1999.

Gramaglia, P. A. 'Sogni, visioni e locuzioni interiori nell'epigrafia africana'. *Augustinianum* 29 (1989), 497–548.

Greenberg, R., H. Katz, W. Schwartz and C. Pearlman. 'A Research Based Reconsideration of the Psychoanalytic Theory of Dreams'. *Journal of the American Psychoanalytic Association* 40 (1992), 531–550.

Gregory, T. 'I sogni e gli astri'. In Gregory 1985, 111–148.

Gregory, T. (ed.). *I sogni nel medioevo.* Rome, 1985.

Grmek, M. (ed.). *Hippocratica.* Paris, 1980.

Gsteiger, M. *Träume in der Weltliteratur.* Zürich, 1999.

Guidorizzi, G. 'L'opusculo di Galeno *De dignotione ex insomniis*'. *Bollettino del Comitato per l'edizione dei classici*, n.s. 21 (1973), 81–105.

Guidorizzi, G. 'L'interpretazione dei sogni nel mondo tardoantico'. In Gregory 1985, 149–170.

Guidorizzi, G. (ed.). *Il sogno in Grecia.* Rome and Bari, 1988.

Guillon, P. 'L'offrande d'Aristichos et la consultation de l'oracle de Ptoion au début du IIIe s. av. J.-C.'. *Bulletin de Correspondance Hellénique* 70 (1946), 216–232.

Gunderson, K. 'The Dramaturgy of Dreams in Pleistocene Minds and Our Own'. *BBS* 23 (2000), 946–947.

Guthrie, W. K. C. *A History of Greek Philosophy*, 6 vols. Cambridge, 1962–1981.

Haas, H., H. Guitar-Amsterdamer and I. Strauch. 'Die Erfassung bizarrer Elemente im Traum'. *Schweizerische Zeitschrift für Psychologie* 47 (1988), 237–247.

Habermehl, P. *Petronius, Satyrica 79–141: Ein philologisch-literarischer Kommentar.* Berlin, 2006.

Habicht, C. *Die Inschriften des Asklepieions (Altertümer von Pergamon VIII, 3).* Berlin, 1969.

Hankins, J. 'Renaissance Crusaders: Humanist Crusade Literature in the Age of Mehmed II'. *Dumbarton Oaks Papers* 49 (1995), 111–207.

Hankinson, R. J. 'Greek Medical Models of Mind'. In Everson 1991, 194–217.

Hankinson, R. J. *Cause and Explanation in Ancient Greek Thought.* Oxford, 1998.

Hanson, J. S. 'Dreams and Visions in the Graeco-Roman World and Early Christianity'. In *ANRW* II.23.2 (1980), 1395–.

Harlow, J., and S. Roll. 'Frequency of Day Residue in Dreams of Young Adults'. *Perceptual and Motor Skills* 74 (1992), 832–834.

Harris, W. V. 'On the Applicability of the Concept of Class in Roman History'. In T. Yuge and M. Doi (eds.), *Forms of Control and Subordination in Antiquity.* Tokyo and Leiden, 1988, 598–610.

Harris, W. V. *Ancient Literacy.* Cambridge, Mass., 1989.

Harris, W. V. *Restraining Rage: The Ideology of Anger Control in Classical Antiquity.* Cambridge, Mass., 2002.

Harris, W. V. 'Roman Opinions about the Truthfulness of Dreams'. *JRS* 93 (2003), 18–34.

Harris, W. V. 'Constantine's Dream'. *Klio* 87 (2005), 488–494 (2005a).

Harris, W. V. '*Insomnia:* The Content of Roman Dreams'. In W. V. Harris and E. Lo Cascio (eds.), *Noctes Campanae: Studi di storia ed archeologia dell'Italia preromana e romana in memoria di Martin Frederiksen.* Naples, 2005, 245–261 (2005b).

Harris, W. V. 'History Empathy and Emotions'. Forthcoming.

Harrison, T. *Divinity and History: The Religion of Herodotus.* Oxford, 2000.

Hartmann, E. *Dreams and Nightmares: The New Theory on the Origin and Meaning of Dreams.* New York, 1998.

Headlam, W. G. (ed.). *Herodas: The Mimes and Fragments,* ed. A. D. Knox. Cambridge, 1922.

Heffernan, T. J. 'Philology and Authorship in the *Passio Sanctarum Perpetuae et Felicitatis*'. *Traditio* 50 (1995), 315–325.

Heintz, J.-G. (ed.). *Oracles et Prophéties dans l'Antiquité.* Paris, 1997.

Henrichs, A. 'Two Doxographical Notes: Democritus and Prodicus on Religion'. *Harvard Studies in Classical Philology* 79 (1975), 93–123.

Herman, J. H., S. J. Ellman and H. M. Roffwarg. 'The Problem of NREM Dream Recall Re-examined'. In Arkin et al. 1978, 59–92.

Herzog, R. *Die Wunderheilungen von Epidauros. Philologus* Supplementband 22 no. 3. Leipzig, 1931.

Heubner, H. *Tacitus, Die Historien: Kommentar,* 5 vols. Heidelberg, 1963–1982.

Hey, F. O. *Der Traumglaube der Antike: Ein historischer Versuch,* vol. 1. Progr. Munich, 1907–1908.

Higbie, C. *The Lindian Chronicle and the Greek Creation of Their Past.* Oxford, 2003.

Hobson, J. A. *The Dreaming Brain.* New York, 1988.

Hobson, J. A. *Dreaming: An Introduction to the Science of Sleep.* New York, 2002.

Hobson, J. A., E. F. Pace-Schott and R. Stickgold. 'Dreaming and the Brain: Toward a Cognitive Neuroscience of Conscious States'. *BBS* 23 (2000), 793–842 (2000a).

Hobson, J. A., E. F. Pace-Schott and R. Stickgold. 'Dream Science 2000: A Response to Commentaries on *Dreaming and the Brain*'. *BBS* 23 (2000), 1019–1035 (2000b).

Hofstetter, E. 'Seirenes'. In *Lexicon Iconographicum Mythologiae Classicae,* supp. 1997, 1093–1104.

Holland, P. '"The Interpretation of Dreams" in the Renaissance', in Brown 1999, 125–146.

Holowchak, M. 'Aristotle on Dreaming: What Goes on in Sleep When the "Big Fire" Goes Out'. *Ancient Philosophy* 16 (1996), 405–423.

Holowchak, M. A. 'Interpreting Dreams for Corrective Regimen: Diagnostic Dreams in Greco-Roman Medicine'. *Journal of the History of Medicine and Allied Sciences* 56 (2001), 382–399.

Holowchak, M. *Ancient Science and Dreams: Oneirology in Greco-Roman Antiquity.* Lanham, Md., 2002.

Holy, L. 'Berti Dream Interpretation'. In M. C. Jedrej and R. Shaw (eds.), *Dreaming, Religion and Society in Africa.* Leiden, 1992, 86–99.

Hopkins, J. 'The Interpretation of Dreams'. In J. Neu (ed.), *The Cambridge Companion to Freud.* Cambridge, 1991, 86–135.

Hopkins, K. 'Novel Evidence for Roman Slavery'. *Past and Present* 138 (1993), 3–27. Repr. in R. Osborne (ed.), *Studies in Ancient Greek and Roman Society.* Cambridge, 2004, 206–225.

Hopkins, K. 'Christian Number and Its Implications'. *Journal of Early Christian Studies* 6 (1998), 185–226.

Horstmanshoff, H. F. J., and M. Stol (eds.). *Magic and Rationality in Ancient Near Eastern and Graeco-Roman Medicine.* Leiden, 2004.

Hu, P., M. Stylos-Allan and M. P. Walker, 'Sleep Facilitates Consolidation of Emotional Declarative Memory', *Psychological Science* 17 (2006), 891–898.

Huby, P. M. *Theophrastus of Eresus, Sources for His Life, Writings, Thought and Influence, Commentary* IV. Leiden, 1999.

Humphreys, S. C. 'From Riddle to Rigour: Satisfactions of Scientific Prose in Ancient Greece'. In S. Marchand and E. Lunbecke (eds.), *Proof and Persuasion*. Turnhout, 1996, 3–24.

Humphreys, S. C. 'Dynamics of the Greek "Breakthrough": the Dialogue between Philosophy and Religion', in Eisenstadt 1986, 92–110. Cited from the repr. in Humphreys, *The Strangeness of Gods: Historical Perspectives on the Interpretation of Athenian Religion,* Oxford, 2004.

Hundt, J. *Die Traumglaube bei Homer.* Greifswald, 1935.

Hunink, V. J. C. 'Dreams in Apuleius' Metamorphoses', in Lardinois et al., 2006, 18–31.

Hunt, H. T. *The Multiplicity of Dreams: Memory, Imagination, and Consciousness.* New Haven, 1989.

Hunt, L. 'Psychology, Psychoanalysis, and Historical Thought'. In L. Kramer and S. Maza (eds.), *A Companion to Western Historical Thought.* Oxford, 2002, 337–356.

Hunter, R. L. (ed.). *Apollonius of Rhodes: Argonautica Book III.* Cambridge, 1989.

Husser, J.-M. 'Songe'. In *Dictionnaire de la Bible*, supp. Paris, 1996, 12:1439–1544.

Indelli, G. (ed.). *Polistrato: Sul disprezzo irrazionale delle opinioni popolari.* Naples, 1978.

Inwood, B. (ed.). *The Poem of Empedocles.* Toronto, 1992.

Jal, P. (ed.). *Tite-Live: Histoire romaine, Livre XXVI.* Paris, 1991.

Janko, R. 'God, Science and Socrates'. *Bulletin of the Institute of Classical Studies* 46 (2002–2003), 1–18.

Jebb, R. C. (ed.). *Sophocles: Electra,* 3rd ed. Cambridge, 1894.

Jocelyn, H. D. (ed.). *The Tragedies of Ennius: The Fragments.* Cambridge, 1967.

Johnson, J. H. 'Louvre E3229: A Demotic Magical Text'. *Enchoria* 7 (1977), 55–102.

Johnston, S. I., and P. T. Struck (eds.). *Mantikê. Studies in Ancient Divination.* Leiden, 2005.

Joly, R. *Recherches sue le traité pseudo-hippocratique du Régime.* Paris, 1960.

Joly, R. 'Un peu d'épistémologie historique pour hippocratisants'. In Grmek 1980, 285–298.

Joly, R. (ed.). *Hippocrate: Du Régime,* Budé ed. VI:1. Paris, 2003.

Jones, B. E. 'The Interpretation of Physiology'. *BBS* 23 (2000), 955–956.

Jones, C. P. *Plutarch and Rome.* Oxford, 1971.

Jones, C. P. *The Roman World of Dio Chrysostom.* Cambridge, Mass., 1978.

Jouanna, J. 'Le rêve dans l'*Hécube* d'Euripide'. *Ktema* 7 (1982), 43–52.

Jouanna, J. (ed.). *Hippocrate, Des vents, De l'art.* Paris, 1988.

Jouanna, J. (ed.). *Hippocrate: De l'ancienne médicine.* Paris, 1990.

Jouanna, J. *Hippocrates,* trans. M. C. DeBevoise. Baltimore, 1999. Original ed.: Paris, 1992.

Jouanna, J. 'Oracles et devins chez Sophocle'. In Heintz 1997, 283–320.

Jouanna, J. 'L'interpretation des rêves et la théorie micro-macrocosmique dans le traité hippocratique *Du Régime:* Sémiotique et mimesis'. In K.-D. Fischer, D. Nickel and P. Potter (eds.), *Text and Tradition: Studies in Ancient Medicine and Its Transmission.* Leiden, 1998, 161–174.

Jouanna, J. (ed.). *Hippocrate: La maladie sacrée,* Budé ed., II:3. Paris, 2003.

Junod, E., and J.-D. Kaestli (eds.). *Acta Iohannis.* Turnhout, 1983.

Kahn, C. H. 'Sensation and Consciousness in Aristotle's Psychology'. *Archiv für die Gescichte der Philosophie* 48 (1966), 43–81. Repr. in J. Barnes, M. Schofield and R. Sorabji (eds.), *Articles on Aristotle* IV. London, 1979, 1–31.

Kahn, C. H. 'Writing Philosophy: Prose and Poetry from Thales to Plato'. In H. Yunis (ed.), *Written Texts and the Rise of Literate Culture in Ancient Greece.* Cambridge, 2003, 139–161.

Kasprzyk, D. 'Les couleurs du rêve: L'*Onirocriticon* d'Artémidore'. In L. Villard (ed.), *Couleurs et vision dans l'antiquité classique.* Rouen, 2002, 129–152.

Kessels, A. H. M. *Studies on the Dream in Greek Literature.* Utrecht, 1978.

Kessels, A. H. M., 'Dreams in Apollonius' *Argonautica*'. In den Boeft and Kessels 1982, 155–173.

Kessels, A. H. M., and P. W. van der Horst. 'The Vision of Dorotheus (Pap. Bodmer 29)'. *Vigiliae Christianae* 41 (1987), 313–359.

Kidd, I. G. *Poseidonius,* II: *The Commentary,* 2 vols. Cambridge, 1988.

Kilborne, B. 'On Classifying Dreams'. In B. Tedlock (ed.), *Dreaming: Anthropological and Psychological Interpretations.* Cambridge, 1987, 171–193.

Kilroe, P. A. 'The Dream as Text, the Dream as Narrative', *Dreaming* 10 (2000), 125–137.

King, C. 'The Organization of Roman Religious Beliefs'. *Classical Antiquity* 22 (2003), 275–312.

Kingsley, P. *Ancient Philosophy, Mystery, and Magic: Empedocles and Pythagorean Tradition*. Oxford, 1995.

Kraemer, R., and S. L. Lander. 'Perpetua and Felicitas'. In P. Esler (ed.), *The Early Christian World*. London, 2000, 2:1048–1068.

Kragelund, P. 'Epicurus, Priapus and the Dreams in Petronius'. *CQ* 39 (1989), 436–450.

Kragelund, P. 'Epicurus, Pseudo-Quintilian and the Rhetor at Trajan's Forum'. *Classica et Mediaevalia* 42 (1991), 259–275.

Kragelund, P. 'Dreams, Religion and Politics in Republican Rome'. *Historia* 50 (2001), 53–95.

Kruger, S. F. *Dreaming in the Middle Ages*. Cambridge, 1992.

Kudlien, F. *Der Beginn des medizinischen Denkens bei den Griechen, von Homer bis Hippokrates*. Zurich, 1967.

Kudlien, F. 'Galen's Religious Belief'. In V. Nutton (ed.), *Galen: Problems and Prospects*. London, 1981, 117–130.

Kuhn, T. S. *The Structure of Scientific Revolutions*, 2nd ed. Chicago, 1970. Original ed.: 1962.

Kuhn, T. S. *The Road since Structure: Philosophical Essays, 1970–1993*. Chicago, 2000.

Kyriazopoulos, A. 'Les épiphanies des dieux dans les papyrus de l'époque impériale'. In *Akten des 21: Internationalen Papyrologenkongresses Berlin, 13.–19.8.1995*. Archiv für Papyrusforschung Beiheft 3. Stuttgart and Leipzig, 1997, 556–562.

Laks, A. 'Écriture, prose, et les débuts de la philosophie grecque'. *Methodos* 1 (2001), 131–151.

Laks, A. *Introduction à la philosophie présocratique*. Paris, 2006.

Laks, A. and C. Louguet (eds.). *Qu'est-ce que la philosophie présocratique?* Villeneuve d'Ascq, 2002.

Lane Fox, R. *Pagans and Christians*. London, 1986.

Lardinois, A. P. M. H., M. van der Poel, and V. Hunink (eds.). *Land of Dreams: Greek and Latin Studies in Honour of A. H. M. Kessels*. Leiden, 2006.

Le Goff, J. 'Le Christianisme et les rêves (IIe–VIIe siècles)'. In Gregory 1985, 171–218.

Lenk, E. *Die unbewusste Gesellschaft: Über die mimetische Grundstruktur in der Literatur und im Traum.* Munich, 1983.

Leone, G. 'Epicuro, Della natura, libro XXXIV (PHerc. 1431)'. *Cronache ercolanesi* 32 (2002), 7–133.

Leonhardt, J. *Ciceros Kritik der Philosophenschulen.* Munich, 1999.

Lesher, J. H. 'Xenophanes' Scepticism'. *Phronesis* 23 (1978), 1–21.

Leszl, W. 'Democritus' Works: From Their Titles to Their Contents'. In Brancacci and Morel 2007, 11–76.

Leuci, V. A. 'Dream-technical Terms in the Greco-Roman World.' Ph.D. diss., University of Missouri at Columbia, 1993.

Levene, D. S. *Religion in Livy.* Leiden, 1993.

Lévy, C. 'De Chrysippe à Posidonius: Variations stoïciennes sur le thème de la divination'. In Heintz 1997, 321–343.

Lévy, E. 'Le rêve homérique'. *Ktema* 7 (1982), 23–41.

Lewis, R. G. 'Sulla's Autobiography: Scope and Economy'. *Athenaeum* 59 (1991), 509–519.

Liatsi, M. 'Zur Funktion des Traumes in der antiken Medizin (Hippokrates, De victu IV)'. In *Antike Naturwissenschaft und ihre Rezeption* 12 (2003), 7–21.

LiDonnici, L. R. *The Epidaurian Miracle Inscriptions.* Atlanta, 1995.

Lienhardt, G. *Divinity and Experience: The Religion of the Dinka.* Oxford, 1961.

Lincoln, J. S. *The Dream in Primitive Cultures,* 1st ed. London, 1935; 2nd ed. New York, 1970.

Lloyd, G. E. R. *Science, Folklore and Ideology: Studies in the Life Sciences in Ancient Greece.* Cambridge, 1983.

Lloyd, G. E. R. *Revolutions of Wisdom: Studies in the Claims and Practice of Ancient Greek Science.* Berkeley and Los Angeles, 1987.

Lloyd, G. E. R. *Demystifying Mentalities.* Cambridge, 1990.

Lloyd, G. E. R. 'Greek Antiquity: The Invention of Nature'. In J. Torrance (ed.), *The Concept of Nature.* Oxford, 1992, 1–24.

Lloyd, G. E. R. 'Le pluralisme de la vie intellectuelle avant Platon'. In Laks and Louguet 2002, 39–53.

Lloyd, G. E. R. *In the Grip of Disease: Studies in the Greek Imagination.* Oxford, 2003.

Lloyd, G. E. R. 'Mathematics as a Model of Method in Galen', in Sharples 2005, 110–130.

Lorenz, H. *The Brute Within: Appetitive Desire in Plato and Aristotle.* Oxford, 2006.

Macario, M. *Du sommeil, des rêves et du somnambulisme dans l'état de santé et de maladie.* Lyon and Paris, 1857.

MacMullen, R. *Paganism in the Roman Empire.* New Haven, 1981.

MacMullen, R. 'The Epigraphic Habit in the Roman Empire'. *American Journal of Philology* 103 (1982), 233–246.

Mamelak, A. N., and J. Hobson. 'Dream Bizarreness as the Cognitive Correlate of Altered Neuronal Behavior in REM Sleep'. *Journal of Cognitive Neuroscience* 1 (1989), 201–222.

Manselli, R. 'Il sogno come premonizione, consiglio e predizione nella tradizione medioevale'. In Gregory 1985, 219–244.

Manuwald, B. 'Traum und Traumdeutung in der griechischen Antike'. In R. Hiestand (ed.), *Traum und Träumen: Inhalt, Darstellung, Funktionen einer Lebenserfahrung in Mittelalter und Renaissance.* Düsseldorf, 1994, 15–42.

Maquet, P., D. Dive, E. Salmon, B. Sadzot, G. Franco, R. Poirrier, and G. Franck. 'Cerebral Glucose Utilization during Sleep-wake Cycle in Man Determined by Positron Emission Tomography and [18F]-2-fluoro-2-deoxy-D-glucose Method'. *Brain Research* 513 (1990), 136–143.

Marcovich, M. (ed.). *Tatian: Oratio ad Graecos.* Berlin and New York, 1995.

Marcovich, M. (ed.). *Heraclitus,* 2nd ed. Sankt Augustin, 2001.

Marcus, S. *Representations: Essays on Literature and Society.* New York, 1975.

Marquardt, C. J. G., R. A. Bonato, and R. F. Hoffmann. 'An Empirical Investigation into the Day–Residue and Dream-lag Effects'. *Dreaming* 6 (1996), 57–65.

Martin, D. B. *Inventing Superstition: From the Hippocratics to the Christians.* Cambridge, Mass., 2004.

Martínez, L. *La théorie des rêves chez Aristote: Principes physiologiques et psychologiques.* Villeneuve d'Ascq, 2000.

Marx, K. F. H. *Herophilus: Ein Beitrag zur Geschichte der Medicin.* Karlsruhe and Baden, 1838.

Mathieu-Castellani, G. 'Veiller en dormant, dormir en veillant: Le Songe dans les Essais'. In Charpentier 1990, 231–238.

Matthews, J. F. *The Roman Empire of Ammianus.* Baltimore, 1989.

Mayr, E. *The Growth of Biological Thought: Diversity, Evolution, and Inheritance.* Cambridge, Mass., 1982.

Mazzoli, G. 'Il sogno archittetato: Plauto, *Miles gloriosus,* vv. 79–595'. In N. Merola (ed.), *Il sogno raccontato.* Vibo Valentia, 1995, 59–68.

McCarley, R. W., and J. A. Hobson. 'The Neurobiological Origins of Psychoanalytic Dream Theory'. *American Journal of Psychiatry* 134 (1977), 1211–1221.

McNamara, P. *An Evolutionary Psychology of Sleep and Dreams.* Westport, Conn., 2004.

Mejer, J. *Diogenes Laertius and His Hellenistic Background.* Wiesbaden, 1978.

Michenaud, G., and J. Dierkens. *Les Rêves dans les 'Discours Sacrés' d'Aelius Aristide.* Mons, 1972.

Mikalson, J. D. *Athenian Popular Religion.* Chapel Hill and London, 1983.

Millar, F. *A Study in Cassius Dio.* Oxford, 1964.

Miller, P. C. *Dreams in Late Antiquity.* Princeton, 1994.

Monfasani, J. *George of Trebizond: A Biography and a Study of His Rhetoric and Logic.* Leiden, 1976.

Morel, P.-M. *Démocrite et la recherche des causes.* Paris, 1996.

Morel, P.-M. 'Démocrite et les Parva Naturalia d'Aristote'. In Laks and Louguet 2002, 449–464.

Morgan, K. A. *Myth and Philosophy from the Presocratics to Plato.* Cambridge, 2000.

Motschmann, C. *Die Religionspolitik Marc Aurels.* Stuttgart, 2002.

Mouritsen, H. 'Freedmen and Decurions: Epitaphs and Social History in Imperial Italy'. *JRS* 95 (2005), 38–63.

Mrozek, S. 'A propos de la répartition chronologique des inscriptions latines dans le Haut-Empire'. *Epigraphica* 35 (1973), 113–118.

Musurillo, H. (ed.) *Acts of the Christian Martyrs.* Oxford, 1972.

Näf, B. *Traum und Traumdeutung im Altertum.* Darmstadt, 2004.

Needham, R. *Belief, Language, and Experience.* Oxford, 1972.

Nenci, G. (ed.) *Erodoto: Le storie, Libro VI.* Milan, 1996.

Nicosia, S. 'L'autobiografia onirica di Elio Aristide'. In Guidorizzi 1988, 173–189.

Nielsen, T. A. 'A Review of Mentation in REM and NREM Sleep: "Covert" REM Sleep as a Possible Reconciliation of Two Opposing Models'. *BBS* 23 (2000), 851–866.

Nilsson, M. P. *Geschichte der griechischen Religion*, 2 vols., 1st ed. Munich, 1941–1950.

Nisbet, R. G. M., and M. Hubbard. *A Commentary on Horace, Odes, Book II.* Oxford, 1978.

Nock, A. D. 'A Vision of Mandulis Aion'. *Harvard Theological Review* 27 (1934), 53–104. Repr. in *Essays on Religion in the Ancient World.* Oxford, 1972, 1:357–400.

Nock, A. D. Rev. of Edelstein and Edelstein 1945, *Classical Philology* 45 (1950), 45–50.

Noegel, S. B. 'Dreams and Dream Interpreters in Mesopotamia and in the Hebrew Bible (Old Testament)'. In Bulkeley 2001, 45–71.

Noegel, S. B. 'Dreaming and the Ideology of Mantics: Homer and Ancient Near Eastern Oneiromancy'. In A. Panaino and G. Pettinato (eds.), *Ideologies as Intercultural Phenomena.* Melammu Symposia III. Milan, 2002, 167–181.

Noegel, S. B. *Nocturnal Ciphers: The Allusive Language of Dreams in the Ancient Near East.* New Haven, 2007.

Nutton, V. *Ancient Medicine.* London, 2004.

Oberhelman, S. M. 'Galen, *On Diagnosis from Dreams*'. *Journal of the History of Medicine* 38 (1983), 36–47.

Oberhelman, S. M. 'The Diagnostic Dream in Ancient Medical Theory and Practice'. *Bulletin of the History of Medicine and Allied Sciences* 61 (1987), 47–60.

Oberhelman, S. M. 'Dreams in Graeco-Roman Medicine'. In *ANRW* II, 37, 1 (1993), 121–156.

Oberhelman, S. M. 'Hierarchies of Gender, Ideology and Power in Ancient and Medieval Greek and Arabic Dream Literature'. In J. W. Wright and E. K. Rowson (eds.), *Homoeroticism in Classical Arabic Literature.* New York, 1997, 55–93.

Önnerfors, A. 'Traumerzählung und Traumtheorie beim älteren Plinius'. *Rheinisches Museum* 119 (1976), 352–365.

O'Hara, J. J. '*Somnia ficta* in Lucretius and Lucilius'. *CQ* 37 (1987), 517–519.

Olson, D. S. 'Cario and the New World of Aristophanes' *Plutus*'. *Transactions of the American Philological Association* 119 (1989), 193–199.

Oppenheim, A. L. *The Interpretation of Dreams in the Ancient Near East.* Philadelphia, 1956.

Pack, R. 'Artemidorus and His Waking World'. *Transactions of the American Philological Association* 86 (1955), 280–290.

Pack, R. A. *The Greek and Latin Literary Texts from Greco-Roman Egypt,* 2nd ed. Ann Arbor 1965.

Padel, R. *Whom Gods Destroy: Elements of Greek and Tragic Madness.* Princeton, 1995.

Pagel, J. F. 'Dreaming Is *Not* a Non-conscious Electrophysiologic State'. *BBS* 23 (2000), 984–988.

Pakkanen, P. *Interpreting Early Hellenistic Religion: A Study Based on the Mystery Cult of Demeter and the Cult of Isis.* Helsinki, 1996.

Pandya, V. 'Forest Smells and Spider Webs: Ritualized Dream Interpretation among Andaman Islanders'. *Dreaming* 14 (2004), 136–150.

Paravicini Bagliani, A., and G. Stabile (eds.). *Träume im Mittelalter: Ikonologische Studien.* Stuttgart and Zurich, 1989.

Parker, R. *Miasma: Pollution and Purification in Early Greek Religion.* Oxford, 1983.

Parker, R. *Polytheism and Society at Athens.* Oxford, 2005.

Pearcy, L. T. 'Theme, Dream, and Narrative: Reading the *Sacred Tales* of Aelius Aristides'. *Transactions of the American Philological Association* 118 (1988), 377–391.

Pease, A. (ed.). *M. Tulli Ciceronis De divinatione.* Urbana 1920–1923.

Pelling, C. B. R. 'Tragical Dreamer: Some Dreams in the Roman Historians'. *Greece and Rome* 44 (1997), 197–213.

Pelling, C. 'Modern Fantasy and Ancient Dreams'. In C. Sullivan and B. White (eds.), *Writing and Fantasy.* London, 1999, 15–31.

Pendrick, G. J. (ed.). *Antiphon the Sophist: Fragments.* Cambridge, 2002.

Perkell, C. G. *The Poet's Truth: A Study of the Poet in Virgil's Georgics.* Berkeley, 1989.

Perry, B. E. (ed.). *Aesopica.* Urbana, Ill., 1952.

Perutelli, A. 'Il sogno di Medea da Apollonio Rodio a Valerio Flacco', *Materiali e Discussioni* 33 (1994), 33–50.

Pfister, F. 'Epiphanie'. In *RE* supp. IV (1924), cols. 277–323.

Pickering W. S. F. (ed.). *Durkheim on Religion: A Selection of Readings with Bibliographies.* 1975.

Plastira-Valkanou, M. 'Dreams in Xenophon Ephesius'. *Symbolae Osloenses* 76 (2001), 137–149.

Pomeroy, A. J. 'Status and Status-concern in the Greco-Roman Dream-Books'. *Ancient Society* 22 (1991), 51–74.

Price, S. 'The Future of Dreams: From Freud to Artemidorus'. *Past and Present* 113 (1986), 3–37, revised and repr. in R. Osborne (ed.), *Studies In Ancient Greek and Roman Society*, Cambridge, 2004, 226–259.

Price, S. *Religions of the Ancient Greeks.* Cambridge, 1999.

Pritchett, W. K. *The Greek State at War* III. Berkeley, 1979.

Rankin, A. V. 'Penelope's Dreams in Books XIX and XX of the Odyssey'. *Helikon* 2 (1962), 617–624.

Rechtschaffen, A. 'The Single-mindedness and Isolation of Dreams'. *Sleep* 1 (1978), 97–109.

Rechtschaffen, A., and C. Buchignani. 'The Visual Appearance of Dreams'. In Antrobus and Bertini 1992, 143–155.

Reinsel, R., J. S. Antrobus, and M. Wollman. 'Bizarreness in Dreams and Waking Fantasy'. In Antrobus and Bertini 1992, 157–184.

Renberg, G. 'Commanded by the Gods': An Epigraphical Study of Dreams and Visions in Greek and Roman Religious Life. Ph.D. diss., Duke University, 2003.

Renberg, G. 'Was Incubation Practiced in the Latin West?' *Archiv für Religionsgeschichte* 8 (2006), 105–146.

Repici, L. 'Aristotele, gli stoici e il libro dei sogni nel *De Divinatione* di Cicerone'. *Atti dell' Accademia delle Scienze di Torino* 125, 2 (1991), 93–126.

Repici, L. (ed.) *Aristotele: Il sonno e i sogni.* Venice, 2003.

Revonsuo, A. 'The Reinterpretation of Dreams: An Evolutionary Hypothesis of the Function of Dreaming'. *BBS* 23 (2000), 877–901.

Revonsuo, A., and C. Salmivalli. 'A Content Analysis of Bizarre Elements in Dreams'. *Dreaming* 5 (1995), 169–187.

Richardson, N. *Homer, The Iliad: A Commentary, Books 21–24.* Cambridge, 1993.

Richter, G. M. A. 'Ancient Plaster Casts of Greek Metalware'. *American Journal of Archaeology* 62 (1958), 369–377.

Riethmüller, J. W. *Asklepios: Heiligtümer und Kulte*, 2 vols. Heidelberg, 2005.

Rigsby, K. 'Chrysogone's Mother'. *Museum Helveticum* 60 (2003), 60–64.

Riley Smith, J. *The First Crusaders, 1095–1131.* Cambridge, 1997.

Rittenhouse, C., R. Stickgold, and J. A. Hobson. 'Constraint on the Transformation of Characters, Objects, and Settings in Dream Reports'.
Consciousness and Cognition 3 (1994), 100–113.

Robbins, P. R., and R. H. Tanck. 'Interest in Dreams and Dream Recall'.
Perceptual and Motor Skills 66 (1988), 291–294.

Robert, L. 'Trois oracles de la théosophie et un prophète d'Apollon'.
Comptes-Rendus de l'Académie des Inscriptions et Belles-Lettres 1968,
568–599. Repr. in *Opera Minora Selecta* V. Amsterdam, 1989,
584–615.

Robert, L. 'Les inscriptions de Thessalonique'. *Revue de Philologie* 1974,
180–246. Repr. in *Opera Minora Selecta* V. Amsterdam, 1989,
267–333.

Robert, L. 'Une vision de Perpétue martyre à Carthage en 203'. *Comptes-
Rendus de l'Académie des Inscriptions et Belles-Lettres* (1982),
228–276.

Robinson, T. M. *Heraclitus: Fragments.* Toronto, 1987.

Roos, E. 'De incubationis ritu per ludibrium apud Aristophanem detorto'.
Opuscula Atheniensia 3 (1960), 55–97.

Rosenthal, F. 'An Ancient Commentary on the Hippocratic Oath'. *Bulletin of the History of Medicine and Allied Sciences* 30 (1956), 52–87.

Rostovtzeff, M. I. *The Social and Economic History of the Hellenistic
World,* 3 vols. Oxford, 1941.

Rotondaro, S. *Il sogno in Platone.* Naples, 1998.

Rousseau, G. S. 'Dream and Vision in Aeschylus' Oresteia'. *Arion* 2
(1963), 101–136.

Rousselle, R. 'Healing Cults in Antiquity: The Dream Cures of Asclepius
of Epidaurus'. *Journal of Psychohistory* 12 (1984–1985), 339–352.

Roussy, F., C. Camirand, D. Foulkes, J. De Koninck, M. Loftis and N. H.
Kerr. 'Does Early-night REM Dream Content Reliably Reflect
Presleep State of Mind?' *Dreaming* 6 (1996), 121–130.

Roussy, F., M. Brunette, P. Mercier, I. Gonthier, J. Grenier, M. Sirois-
Berliss, M. Lortie-Lussier and J. De Koninck. 'Daily Events and
Dream Content: Unsuccessful Matching Attempts'. *Dreaming* 10
(2000), 77–83.

Rozokoki, A. 'Penelope's Dream in Book 19 of the Odyssey'. *CQ* 51
(2001), 1–6.

Rubensohn, O. 'Das Aushängeschild eines Traumdeuters'. In *Festschrift
Johannes Vahlen zum siebenzigsten Geburtstag.* Berlin, 1900, 3–15.

Rupprecht, C. S. (ed.). *The Dream and the Text: Essays on Literature and Language*. Albany, N.Y., 1993.

Ryholt, K. 'Nectanebo's Dream or the Prophecy of Petesis'. In Blasius and Schipper 2002, 221–241.

Ryle, G. *The Concept of Mind*. London, 1949.

Said, S. 'Oracles et devins dans le roman grec'. In Heintz 1997, 367–403.

Samama, E. *Les médecins dans le monde grec: Sources épigraphiques sur la naissance d'un corps médical*. Geneva, 2003.

Sandwell, I. 'Outlawing "Magic" or Outlawing "Religion"? Libanius and the Theodosian Code as Evidence for Legislation against "Pagan" Practices'. In W. V. Harris, *The Spread of Christianity in the First Four Centuries: Essays in Explanation*. Columbia Studies in the Classical Tradition 27. Leiden, 2005, 87–123.

Saredi, R., G. W. Baylor, B. Meier and I. Strauch. 'Current Concerns and REM-Dreams: A Laboratory Study of Dream Incubation'. *Dreaming* 7 (1997), 195–208.

Sassi, M. M. *The Science of Man in Ancient Greece*, trans. P. Tucker. Chicago and London, 2001. (Original ed.: *Scienza dell'uomo nella Grecia antica*, Turin, 1988.)

Sassi, M. M. 'Da Senofane al *Timeo:* Il problema del discorso verosimile'. In M. Bugno (ed.), *Senofane ed Elea tra Ionia e Magna Grecia*. Naples, 2005, 141–146.

Scheid, J. *Quand faire, c'est croire: Les rites sacrificiels des Romains*. Paris, 2005.

Schiappa, E. *Protagoras and logos: A Study in Greek Philosophy and Rhetoric*. Columbia, S.C., 1991.

Schmekel, A. *Die Philosophie der mittleren Stoa in ihrem geschichtlichen Zusammenhange*. Berlin, 1892.

Schmitt, J.-C. 'Rêver au XIIe siècle'. In Gregory 1985, 291–316.

Schmitt, J.-C. 'The Liminality and Centrality of Dreams in the Medieval West'. In Shulman and Stroumsa 1999, 274–287.

Schneeweiss, G. (ed.). *Aristoteles, Protreptikos: Hinführung zur Philosophie*. Darmstadt, 2005.

Schörner, G. *Votive im römischen Griechenland*. Stuttgart, 2003.

Schofield, M. 'Cicero for and against Divination'. *JRS* 76 (1986), 47–65.

Schofield, M. 'Heraclitus' Theory of Soul and Its Antecedents'. In Everson 1991, 13–34.

Schredl, M. 'Dream Recall, Attitude toward Dreams, and Personality'.
   Personality and Individual Differences 20 (1996), 613–618.

Schredl, M. 'Messung der Traumerinnerung: Siebenstufige Skala und
   Daten gesunder Personen'. *Somnologie* 6 (2002), 34–38.

Schredl, M. 'REM Sleep, Dreaming, and Procedural Memory'. *BBS* 28
   (2005), 80–81.

Schredl, M., P. Ciric, S. Götz, and L. Wittmann. 'Dream Recall
   Frequency, Attitude towards Dreams and Openness to Experience'.
   Dreaming 13 (2003), 145–153.

Schredl, M., S. Frauscher and A. Shendi. 'Dream Recall and Visual Memory'. *Perceptual and Motor Skills* 81 (1995), 256–258.

Schredl, M., and F. Hofmann. 'Continuity between Waking Activities and
   Dream Activities'. *Consciousness and Cognition* 12 (2003), 298–308.

Schredl, M., and E. Piel. 'Gender Differences in Dream Recall'. *Personality and Individual Differences* 35 (2003), 1185–1189.

Schrijvers, P. H. 'La classification des rêves selon Hérophile'. *Mnemosyne*
   30 (1977), 13–27.

Schrijvers, P. H. 'Die Traumtheorie des Lukrez'. *Mnemosyne* 33 (1980),
   128–151.

Schwabl, H. 'Zu den Träumen bei Homer und Herodot'. In ΑΡΕΤΗΣ
   ΜΝΗΜΗ: Ἀφιέρωμα εἰς μνήμην τοῦ Κωνσταντίνου Ἰ. Βουρβέρη.
   Athens, 1983, 17–27.

Schwartz, E. *De Pionio et Polycarpo*. Göttingen, 1905.

Schwartz, Seth. *Imperialism and Jewish Society, 200 B.C.E. to 640 A.D.*
   Princeton, 2001.

Schwartz, Sophie. 'A Historical Loop of One Hundred Years: Similarities
   between Nineteenth-century and Contemporary Dream Research'.
   Dreaming 10 (2000), 55–66.

Seaford, R. *Money and the Early Greek Mind*. Cambridge, 2004.

Seaford, R. 'Money and Tragedy'. In W. V. Harris (ed.), *Monetary Systems
   of the Greeks and Romans*. Oxford, 2008, 49–65.

Sedley, D. N. *Lucretius and the Transformation of Greek Wisdom*. Cambridge, 1998.

Segall, S. R. 'A Test of Two Theories of Dream Forgetting'. *Journal of
   Clinical Psychology* 36 (1980), 739–742.

Seligman, C. G. 'Anthropology and Psychology: A Study of Some Points
   of Contact'. *Journal of the Royal Anthropological Institute* 54 (1924),
   13–46.

Sharples, R. W. 'Dicaearchus on the Soul and on Divination'. In W. W. Fortenbaugh and E. Schütrumpf (eds.), *Dicaearchus of Messana: Text, Translation, and Discussion.* New Brunswick and London, 2000, 143–173.

Sharples, R. W. 'Introduction: Philosophy and the Sciences in Antiquity'. In Sharples 2005, 1–7.

Sharples, R. W. (ed.). *Philosophy and the Sciences in Antiquity.* Aldershot and Burlington, Vermont, 2005.

Shaw, B. D. 'The Passion of Perpetua'. *Past and Present* 139 (1993), 3–45.

Sherwin-White, S. M. *Ancient Cos.* Göttingen, 1978.

Shevrin, H., and A. S. Eiser. 'Continued Vitality of the Freudian Theory of Dreaming'. *BBS* 23 (2000), 1004–1006.

Shewring, W. H. 'En marge de la *Passion des Saintes Perpétue et Félicité*'. *Revue bénédictine* 43 (1931), 15–22.

Shulman, D., and Stroumsa, G. G. *Dream Cultures: Explorations in the Comparative History of Dreaming.* New York and Oxford, 1999.

Singer, P. N. *Galen: Selected Works.* Oxford, 1997.

Sinos, R. H. 'Divine Selection: Epiphany and Politics in Archaic Greece'. In C. Dougherty and L. Kurke (eds.), *Cultural Poetics in Archaic Greece: Cult, Performance, Politics.* Cambridge, 1993, 73–91.

Slaveva-Griffin, S. 'A Feast of Speeches: Form and Content in Plato's *Timaeus*'. *Hermes* 133 (2005), 312–337.

Smith, C. R. 'Content Analysis and Narrative Analysis'. In H. T. Reis and C. M. Judd (eds.), *Handbook of Research Methods in Social and Personality Psychology.* New York, 2000, 313–335.

Smith, M. F. (ed.). *Diogenes of Oinoanda: The Epicurean Inscription.* Naples, 1993.

Smith, M. F. *Supplement to Diogenes of Oenoanda, The Epicurean Inscription.* Naples, 2003.

Smith, J. Z. 'Towards Interpreting Demonic Powers in Hellenistic and Roman Antiquity'. In *ANRW* II.16.1 (1978), 425–439.

Smith, N. D. 'Diviners and Divination in Aristophanic Comedy'. *Classical Antiquity* 8 (1989), 140–158.

Smith, W. D. *Hippocrates: Pseudepigraphic Writings.* Leiden, 1990.

Snyder, F. 'The Phenomenology of Dreaming'. In L. Madow and L. H. Snow (eds.), *The Psychodynamic Implications of the Physiological Studies on Dreams.* Springfield, Ill., 1970, 124–151.

Sollenberger, M. J. 'Diogenes Laertius' Life of Demetrius of Phalerum'. In W. W. Fortenbaugh and E. Schütrumpf (eds.), *Demetrius of Phalerum: Text, Translation and Discussion.* New Brunswick, N.J., 2000, 311–329.

Solms, M. *The Neuropsychology of Dreams.* Mahwah, N.J., 1997.

Solms, M. 'Dreaming and REM Sleep Are Controlled by Different Brain Mechanisms'. *BBS* 23 (2000), 843–850 (2000a).

Solms, M. 'Forebrain Mechanisms of Dreaming Are Activated from a Variety of Sources'. *BBS* 23 (2000), 1035–1040 (2000b).

Solmsen, F. *Intellectual Experiments of the Greek Enlightenment.* Princeton, 1975.

Sommerstein, A. H. (ed.). *Aristophanes: Wasps.* Warminster, 1983.

Sommerstein, A. H. (ed.). *Aeschylus: Eumenides.* Cambridge, 1989.

Sommerstein, A. H. (ed.). *Aristophanes: Wealth.* Warminster, 2001.

Spearing, A. C. Introduction to Brown 1999, 1–21.

Sperber, D. 'Intuitive and Reflective Beliefs'. *Mind and Language* 12 (1997), 67–83.

Stadter, P. A. *A Commentary on Plutarch's Pericles.* Chapel Hill, NC, 1989.

States, B. O. 'Bizarreness in Dreams and Other Fictions'. In Rupprecht 1993, 13–31.

States, B. O. 'Dream Bizarreness and Inner Thought'. *Dreaming* 10 (2000), 179–192.

Steiner, H. *Der Traum in der Aeneis.* Bern, 1952.

Stewart, C. 'Erotic Dreams and Nightmares from Antiquity to the Present'. *Journal of the Royal Anthropological Institute,* n.s., 8 (2002), 279–309.

Stewart, C. 'Dreams of Treasure: Temporality, Historicization and the Unconscious'. *Anthropological Theory* 3 (2003), 481–500.

Stewart, P. *Statues in Roman Society: Representation and Response.* Oxford, 2003.

Stewart, Z. 'La religione', in R. Bianchi bandinelli (ed.), *Storia e civiltà dei greci, VIII. La società ellenistica. Economia, diritto, religione,* Milan, 1977, 503–616.

Stoddard, F. J., D. S. Chedekel and L. Shakun. 'Dreams and Nightmares of Burned Children'. In D. Barrett 1996, 25–45.

Strauch, I., and B. Meier. *Den Träumen auf der Spur: Ergebnisse der experimentellen Traumforschung.* Bern, 1992; *In Search of Dreams:*

Results of Experimental Dream Research, trans. M. Ebon. Albany, N.Y., 1996.

Stroumsa, G. G. 'Dreams and Visions in Early Christian Discourse'. In Shulman and Stroumsa 1999, 189–212.

Syme, R. *Tacitus,* 2 vols. Oxford, 1958.

Syme R. *Ammianus and the Historia Augusta.* Oxford, 1968.

Syme, R. 'Hadrian's Autobiography: Servianus and Sura'. In *Roman Papers* VI. Oxford, 1991, 398–408.

Szidat, J. 'Der Neuplatonismus und die Gebildeten im Westen des Reiches'. *Museum Helveticum* 39 (1982), 132–145.

Szpakowska, K. *Behind Closed Eyes: Dreams and Nightmares in Ancient Egypt.* Swansea, 2003.

Taffin, A. 'Comment on rêvait dans les temples d'Ésculape', *Bulletin de la Société G. Budé* 1960, 325–366.

Taylor, C. C. W. *The Atomists Leucippus and Democritus: Fragments.* Toronto, 1999.

Tedlock, B. 'The New Anthropology of Dreaming'. *Dreaming* 1 (1991), 161–178.

Teodorsson, S.-V. *A Commentary on Plutarch's Table Talks,* 3 vols. Göteborg, 1989–1998.

Thériault, G. *Le culte d'homonoia dans les cités grecques.* Lyon and Quebec, 1996.

Thomas, K. *Religion and the Decline of Magic.* London, 1971.

Thomas, R. *Literacy and Orality in Ancient Greece.* Cambridge, 1992.

Thompson, D. J. *Memphis under the Ptolemies.* Princeton, 1988.

Thompson, N. S. 'Evolutionary Psychology Can Ill Afford Adaptionist and Mentalist Credulity'. *BBS* 23 (2000), 1013–1014.

Timpanaro, S. *The Freudian Slip.* London, 1976 (Original: *Il lapsus freudiano.* Florence, 1974.)

Timpanaro, S. *Nuovi contributi di filologia e storia della lingua latina.* Bologna, 1994.

Tonay, V. K. 'Personality Correlates of Dream Recall: Who Remembers?' *Dreaming* 3 (1993), 1–8.

Totti, M. (ed.). *Ausgewählte Texte der Isis- und Sarapis-Religion.* Hildesheim, 1985.

Traill, A. E. 'A Haruspicy Joke in Plautus'. *CQ* 54 (2004), 117–127.

Valli, K., T. Strandholm, L. Sillanmäki and A. Revonsuo, 'Dreams Are More Negative than Real Life: Implications for the Function of Dreaming', *Cognition & Emotion* 22 (2008), 833–861.

van der Eijk, P. J. 'Aristotelian Elements in Cicero's "De divinatione"', *Philologus* 137 (1993), 223–231.

van der Eijk, P. J. (trans. and ed.). *Aristoteles: De insomniis, De divinatione per somnum.* Berlin, 1994.

van der Eijk, P. J. *Diocles of Carystus: A Collection of the Fragments with Translation and Commentary,* 2 vols. Leiden, 2000–2001.

van der Eijk, P. J. 'Introduction to Horstmanshoff and Stol 2004, 1–10.

van der Eijk, P. J. 'Divination, Prognosis and Prophylaxis: The Hippocratic Work on Dreams and Its Near Eastern Background'. In Horstmanshoff and Stol 2004, 187–218.

van der Eijk, P. J. *Medicine and Philosophy in Classical Antiquity.* Cambridge, 2005.

Vanderlinden, S. 'Revelatio Sancti Stephani (B.H.L. 7850–6)'. *Revue des Etudes Byzantines* 4 (1946), 178–217.

van Lieshout, R. G. A. *Greeks on Dreams.* Utrecht, 1980.

van Straten, F. T. 'Daikrates' Dream: A Votive Relief from Kos, and Some Other *kat'onar* Dedications'. *Bulletin Antieke Beschaving* 51 (1976), 1–27.

Vauchez, A. 'Sainteté laïque au XIIIe siècle: La vie du bienheureux Facio de Crémone (v. 1196–1272)'. *Mélanges de l'École Française de Rome, Moyen Âge* 84 (1972), 13–53.

Vegléris, E. 'Platon et le rêve de la nuit'. *Ktema* 7 (1982), 53–65.

Verdenius, W. J. *Parmenides: Some Comments on His Poem.* Groningen, 1942.

Vermeule, C. 'Greek, Etruscan, and Roman Sculptures in the Museum of Fine Arts, Boston'. *American Journal of Archaeology* 68 (1964), 323–341.

Versnel, H. 'What Did Ancient Man See When He Saw a God?' In D. van der Plas (ed.), *Effigies Dei.* Leiden, 1987, 42–55.

Vertes, R. P., and K. E. Eastman. 'The Case against Memory Consolidation in REM Sleep'. *BBS* 23 (2000), 867–876.

Veyne, P. *Les Grecs ont-ils cru à leur mythes?* Paris, 1983.

Veyne, P. 'Une évolution du paganisme gréco-romain: Injustice et piété des dieux, leurs ordres ou "oracles"'. *Latomus* 45 (1986), 259–283.

Veyne, P. 'De Halai en Dalmatie: Un voeu de voyageur et les rêves chez Virgile'. In *Poikilia: Études offertes à Jean-Pierre Vernant*. Paris, 1987, 381–395.

Vigourt, A. *Les présages impériaux d'Auguste à Domitien*. Paris, 2001.

Vlastos, G. 'Religion and Medicine in the Cult of Asclepius: A Review Article'. *Review of Religion* 13 (1949), 269–290.

Vollenweider, M.-L. 'Der Traum des Sulla Felix'. *Schweizerische Numismatische Rundschau* 39 (1958–1959), 22–34.

Volten, A. *Demotische Traumdeutung (Pap. Carlsberg XIII und XIV Verso)*. Copenhagen, 1942.

von Staden, H. 'Hairesis and Heresy: The Case of the *iatrikai haireseis*'. In B. F. Meyer and E. P. Sanders (eds.), *Jewish and Christian Self-Definition* III. London, 1982, 76–100.

von Staden, H. *Herophilus: The Art of Medicine in Early Alexandria*. Cambridge 1989.

von Staden, H. 'Galen's Daimon: Reflections on "Irrational" and "Rational"'. In N. Palmieri (ed.), *Rationnel et irrationnel dans la médecine antique et médiévale*. Saint-Etienne, 2003, 15–43.

Wacht, M. 'Inkubation'. In *Reallexikon für Antike und Christentum* XVIII (1997), cols. 179–265.

Walbank, F. W. *A Historical Commentary on Polybius*, 3 vols. Oxford, 1957–1979.

Walde, C. 'Dream Interpretation in a Prosperous Age? Artemidorus, the Greek Interpreter of Dreams'. In Shulman and Stroumsa 1999, 121–142.

Walde, C. *Die Traumdarstellungen in der griechisch-römischen Dichtung*. Munich and Leipzig, 2001.

Walker, M. P., and R. Stickgold. 'Sleep-dependent Learning and Memory Consolidation'. *Neuron* 44 (2004), 121–133.

Walzer, R. (ed.). *Galen on Medical Experience*. Oxford, 1944.

Wardle, D. (ed.). *Cicero on Divination: De Divinatione, Book I*. Oxford, 2006.

Warren, J. 'Democritus on Social and Psychological Harm'. In Brancacci and Morel 2007, 87–104.

Waszink, J. H. (ed.). *Tertulliani De Anima*. Amsterdam, 1947.

Wax, M. L. 'Dream Sharing as Social Practice'. *Dreaming* 14 (2004), 83–93.

Weber, G. 'Traum und Alltag in hellenistischer Zeit'. *Zeitschrift für Religions- und Geistesgeschichte* 50 (1998), 22–39.

Weber, G. 'Herrscher und Traum in hellenistischer Zeit'. *Archiv für Kulturgeschichte* 81 (1999), 1–33.

Weber, G. *Kaiser, Träume und Visionen in Prinzipat und Spätantike.* Stuttgart, 2000.

Weber, G. 'Träume und Visionen im Alltag der römischen Kaiserzeit: Das Zeugnis der Inschriften und Papyri'. *Quaderni Catanesi di Studi Antichi e Medievali* 4–5 (2005–2006), 55–121.

Weidhorn, M. *Dreams in Seventeenth-century English Literature.* The Hague and Paris, 1970.

West, M. L. (ed.). *Hesiod: Theogony.* Oxford, 1966.

West, M. L. *Studies in Aeschylus.* 1990.

West, S. 'And It Came to Pass That Pharaoh Dreamed: Notes on Herodotus 2.139, 141'. *CQ* 37 (1987), 262–271.

White, R. J. *Artemidorus, Oneirocritica: Translation and Commentary.* Park Ridge, N.J., 1975.

Wijsenbeek-Wijler, H. *Aristotle's Concept of Soul, Sleep and Dreams.* Amsterdam, 1978.

Wikenhauser, A. 'Doppelträume'. *Biblica* 29 (1948), 100–111.

Wilamowitz-Moellendorff, U. von. *Die Ilias und Homer.* Berlin, 1916.

Wilamowitz-Moellendorff, U. von. *Der Glaube der Hellenen,* 2 vols. Berlin, 1931–1932.

Willink, C. W. (ed.). *Euripides: Orestes.* Oxford, 1986.

Winnington-Ingram, R. P. *Sophocles: An Interpretation.* Cambridge, 1980.

Wiseman, T. P. 'Lying Historians: Seven Types of Mendacity'. In C. Gill and T. P. Wiseman (eds.), *Lies and Fiction in the Ancient World.* Exeter, 1993, 122–146.

Wittgenstein, L. 'Bemerkungen über Frazers *The Golden Bough*'. *Synthese* 17 (1967), 233–253.

Wolcott, S., and C. M. Strapp 'Dream Recall Frequency and Dream Detail as Mediated by Personality, Behavior, and Attitude'. *Dreaming* 12 (2002), 27–44.

Wright, D. H. *The Vatican Vergil: A Masterpiece of Late Antique Art.* Berkeley and Los Angeles, 1993.

Wright, M. R. (ed.). *Empedocles: The Extant Fragments.* New Haven, 1981.

Zadra, A., S. Desjardins and E. Marcotte, 'Evolutionary Function of Dreams: A Test of the Threat Simulation Theory in Recurrent Dreams', *Consciousness and Cognition* 15 (2006), 450–463.

Zane, M. D. 'Significance of Differing Responses among Psychoanalysts to the Same Dream'. In J. H. Masserman (ed.), *Dream Dynamics*. New York, 1971, 174–177.

Zauzich, K.-T. 'Aus zwei demotischen Traumbüchern'. *Archiv für Papyrusforschung* 27 (1980), 91–98.

Žižek, S. 'Freud Lives!' *London Review of Books*, 25 May 2006.

Index